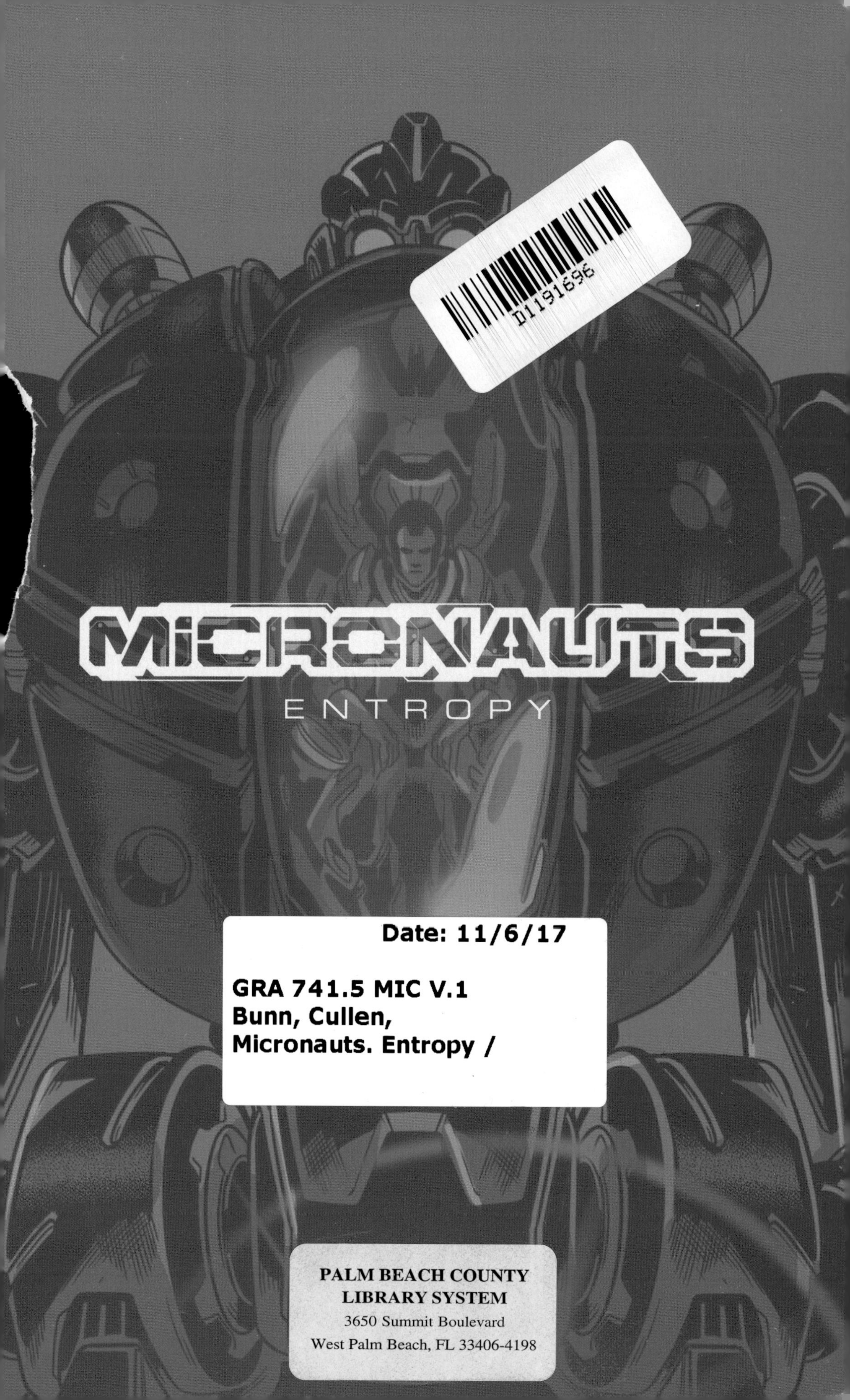
MICRONAUTS
ENTROPY

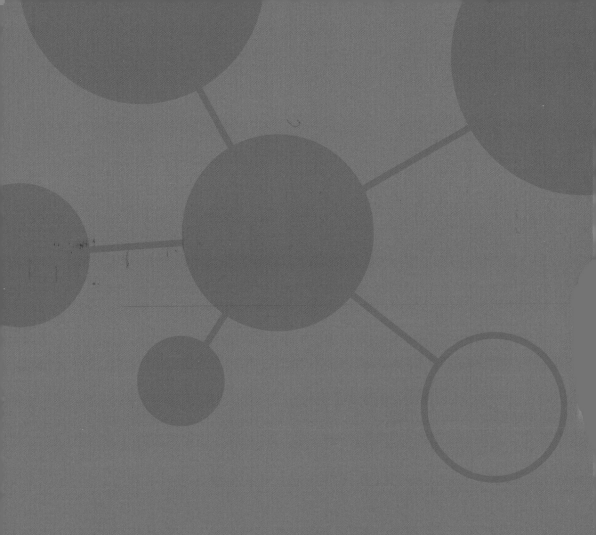

IDW

Facebook: **facebook.com/idwpublishing**
Twitter: **@idwpublishing**
YouTube: **youtube.com/idwpublishing**
Tumblr: **tumblr.idwpublishing.com**
Instagram: **instagram.com/idwpublishing**

COVER ART BY
J.H. WILLIAMS III

COLLECTION EDITS BY
JUSTIN EISINGER
AND ALONZO SIMON

COLLECTION DESIGN BY
JEFF POWELL

PUBLISHER
TED ADAMS

ISBN: 978-1-63140-755-0   19 18 17 16   1 2 3 4

Ted Adams, CEO & Publisher
Greg Goldstein, President & COO
Robbie Robbins, EVP/Sr. Graphic Artist
Chris Ryall, Chief Creative Officer
David Hedgecock, Editor-in-Chief
Laurie Windrow, Senior VP of Sales & Marketing
Matthew Ruzicka, CPA, Chief Financial Officer
Dirk Wood, VP of Marketing
Lorelei Bunjes, VP of Digital Services
Jeff Webber, VP of Digital and Subsidiary Rights
Jerry Bennington, VP of New Product Development

WRITTEN BY
CULLEN BUNN

ART BY
MAX DUNBAR

BREAKDOWNS FOR ISSUE #1 BY
DAVID BALDEÓN

FINISHES FOR ISSUE #1 BY
FICO OSSIO, MAX DUNBAR,
JACK LAWRENCE,
AND DAVID BALDEÓN

COLORS BY
DAVID GARCIA CRUZ

ADDITIONAL COLORS BY
JOANA LAFUENTE,
THOMAS DEER,
JOHN-PAUL BOVE,
AND ANDER ZARATE

LETTERS BY
TOM B. LONG

SERIES EDITS BY
JOHN BARBER

MICRONAUTS

ENTROPY

01

ART BY **J.H. WILLIAMS III**

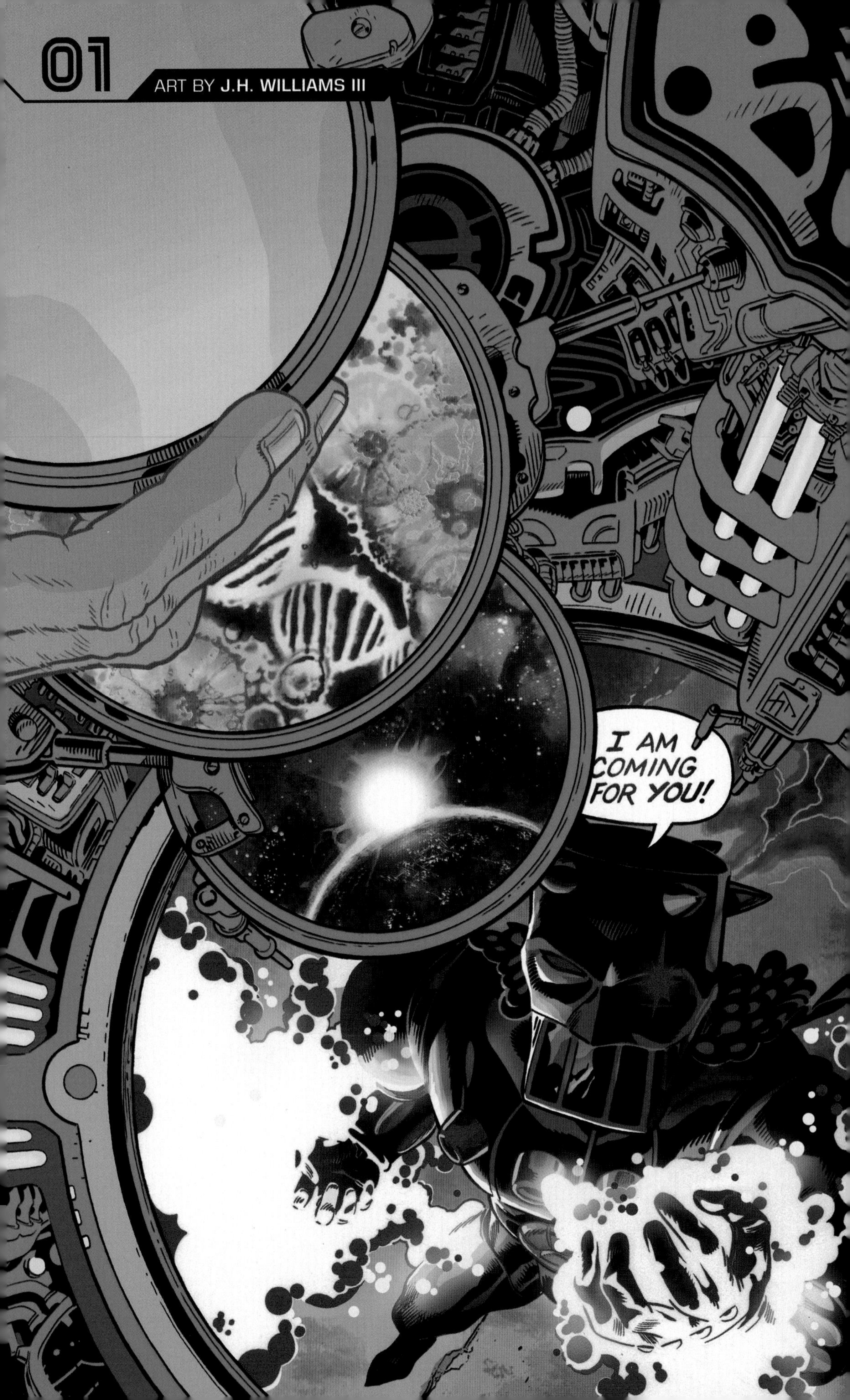

I AM COMING FOR YOU!

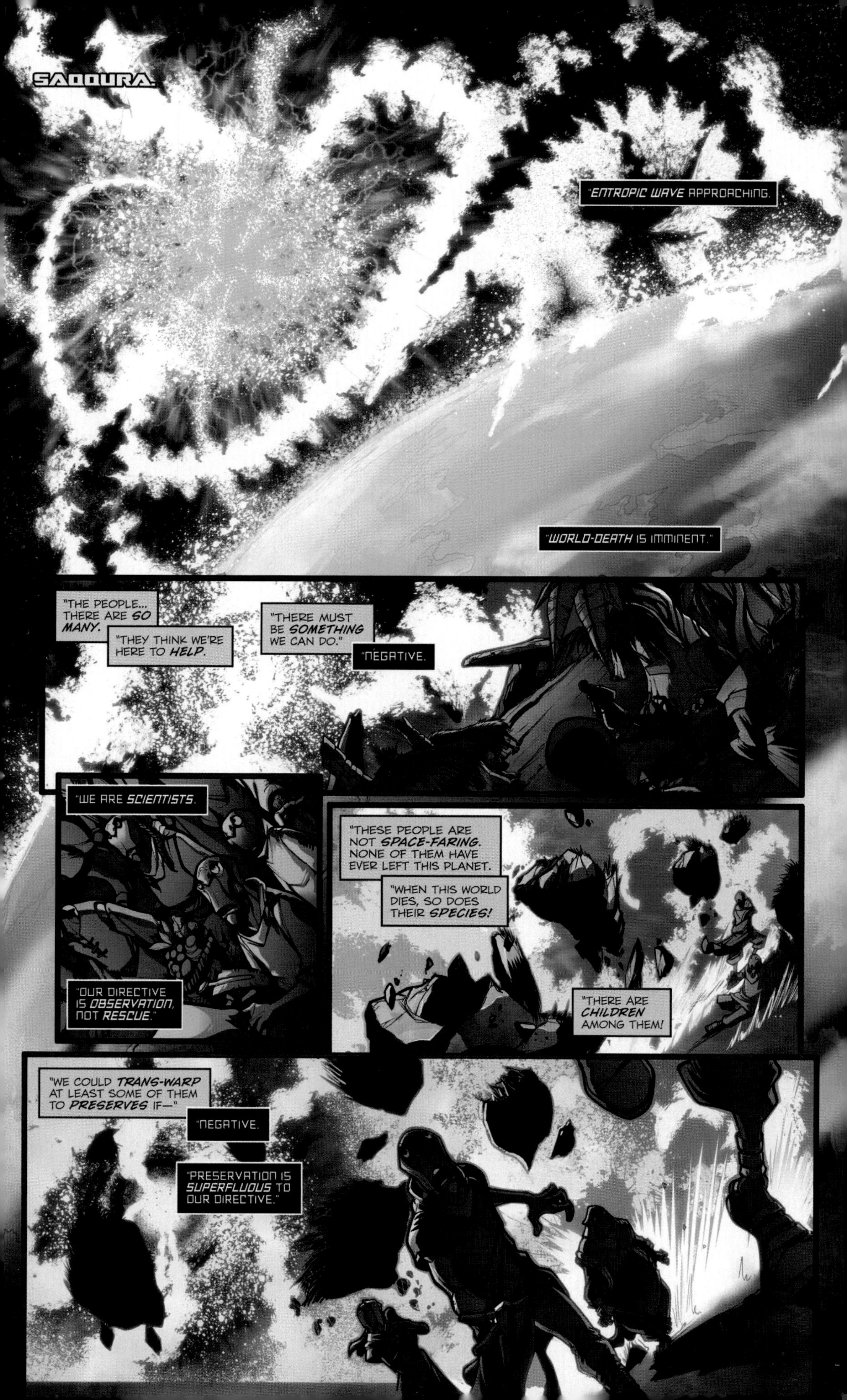
SADQURA.
"ENTROPIC WAVE APPROACHING.
"WORLD-DEATH IS IMMINENT."
"THE PEOPLE... THERE ARE SO MANY.
"THEY THINK WE'RE HERE TO HELP.
"THERE MUST BE SOMETHING WE CAN DO."
"NEGATIVE.
"WE ARE SCIENTISTS.
"OUR DIRECTIVE IS OBSERVATION, NOT RESCUE."
"THESE PEOPLE ARE NOT SPACE-FARING. NONE OF THEM HAVE EVER LEFT THIS PLANET.
"WHEN THIS WORLD DIES, SO DOES THEIR SPECIES!
"THERE ARE CHILDREN AMONG THEM!
"WE COULD TRANS-WARP AT LEAST SOME OF THEM TO PRESERVES IF—"
"NEGATIVE.
"PRESERVATION IS SUPERFLUOUS TO OUR DIRECTIVE."

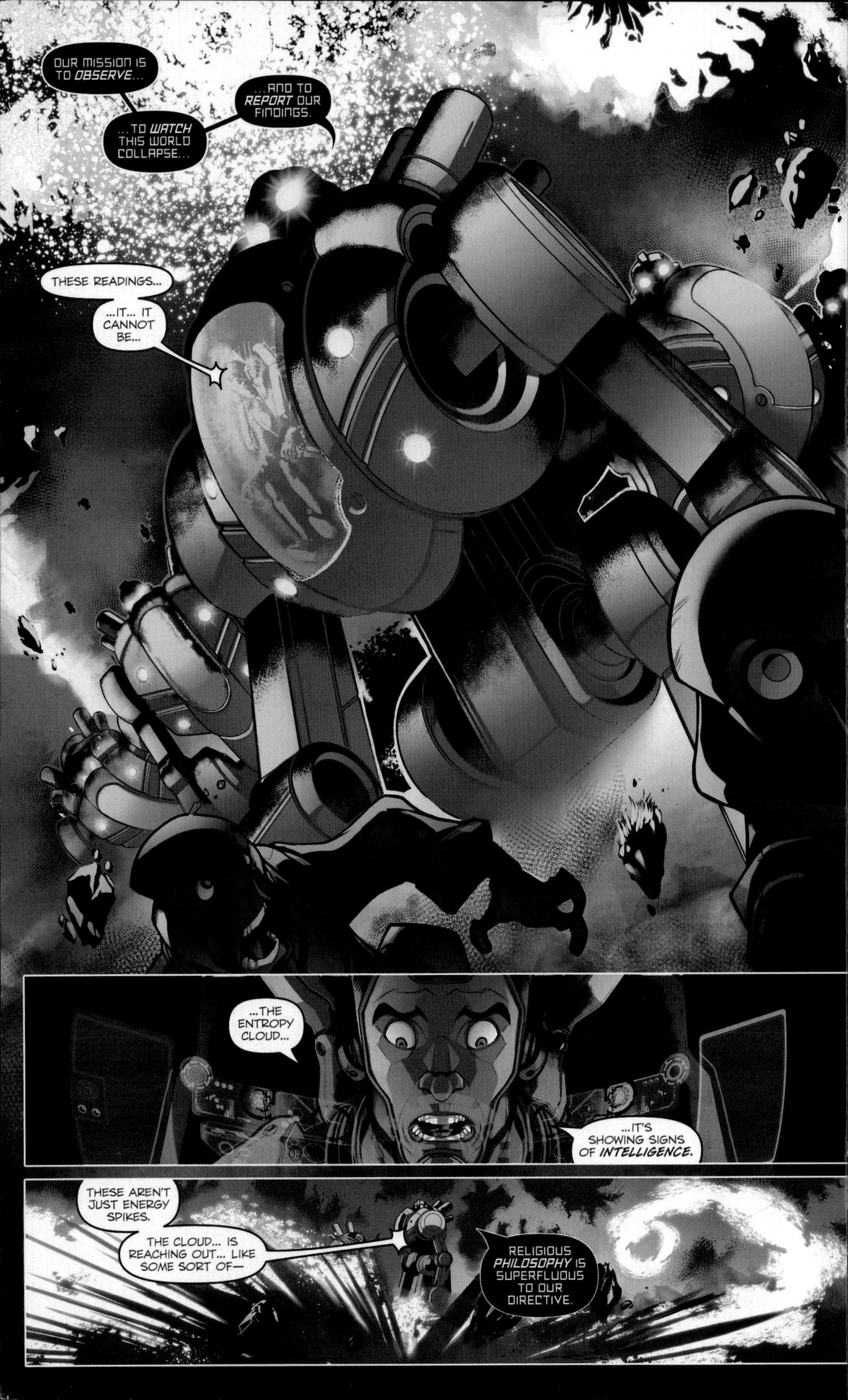
OUR MISSION IS TO OBSERVE...
...TO WATCH THIS WORLD COLLAPSE...
...AND TO REPORT OUR FINDINGS.
THESE READINGS...
...IT... IT CANNOT BE...
...THE ENTROPY CLOUD...
...IT'S SHOWING SIGNS OF INTELLIGENCE.
THESE AREN'T JUST ENERGY SPIKES.
THE CLOUD... IS REACHING OUT... LIKE SOME SORT OF—
RELIGIOUS PHILOSOPHY IS SUPERFLUOUS TO OUR DIRECTIVE.

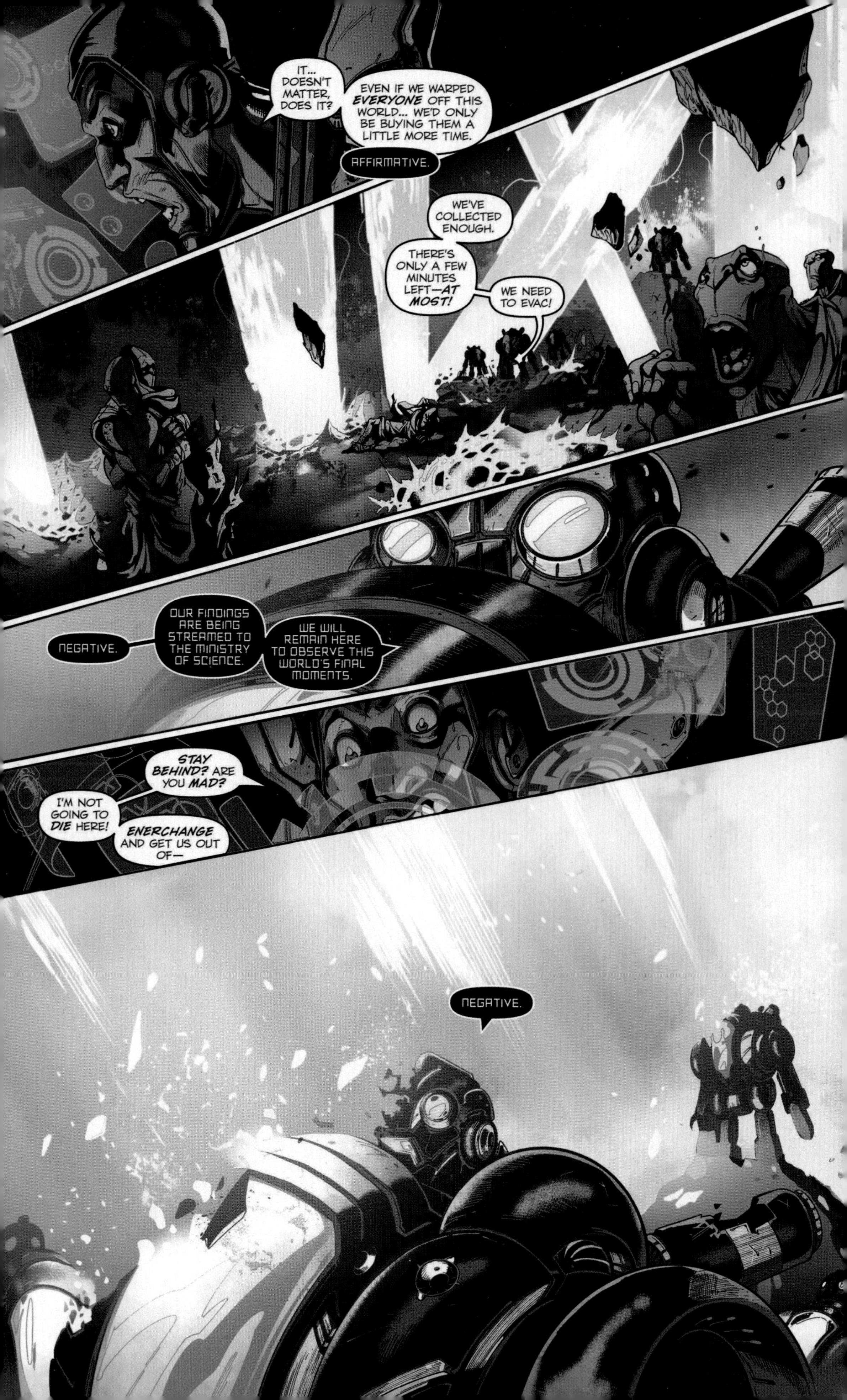
IT... DOESN'T MATTER, DOES IT?
EVEN IF WE WARPED EVERYONE OFF THIS WORLD... WE'D ONLY BE BUYING THEM A LITTLE MORE TIME.
AFFIRMATIVE.
WE'VE COLLECTED ENOUGH.
THERE'S ONLY A FEW MINUTES LEFT—AT MOST!
WE NEED TO EVAC!
NEGATIVE.
OUR FINDINGS ARE BEING STREAMED TO THE MINISTRY OF SCIENCE.
WE WILL REMAIN HERE TO OBSERVE THIS WORLD'S FINAL MOMENTS.
STAY BEHIND? ARE YOU MAD?
I'M NOT GOING TO DIE HERE!
ENERCHANGE AND GET US OUT OF—
NEGATIVE.

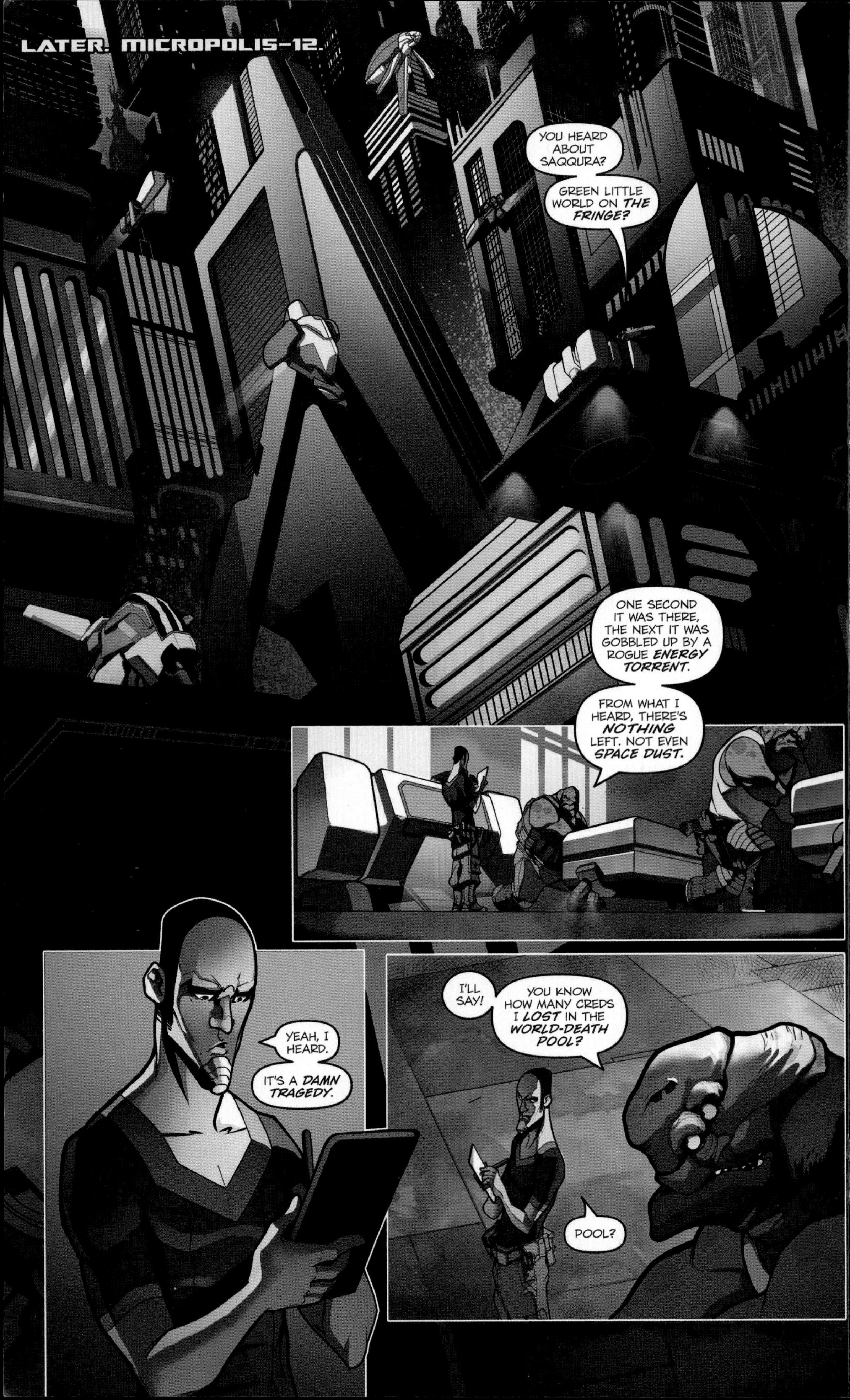
LATER. MICROPOLIS-12.
YOU HEARD ABOUT SAQQURA?
GREEN LITTLE WORLD ON THE FRINGE?
ONE SECOND IT WAS THERE, THE NEXT IT WAS GOBBLED UP BY A ROGUE ENERGY TORRENT.
FROM WHAT I HEARD, THERE'S NOTHING LEFT. NOT EVEN SPACE DUST.
YEAH, I HEARD.
IT'S A DAMN TRAGEDY.
I'LL SAY!
YOU KNOW HOW MANY CREDS I LOST IN THE WORLD-DEATH POOL?
POOL?

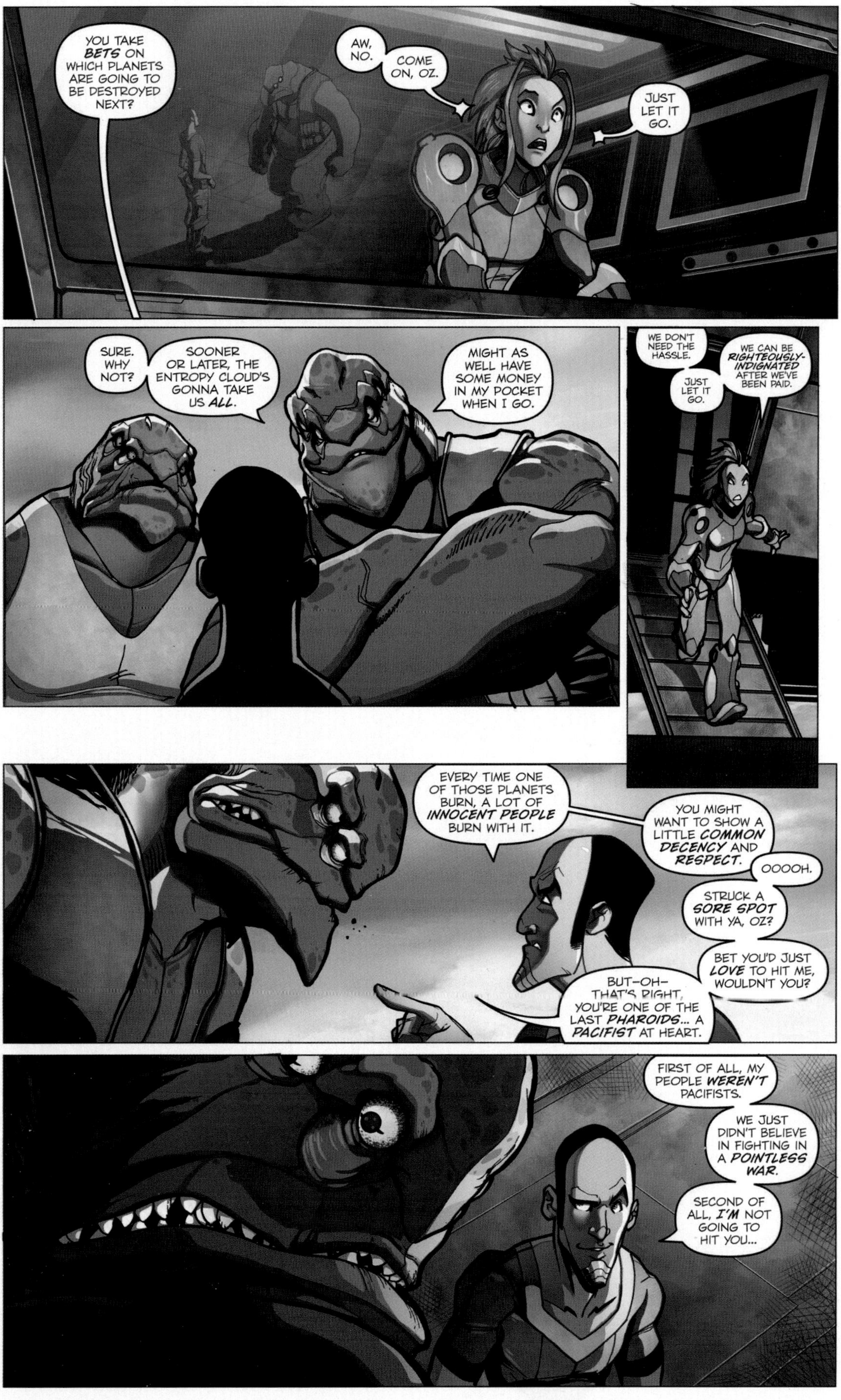
YOU TAKE BETS ON WHICH PLANETS ARE GOING TO BE DESTROYED NEXT?
AW, NO.
COME ON, OZ.
JUST LET IT GO.
SURE. WHY NOT?
SOONER OR LATER, THE ENTROPY CLOUD'S GONNA TAKE US ALL.
MIGHT AS WELL HAVE SOME MONEY IN MY POCKET WHEN I GO.
WE DON'T NEED THE HASSLE.
JUST LET IT GO.
WE CAN BE RIGHTEOUSLY-INDIGNATED AFTER WE'VE BEEN PAID.
EVERY TIME ONE OF THOSE PLANETS BURN, A LOT OF INNOCENT PEOPLE BURN WITH IT.
YOU MIGHT WANT TO SHOW A LITTLE COMMON DECENCY AND RESPECT.
OOOOH.
STRUCK A SORE SPOT WITH YA, OZ?
BET YOU'D JUST LOVE TO HIT ME, WOULDN'T YOU?
BUT—OH—THAT'S RIGHT, YOU'RE ONE OF THE LAST PHAROIDS... A PACIFIST AT HEART.
FIRST OF ALL, MY PEOPLE WEREN'T PACIFISTS.
WE JUST DIDN'T BELIEVE IN FIGHTING IN A POINTLESS WAR.
SECOND OF ALL, I'M NOT GOING TO HIT YOU...

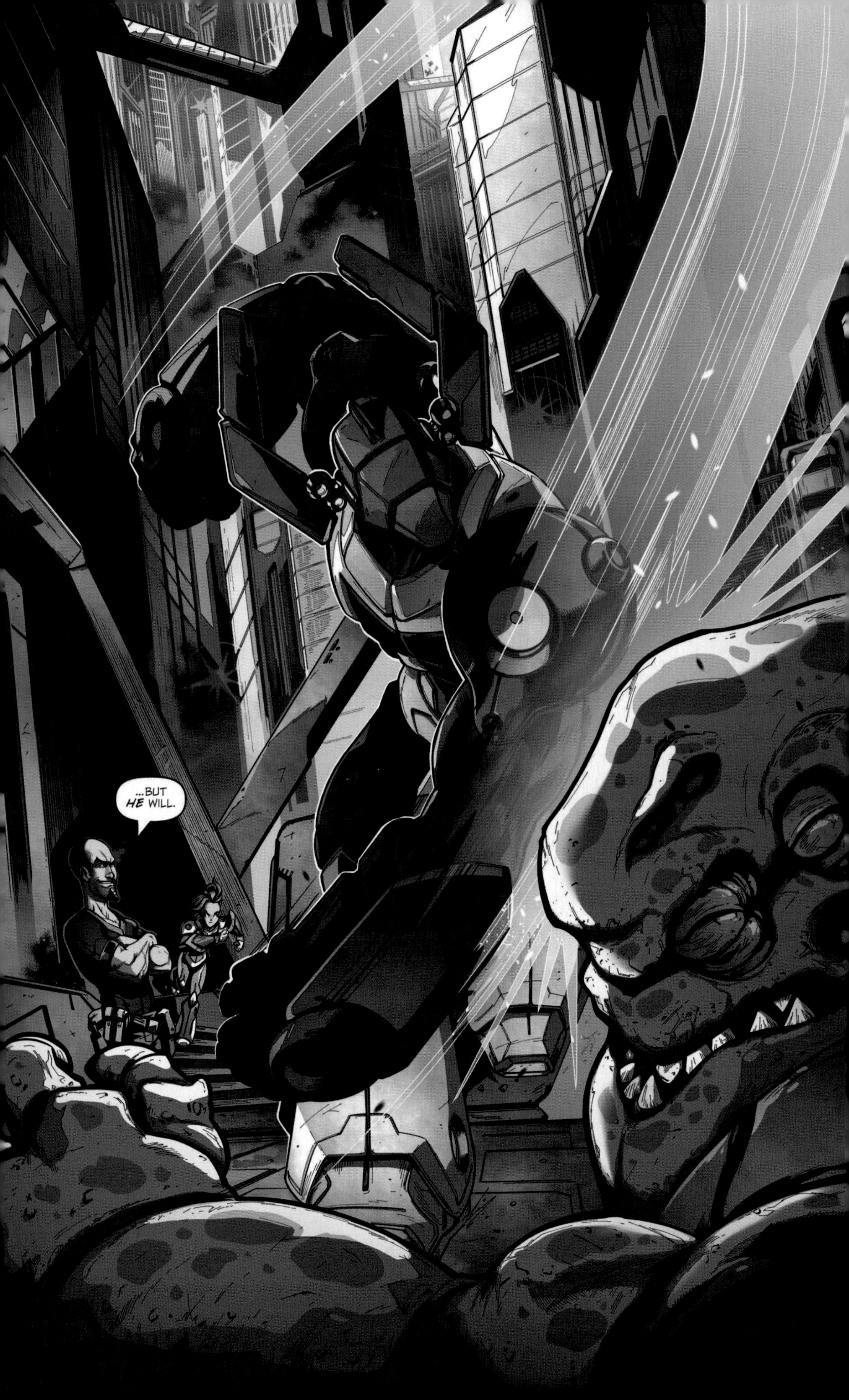
...BUT *HE* WILL.

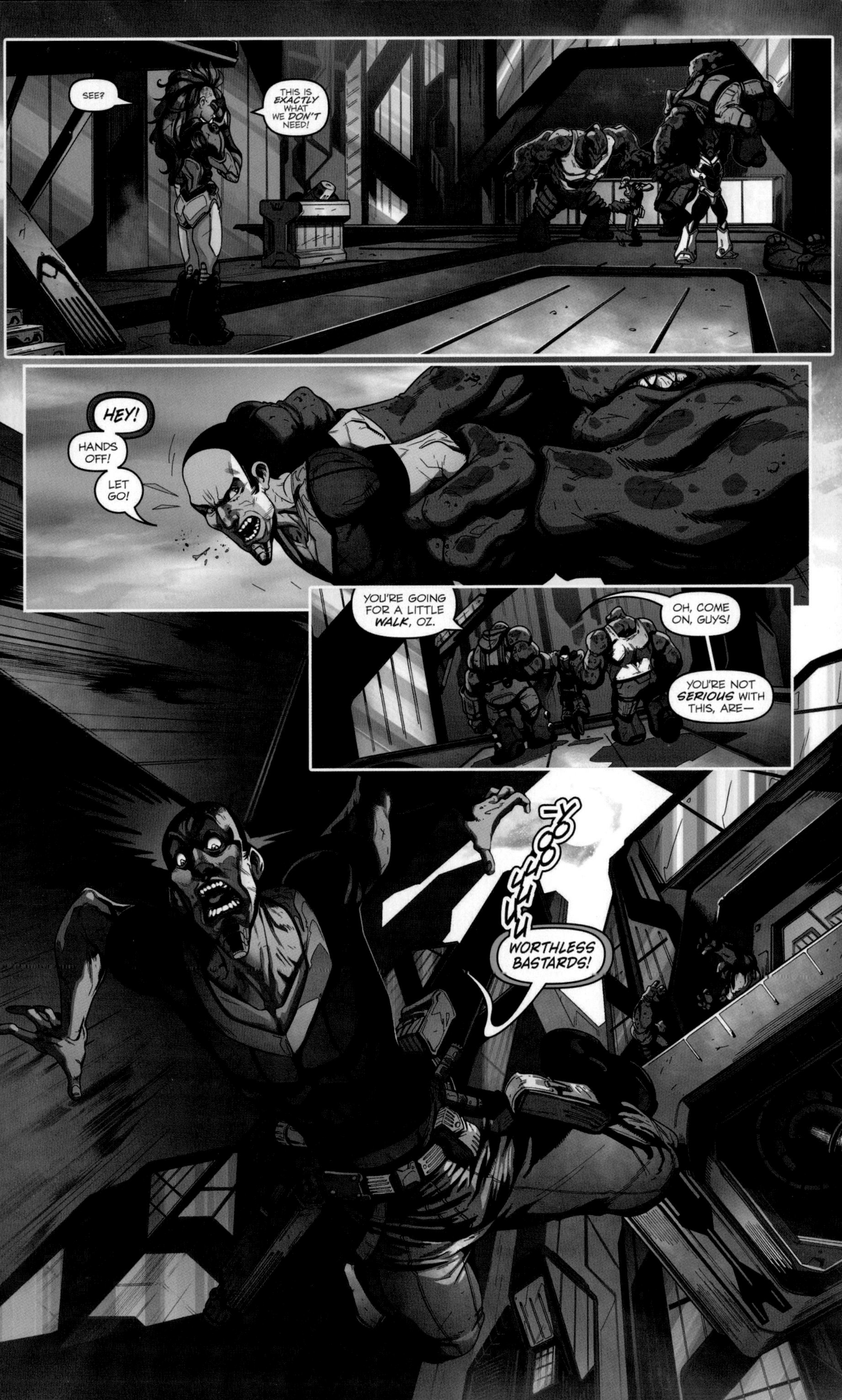
SEE?
THIS IS EXACTLY WHAT WE DON'T NEED!
HEY!
HANDS OFF!
LET GO!
YOU'RE GOING FOR A LITTLE WALK, OZ.
OH, COME ON, GUYS!
YOU'RE NOT SERIOUS WITH THIS, ARE—
YOOOUUUU
WORTHLESS BASTARDS!

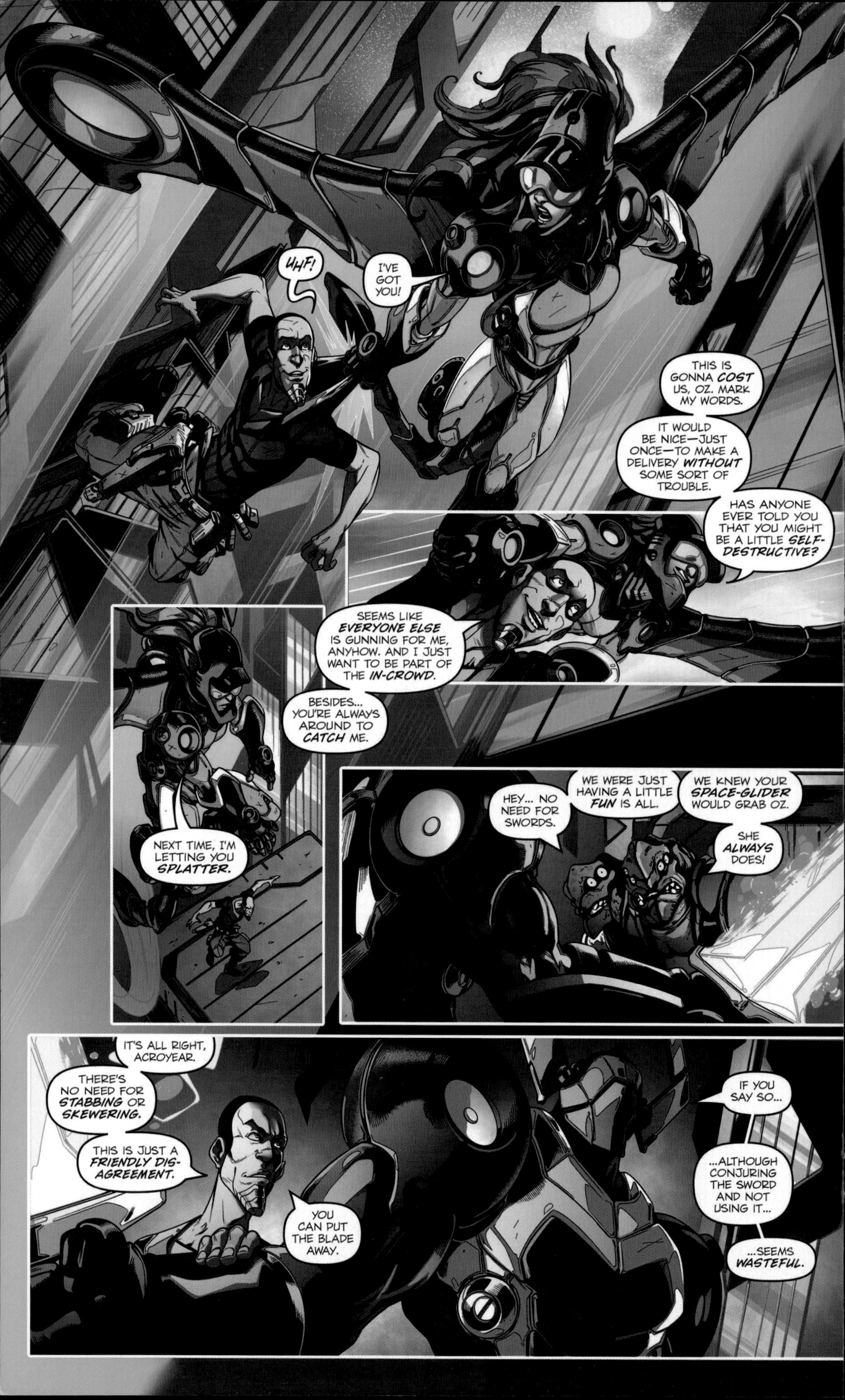
UHF!
I'VE GOT YOU!
THIS IS GONNA COST US, OZ. MARK MY WORDS.
IT WOULD BE NICE—JUST ONCE—TO MAKE A DELIVERY WITHOUT SOME SORT OF TROUBLE.
HAS ANYONE EVER TOLD YOU THAT YOU MIGHT BE A LITTLE SELF-DESTRUCTIVE?
SEEMS LIKE EVERYONE ELSE IS GUNNING FOR ME, ANYHOW. AND I JUST WANT TO BE PART OF THE IN-CROWD.
BESIDES... YOU'RE ALWAYS AROUND TO CATCH ME.
NEXT TIME, I'M LETTING YOU SPLATTER.
HEY... NO NEED FOR SWORDS.
WE WERE JUST HAVING A LITTLE FUN IS ALL.
WE KNEW YOUR SPACE-GLIDER WOULD GRAB OZ.
SHE ALWAYS DOES!
IT'S ALL RIGHT, ACROYEAR.
THERE'S NO NEED FOR STABBING OR SKEWERING.
THIS IS JUST A FRIENDLY DIS-AGREEMENT.
YOU CAN PUT THE BLADE AWAY.
IF YOU SAY SO...
...ALTHOUGH CONJURING THE SWORD AND NOT USING IT...
...SEEMS WASTEFUL.

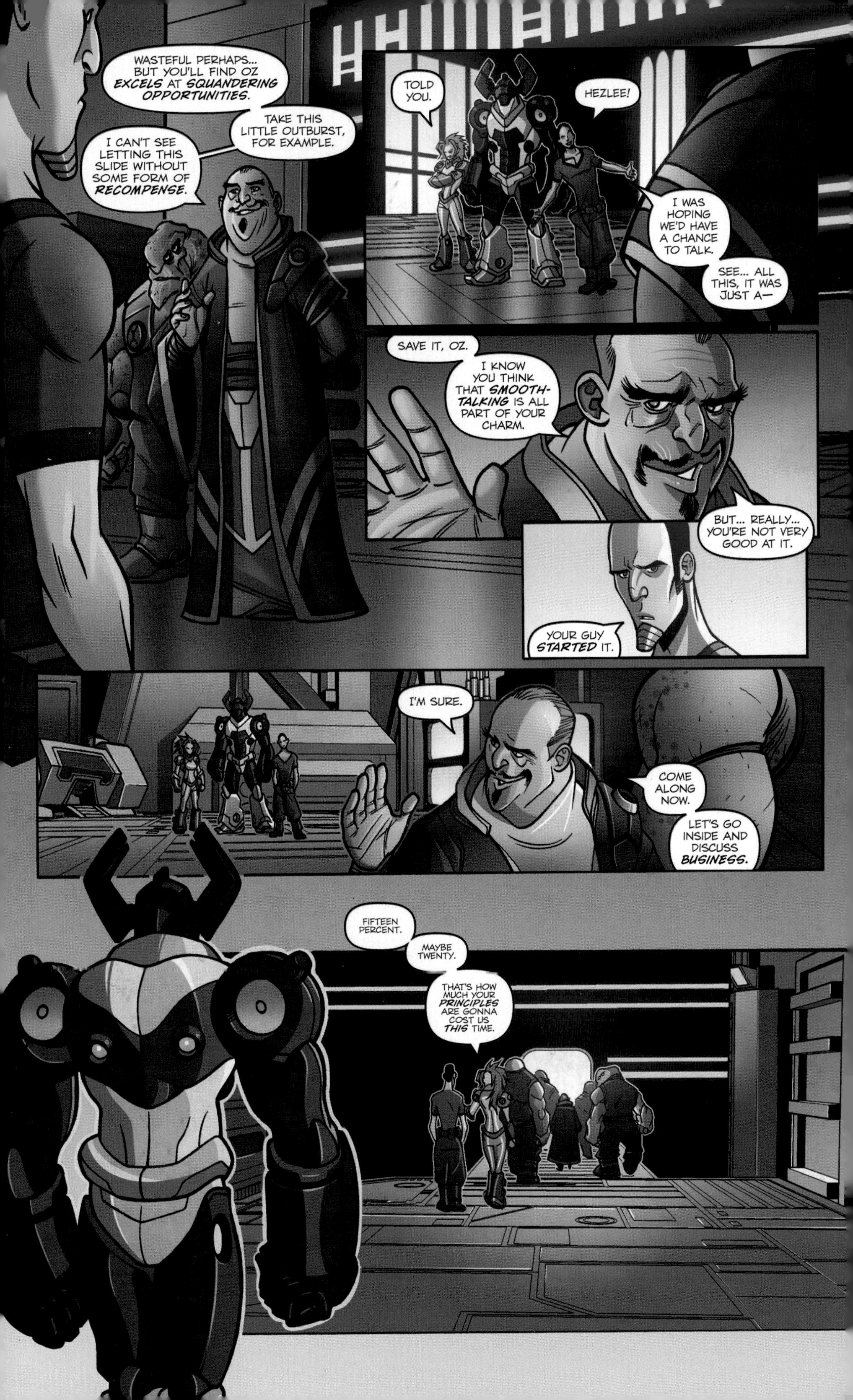
WASTEFUL PERHAPS... BUT YOU'LL FIND OZ *EXCELS* AT *SQUANDERING OPPORTUNITIES*.
TAKE THIS LITTLE OUTBURST, FOR EXAMPLE.
I CAN'T SEE LETTING THIS SLIDE WITHOUT SOME FORM OF *RECOMPENSE*.
TOLD YOU.
HEZLEE!
I WAS HOPING WE'D HAVE A CHANCE TO TALK.
SEE... ALL THIS, IT WAS JUST A—
SAVE IT, OZ.
I KNOW YOU THINK THAT *SMOOTH-TALKING* IS ALL PART OF YOUR CHARM.
BUT... REALLY... YOU'RE NOT VERY GOOD AT IT.
YOUR GUY *STARTED* IT.
I'M SURE.
COME ALONG NOW.
LET'S GO INSIDE AND DISCUSS *BUSINESS*.
FIFTEEN PERCENT.
MAYBE TWENTY.
THAT'S HOW MUCH YOUR *PRINCIPLES* ARE GONNA COST US *THIS* TIME.

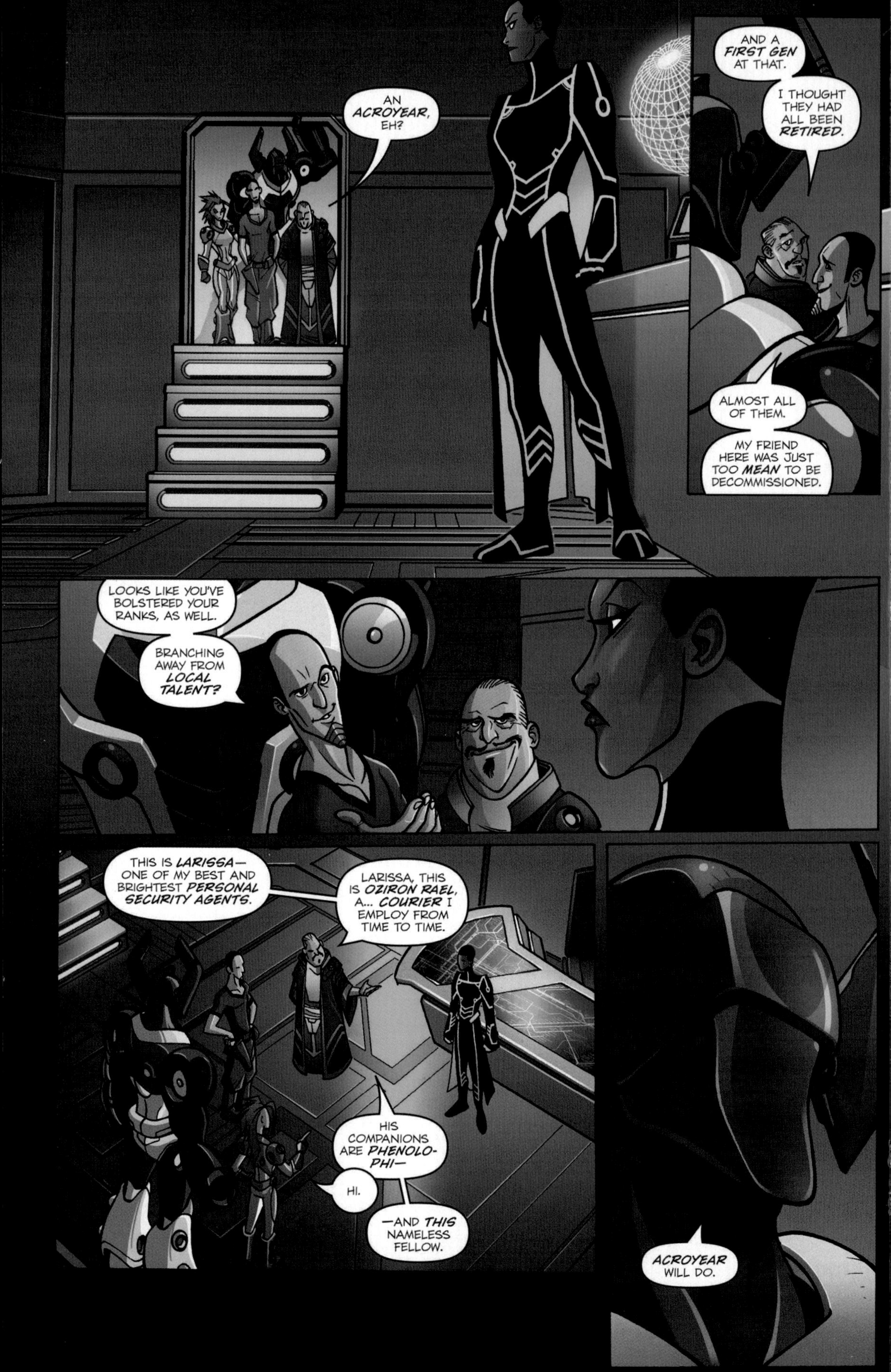
AN ACROYEAR, EH?
AND A FIRST GEN AT THAT.
I THOUGHT THEY HAD ALL BEEN RETIRED.
ALMOST ALL OF THEM.
MY FRIEND HERE WAS JUST TOO MEAN TO BE DECOMMISSIONED.
LOOKS LIKE YOU'VE BOLSTERED YOUR RANKS, AS WELL.
BRANCHING AWAY FROM LOCAL TALENT?
THIS IS LARISSA— ONE OF MY BEST AND BRIGHTEST PERSONAL SECURITY AGENTS.
LARISSA, THIS IS OZIRON RAEL, A... COURIER I EMPLOY FROM TIME TO TIME.
HIS COMPANIONS ARE PHENOLO-PHI—
HI.
—AND THIS NAMELESS FELLOW.
ACROYEAR WILL DO.

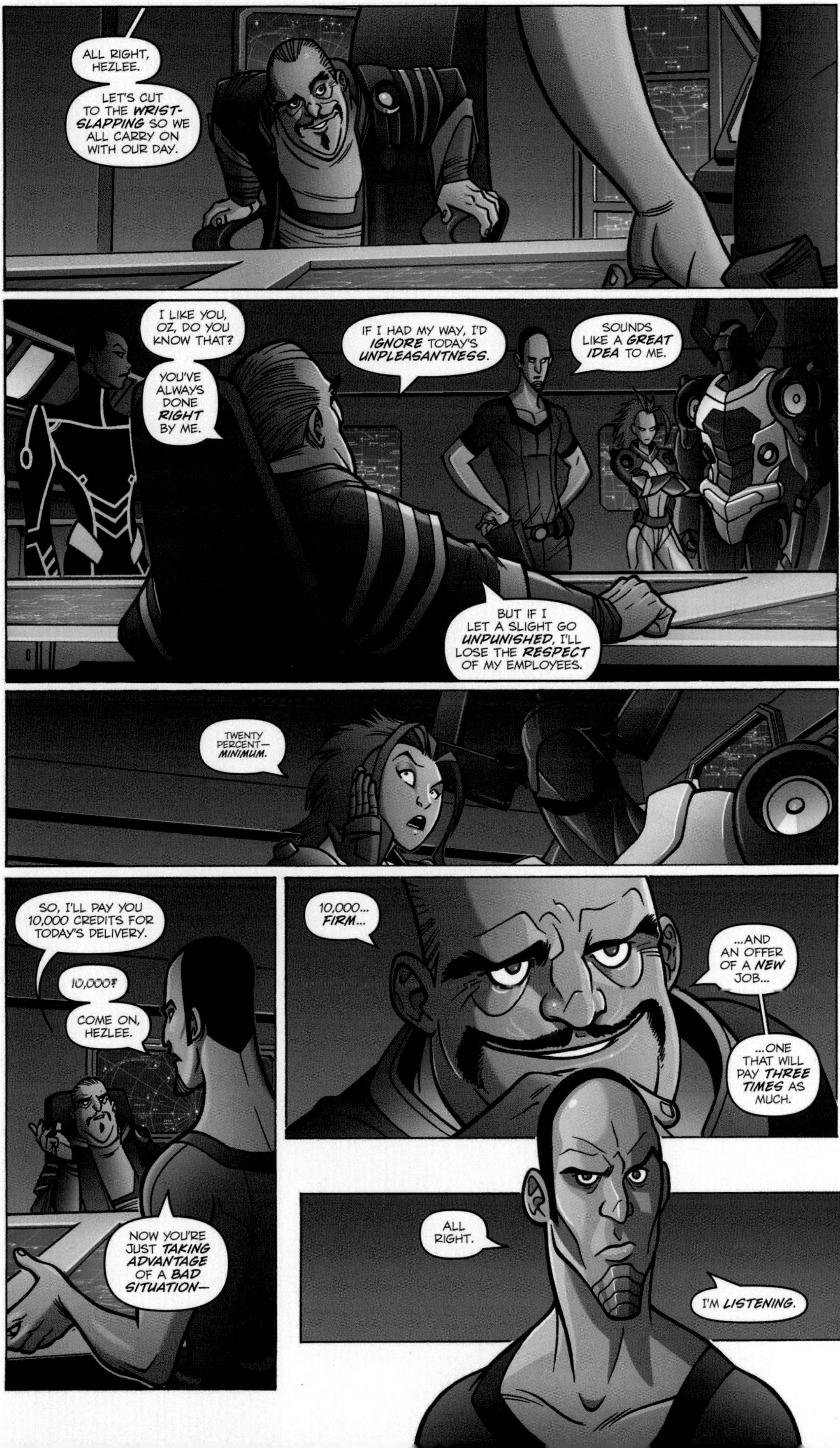
ALL RIGHT, HEZLEE.
LET'S CUT TO THE WRIST-SLAPPING SO WE ALL CARRY ON WITH OUR DAY.
I LIKE YOU, OZ, DO YOU KNOW THAT?
YOU'VE ALWAYS DONE RIGHT BY ME.
IF I HAD MY WAY, I'D IGNORE TODAY'S UNPLEASANTNESS.
SOUNDS LIKE A GREAT IDEA TO ME.
BUT IF I LET A SLIGHT GO UNPUNISHED, I'LL LOSE THE RESPECT OF MY EMPLOYEES.
TWENTY PERCENT—MINIMUM.
SO, I'LL PAY YOU 10,000 CREDITS FOR TODAY'S DELIVERY.
10,000?
COME ON, HEZLEE.
NOW YOU'RE JUST TAKING ADVANTAGE OF A BAD SITUATION—
10,000... FIRM...
...AND AN OFFER OF A NEW JOB...
...ONE THAT WILL PAY THREE TIMES AS MUCH.
ALL RIGHT.
I'M LISTENING.

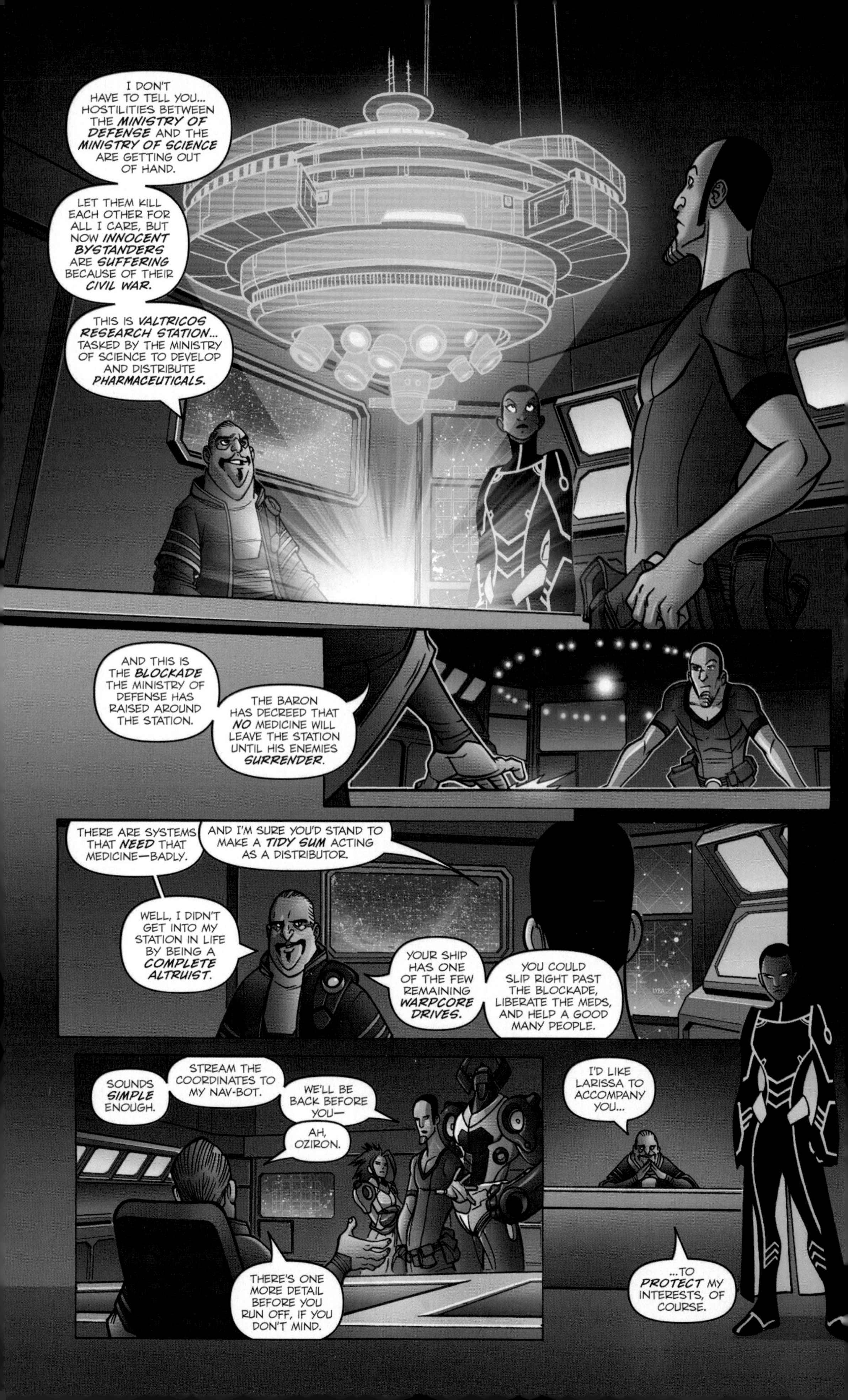
I DON'T HAVE TO TELL YOU... HOSTILITIES BETWEEN THE MINISTRY OF DEFENSE AND THE MINISTRY OF SCIENCE ARE GETTING OUT OF HAND.
LET THEM KILL EACH OTHER FOR ALL I CARE, BUT NOW INNOCENT BYSTANDERS ARE SUFFERING BECAUSE OF THEIR CIVIL WAR.
THIS IS VALTRICOS RESEARCH STATION... TASKED BY THE MINISTRY OF SCIENCE TO DEVELOP AND DISTRIBUTE PHARMACEUTICALS.
AND THIS IS THE BLOCKADE THE MINISTRY OF DEFENSE HAS RAISED AROUND THE STATION.
THE BARON HAS DECREED THAT NO MEDICINE WILL LEAVE THE STATION UNTIL HIS ENEMIES SURRENDER.
THERE ARE SYSTEMS THAT NEED THAT MEDICINE—BADLY.
AND I'M SURE YOU'D STAND TO MAKE A TIDY SUM ACTING AS A DISTRIBUTOR.
WELL, I DIDN'T GET INTO MY STATION IN LIFE BY BEING A COMPLETE ALTRUIST.
YOUR SHIP HAS ONE OF THE FEW REMAINING WARPCORE DRIVES.
YOU COULD SLIP RIGHT PAST THE BLOCKADE, LIBERATE THE MEDS, AND HELP A GOOD MANY PEOPLE.
SOUNDS SIMPLE ENOUGH.
STREAM THE COORDINATES TO MY NAV-BOT.
WE'LL BE BACK BEFORE YOU—
AH, OZIRON.
THERE'S ONE MORE DETAIL BEFORE YOU RUN OFF, IF YOU DON'T MIND.
I'D LIKE LARISSA TO ACCOMPANY YOU...
...TO PROTECT MY INTERESTS, OF COURSE.

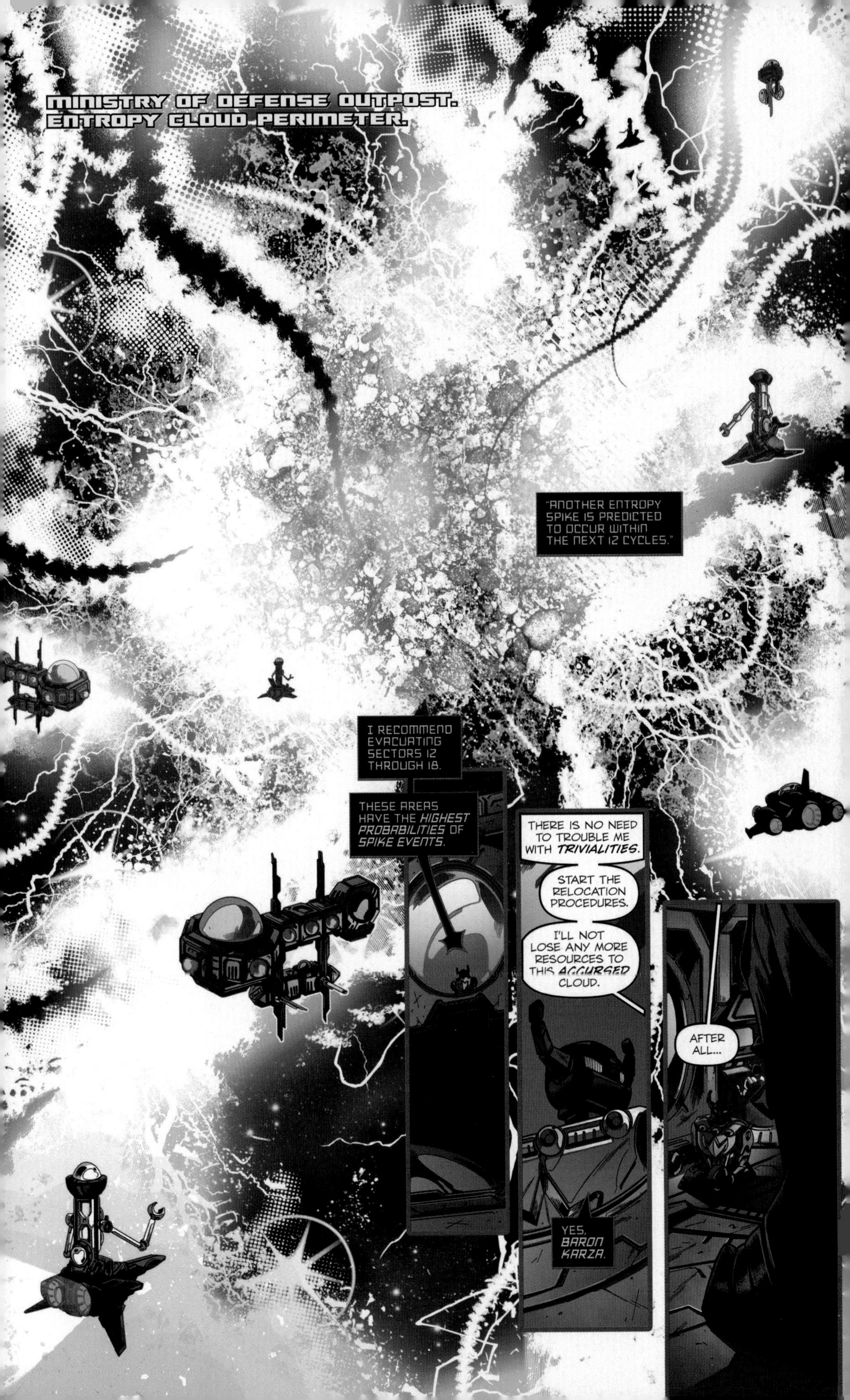
MINISTRY OF DEFENSE OUTPOST.
ENTROPY CLOUD PERIMETER.
"ANOTHER ENTROPY SPIKE IS PREDICTED TO OCCUR WITHIN THE NEXT 12 CYCLES."
I RECOMMEND EVACUATING SECTORS 12 THROUGH 18.
THESE AREAS HAVE THE *HIGHEST PROBABILITIES* OF *SPIKE EVENTS*.
THERE IS NO NEED TO TROUBLE ME WITH *TRIVIALITIES*.
START THE RELOCATION PROCEDURES.
I'LL NOT LOSE ANY MORE RESOURCES TO THIS *ACCURSED* CLOUD.
YES, *BARON KARZA*.
AFTER ALL...

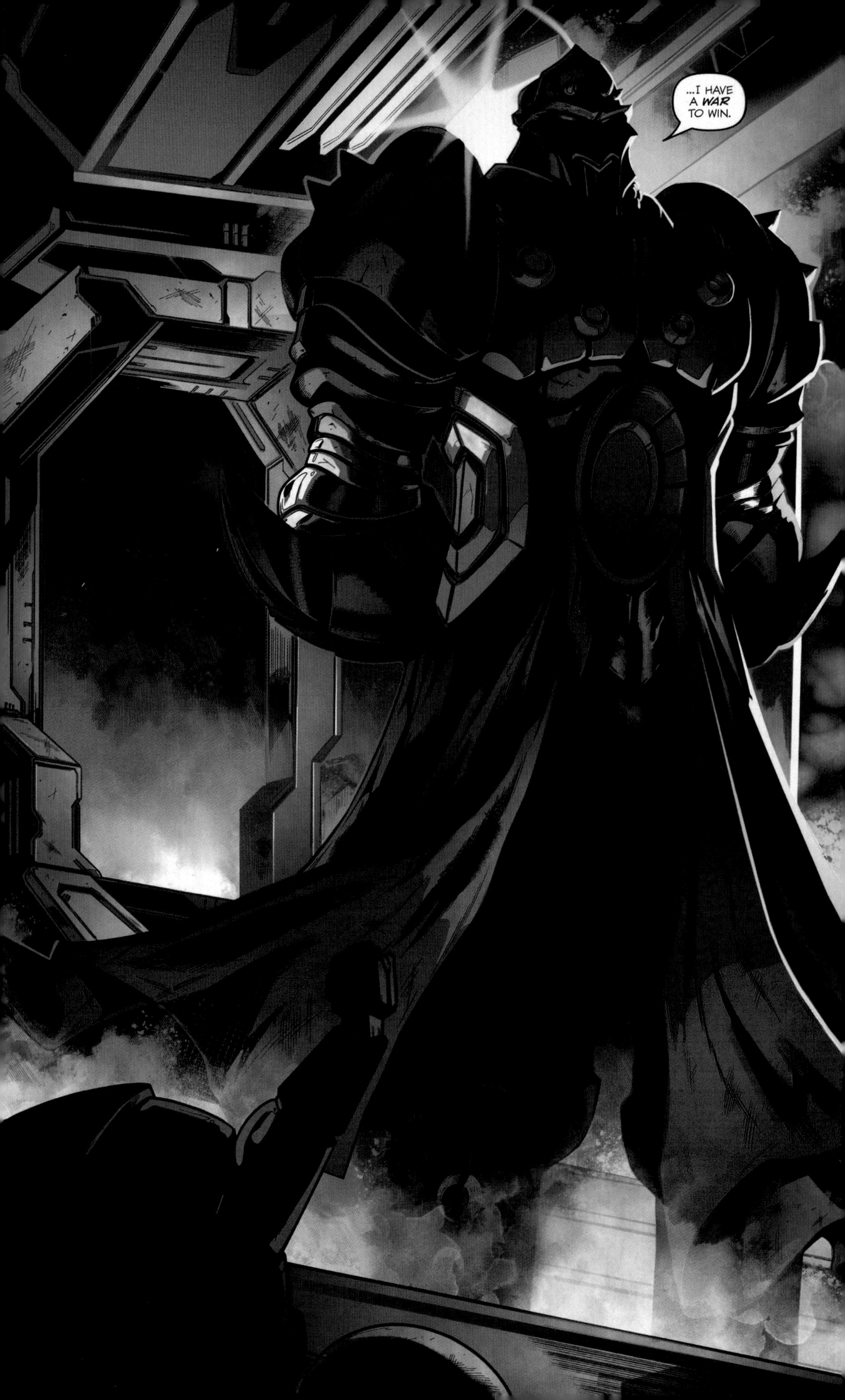
...I HAVE A WAR TO WIN.

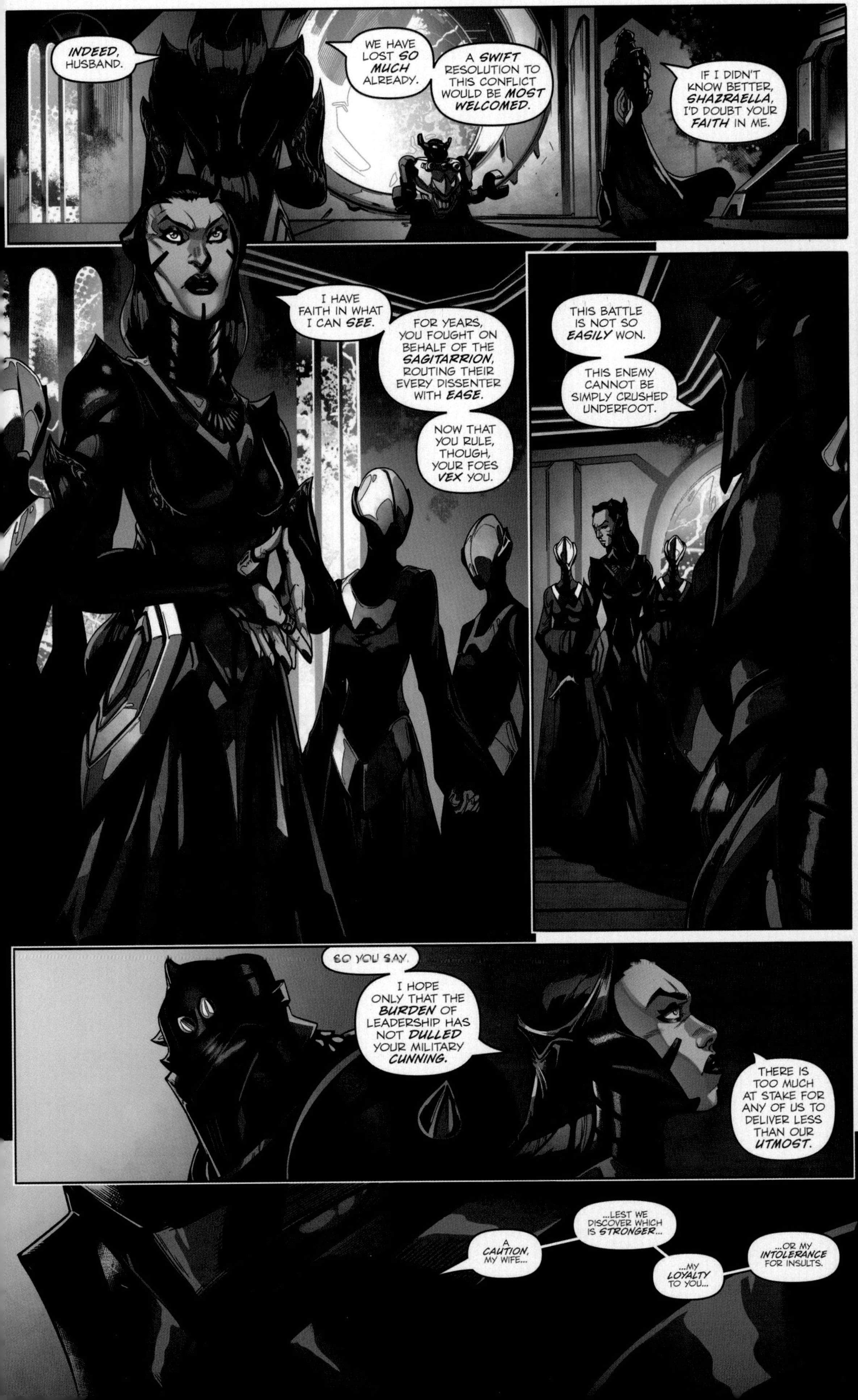

INDEED, HUSBAND.
WE HAVE LOST SO MUCH ALREADY.
A SWIFT RESOLUTION TO THIS CONFLICT WOULD BE MOST WELCOMED.
IF I DIDN'T KNOW BETTER, SHAZRAELLA, I'D DOUBT YOUR FAITH IN ME.
I HAVE FAITH IN WHAT I CAN SEE.
FOR YEARS, YOU FOUGHT ON BEHALF OF THE SAGITARRION, ROUTING THEIR EVERY DISSENTER WITH EASE.
NOW THAT YOU RULE, THOUGH, YOUR FOES VEX YOU.
THIS BATTLE IS NOT SO EASILY WON.
THIS ENEMY CANNOT BE SIMPLY CRUSHED UNDERFOOT.
SO YOU SAY.
I HOPE ONLY THAT THE BURDEN OF LEADERSHIP HAS NOT DULLED YOUR MILITARY CUNNING.
THERE IS TOO MUCH AT STAKE FOR ANY OF US TO DELIVER LESS THAN OUR UTMOST.
A CAUTION, MY WIFE...
...LEST WE DISCOVER WHICH IS STRONGER...
...MY LOYALTY TO YOU...
...OR MY INTOLERANCE FOR INSULTS.

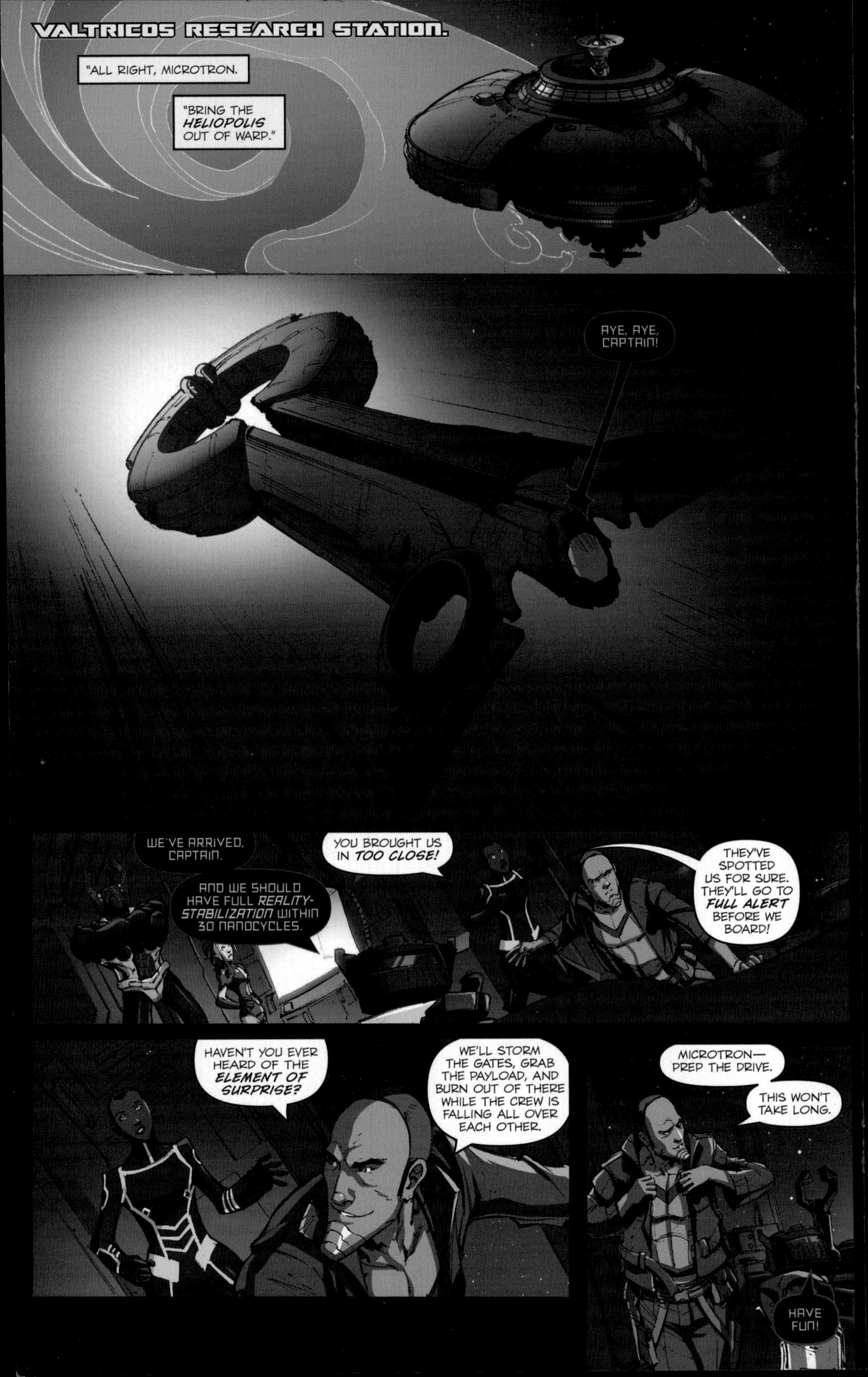
VALTRICOS RESEARCH STATION.
"ALL RIGHT, MICROTRON.
"BRING THE *HELIOPOLIS* OUT OF WARP."
AYE, AYE, CAPTAIN!
WE'VE ARRIVED, CAPTAIN.
AND WE SHOULD HAVE FULL *REALITY-STABILIZATION* WITHIN 30 NANOCYCLES.
YOU BROUGHT US IN *TOO CLOSE!*
THEY'VE SPOTTED US FOR SURE. THEY'LL GO TO *FULL ALERT* BEFORE WE BOARD!
HAVEN'T YOU EVER HEARD OF THE *ELEMENT OF SURPRISE?*
WE'LL STORM THE GATES, GRAB THE PAYLOAD, AND BURN OUT OF THERE WHILE THE CREW IS FALLING ALL OVER EACH OTHER.
MICROTRON— PREP THE DRIVE.
THIS WON'T TAKE LONG.
HAVE FUN!

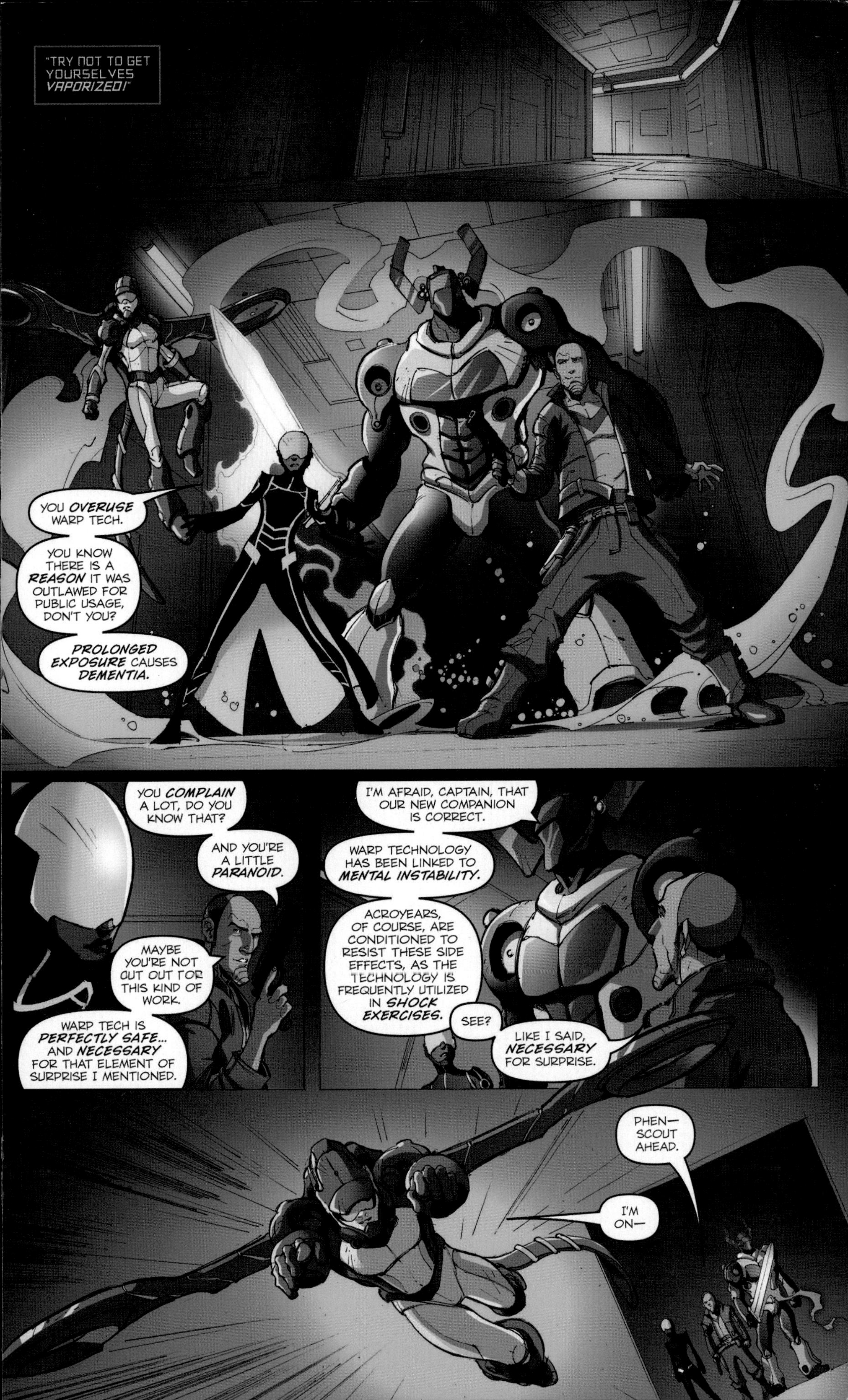
"TRY NOT TO GET YOURSELVES VAPORIZED!"
YOU OVERUSE WARP TECH.
YOU KNOW THERE IS A REASON IT WAS OUTLAWED FOR PUBLIC USAGE, DON'T YOU?
PROLONGED EXPOSURE CAUSES DEMENTIA.
YOU COMPLAIN A LOT, DO YOU KNOW THAT?
AND YOU'RE A LITTLE PARANOID.
MAYBE YOU'RE NOT CUT OUT FOR THIS KIND OF WORK.
WARP TECH IS PERFECTLY SAFE... AND NECESSARY FOR THAT ELEMENT OF SURPRISE I MENTIONED.
I'M AFRAID, CAPTAIN, THAT OUR NEW COMPANION IS CORRECT.
WARP TECHNOLOGY HAS BEEN LINKED TO MENTAL INSTABILITY.
ACROYEARS, OF COURSE, ARE CONDITIONED TO RESIST THESE SIDE EFFECTS, AS THE TECHNOLOGY IS FREQUENTLY UTILIZED IN SHOCK EXERCISES.
SEE?
LIKE I SAID, NECESSARY FOR SURPRISE.
PHEN— SCOUT AHEAD.
I'M ON—

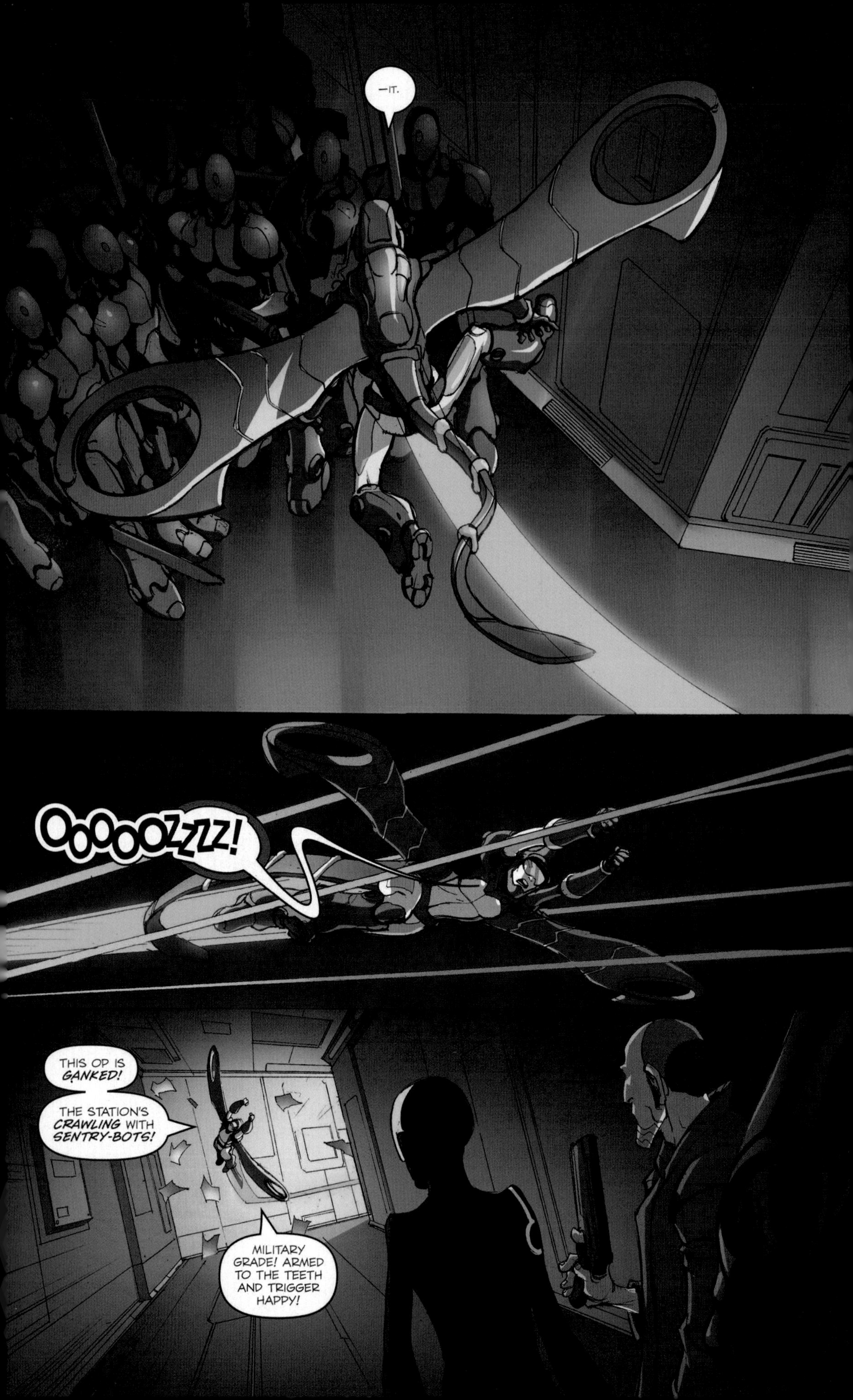
—IT.
OOOOOZZZZ!
THIS OP IS *GANKED!*
THE STATION'S *CRAWLING* WITH *SENTRY-BOTS!*
MILITARY GRADE! ARMED TO THE TEETH AND TRIGGER HAPPY!

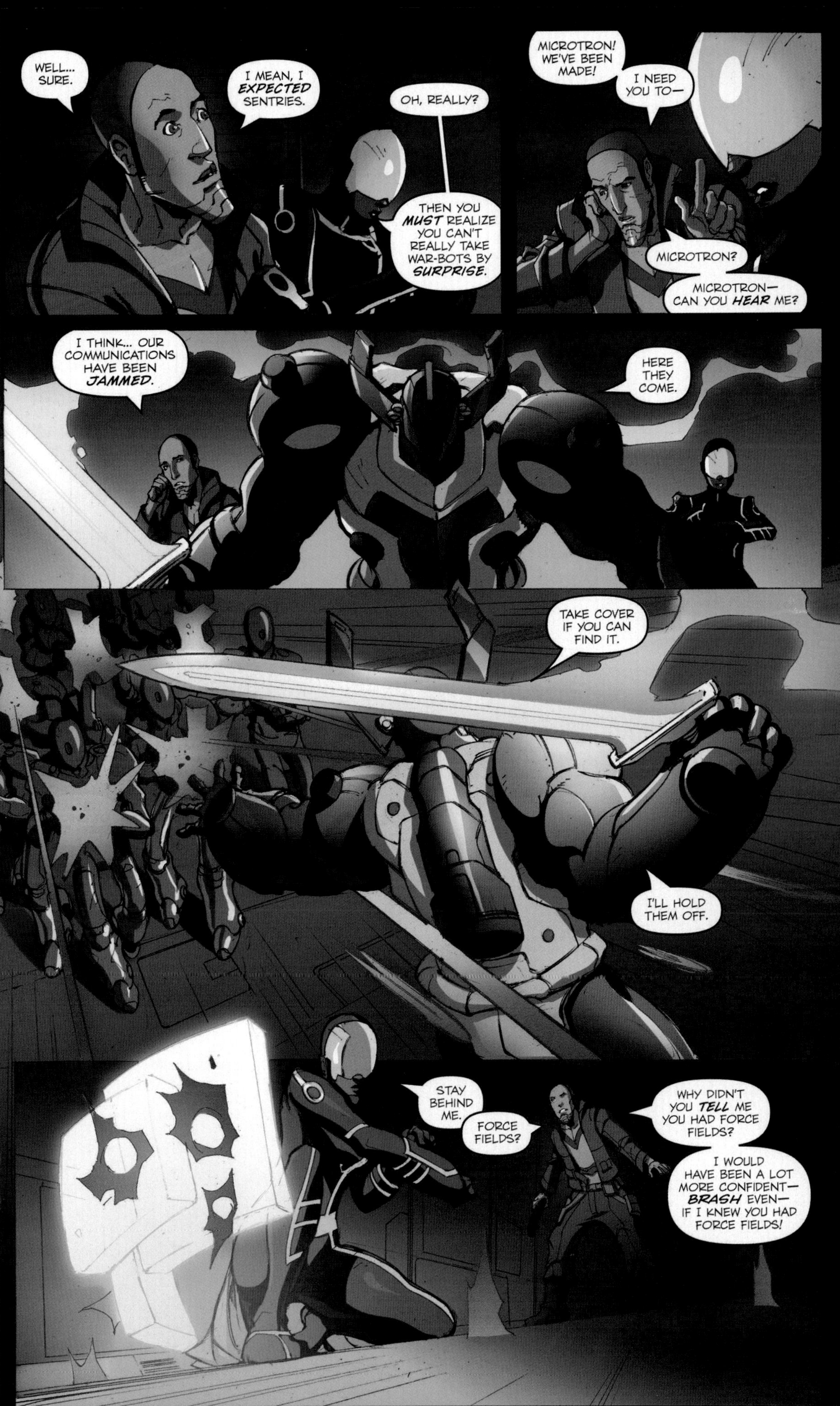

WELL... SURE.
I MEAN, I EXPECTED SENTRIES.
OH, REALLY?
THEN YOU MUST REALIZE YOU CAN'T REALLY TAKE WAR-BOTS BY SURPRISE.
MICROTRON! WE'VE BEEN MADE!
I NEED YOU TO—
MICROTRON?
MICROTRON— CAN YOU HEAR ME?
I THINK... OUR COMMUNICATIONS HAVE BEEN JAMMED.
HERE THEY COME.
TAKE COVER IF YOU CAN FIND IT.
I'LL HOLD THEM OFF.
STAY BEHIND ME.
FORCE FIELDS?
WHY DIDN'T YOU TELL ME YOU HAD FORCE FIELDS?
I WOULD HAVE BEEN A LOT MORE CONFIDENT— BRASH EVEN— IF I KNEW YOU HAD FORCE FIELDS!

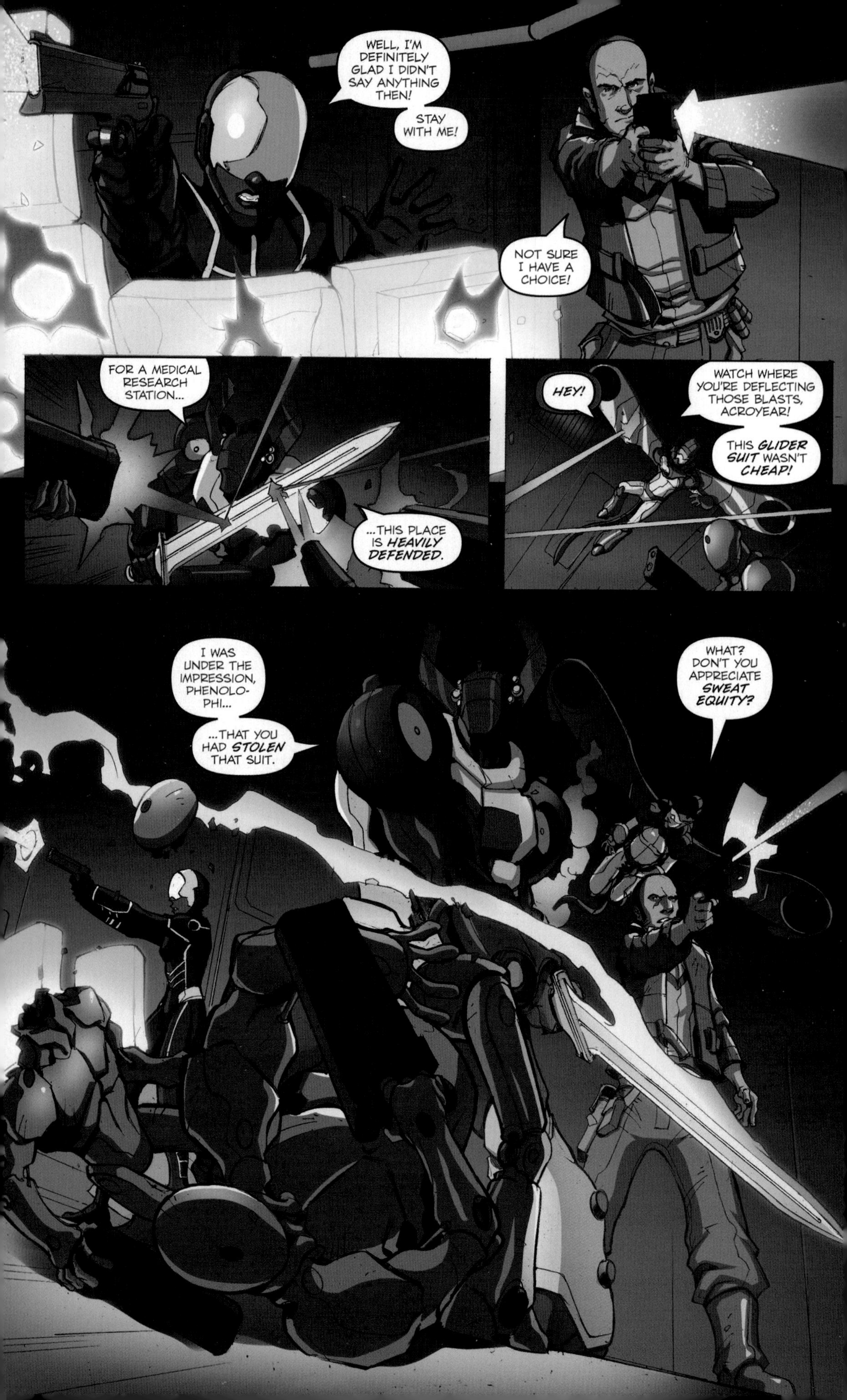
WELL, I'M DEFINITELY GLAD I DIDN'T SAY ANYTHING THEN!
STAY WITH ME!
NOT SURE I HAVE A CHOICE!
FOR A MEDICAL RESEARCH STATION...
...THIS PLACE IS HEAVILY DEFENDED.
HEY!
WATCH WHERE YOU'RE DEFLECTING THOSE BLASTS, ACROYEAR!
THIS GLIDER SUIT WASN'T CHEAP!
I WAS UNDER THE IMPRESSION, PHENOLO-PHI...
...THAT YOU HAD STOLEN THAT SUIT.
WHAT? DON'T YOU APPRECIATE SWEAT EQUITY?

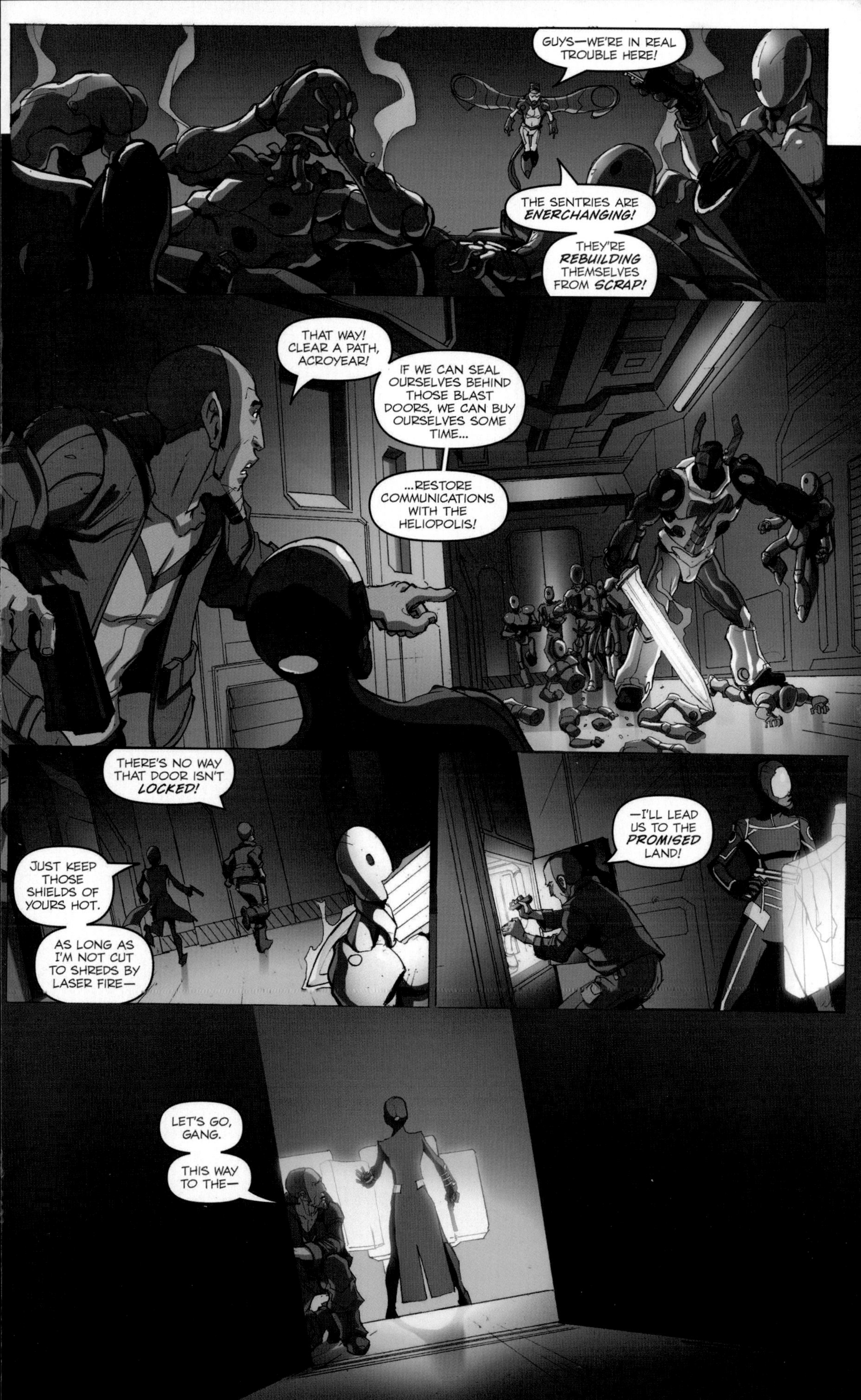
GUYS—WE'RE IN REAL TROUBLE HERE!
THE SENTRIES ARE ENERCHANGING!
THEY'RE REBUILDING THEMSELVES FROM SCRAP!
THAT WAY! CLEAR A PATH, ACROYEAR!
IF WE CAN SEAL OURSELVES BEHIND THOSE BLAST DOORS, WE CAN BUY OURSELVES SOME TIME...
...RESTORE COMMUNICATIONS WITH THE HELIOPOLIS!
THERE'S NO WAY THAT DOOR ISN'T LOCKED!
JUST KEEP THOSE SHIELDS OF YOURS HOT.
AS LONG AS I'M NOT CUT TO SHREDS BY LASER FIRE—
—I'LL LEAD US TO THE PROMISED LAND!
LET'S GO, GANG.
THIS WAY TO THE—

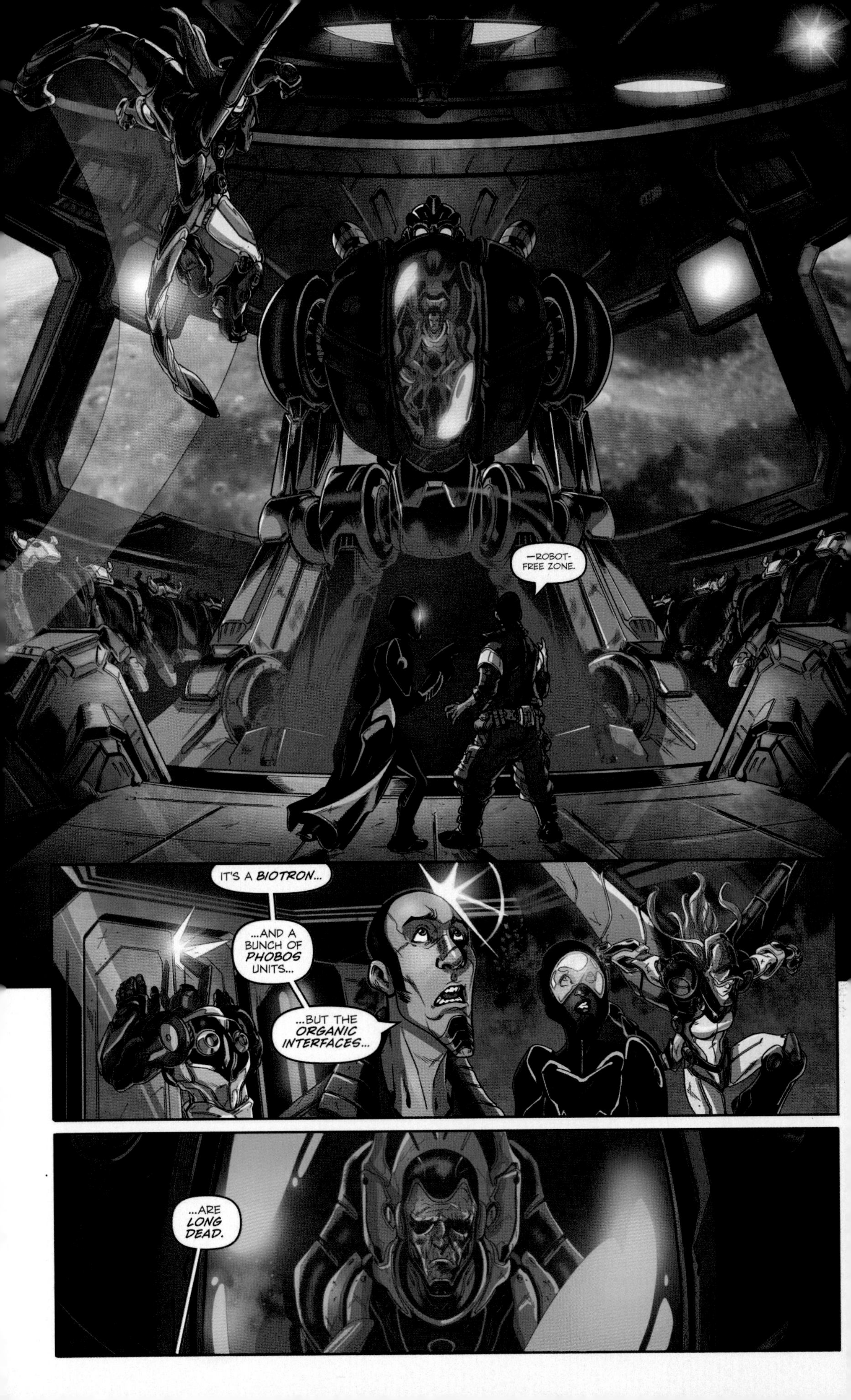
—ROBOT-FREE ZONE.
IT'S A BIOTRON...
...AND A BUNCH OF PHOBOS UNITS...
...BUT THE ORGANIC INTERFACES...
...ARE LONG DEAD.

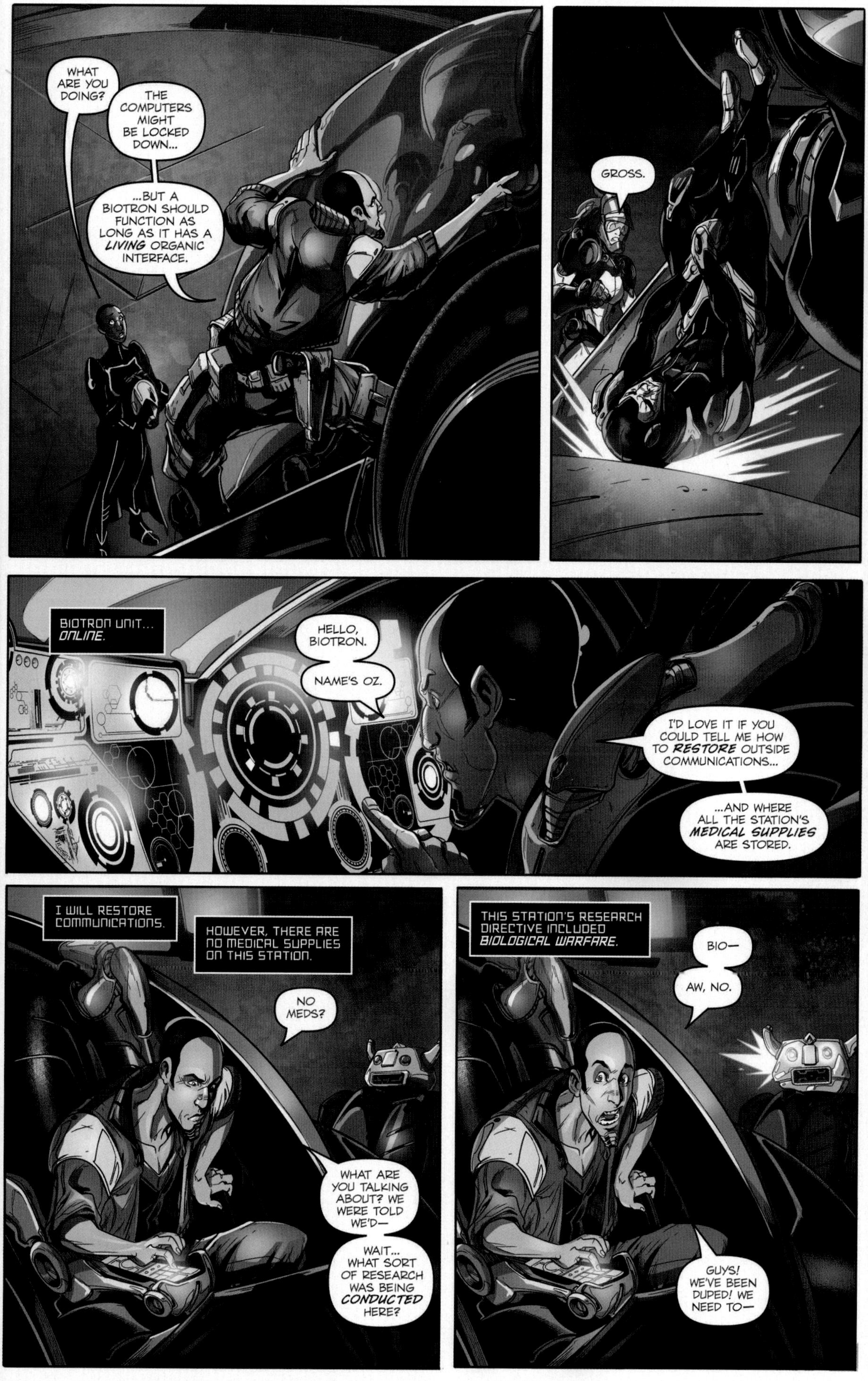
WHAT ARE YOU DOING?
THE COMPUTERS MIGHT BE LOCKED DOWN...
...BUT A BIOTRON SHOULD FUNCTION AS LONG AS IT HAS A LIVING ORGANIC INTERFACE.
GROSS.
BIOTRON UNIT... ONLINE.
HELLO, BIOTRON.
NAME'S OZ.
I'D LOVE IT IF YOU COULD TELL ME HOW TO RESTORE OUTSIDE COMMUNICATIONS...
...AND WHERE ALL THE STATION'S MEDICAL SUPPLIES ARE STORED.
I WILL RESTORE COMMUNICATIONS.
HOWEVER, THERE ARE NO MEDICAL SUPPLIES ON THIS STATION.
NO MEDS?
WHAT ARE YOU TALKING ABOUT? WE WERE TOLD WE'D—
WAIT... WHAT SORT OF RESEARCH WAS BEING CONDUCTED HERE?
THIS STATION'S RESEARCH DIRECTIVE INCLUDED BIOLOGICAL WARFARE.
BIO—
AW, NO.
GUYS! WE'VE BEEN DUPED! WE NEED TO—

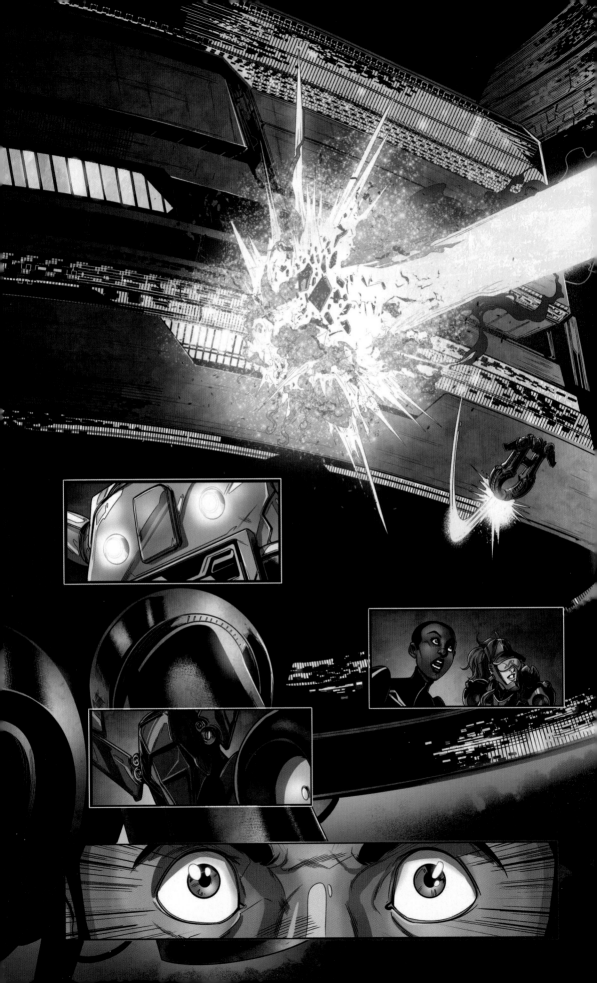

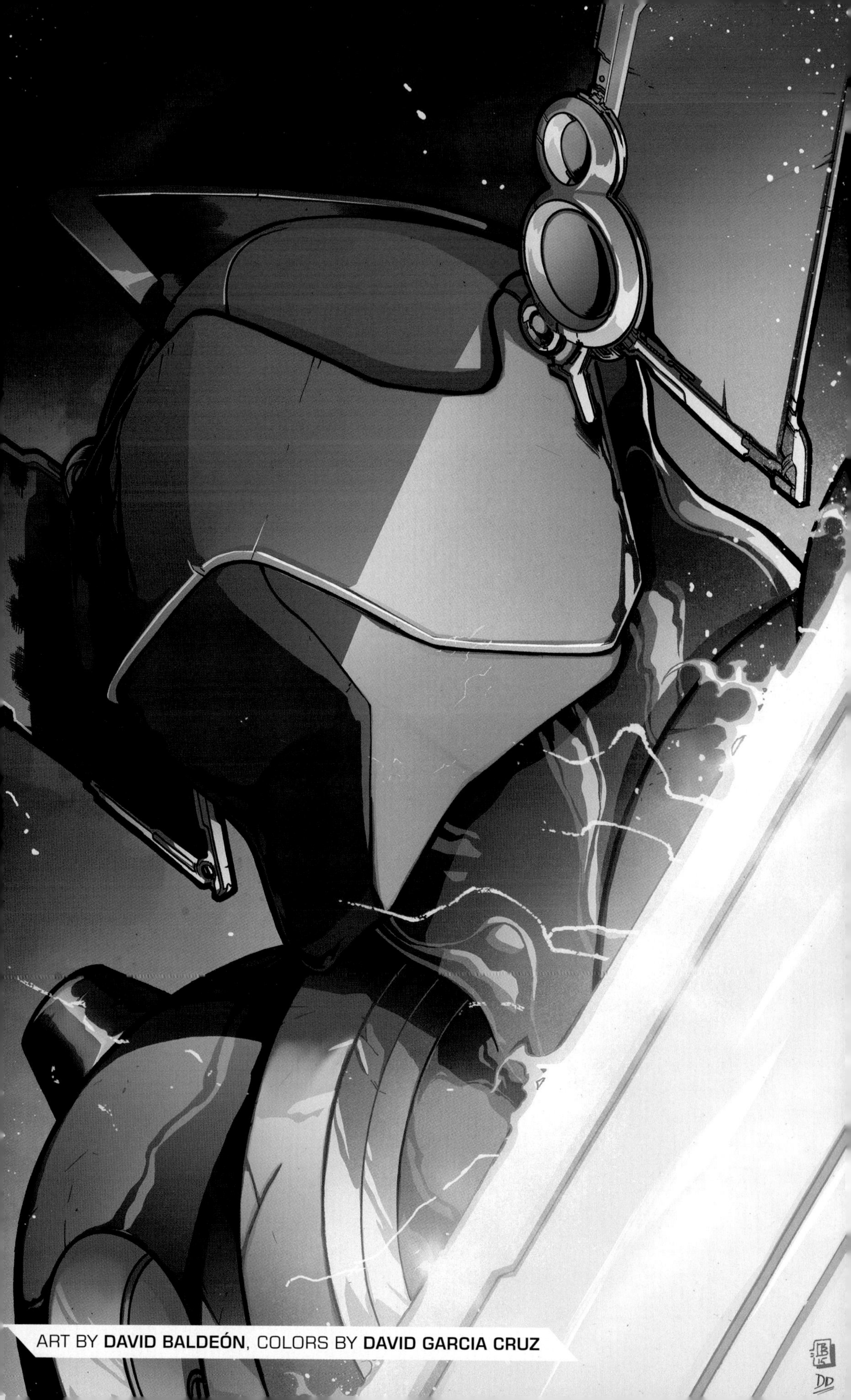

ART BY **DAVID BALDEÓN**, COLORS BY **DAVID GARCIA CRUZ**

02

ART BY **J.H. WILLIAMS III**

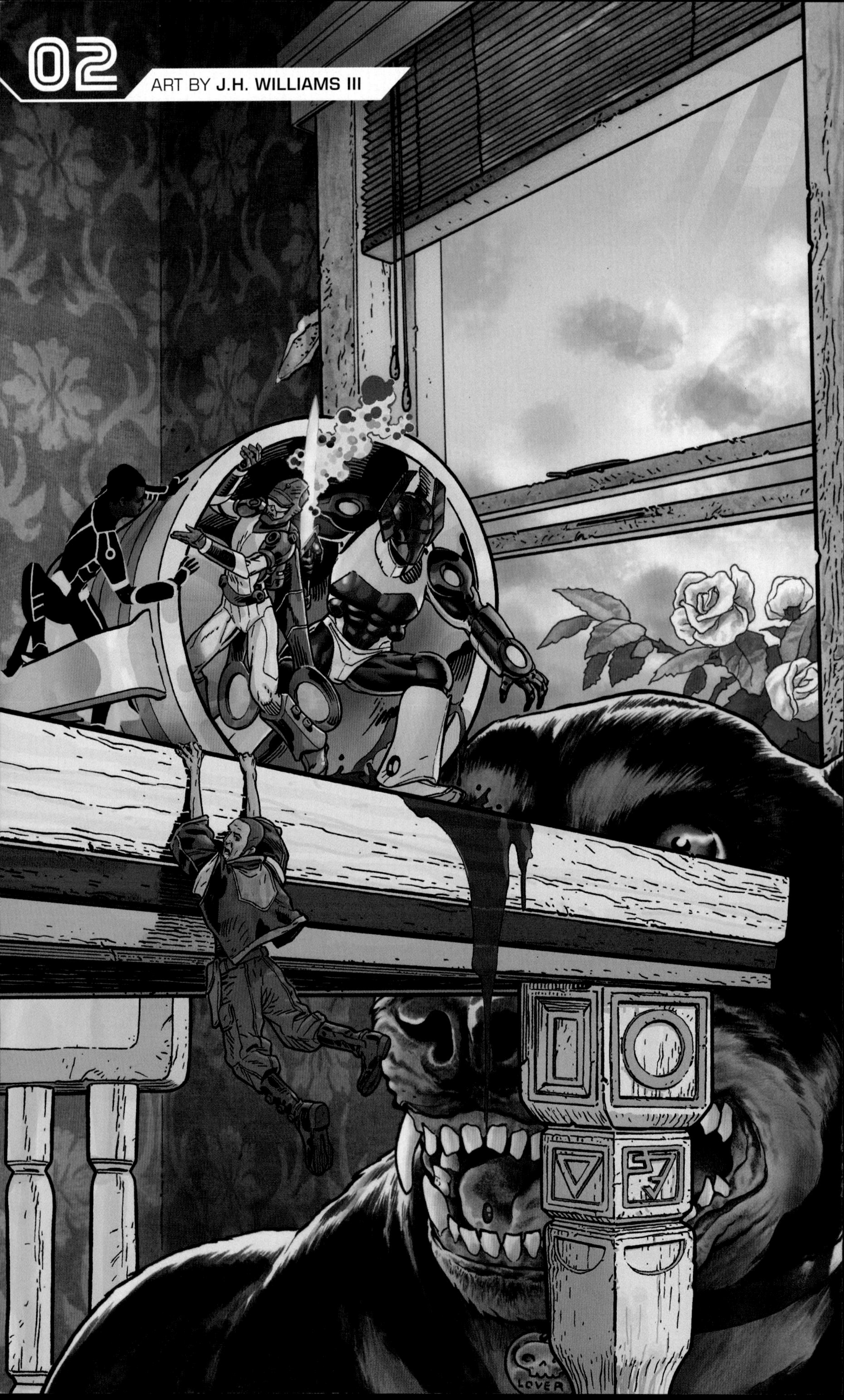
LOVER

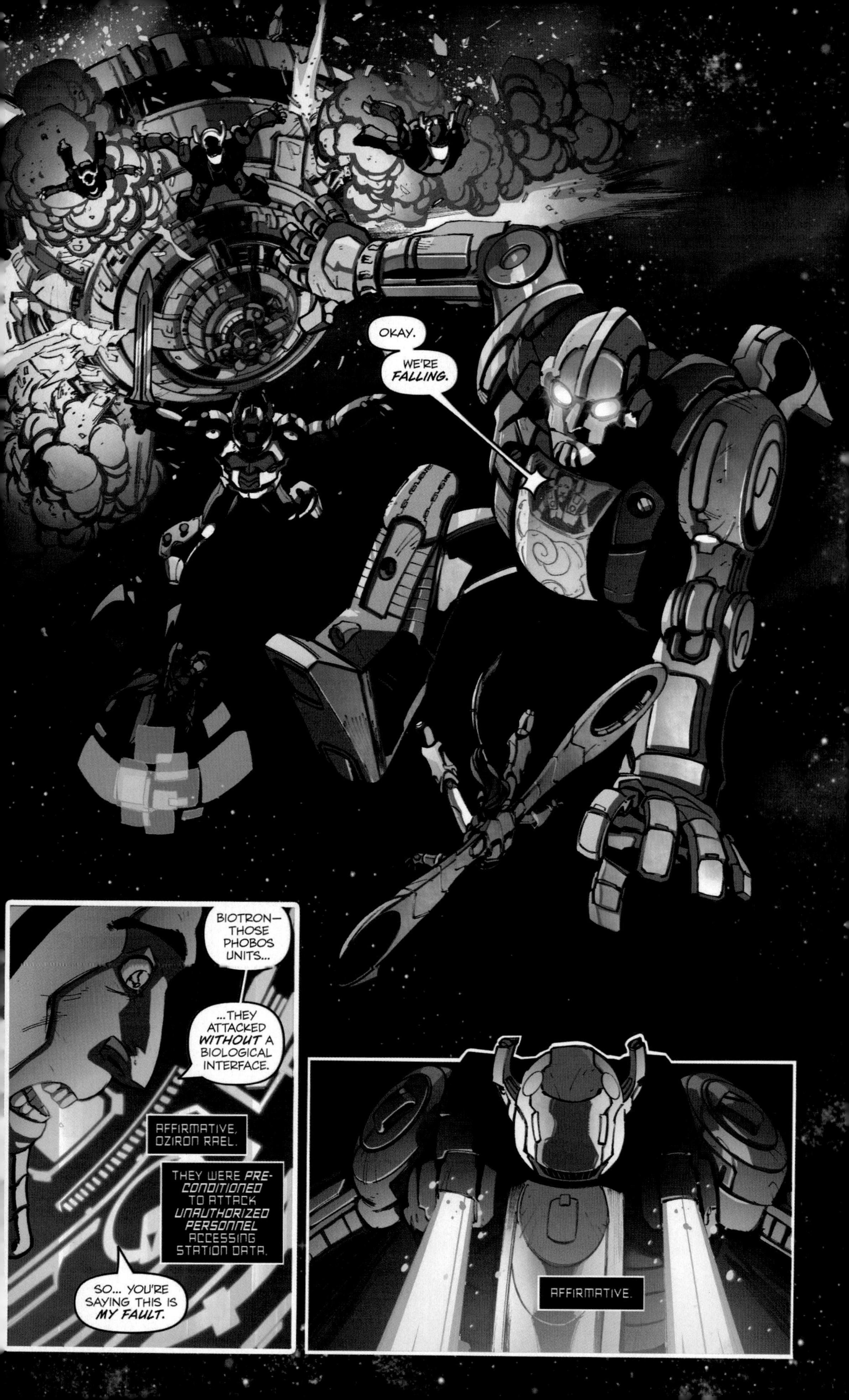

OKAY.
WE'RE FALLING.
BIOTRON— THOSE PHOBOS UNITS...
...THEY ATTACKED WITHOUT A BIOLOGICAL INTERFACE.
AFFIRMATIVE, OZIRON RAEL.
THEY WERE PRE-CONDITIONED TO ATTACK UNAUTHORIZED PERSONNEL ACCESSING STATION DATA.
SO... YOU'RE SAYING THIS IS MY FAULT.
AFFIRMATIVE.

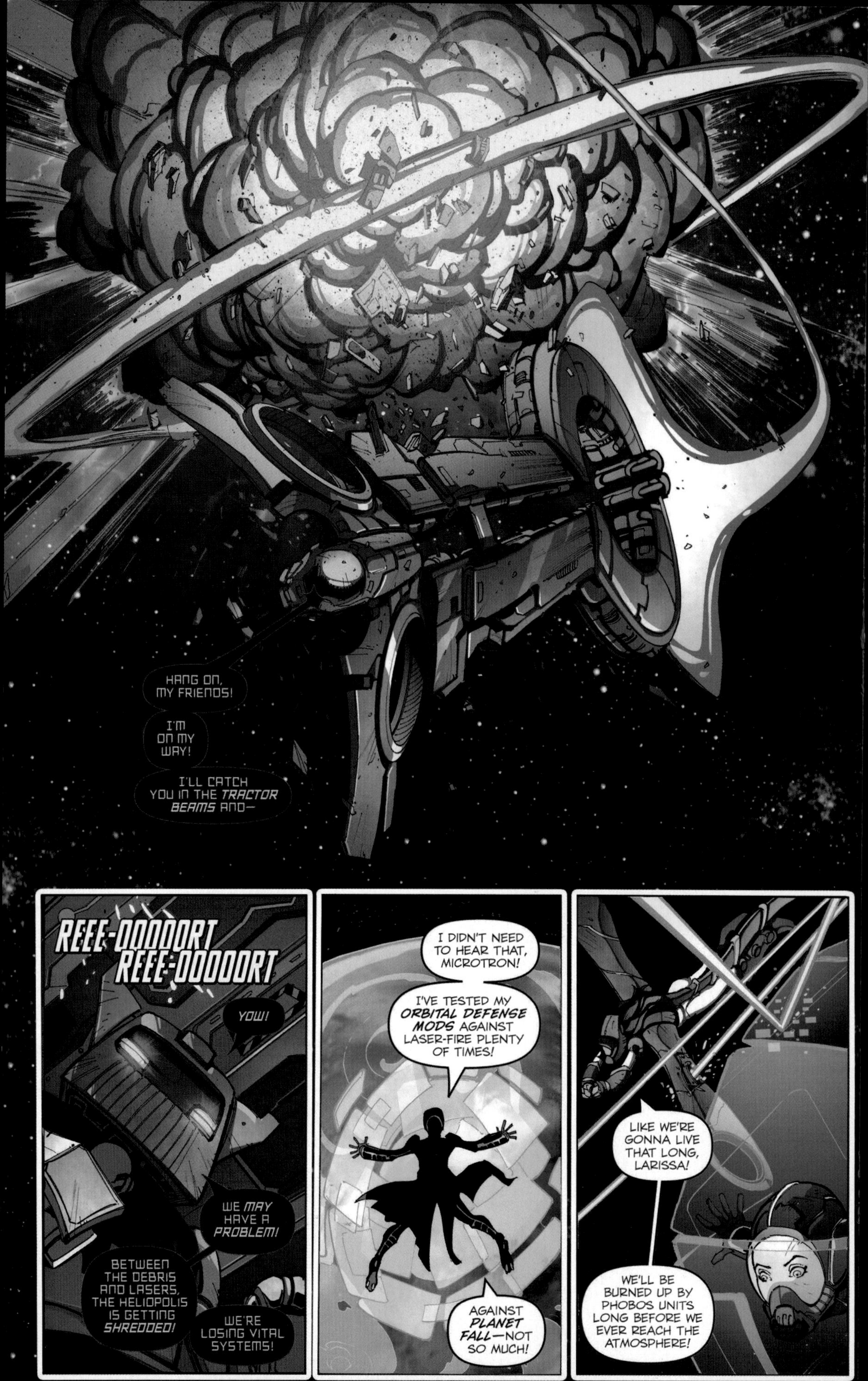

HANG ON, MY FRIENDS!
I'M ON MY WAY!
I'LL CATCH YOU IN THE *TRACTOR BEAMS* AND—
REEE-OOOOORT REEE-OOOOORT
YOW!
WE *MAY* HAVE A *PROBLEM!*
BETWEEN THE DEBRIS AND LASERS, THE HELIOPOLIS IS GETTING *SHREDDED!*
WE'RE LOSING VITAL SYSTEMS!
I DIDN'T NEED TO HEAR THAT, MICROTRON!
I'VE TESTED MY ***ORBITAL DEFENSE MODS*** AGAINST LASER-FIRE PLENTY OF TIMES!
AGAINST ***PLANET FALL***—NOT SO MUCH!
LIKE WE'RE GONNA LIVE THAT LONG, LARISSA!
WE'LL BE BURNED UP BY PHOBOS UNITS LONG BEFORE WE EVER REACH THE ATMOSPHERE!

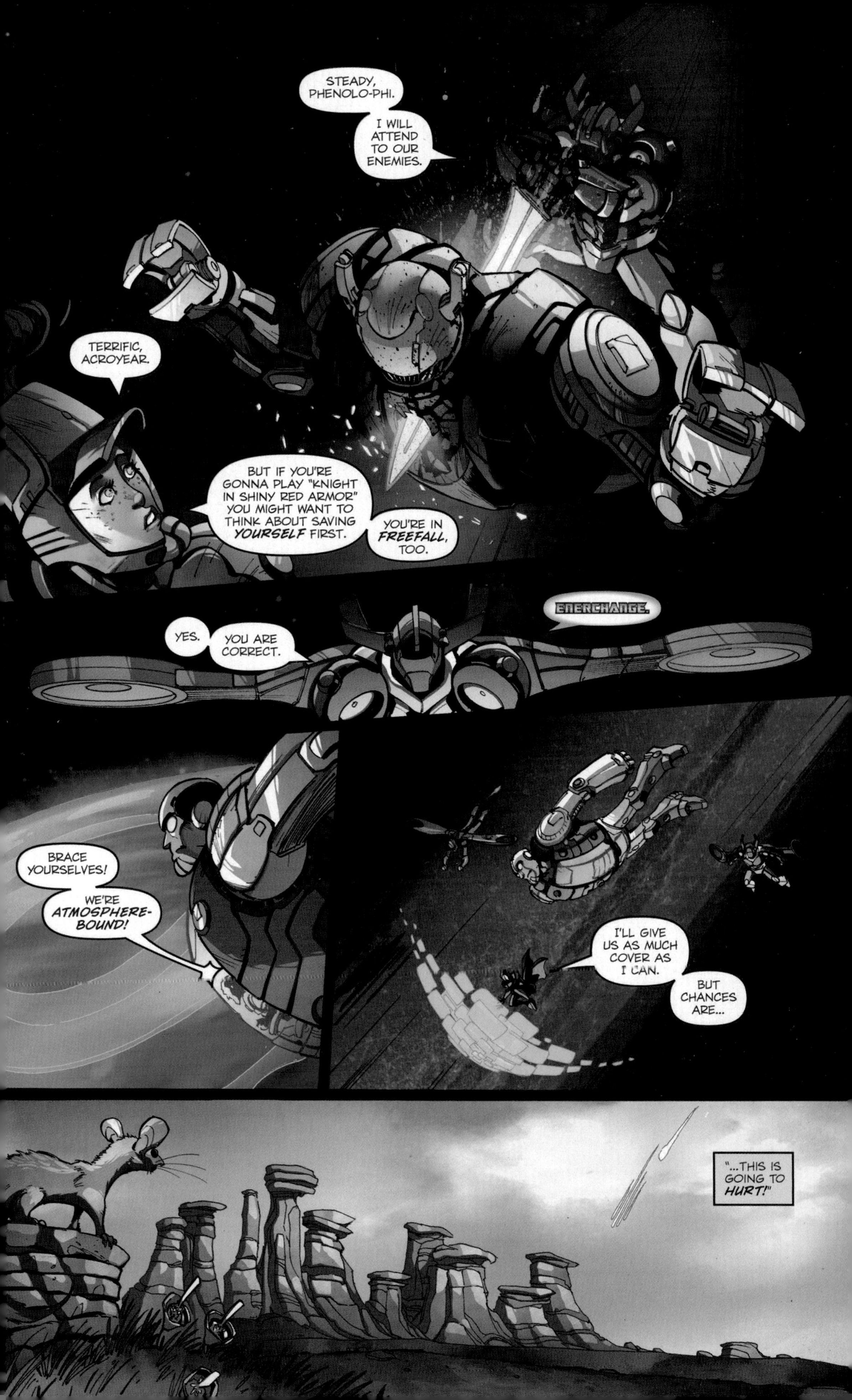
STEADY, PHENOLO-PHI.
I WILL ATTEND TO OUR ENEMIES.
TERRIFIC, ACROYEAR.
BUT IF YOU'RE GONNA PLAY "KNIGHT IN SHINY RED ARMOR" YOU MIGHT WANT TO THINK ABOUT SAVING *YOURSELF* FIRST.
YOU'RE IN *FREEFALL*, TOO.
YES.
YOU ARE CORRECT.
ENERCHANGE.
BRACE YOURSELVES!
WE'RE *ATMOSPHERE-BOUND!*
I'LL GIVE US AS MUCH COVER AS I CAN.
BUT CHANCES ARE...
"...THIS IS GOING TO *HURT!*"

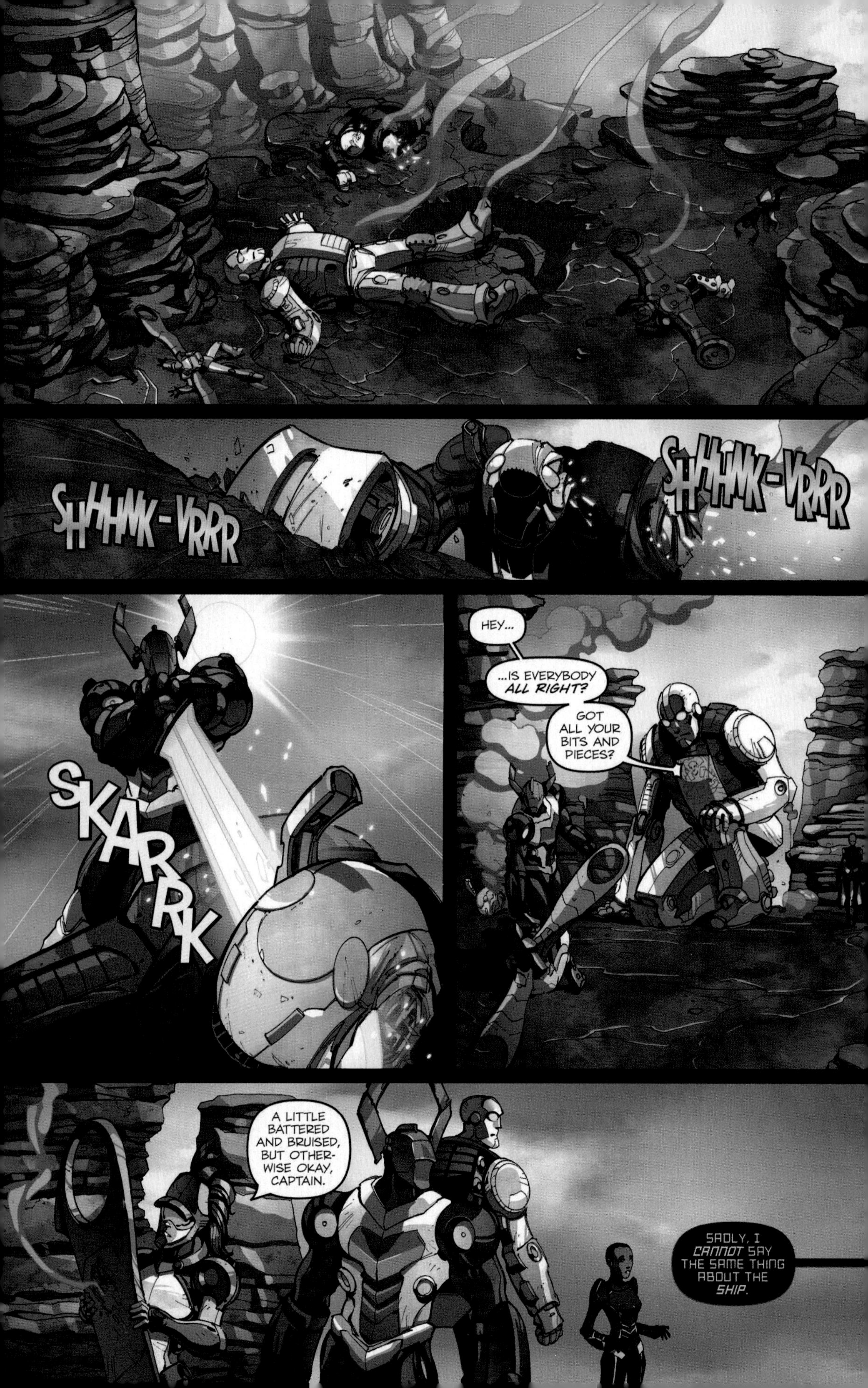
SHHHNK-VRRR
SHHHNK-VRRR
SKARRRK
HEY...
...IS EVERYBODY *ALL RIGHT?*
GOT ALL YOUR BITS AND PIECES?
A LITTLE BATTERED AND BRUISED, BUT OTHER-WISE OKAY, CAPTAIN.
SADLY, I *CANNOT* SAY THE SAME THING ABOUT THE *SHIP*.

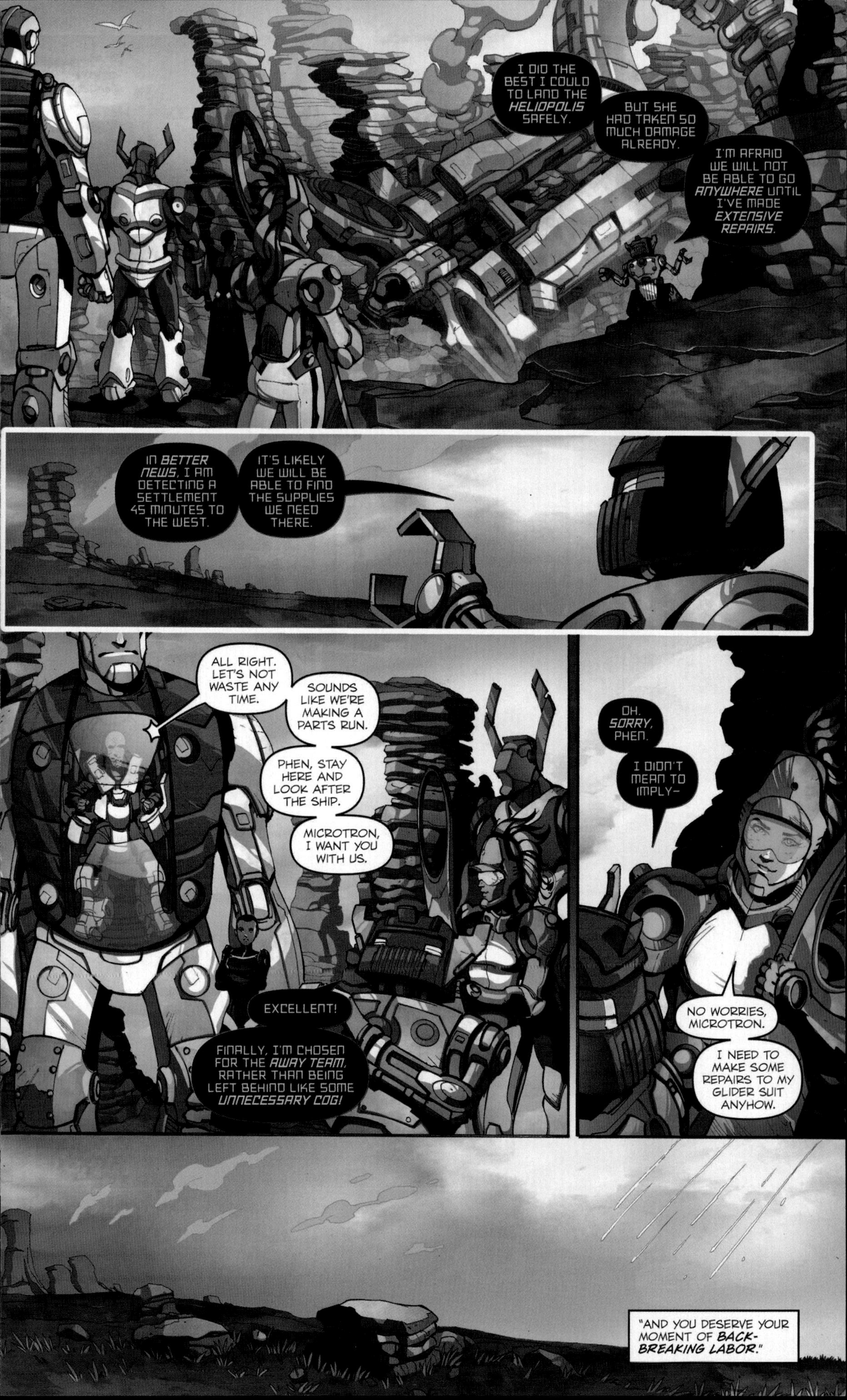
I DID THE BEST I COULD TO LAND THE *HELIOPOLIS* SAFELY.
BUT SHE HAD TAKEN SO MUCH DAMAGE ALREADY.
I'M AFRAID WE WILL NOT BE ABLE TO GO *ANYWHERE* UNTIL I'VE MADE *EXTENSIVE REPAIRS*.
IN *BETTER NEWS*, I AM DETECTING A SETTLEMENT 45 MINUTES TO THE WEST.
IT'S LIKELY WE WILL BE ABLE TO FIND THE SUPPLIES WE NEED THERE.
ALL RIGHT. LET'S NOT WASTE ANY TIME.
SOUNDS LIKE WE'RE MAKING A PARTS RUN.
PHEN, STAY HERE AND LOOK AFTER THE SHIP.
MICROTRON, I WANT YOU WITH US.
EXCELLENT!
FINALLY, I'M CHOSEN FOR THE *AWAY TEAM*, RATHER THAN BEING LEFT BEHIND LIKE SOME *UNNECESSARY COG!*
OH. *SORRY*, PHEN.
I DIDN'T MEAN TO IMPLY–
NO WORRIES, MICROTRON.
I NEED TO MAKE SOME REPAIRS TO MY GLIDER SUIT ANYHOW.
"AND YOU DESERVE YOUR MOMENT OF **BACK-BREAKING LABOR**."

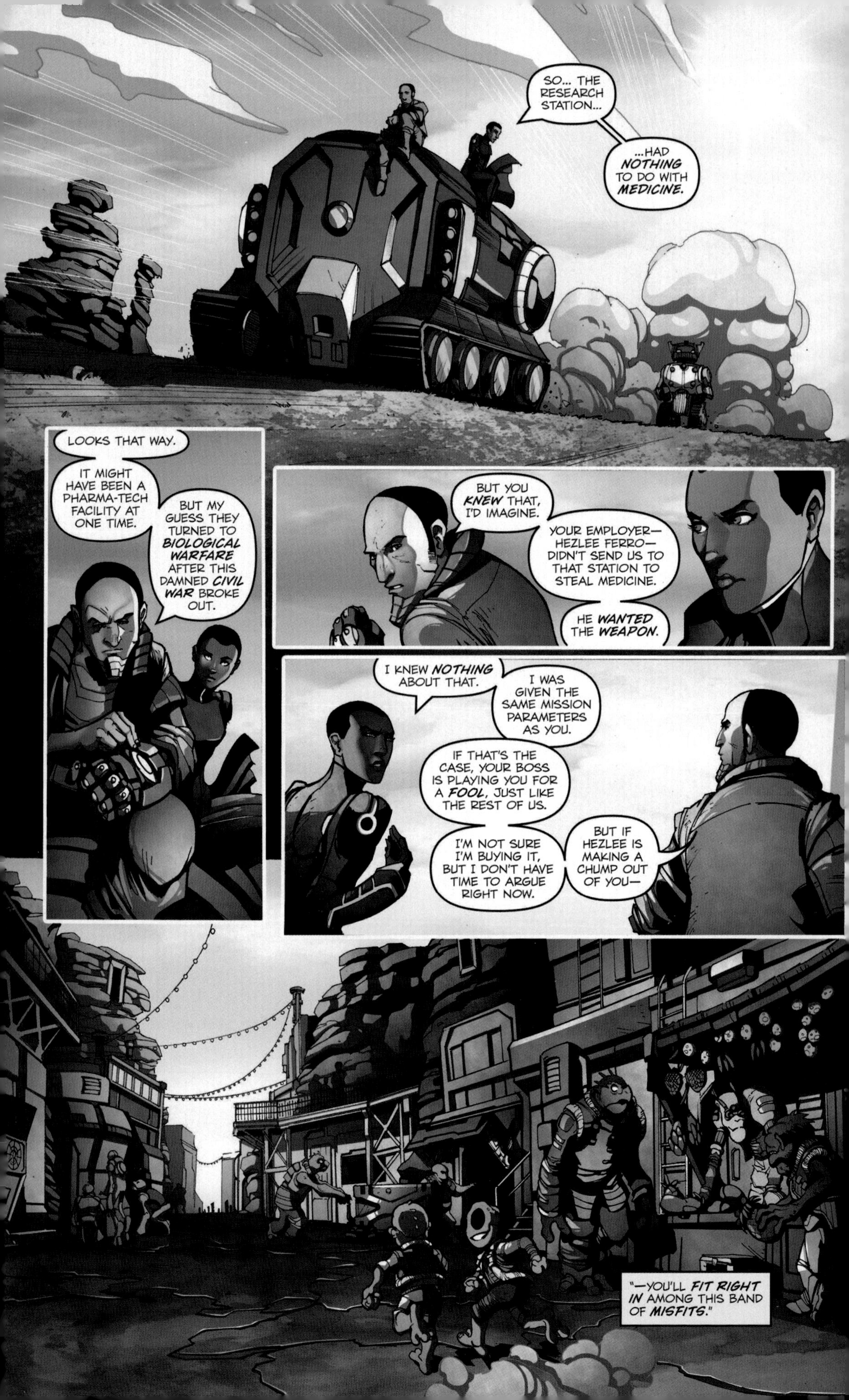
SO... THE RESEARCH STATION...
...HAD NOTHING TO DO WITH MEDICINE.
LOOKS THAT WAY.
IT MIGHT HAVE BEEN A PHARMA-TECH FACILITY AT ONE TIME.
BUT MY GUESS THEY TURNED TO BIOLOGICAL WARFARE AFTER THIS DAMNED CIVIL WAR BROKE OUT.
BUT YOU KNEW THAT, I'D IMAGINE.
YOUR EMPLOYER—HEZLEE FERRO—DIDN'T SEND US TO THAT STATION TO STEAL MEDICINE.
HE WANTED THE WEAPON.
I KNEW NOTHING ABOUT THAT.
I WAS GIVEN THE SAME MISSION PARAMETERS AS YOU.
IF THAT'S THE CASE, YOUR BOSS IS PLAYING YOU FOR A FOOL, JUST LIKE THE REST OF US.
I'M NOT SURE I'M BUYING IT, BUT I DON'T HAVE TIME TO ARGUE RIGHT NOW.
BUT IF HEZLEE IS MAKING A CHUMP OUT OF YOU—
"—YOU'LL FIT RIGHT IN AMONG THIS BAND OF MISFITS."

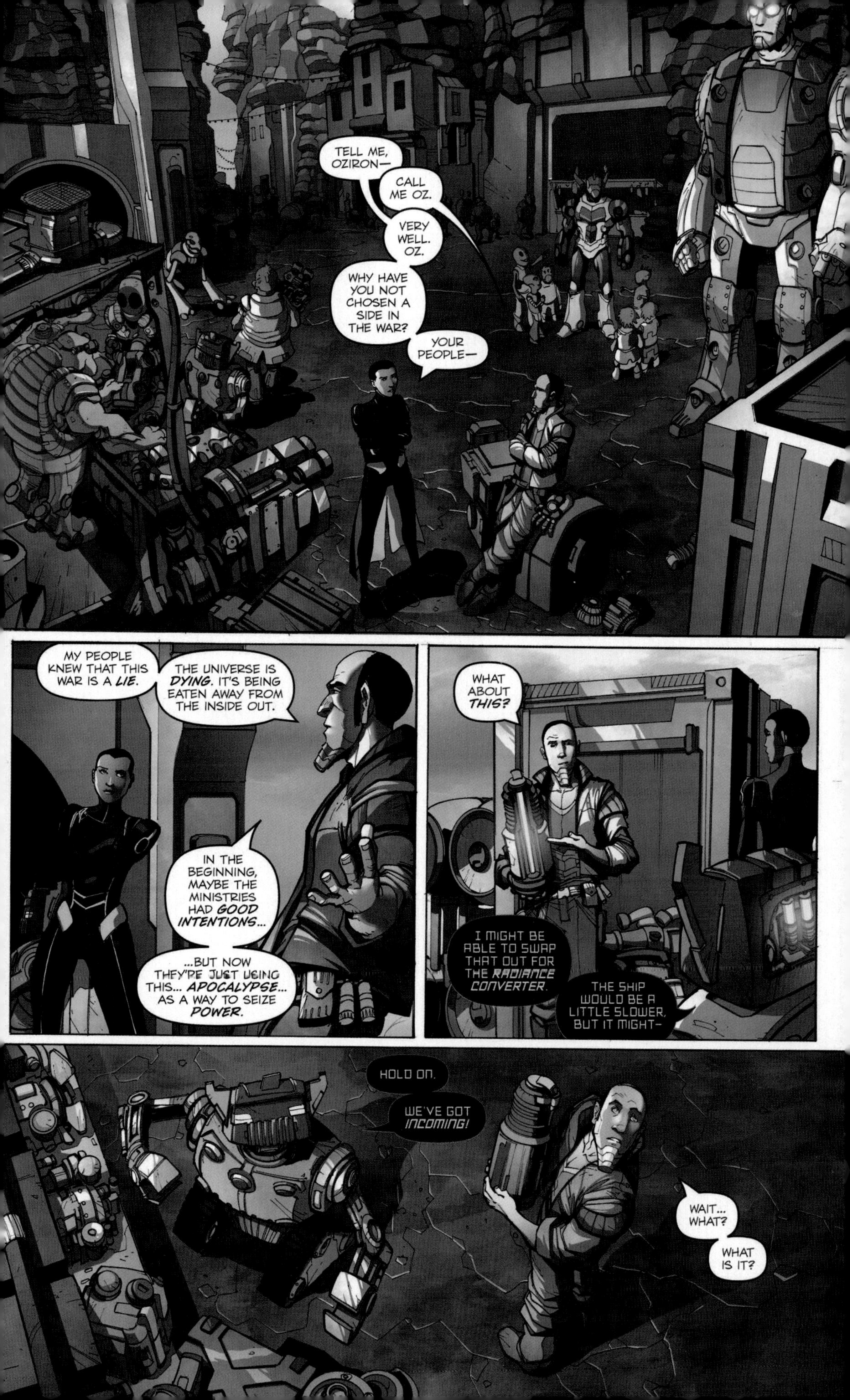
TELL ME, OZIRON—
CALL ME OZ.
VERY WELL. OZ.
WHY HAVE YOU NOT CHOSEN A SIDE IN THE WAR?
YOUR PEOPLE—
MY PEOPLE KNEW THAT THIS WAR IS A LIE.
THE UNIVERSE IS DYING. IT'S BEING EATEN AWAY FROM THE INSIDE OUT.
IN THE BEGINNING, MAYBE THE MINISTRIES HAD GOOD INTENTIONS...
...BUT NOW THEY'RE JUST USING THIS... APOCALYPSE... AS A WAY TO SEIZE POWER.
WHAT ABOUT THIS?
I MIGHT BE ABLE TO SWAP THAT OUT FOR THE RADIANCE CONVERTER.
THE SHIP WOULD BE A LITTLE SLOWER, BUT IT MIGHT—
HOLD ON.
WE'VE GOT INCOMING!
WAIT... WHAT?
WHAT IS IT?

THOOM

IS... THAT...?

BIOTRON—WHATEVER THAT IS... IT CAME FROM THE RESEARCH STATION.

BUT IT DOESN'T LOOK LIKE RANDOM DEBRIS.

AFFIRMATIVE.

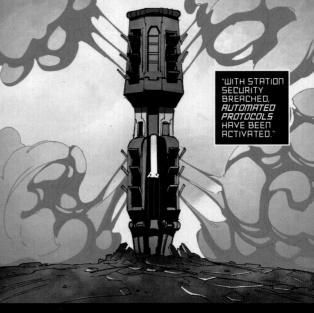

"WITH STATION SECURITY BREACHED, *AUTOMATED PROTOCOLS* HAVE BEEN ACTIVATED."

TESTING OF *BIOLOGICAL AGENT* HAS BEGUN.

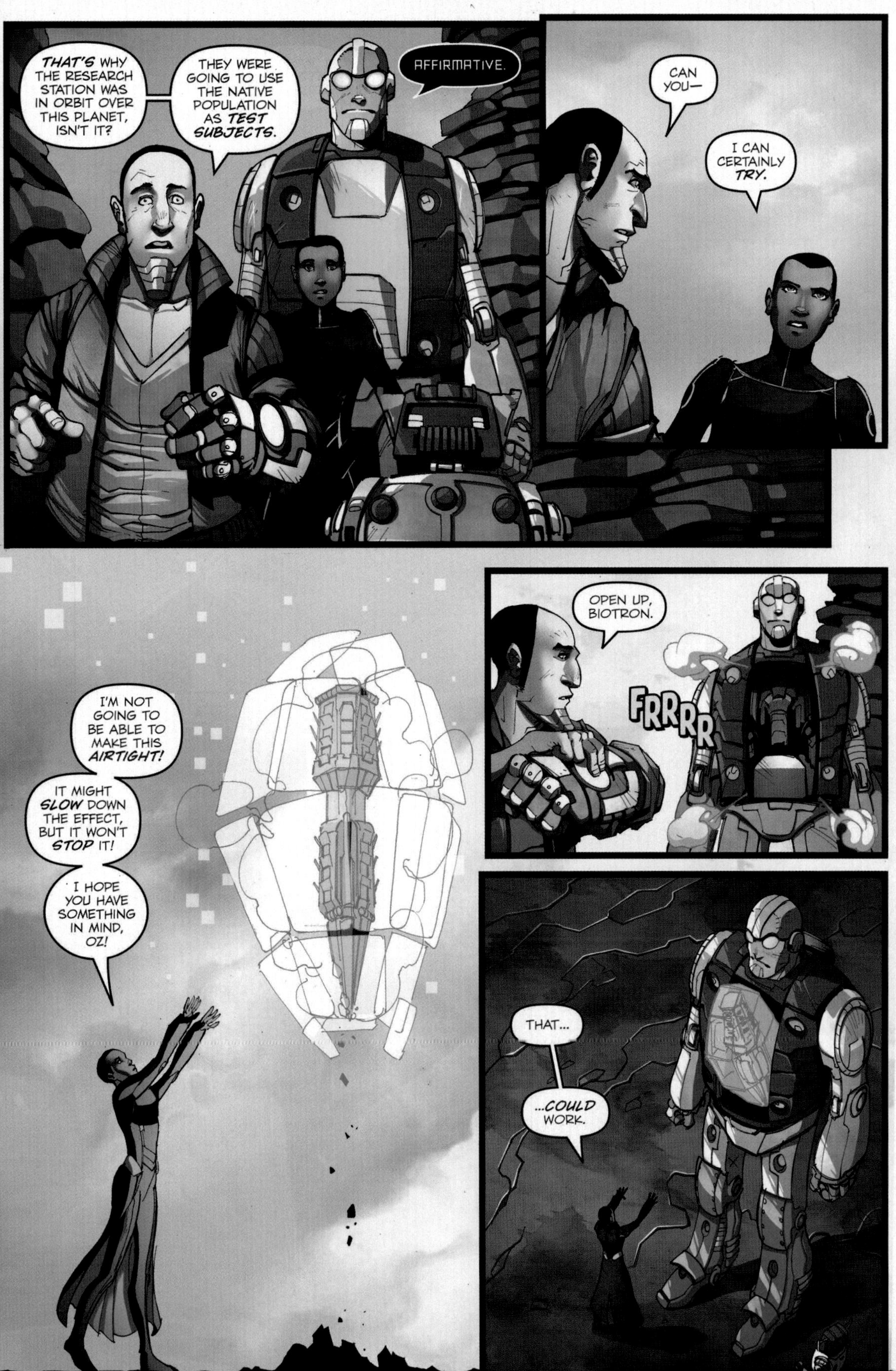
THAT'S WHY THE RESEARCH STATION WAS IN ORBIT OVER THIS PLANET, ISN'T IT?
THEY WERE GOING TO USE THE NATIVE POPULATION AS TEST SUBJECTS.
AFFIRMATIVE.
CAN YOU—
I CAN CERTAINLY TRY.
I'M NOT GOING TO BE ABLE TO MAKE THIS AIRTIGHT!
IT MIGHT SLOW DOWN THE EFFECT, BUT IT WON'T STOP IT!
I HOPE YOU HAVE SOMETHING IN MIND, OZ!
OPEN UP, BIOTRON.
FRRRR
THAT...
...COULD WORK.

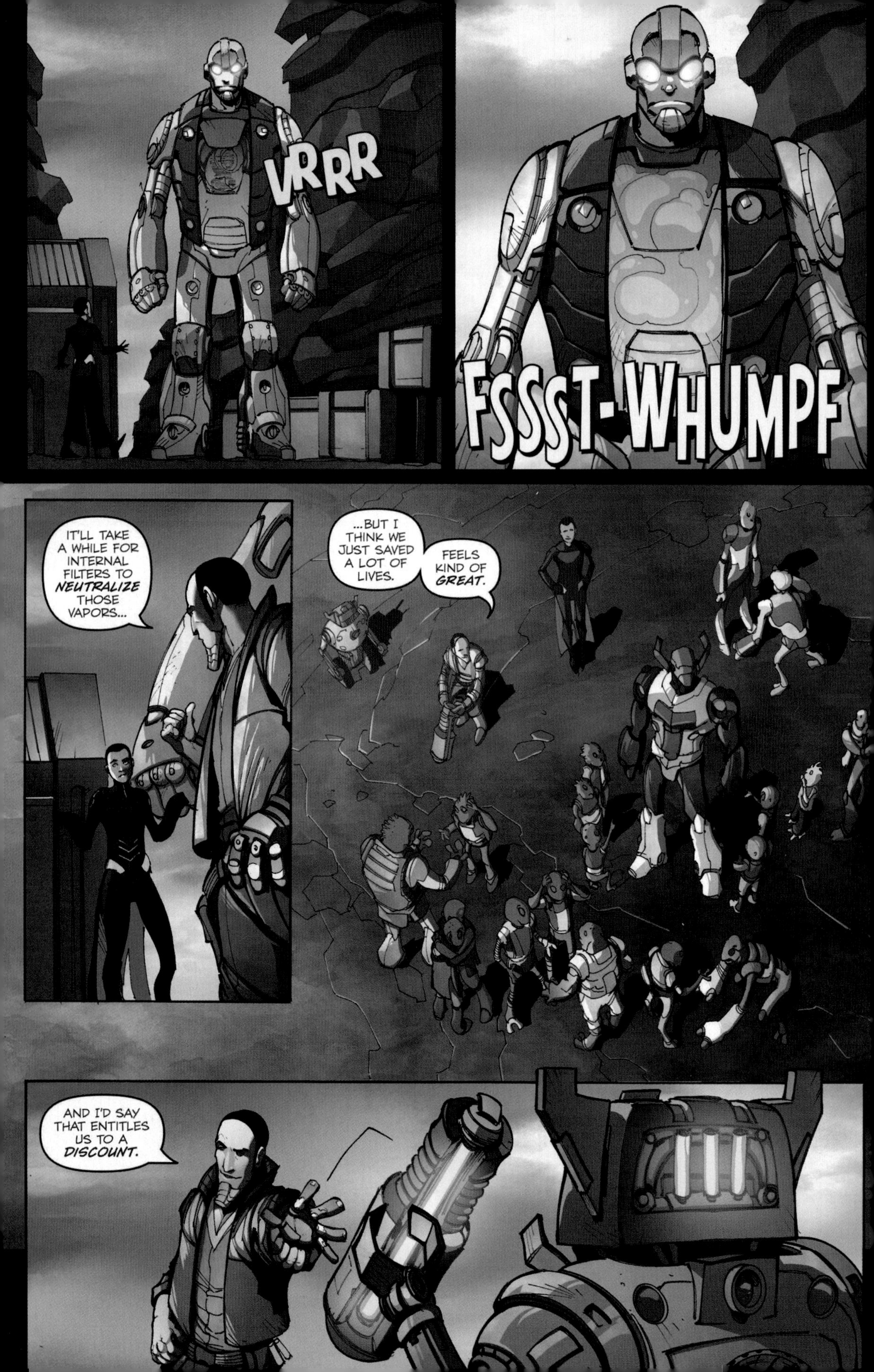
VRRR
FSSST-WHUMPF
IT'LL TAKE A WHILE FOR INTERNAL FILTERS TO NEUTRALIZE THOSE VAPORS...
...BUT I THINK WE JUST SAVED A LOT OF LIVES.
FEELS KIND OF GREAT.
AND I'D SAY THAT ENTITLES US TO A DISCOUNT.

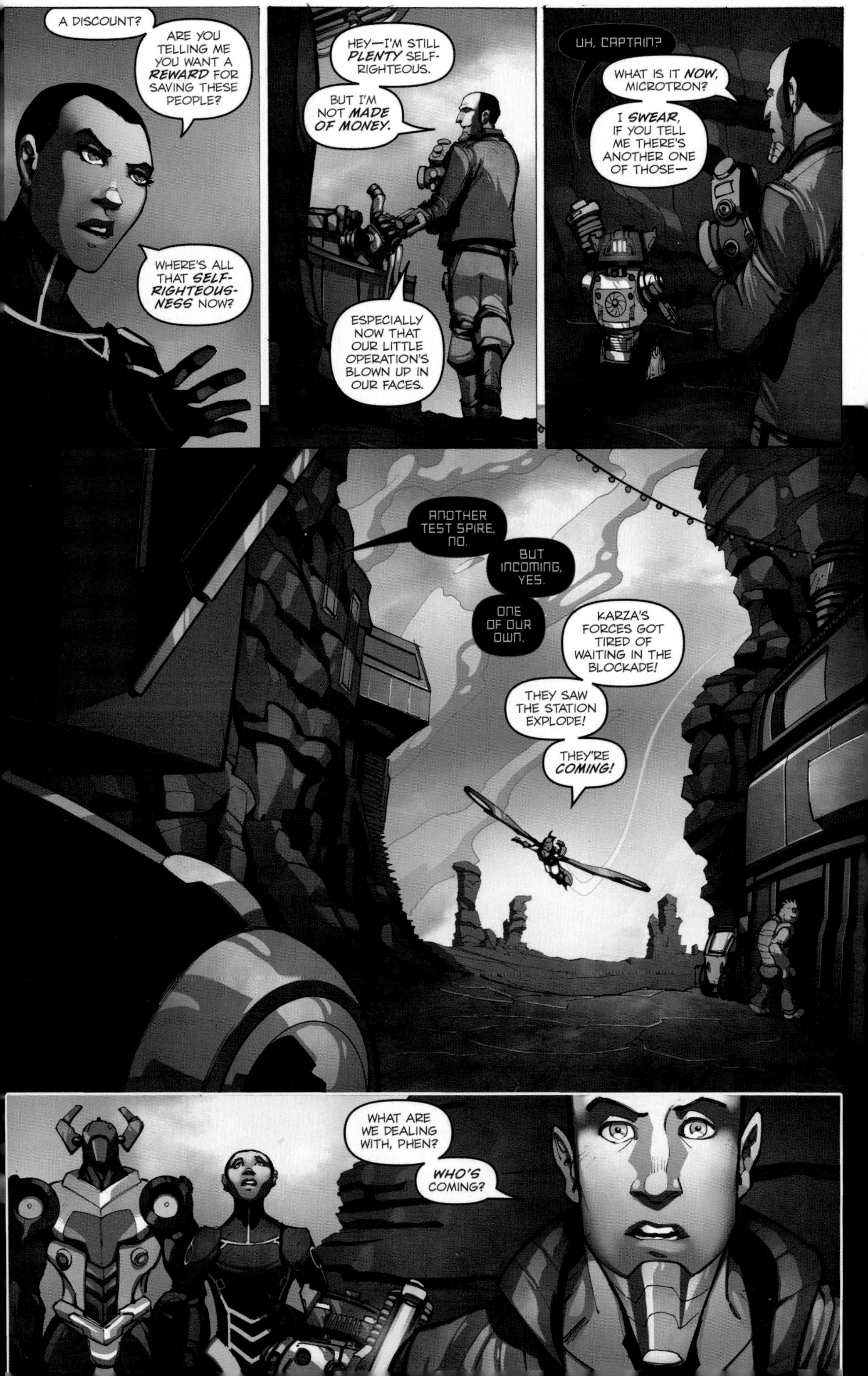
A DISCOUNT?
ARE YOU TELLING ME YOU WANT A REWARD FOR SAVING THESE PEOPLE?
WHERE'S ALL THAT SELF-RIGHTEOUSNESS NOW?
HEY—I'M STILL PLENTY SELF-RIGHTEOUS.
BUT I'M NOT MADE OF MONEY.
ESPECIALLY NOW THAT OUR LITTLE OPERATION'S BLOWN UP IN OUR FACES.
UH, CAPTAIN?
WHAT IS IT NOW, MICROTRON?
I SWEAR, IF YOU TELL ME THERE'S ANOTHER ONE OF THOSE—
ANOTHER TEST SPIRE, NO.
BUT INCOMING, YES.
ONE OF OUR OWN.
KARZA'S FORCES GOT TIRED OF WAITING IN THE BLOCKADE!
THEY SAW THE STATION EXPLODE!
THEY'RE COMING!
WHAT ARE WE DEALING WITH, PHEN?
WHO'S COMING?

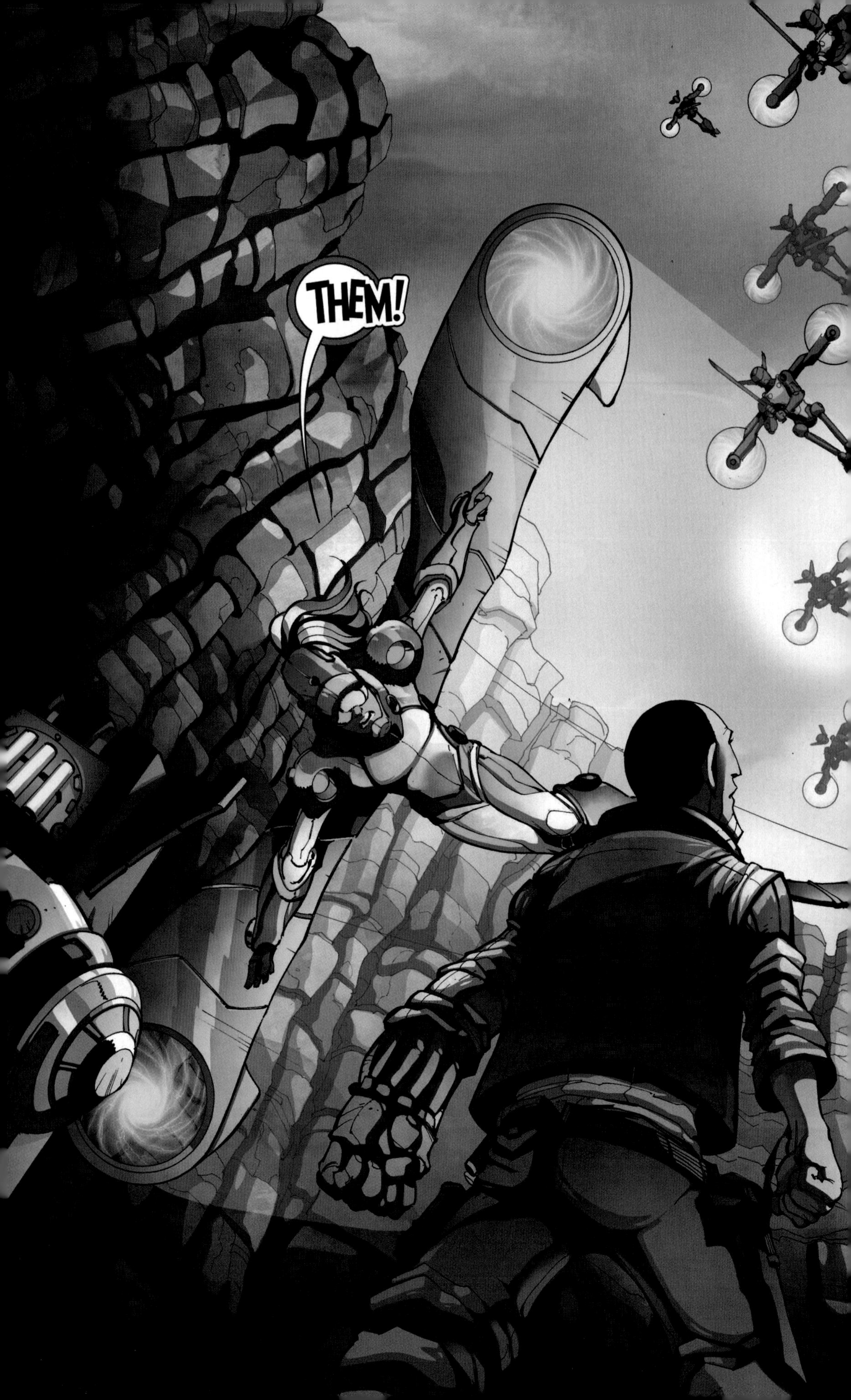
THEM!

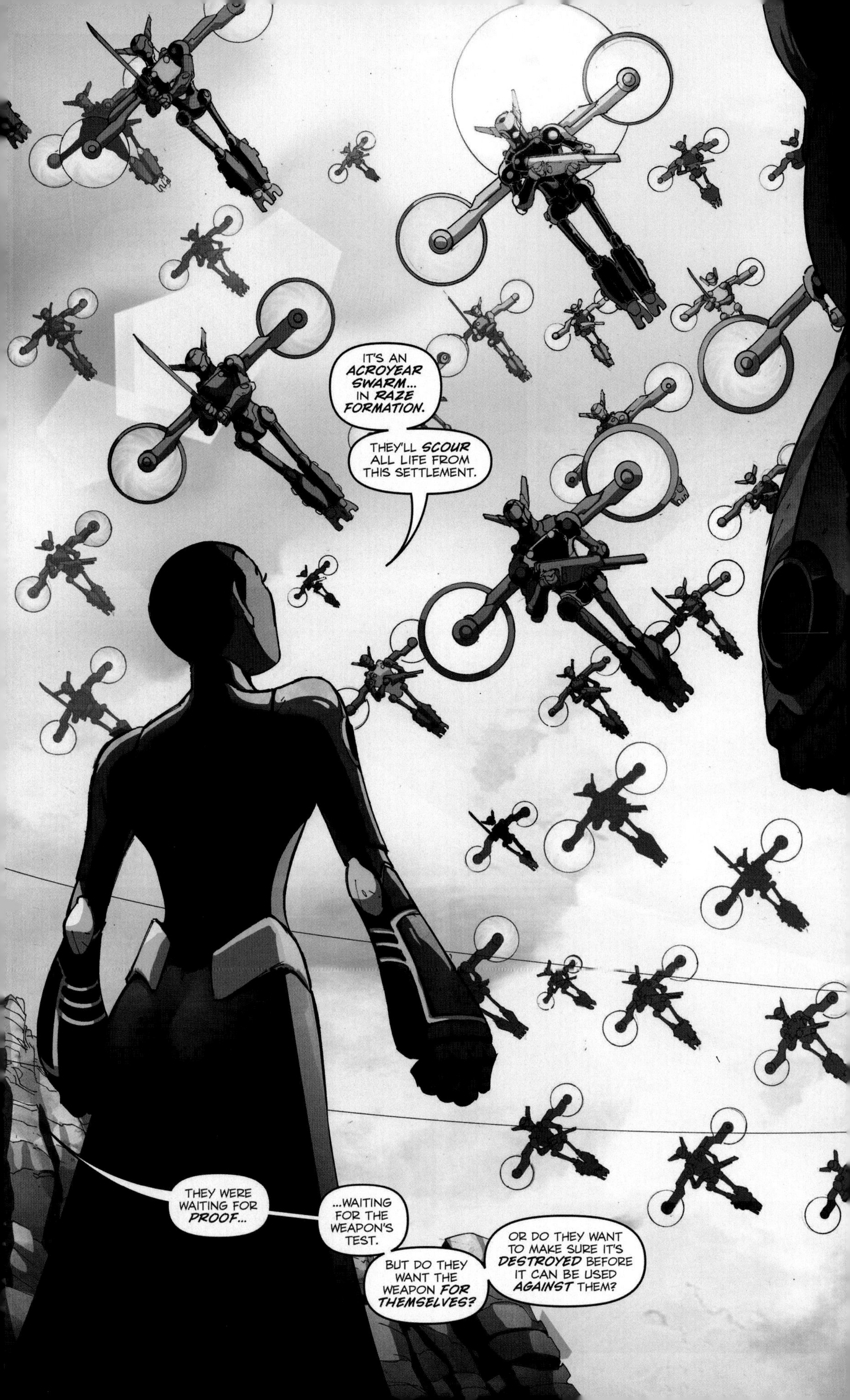
IT'S AN ACROYEAR SWARM... IN RAZE FORMATION.
THEY'LL SCOUR ALL LIFE FROM THIS SETTLEMENT.
THEY WERE WAITING FOR PROOF...
...WAITING FOR THE WEAPON'S TEST.
BUT DO THEY WANT THE WEAPON FOR THEMSELVES?
OR DO THEY WANT TO MAKE SURE IT'S DESTROYED BEFORE IT CAN BE USED AGAINST THEM?

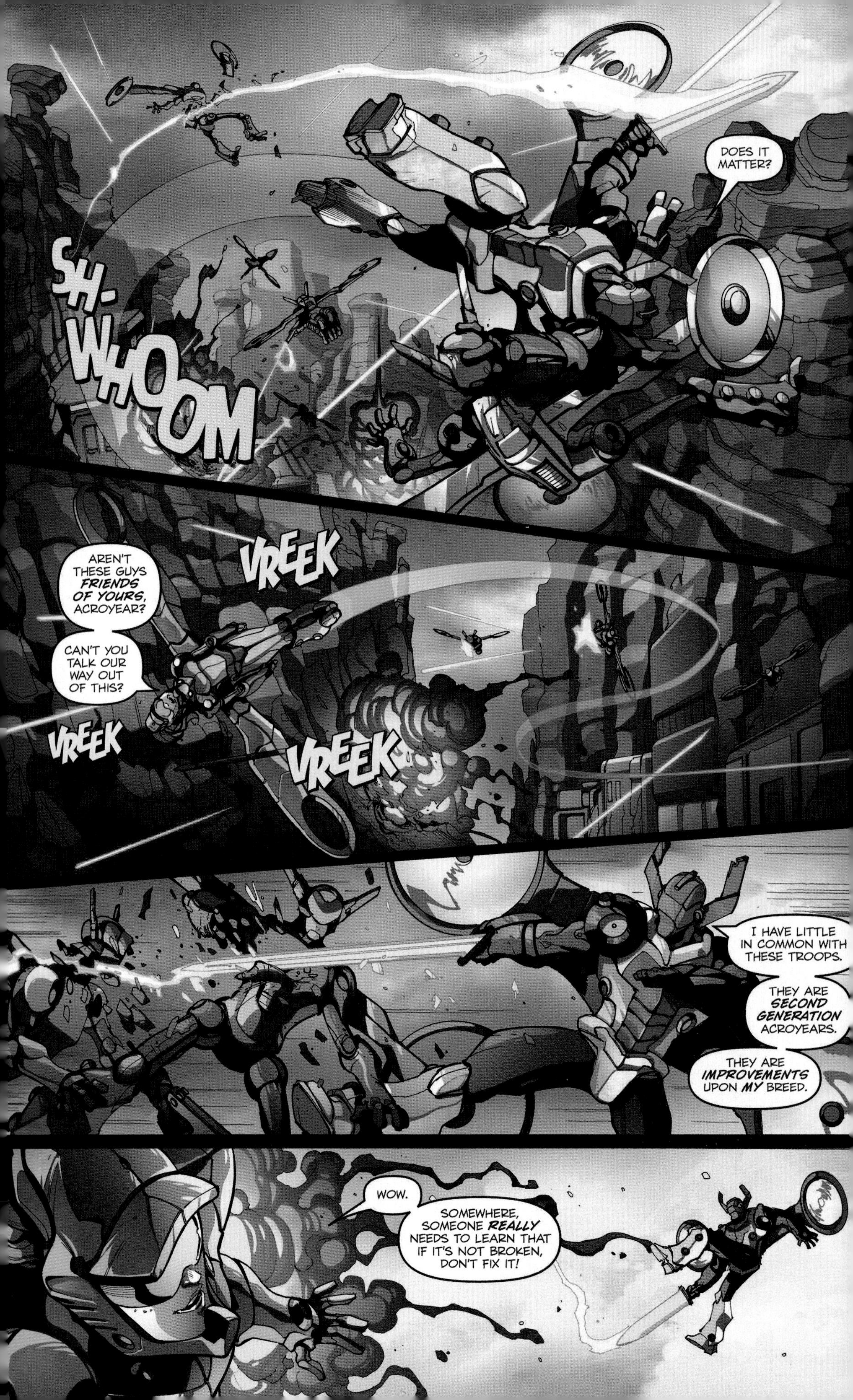
DOES IT MATTER?
SH-WHOOM
VREEK
AREN'T THESE GUYS FRIENDS OF YOURS, ACROYEAR?
CAN'T YOU TALK OUR WAY OUT OF THIS?
VREEK
VREEK
I HAVE LITTLE IN COMMON WITH THESE TROOPS.
THEY ARE SECOND GENERATION ACROYEARS.
THEY ARE IMPROVEMENTS UPON MY BREED.
WOW.
SOMEWHERE, SOMEONE REALLY NEEDS TO LEARN THAT IF IT'S NOT BROKEN, DON'T FIX IT!

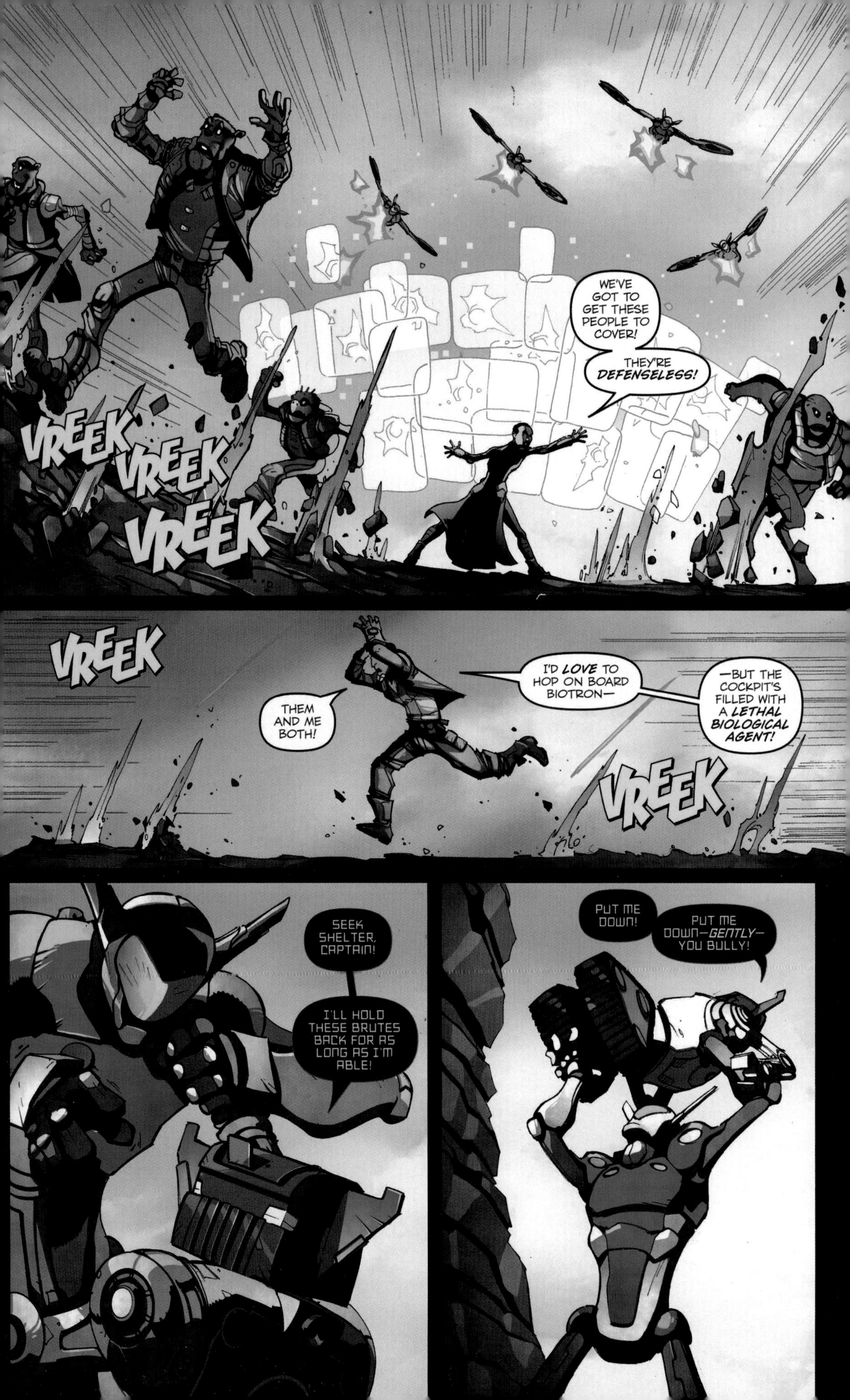
WE'VE GOT TO GET THESE PEOPLE TO COVER!
THEY'RE DEFENSELESS!
VREEK VREEK VREEK
VREEK
THEM AND ME BOTH!
I'D LOVE TO HOP ON BOARD BIOTRON—
—BUT THE COCKPIT'S FILLED WITH A LETHAL BIOLOGICAL AGENT!
VREEK
SEEK SHELTER, CAPTAIN!
I'LL HOLD THESE BRUTES BACK FOR AS LONG AS I'M ABLE!
PUT ME DOWN!
PUT ME DOWN—GENTLY—YOU BULLY!

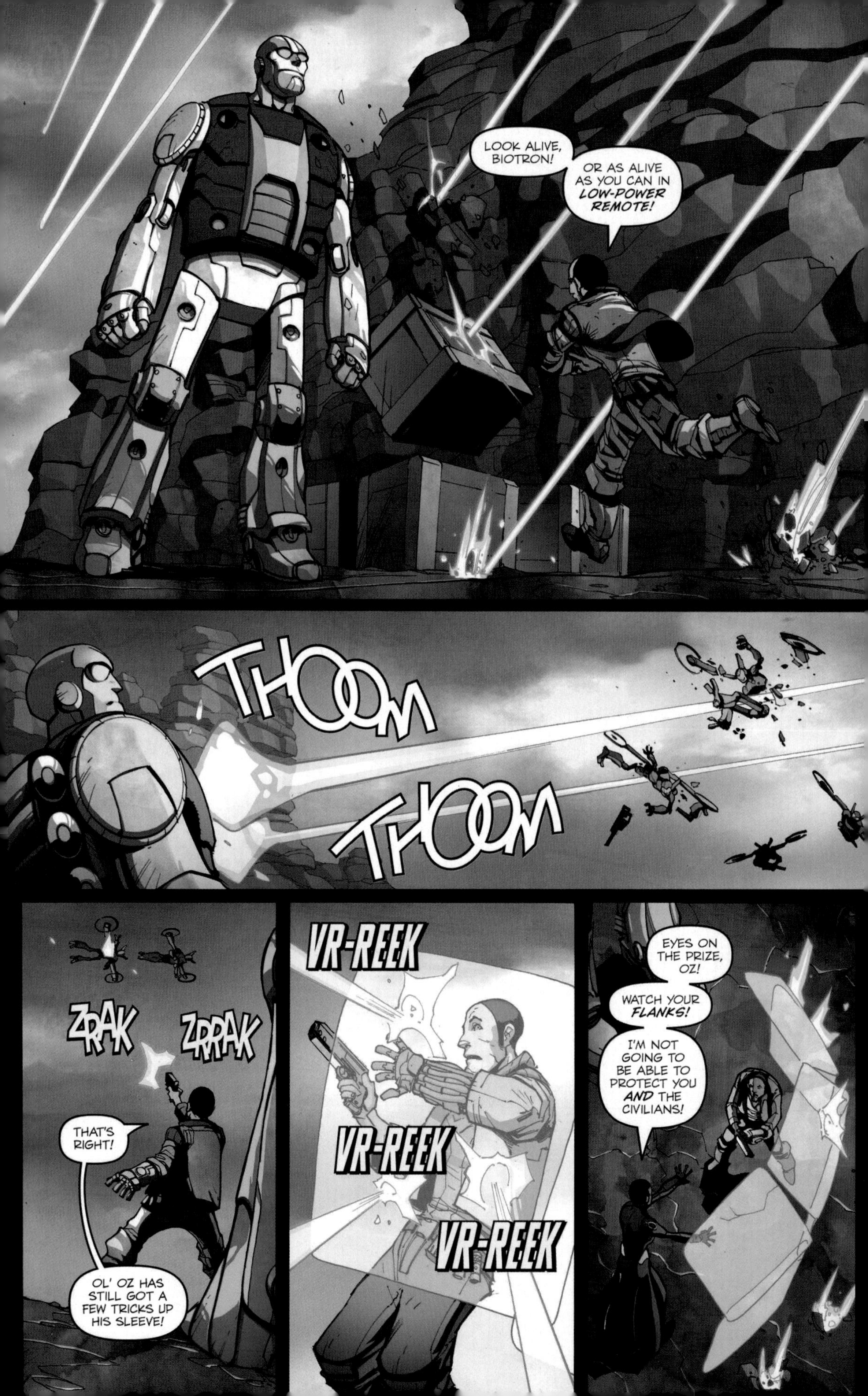
LOOK ALIVE, BIOTRON!
OR AS ALIVE AS YOU CAN IN LOW-POWER REMOTE!
THOOM
THOOM
ZRAK
ZRRAK
THAT'S RIGHT!
OL' OZ HAS STILL GOT A FEW TRICKS UP HIS SLEEVE!
VR-REEK
VR-REEK
VR-REEK
EYES ON THE PRIZE, OZ!
WATCH YOUR FLANKS!
I'M NOT GOING TO BE ABLE TO PROTECT YOU AND THE CIVILIANS!

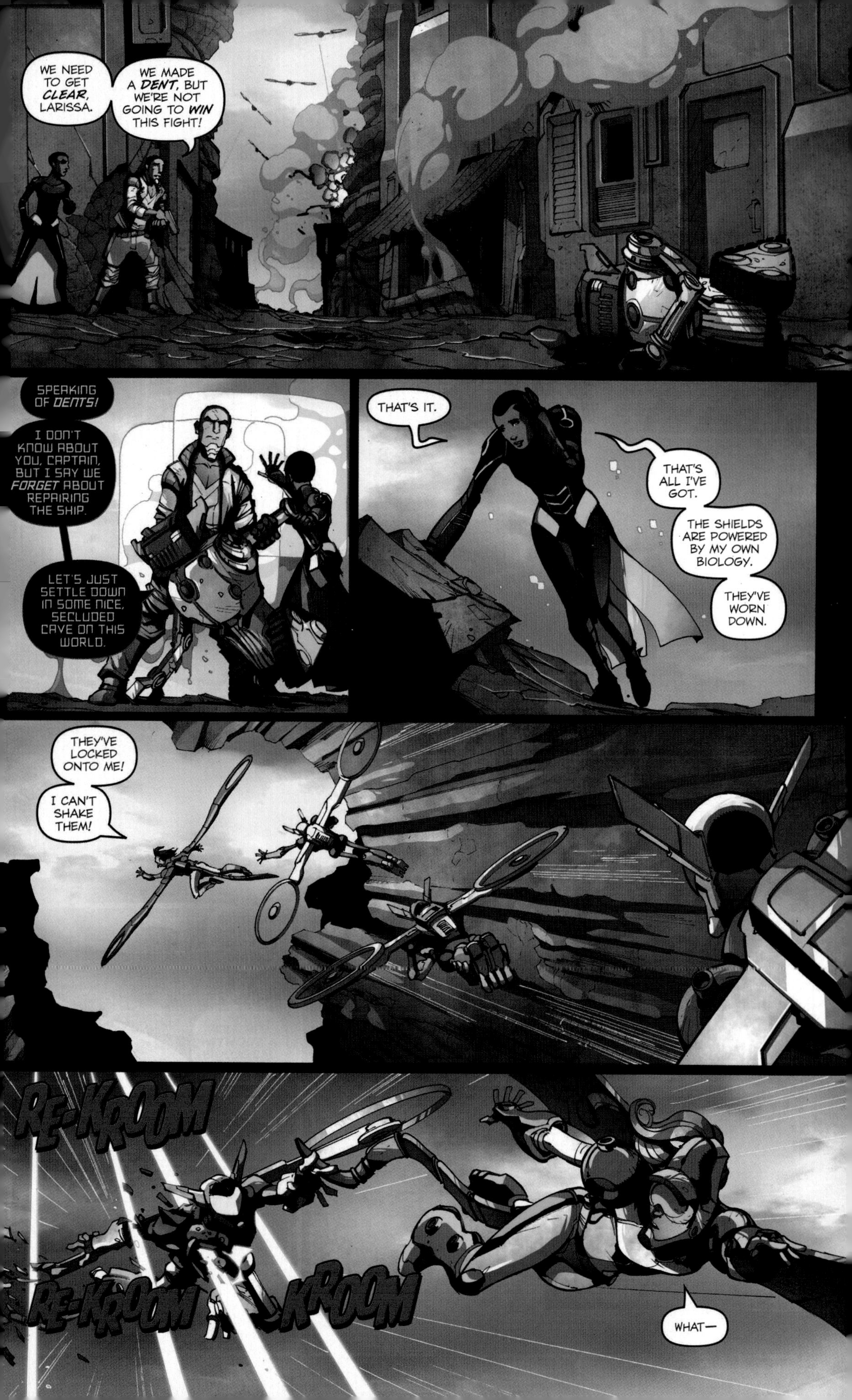
WE NEED TO GET CLEAR, LARISSA.
WE MADE A DENT, BUT WE'RE NOT GOING TO WIN THIS FIGHT!
SPEAKING OF DENTS!
I DON'T KNOW ABOUT YOU, CAPTAIN, BUT I SAY WE FORGET ABOUT REPAIRING THE SHIP.
LET'S JUST SETTLE DOWN IN SOME NICE, SECLUDED CAVE ON THIS WORLD.
THAT'S IT.
THAT'S ALL I'VE GOT.
THE SHIELDS ARE POWERED BY MY OWN BIOLOGY.
THEY'VE WORN DOWN.
THEY'VE LOCKED ONTO ME!
I CAN'T SHAKE THEM!
RE-KROOM
RE-KROOM
KROOM
WHAT—

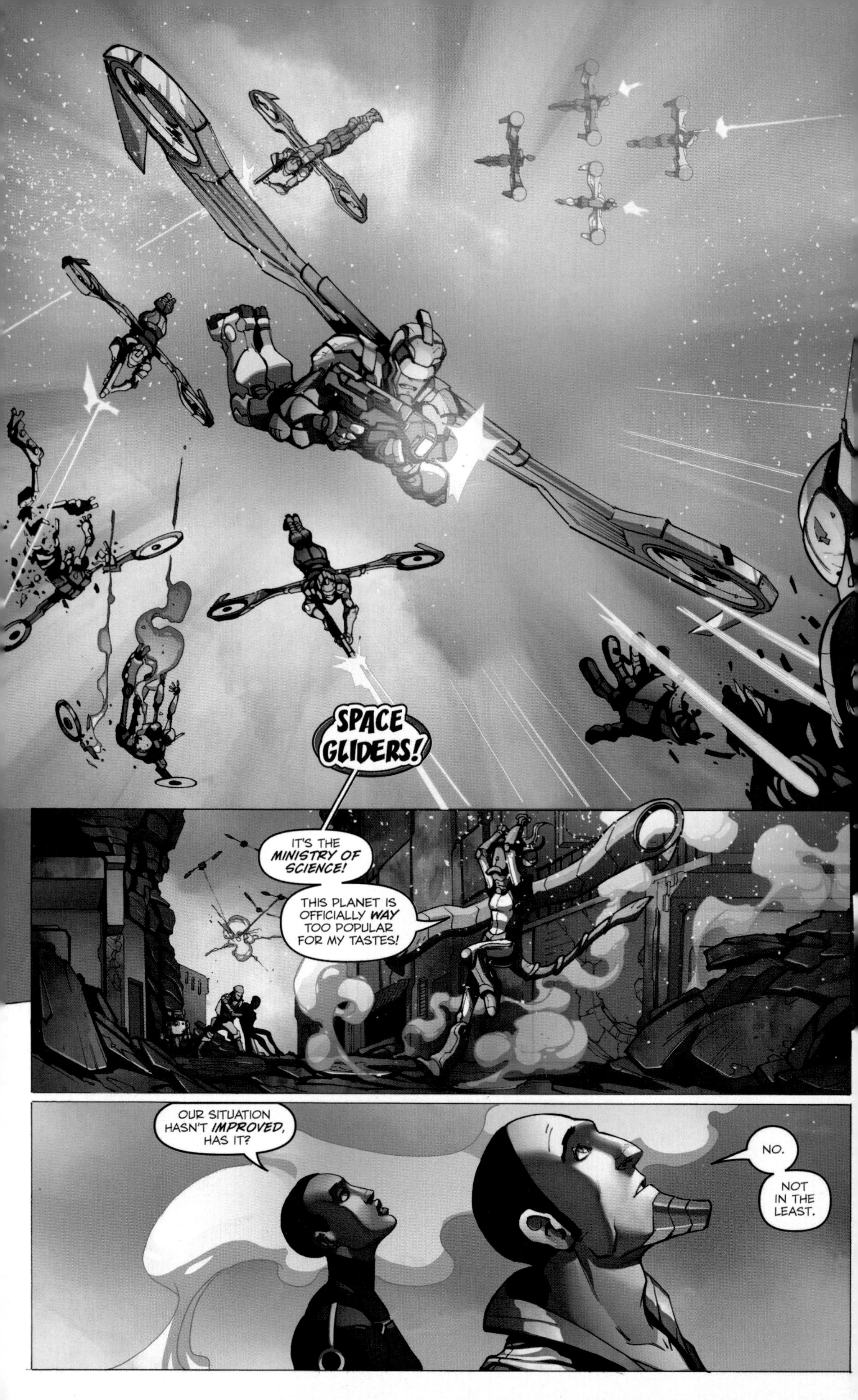
SPACE GLIDERS!
IT'S THE MINISTRY OF SCIENCE!
THIS PLANET IS OFFICIALLY WAY TOO POPULAR FOR MY TASTES!
OUR SITUATION HASN'T IMPROVED, HAS IT?
NO.
NOT IN THE LEAST.

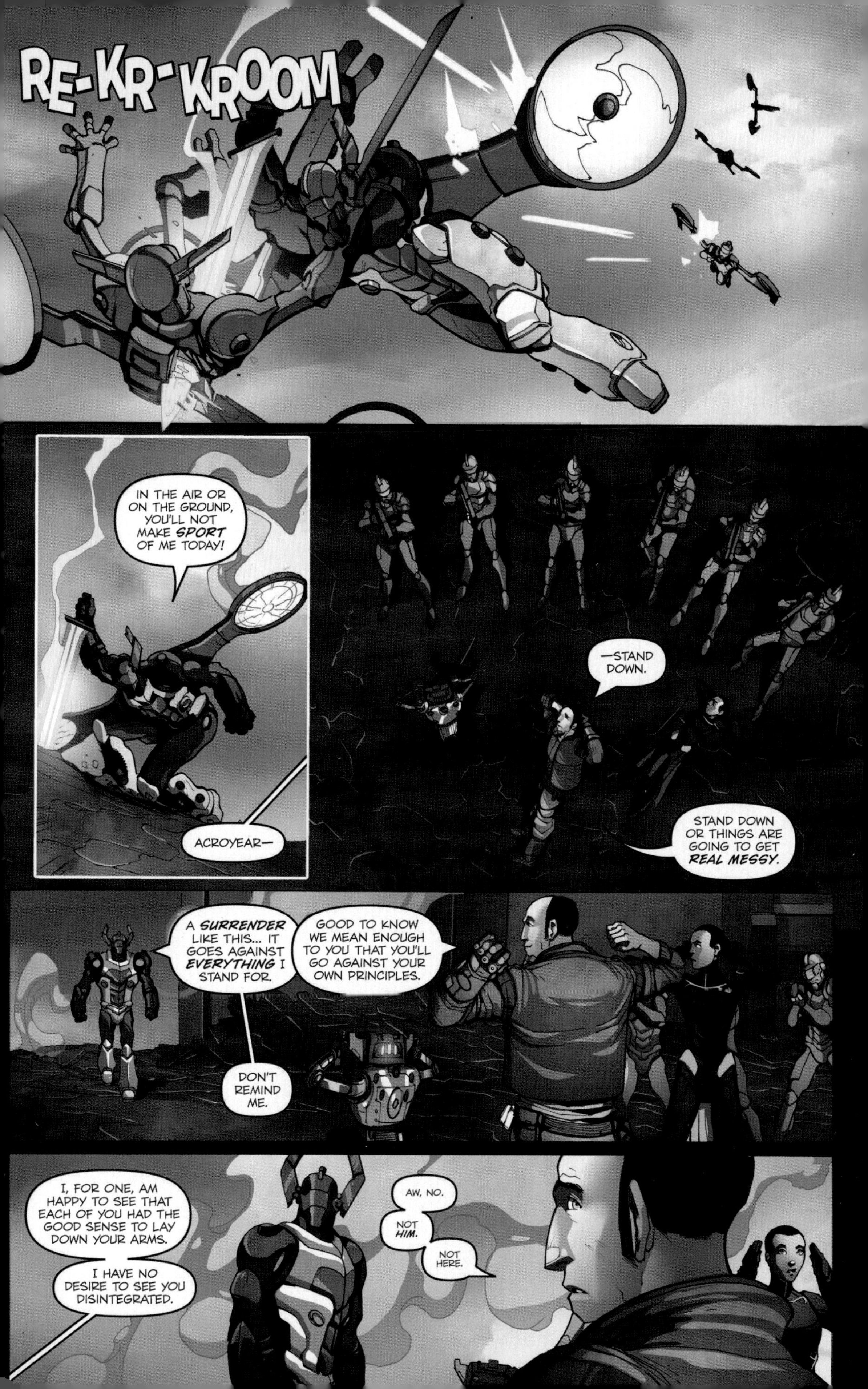
RE-KR-KROOM
IN THE AIR OR ON THE GROUND, YOU'LL NOT MAKE SPORT OF ME TODAY!
ACROYEAR—
—STAND DOWN.
STAND DOWN OR THINGS ARE GOING TO GET REAL MESSY.
A SURRENDER LIKE THIS... IT GOES AGAINST EVERYTHING I STAND FOR.
GOOD TO KNOW WE MEAN ENOUGH TO YOU THAT YOU'LL GO AGAINST YOUR OWN PRINCIPLES.
DON'T REMIND ME.
I, FOR ONE, AM HAPPY TO SEE THAT EACH OF YOU HAD THE GOOD SENSE TO LAY DOWN YOUR ARMS.
I HAVE NO DESIRE TO SEE YOU DISINTEGRATED.
AW, NO.
NOT HIM.
NOT HERE.

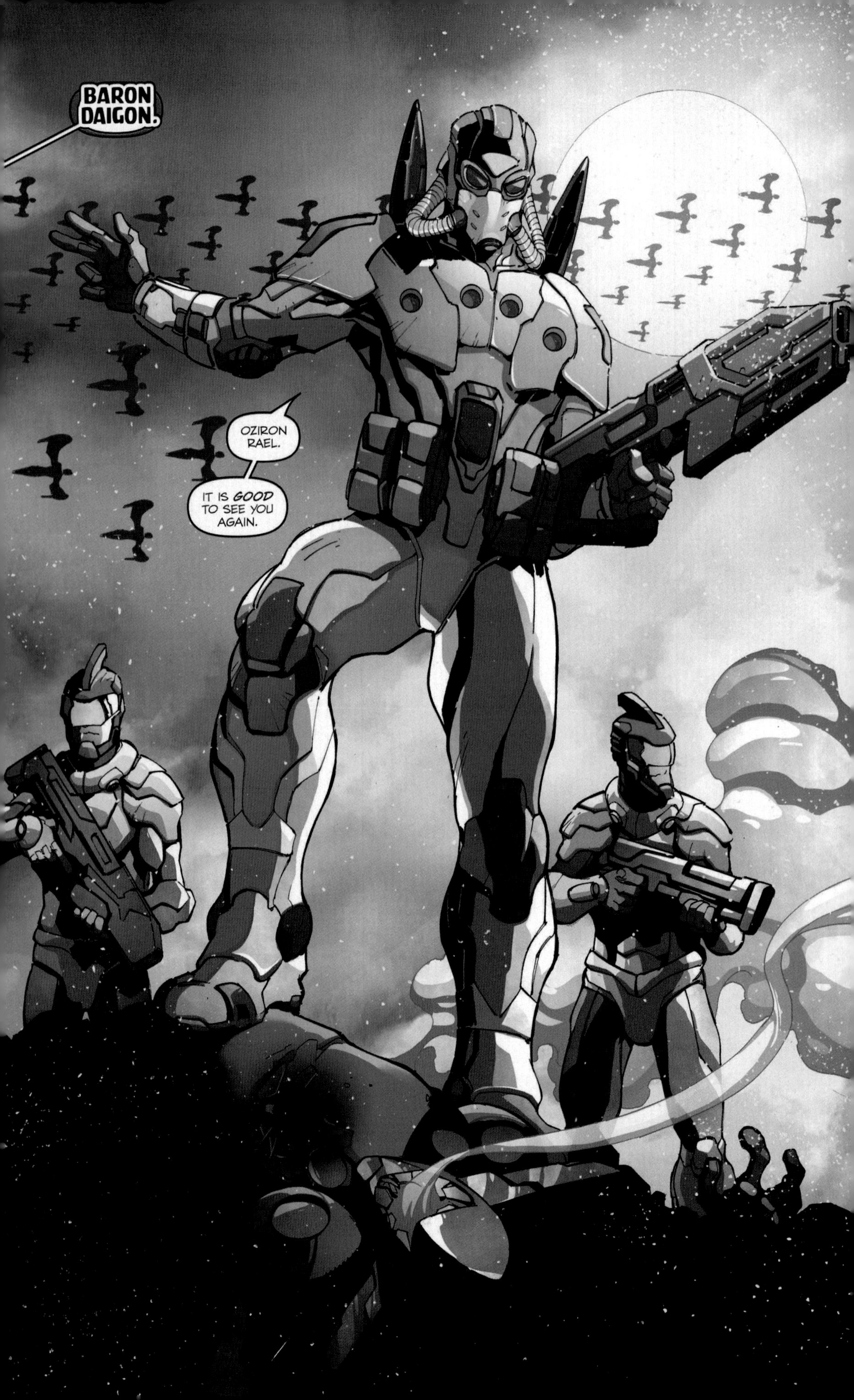
BARON DAIGON.
OZIRON RAEL.
IT IS *GOOD* TO SEE YOU AGAIN.

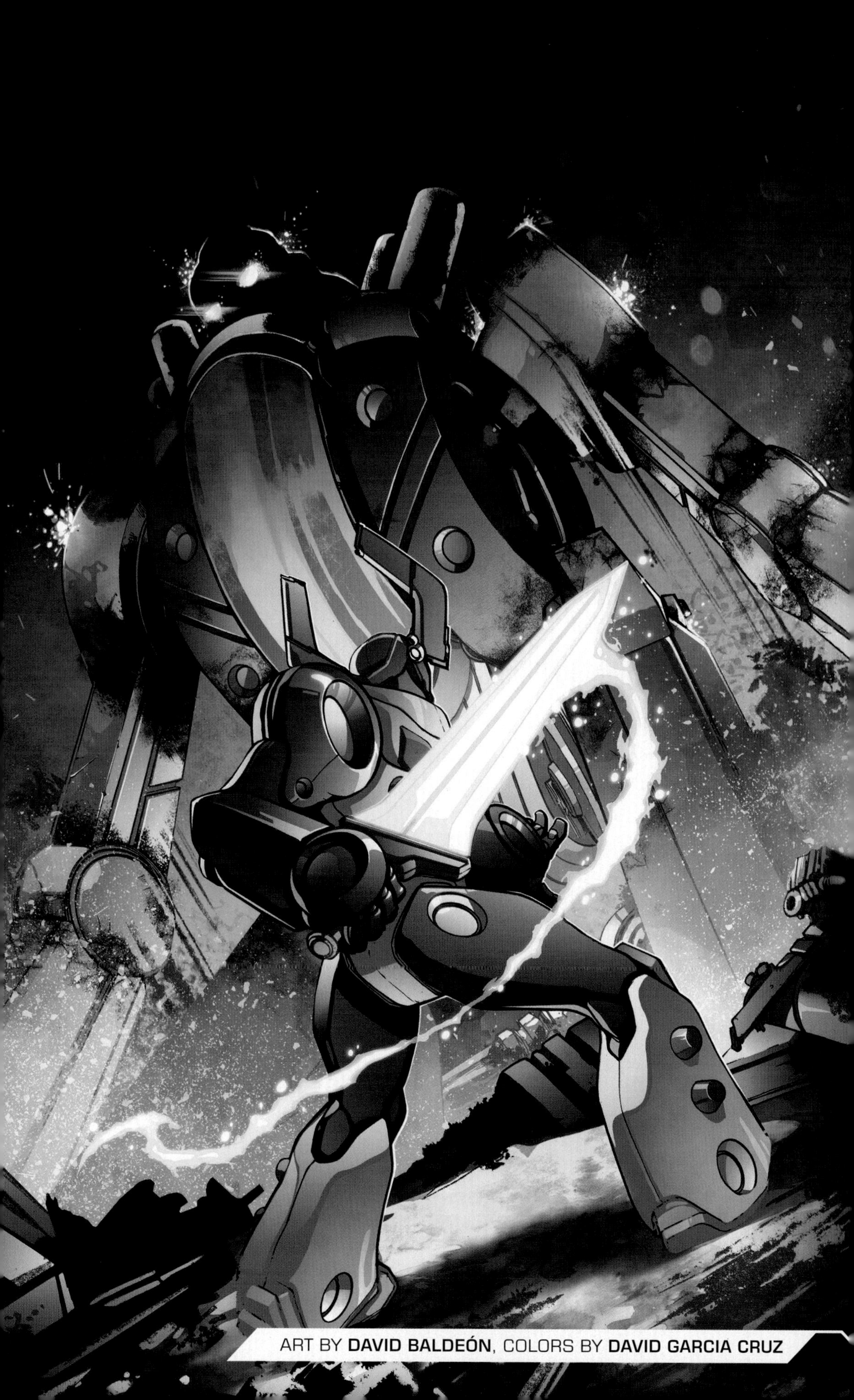

ART BY **DAVID BALDEÓN**, COLORS BY **DAVID GARCIA CRUZ**

03

ART BY **J.H. WILLIAMS III**

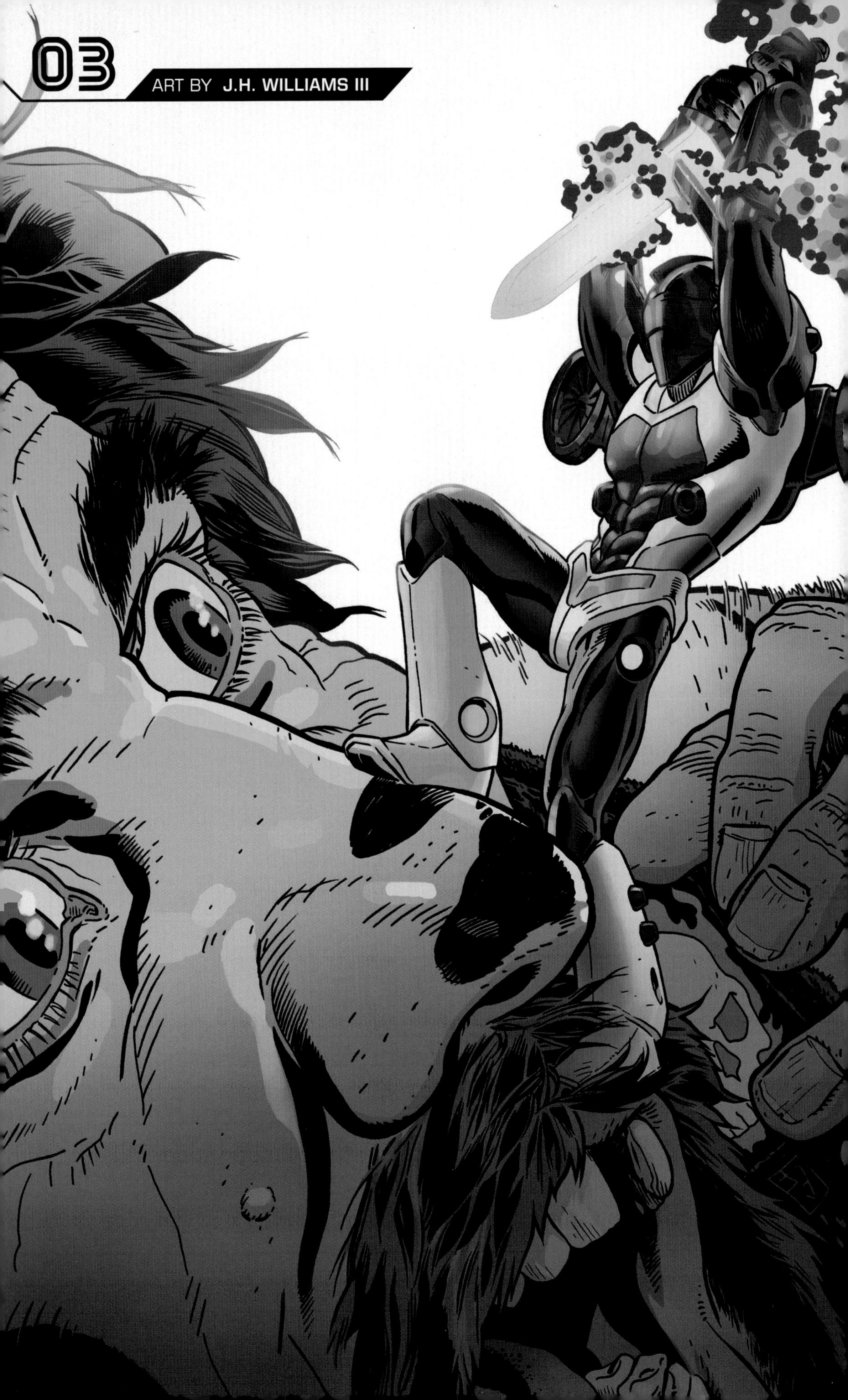

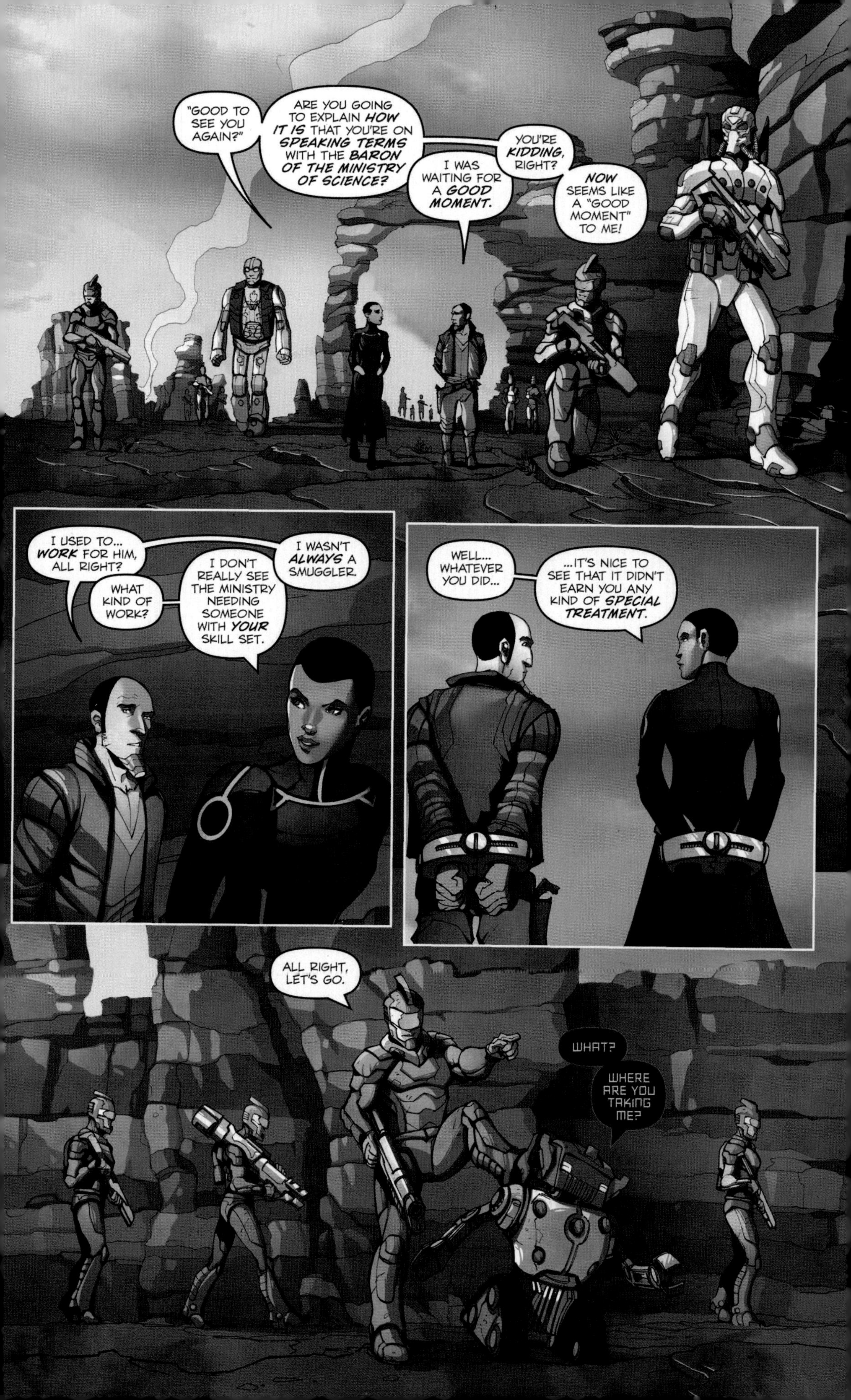
"GOOD TO SEE YOU AGAIN?"
ARE YOU GOING TO EXPLAIN *HOW IT IS* THAT YOU'RE ON *SPEAKING TERMS* WITH THE *BARON OF THE MINISTRY OF SCIENCE?*
I WAS WAITING FOR A *GOOD MOMENT.*
YOU'RE *KIDDING,* RIGHT?
NOW SEEMS LIKE A "GOOD MOMENT" TO ME!
I USED TO... *WORK* FOR HIM, ALL RIGHT?
I WASN'T *ALWAYS* A SMUGGLER.
WHAT KIND OF WORK?
I DON'T REALLY SEE THE MINISTRY NEEDING SOMEONE WITH *YOUR* SKILL SET.
WELL... WHATEVER YOU DID...
...IT'S NICE TO SEE THAT IT DIDN'T EARN YOU ANY KIND OF *SPECIAL TREATMENT.*
ALL RIGHT, LET'S GO.
WHAT?
WHERE ARE YOU TAKING ME?

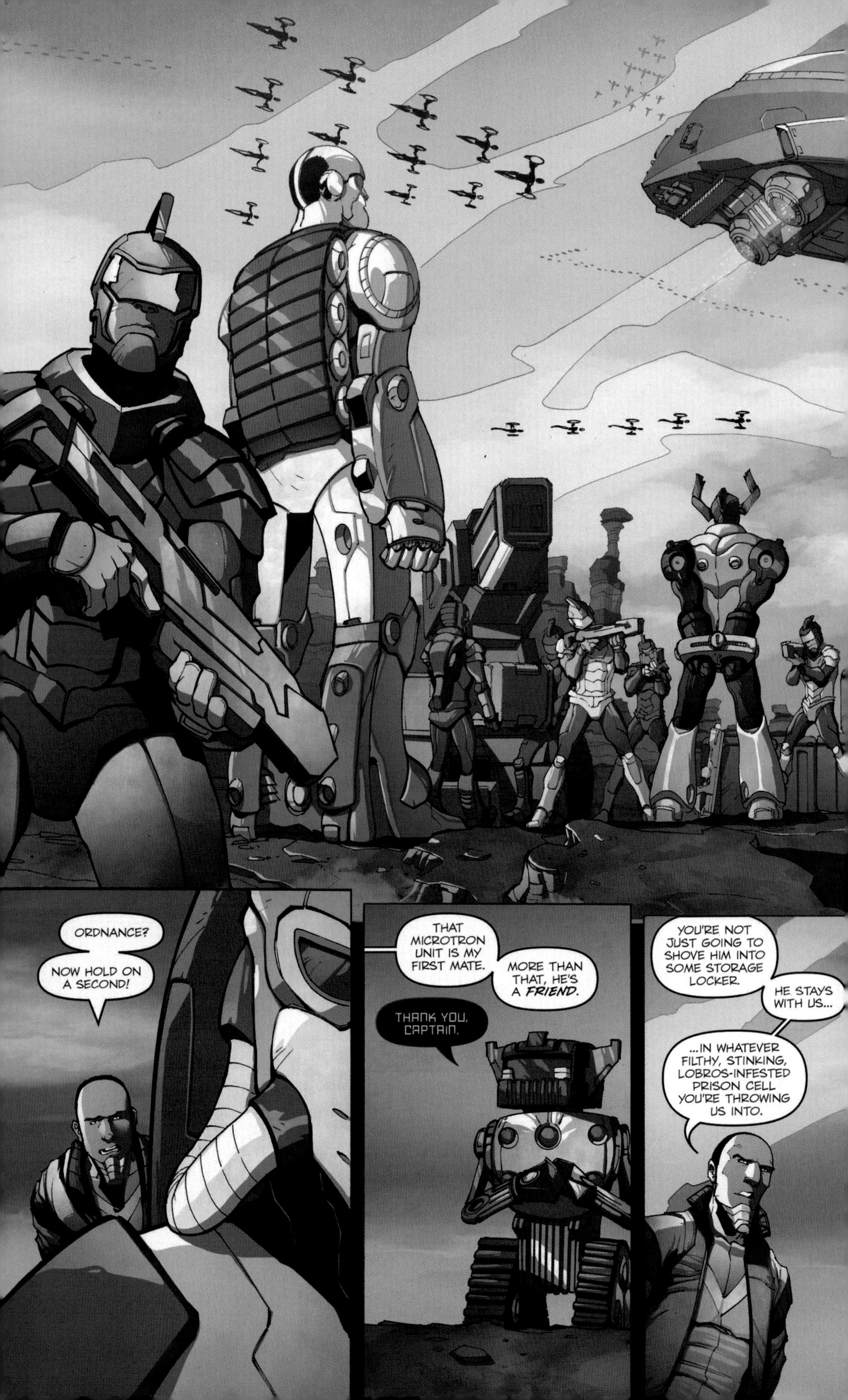
ORDNANCE?
NOW HOLD ON A SECOND!
THAT MICROTRON UNIT IS MY FIRST MATE.
MORE THAN THAT, HE'S A *FRIEND*.
THANK YOU, CAPTAIN.
YOU'RE NOT JUST GOING TO SHOVE HIM INTO SOME STORAGE LOCKER.
HE STAYS WITH US...
...IN WHATEVER FILTHY, STINKING, LOBROS-INFESTED PRISON CELL YOU'RE THROWING US INTO.

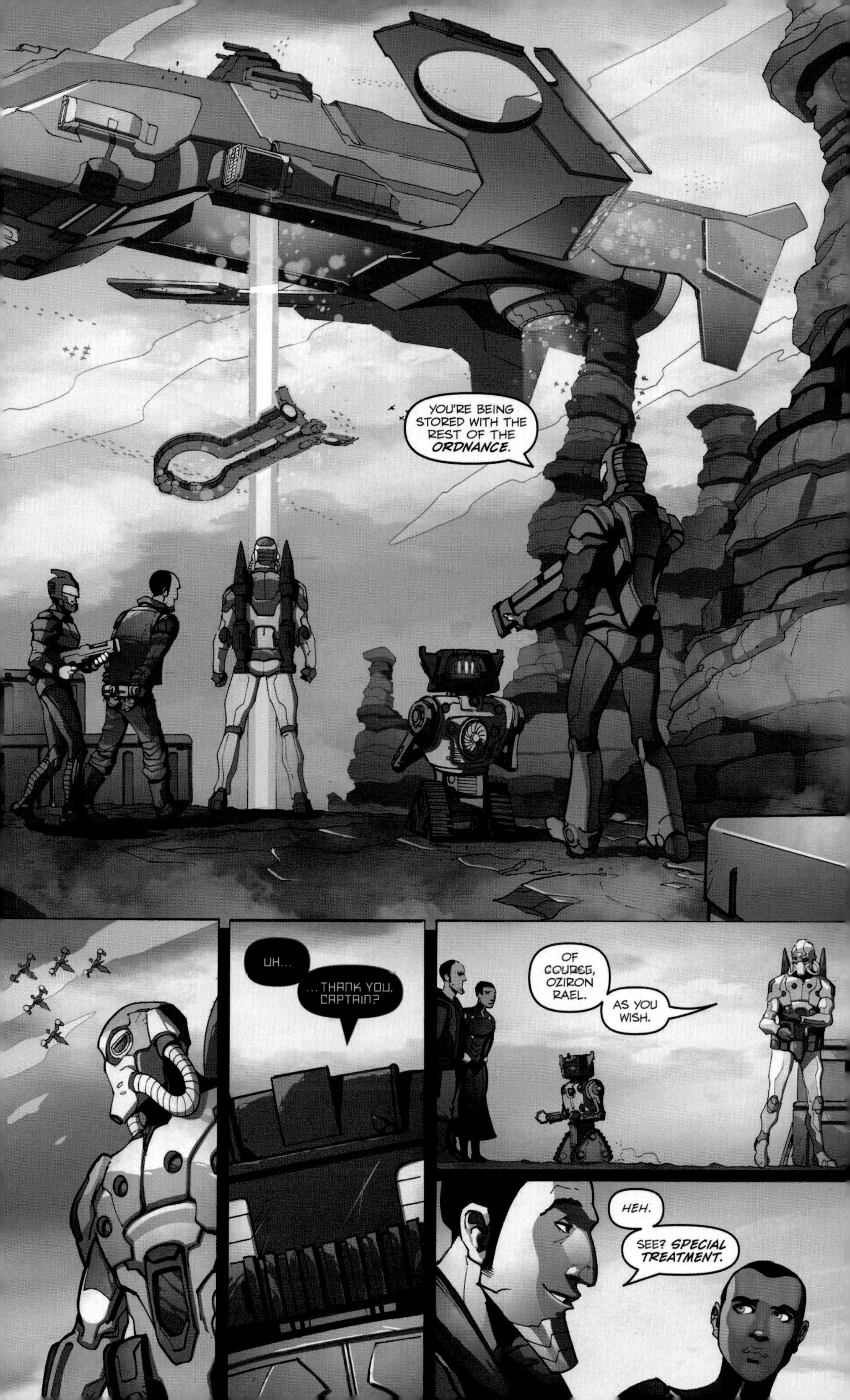
YOU'RE BEING STORED WITH THE REST OF THE *ORDNANCE*.
UH...
...THANK YOU, CAPTAIN?
OF COURSE, OZIRON RAEL.
AS YOU WISH.
HEH.
SEE? *SPECIAL TREATMENT*.

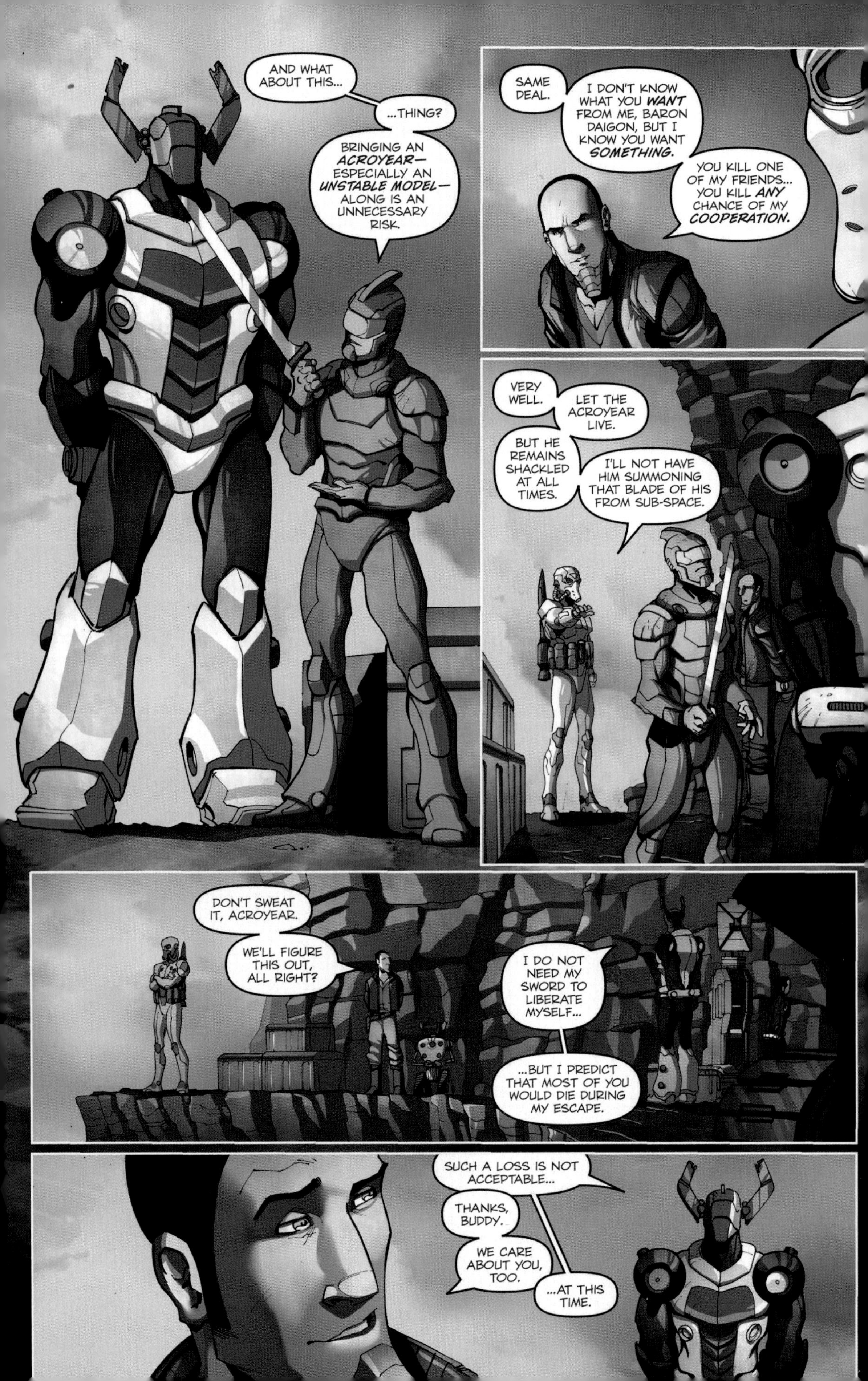
AND WHAT ABOUT THIS...
...THING?
BRINGING AN ACROYEAR— ESPECIALLY AN UNSTABLE MODEL— ALONG IS AN UNNECESSARY RISK.
SAME DEAL.
I DON'T KNOW WHAT YOU WANT FROM ME, BARON DAIGON, BUT I KNOW YOU WANT SOMETHING.
YOU KILL ONE OF MY FRIENDS... YOU KILL ANY CHANCE OF MY COOPERATION.
VERY WELL.
LET THE ACROYEAR LIVE.
BUT HE REMAINS SHACKLED AT ALL TIMES.
I'LL NOT HAVE HIM SUMMONING THAT BLADE OF HIS FROM SUB-SPACE.
DON'T SWEAT IT, ACROYEAR.
WE'LL FIGURE THIS OUT, ALL RIGHT?
I DO NOT NEED MY SWORD TO LIBERATE MYSELF...
...BUT I PREDICT THAT MOST OF YOU WOULD DIE DURING MY ESCAPE.
SUCH A LOSS IS NOT ACCEPTABLE...
THANKS, BUDDY.
WE CARE ABOUT YOU, TOO.
...AT THIS TIME.

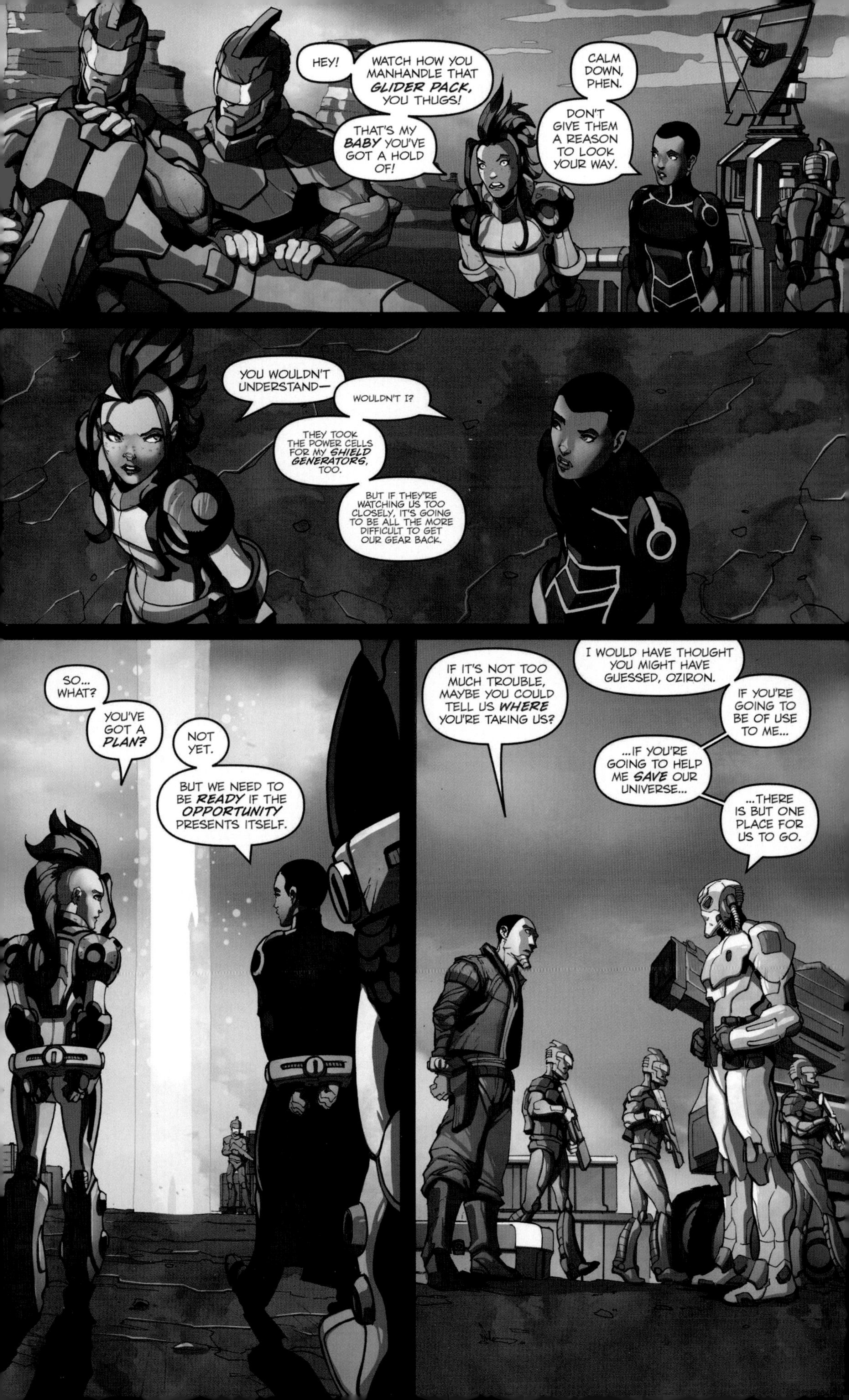
HEY!
WATCH HOW YOU MANHANDLE THAT GLIDER PACK, YOU THUGS!
THAT'S MY BABY YOU'VE GOT A HOLD OF!
CALM DOWN, PHEN.
DON'T GIVE THEM A REASON TO LOOK YOUR WAY.
YOU WOULDN'T UNDERSTAND—
WOULDN'T I?
THEY TOOK THE POWER CELLS FOR MY SHIELD GENERATORS, TOO.
BUT IF THEY'RE WATCHING US TOO CLOSELY, IT'S GOING TO BE ALL THE MORE DIFFICULT TO GET OUR GEAR BACK.
SO... WHAT?
YOU'VE GOT A PLAN?
NOT YET.
BUT WE NEED TO BE READY IF THE OPPORTUNITY PRESENTS ITSELF.
IF IT'S NOT TOO MUCH TROUBLE, MAYBE YOU COULD TELL US WHERE YOU'RE TAKING US?
I WOULD HAVE THOUGHT YOU MIGHT HAVE GUESSED, OZIRON.
IF YOU'RE GOING TO BE OF USE TO ME...
...IF YOU'RE GOING TO HELP ME SAVE OUR UNIVERSE...
...THERE IS BUT ONE PLACE FOR US TO GO.

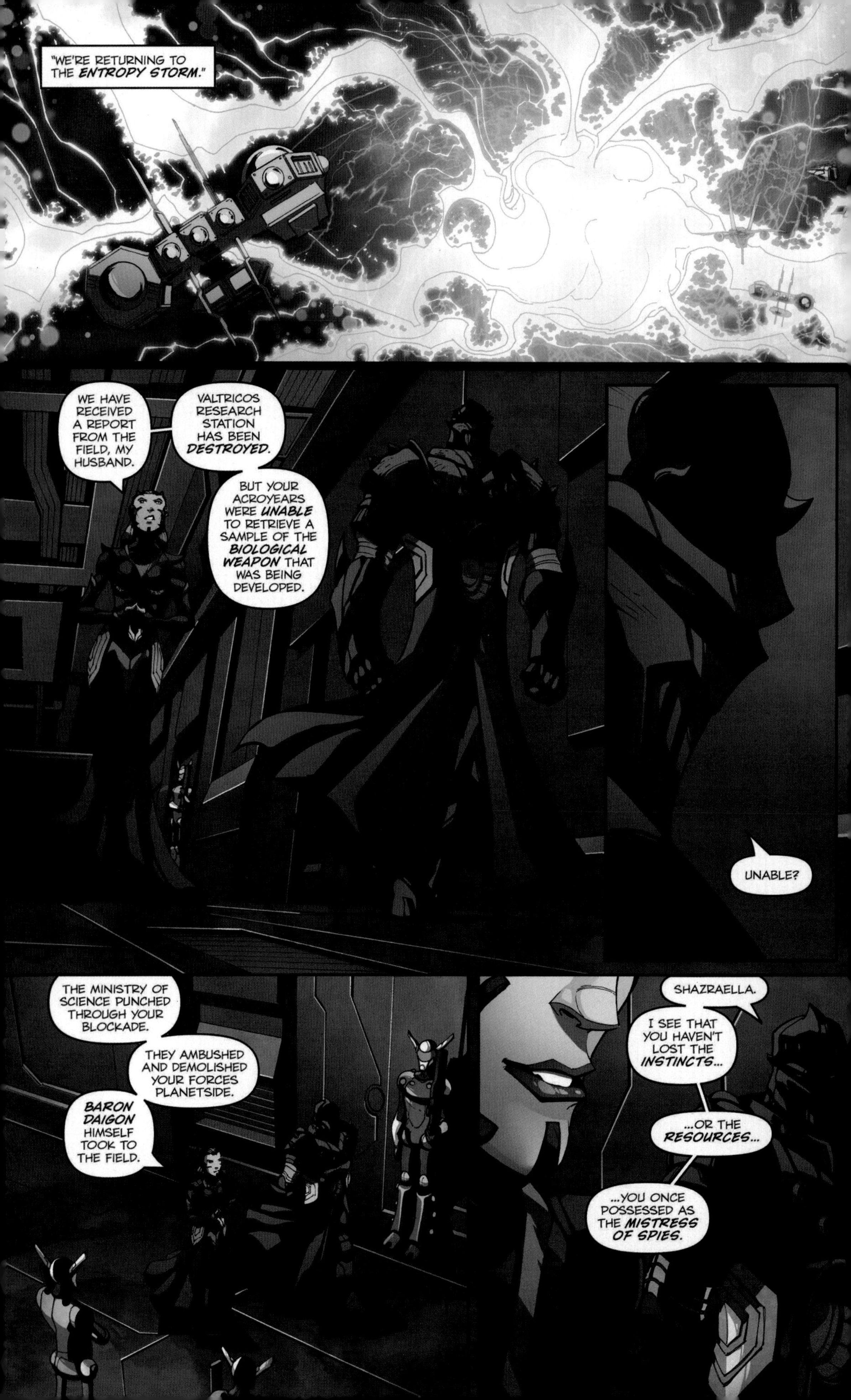
"WE'RE RETURNING TO THE *ENTROPY STORM*."
WE HAVE RECEIVED A REPORT FROM THE FIELD, MY HUSBAND.
VALTRICOS RESEARCH STATION HAS BEEN *DESTROYED*.
BUT YOUR ACROYEARS WERE *UNABLE* TO RETRIEVE A SAMPLE OF THE *BIOLOGICAL WEAPON* THAT WAS BEING DEVELOPED.
UNABLE?
THE MINISTRY OF SCIENCE PUNCHED THROUGH YOUR BLOCKADE.
THEY AMBUSHED AND DEMOLISHED YOUR FORCES PLANETSIDE.
BARON DAIGON HIMSELF TOOK TO THE FIELD.
SHAZRAELLA.
I SEE THAT YOU HAVEN'T LOST THE *INSTINCTS*...
...OR THE *RESOURCES*...
...YOU ONCE POSSESSED AS THE *MISTRESS OF SPIES*.

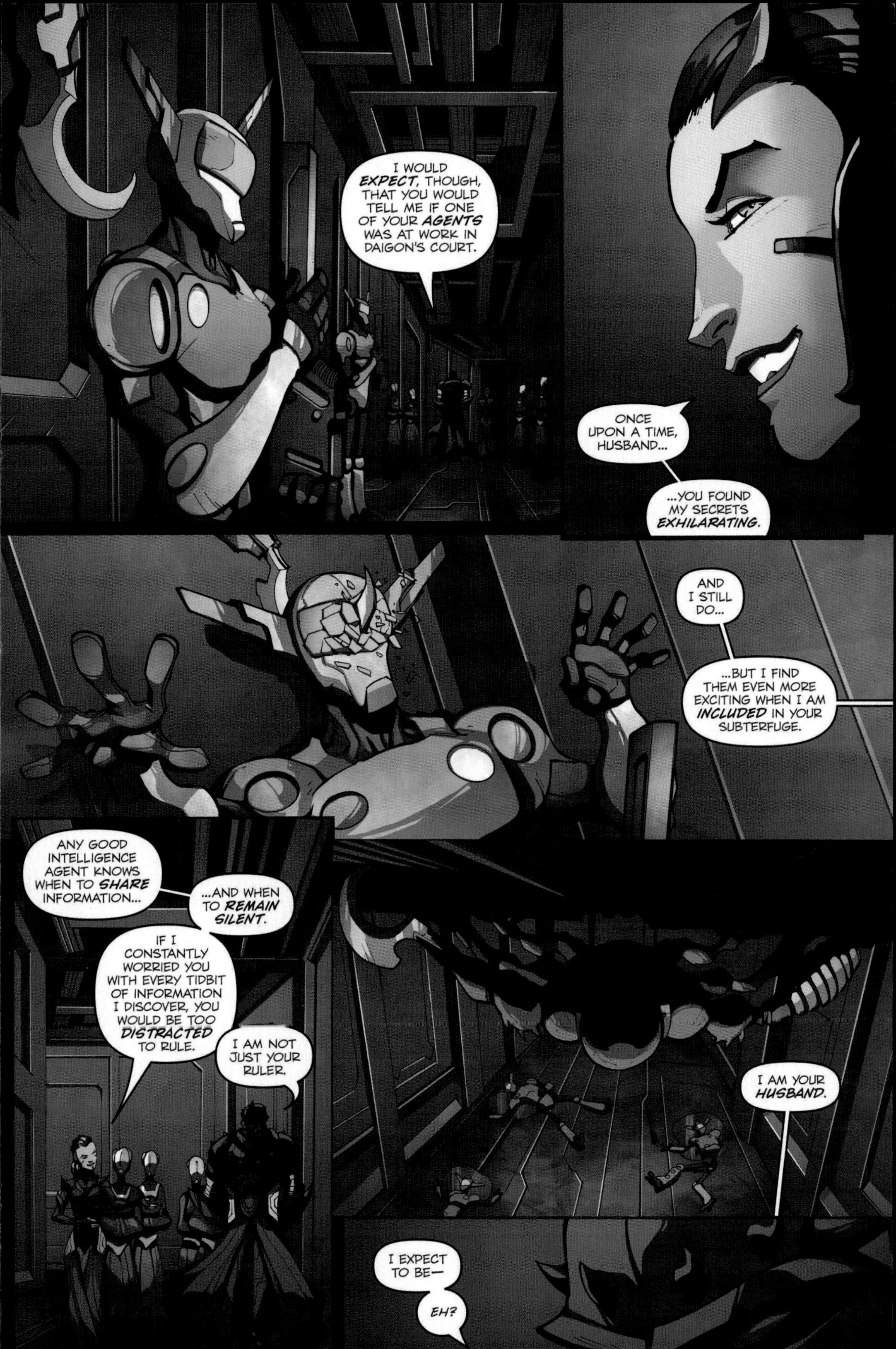
I WOULD EXPECT, THOUGH, THAT YOU WOULD TELL ME IF ONE OF YOUR AGENTS WAS AT WORK IN DAIGON'S COURT.
ONCE UPON A TIME, HUSBAND...
...YOU FOUND MY SECRETS EXHILARATING.
AND I STILL DO...
...BUT I FIND THEM EVEN MORE EXCITING WHEN I AM INCLUDED IN YOUR SUBTERFUGE.
ANY GOOD INTELLIGENCE AGENT KNOWS WHEN TO SHARE INFORMATION...
...AND WHEN TO REMAIN SILENT.
IF I CONSTANTLY WORRIED YOU WITH EVERY TIDBIT OF INFORMATION I DISCOVER, YOU WOULD BE TOO DISTRACTED TO RULE.
I AM NOT JUST YOUR RULER.
I AM YOUR HUSBAND.
I EXPECT TO BE—
EH?

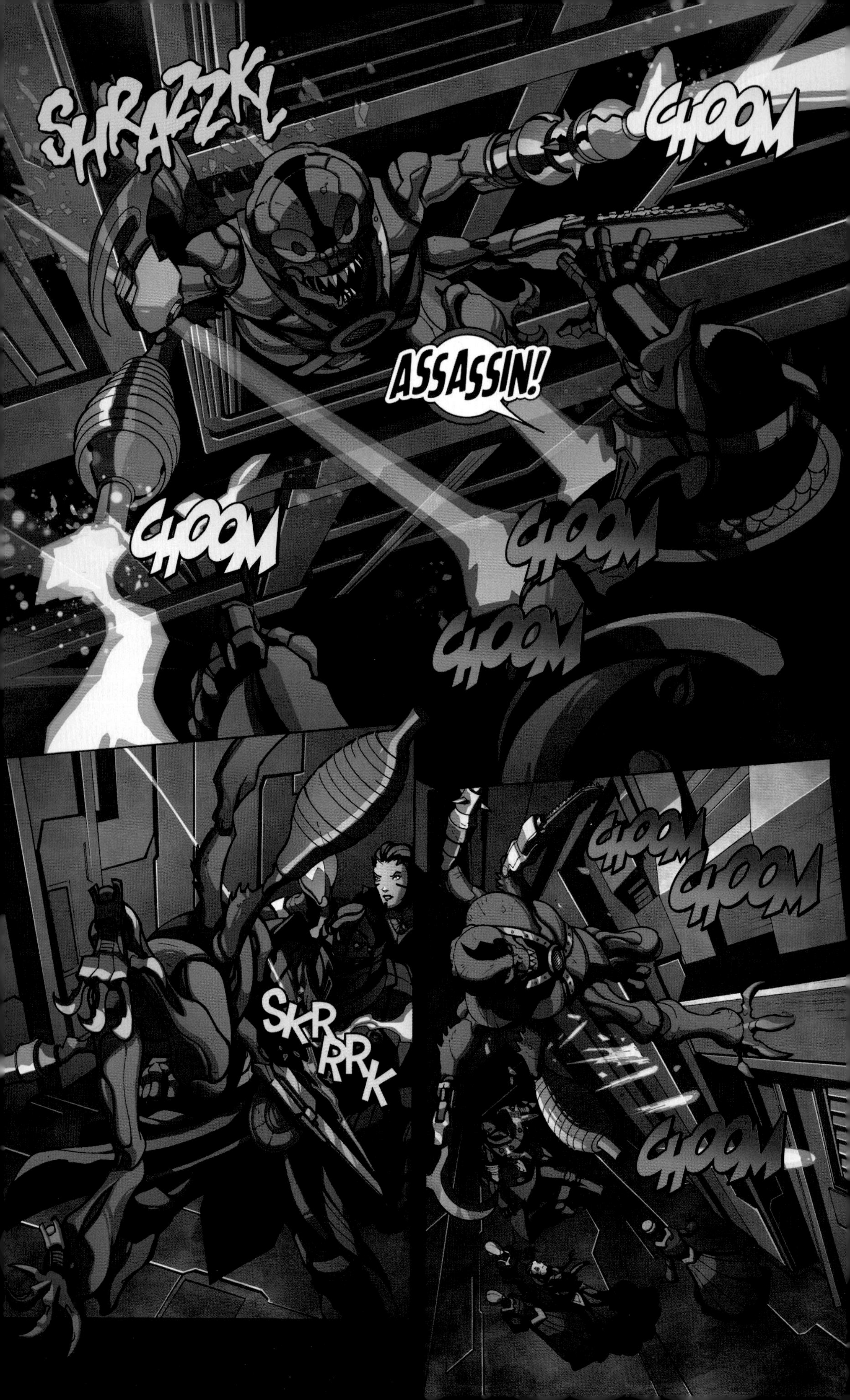
SHRAZZK!
CHOOM
ASSASSIN!
CHOOM
CHOOM
CHOOM
SKRRRK
CHOOM
CHOOM
CHOOM

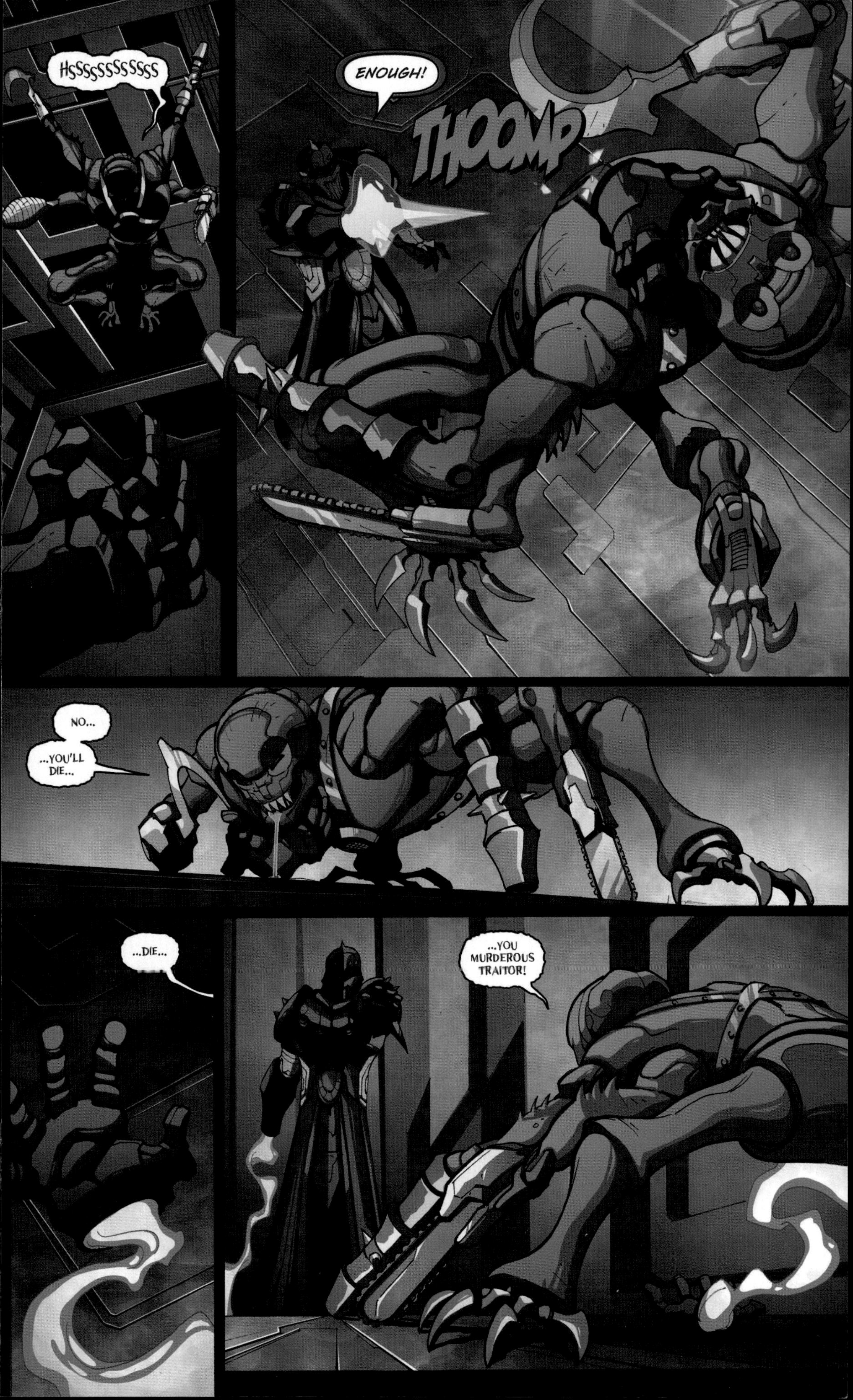
HSSSSSSSSSSSS
ENOUGH!
THOOMP
NO,...
...YOU'LL DIE...
...DIE...
...YOU MURDEROUS TRAITOR!

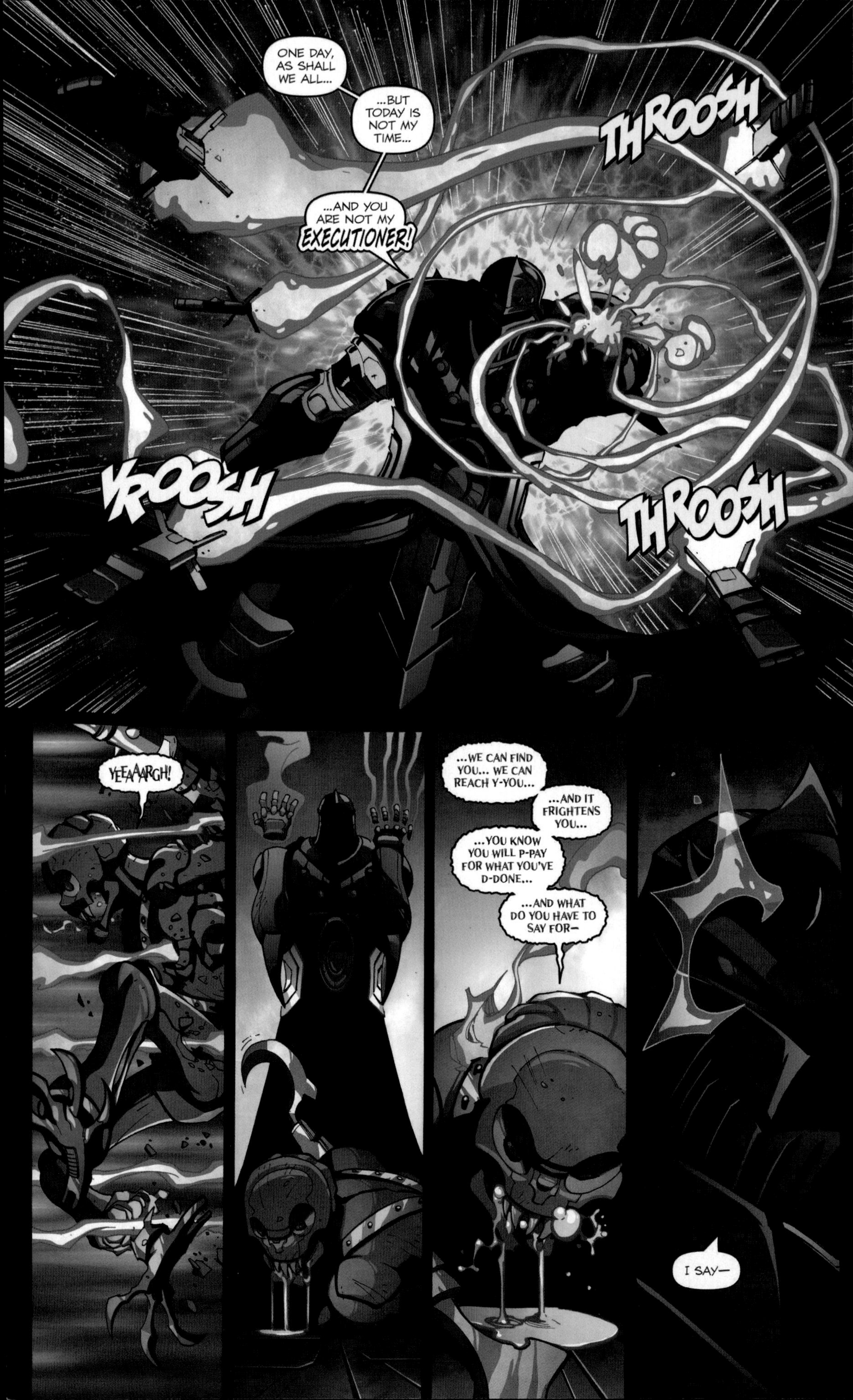
ONE DAY, AS SHALL WE ALL...
...BUT TODAY IS NOT MY TIME...
...AND YOU ARE NOT MY EXECUTIONER!
THROOSH
VROOSH
THROOSH
YEEAAARGH!
...WE CAN FIND YOU... WE CAN REACH Y-YOU...
...AND IT FRIGHTENS YOU...
...YOU KNOW YOU WILL P-PAY FOR WHAT YOU'VE D-DONE...
...AND WHAT DO YOU HAVE TO SAY FOR—
I SAY—

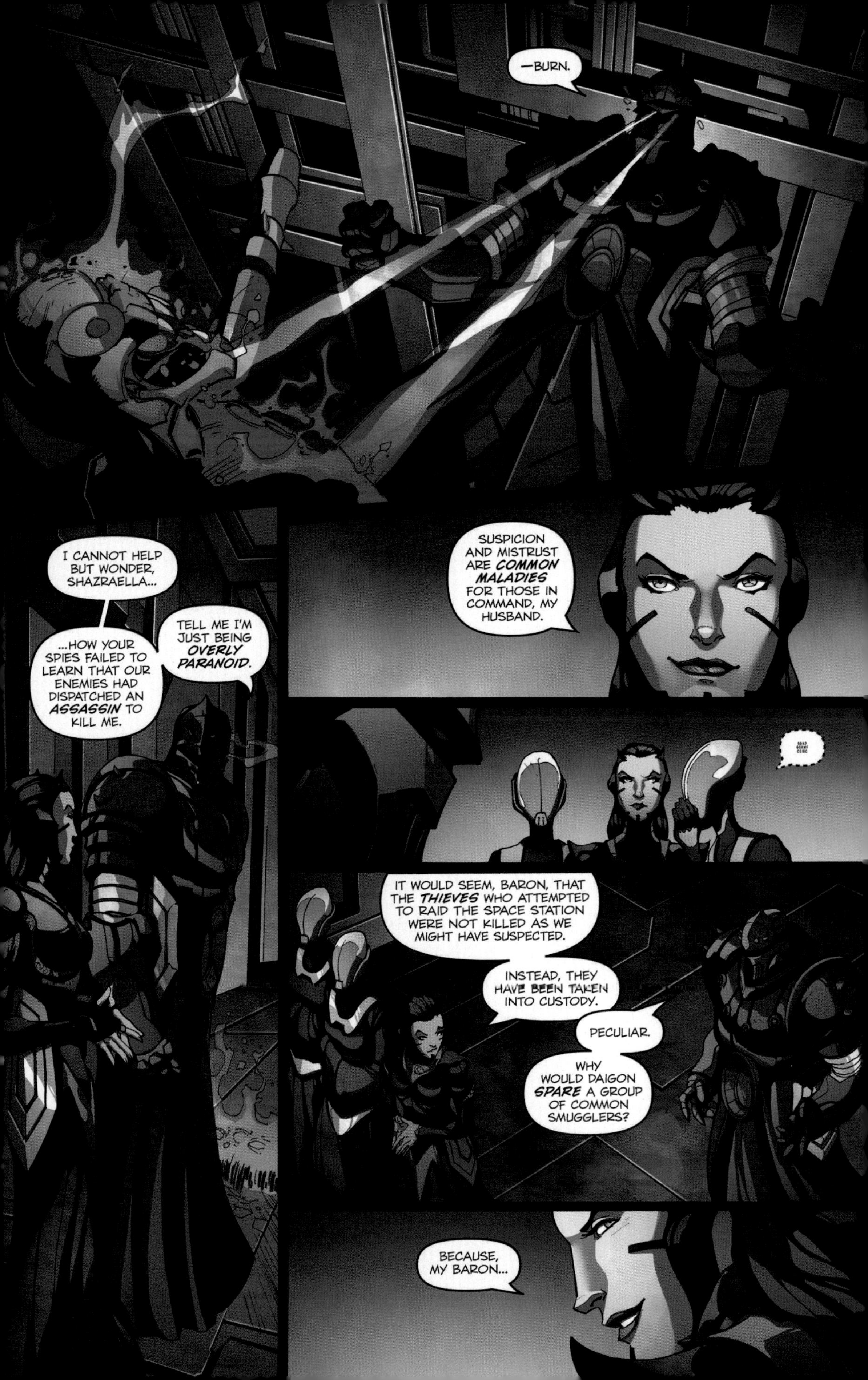
—BURN.
I CANNOT HELP BUT WONDER, SHAZRAELLA...
...HOW YOUR SPIES FAILED TO LEARN THAT OUR ENEMIES HAD DISPATCHED AN ASSASSIN TO KILL ME.
TELL ME I'M JUST BEING OVERLY PARANOID.
SUSPICION AND MISTRUST ARE COMMON MALADIES FOR THOSE IN COMMAND, MY HUSBAND.
IT WOULD SEEM, BARON, THAT THE THIEVES WHO ATTEMPTED TO RAID THE SPACE STATION WERE NOT KILLED AS WE MIGHT HAVE SUSPECTED.
INSTEAD, THEY HAVE BEEN TAKEN INTO CUSTODY.
PECULIAR.
WHY WOULD DAIGON SPARE A GROUP OF COMMON SMUGGLERS?
BECAUSE, MY BARON...

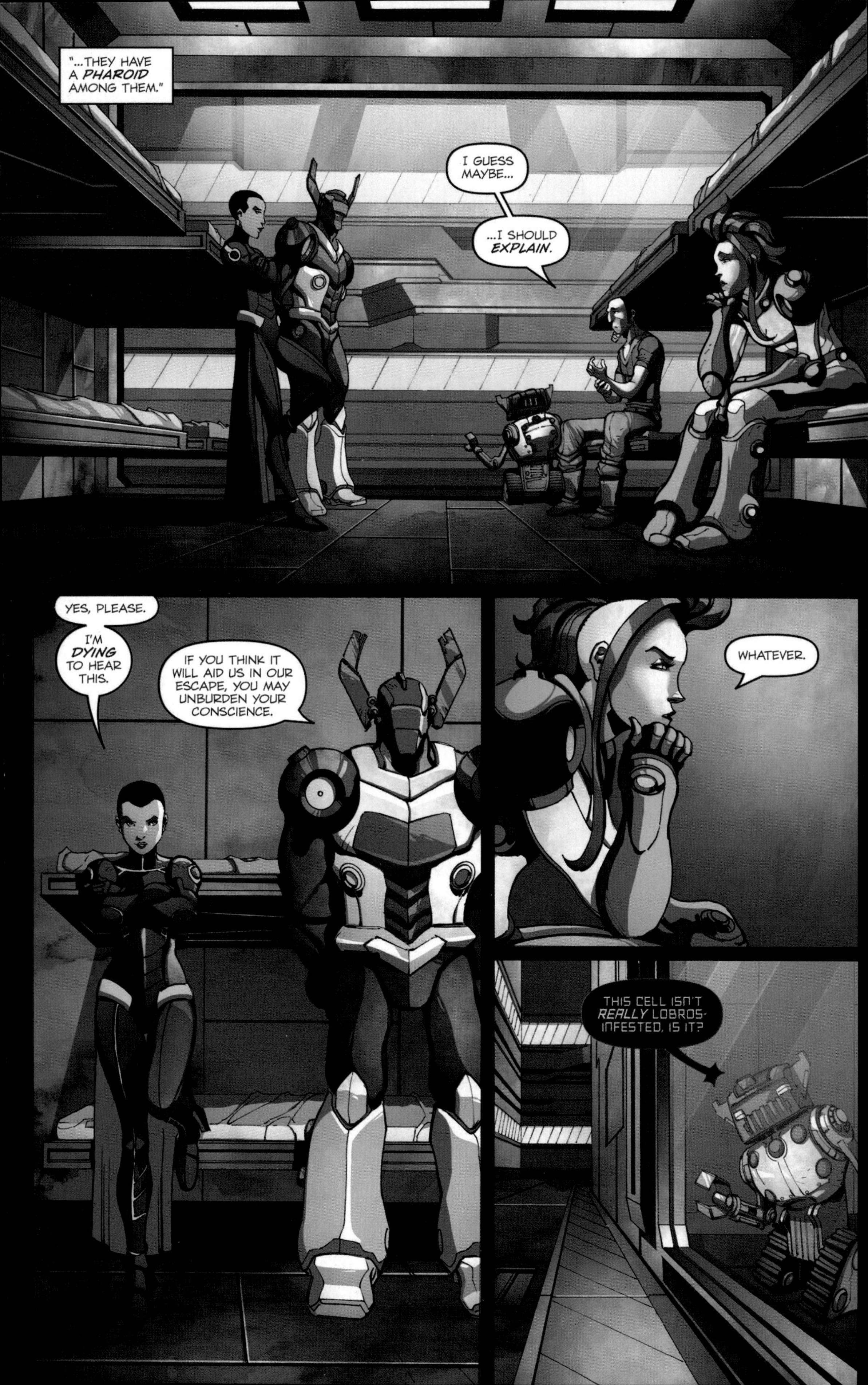
"...THEY HAVE A *PHAROID* AMONG THEM."
I GUESS MAYBE...
...I SHOULD ***EXPLAIN***.
YES, PLEASE.
I'M ***DYING*** TO HEAR THIS.
IF YOU THINK IT WILL AID US IN OUR ESCAPE, YOU MAY UNBURDEN YOUR CONSCIENCE.
WHATEVER.
THIS CELL ISN'T *REALLY* LOBROS-INFESTED, IS IT?

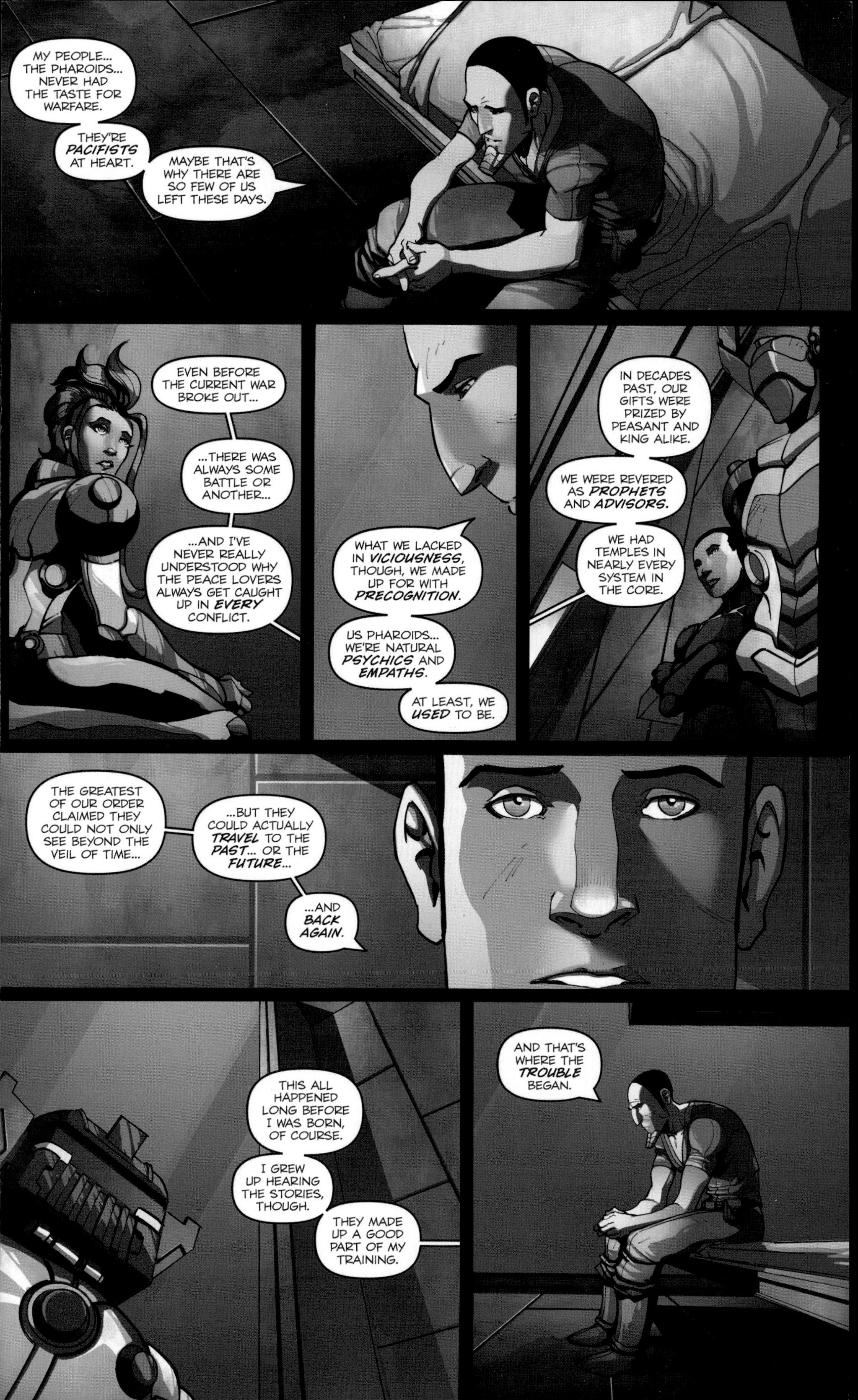
MY PEOPLE... THE PHAROIDS... NEVER HAD THE TASTE FOR WARFARE.
THEY'RE PACIFISTS AT HEART.
MAYBE THAT'S WHY THERE ARE SO FEW OF US LEFT THESE DAYS.
EVEN BEFORE THE CURRENT WAR BROKE OUT...
...THERE WAS ALWAYS SOME BATTLE OR ANOTHER...
...AND I'VE NEVER REALLY UNDERSTOOD WHY THE PEACE LOVERS ALWAYS GET CAUGHT UP IN EVERY CONFLICT.
WHAT WE LACKED IN VICIOUSNESS, THOUGH, WE MADE UP FOR WITH PRECOGNITION.
US PHAROIDS... WE'RE NATURAL PSYCHICS AND EMPATHS.
AT LEAST, WE USED TO BE.
IN DECADES PAST, OUR GIFTS WERE PRIZED BY PEASANT AND KING ALIKE.
WE WERE REVERED AS PROPHETS AND ADVISORS.
WE HAD TEMPLES IN NEARLY EVERY SYSTEM IN THE CORE.
THE GREATEST OF OUR ORDER CLAIMED THEY COULD NOT ONLY SEE BEYOND THE VEIL OF TIME...
...BUT THEY COULD ACTUALLY TRAVEL TO THE PAST... OR THE FUTURE...
...AND BACK AGAIN.
THIS ALL HAPPENED LONG BEFORE I WAS BORN, OF COURSE.
I GREW UP HEARING THE STORIES, THOUGH.
THEY MADE UP A GOOD PART OF MY TRAINING.
AND THAT'S WHERE THE TROUBLE BEGAN.

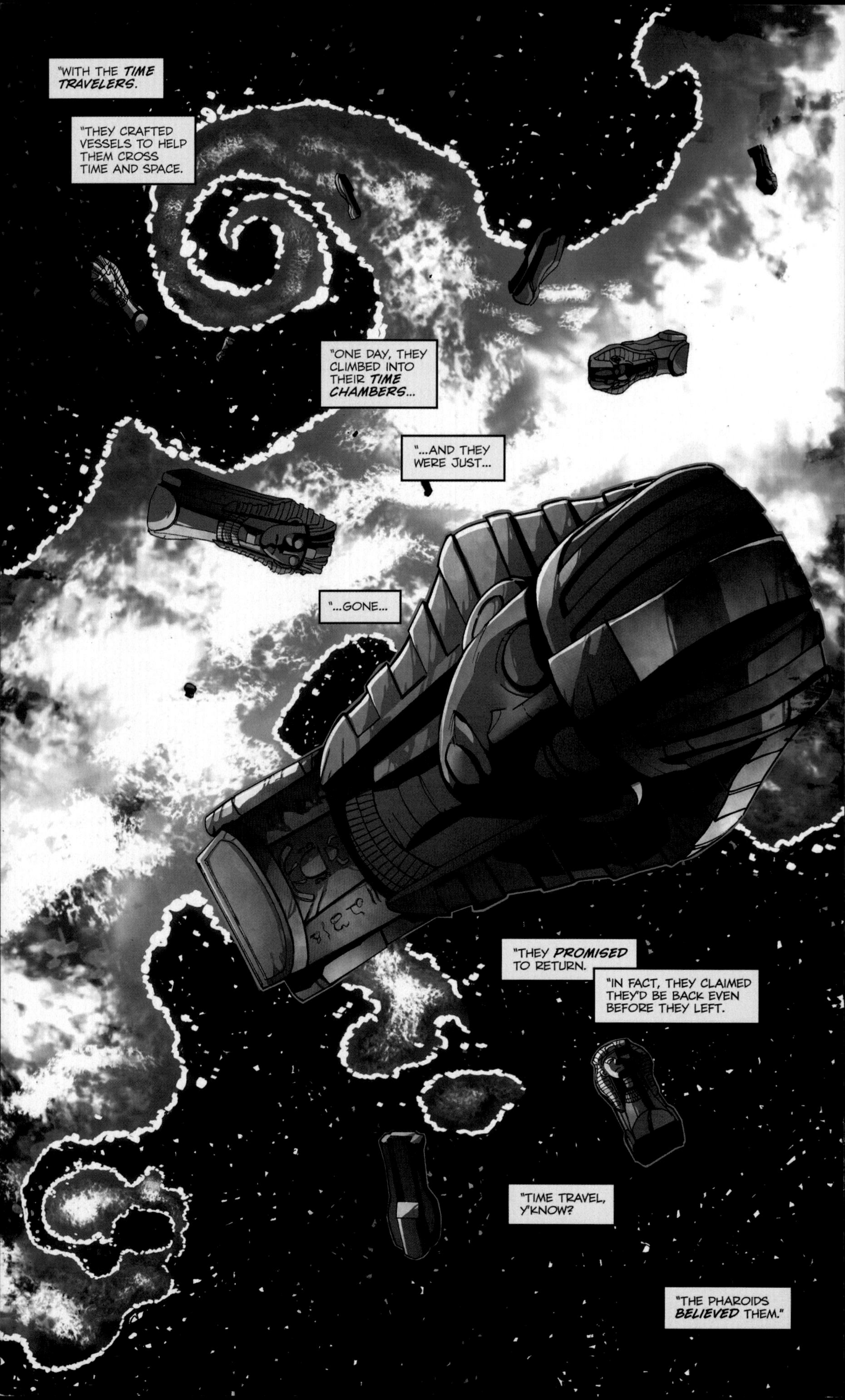
"WITH THE *TIME TRAVELERS*.
"THEY CRAFTED VESSELS TO HELP THEM CROSS TIME AND SPACE.
"ONE DAY, THEY CLIMBED INTO THEIR *TIME CHAMBERS*...
"...AND THEY WERE JUST...
"...GONE...
"THEY *PROMISED* TO RETURN.
"IN FACT, THEY CLAIMED THEY'D BE BACK EVEN BEFORE THEY LEFT.
"TIME TRAVEL, Y'KNOW?
"THE PHAROIDS *BELIEVED* THEM."

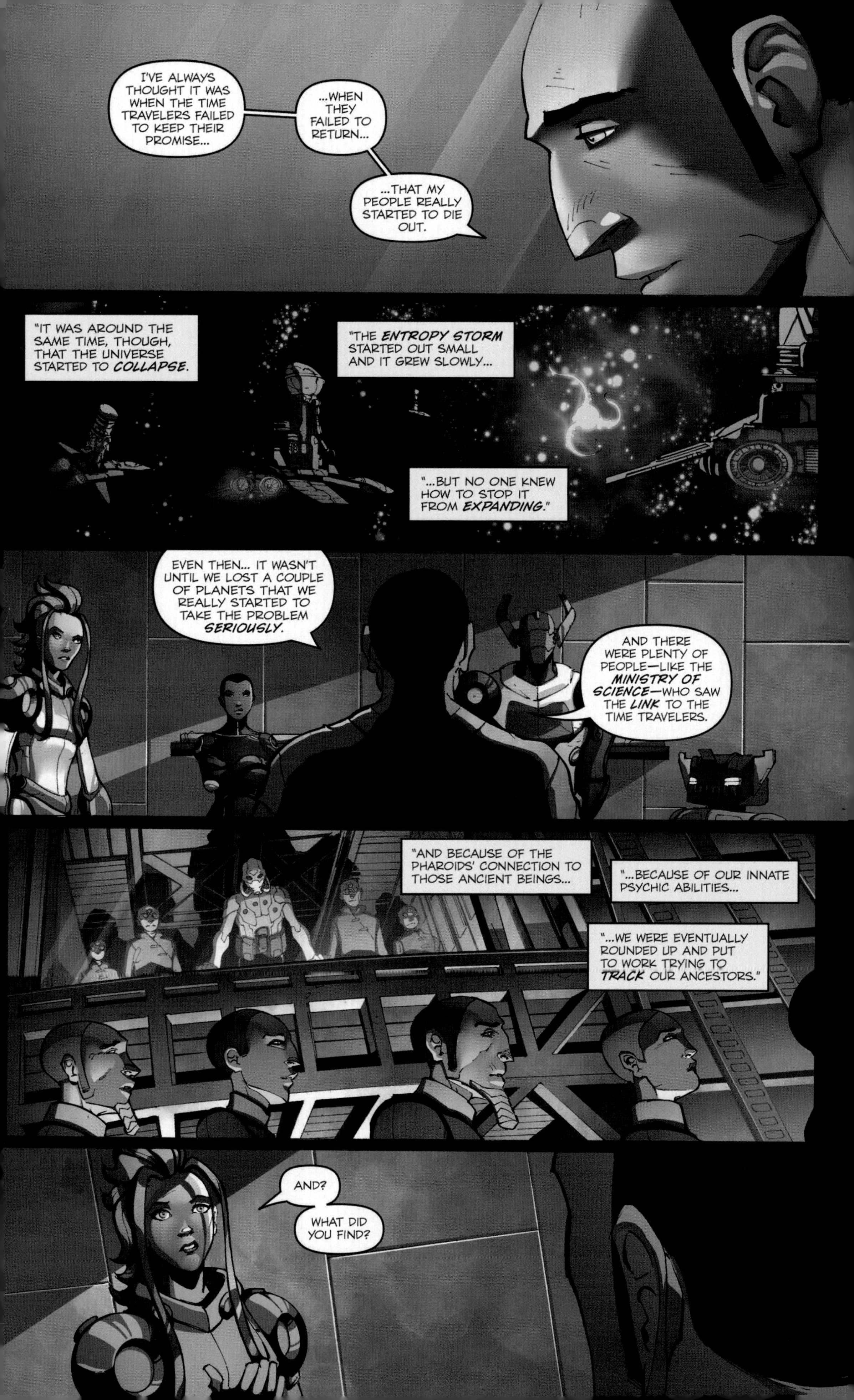

I'VE ALWAYS THOUGHT IT WAS WHEN THE TIME TRAVELERS FAILED TO KEEP THEIR PROMISE...
...WHEN THEY FAILED TO RETURN...
...THAT MY PEOPLE REALLY STARTED TO DIE OUT.
"IT WAS AROUND THE SAME TIME, THOUGH, THAT THE UNIVERSE STARTED TO COLLAPSE.
"THE ENTROPY STORM STARTED OUT SMALL AND IT GREW SLOWLY...
"...BUT NO ONE KNEW HOW TO STOP IT FROM EXPANDING."
EVEN THEN... IT WASN'T UNTIL WE LOST A COUPLE OF PLANETS THAT WE REALLY STARTED TO TAKE THE PROBLEM SERIOUSLY.
AND THERE WERE PLENTY OF PEOPLE—LIKE THE MINISTRY OF SCIENCE—WHO SAW THE LINK TO THE TIME TRAVELERS.
"AND BECAUSE OF THE PHAROIDS' CONNECTION TO THOSE ANCIENT BEINGS...
"...BECAUSE OF OUR INNATE PSYCHIC ABILITIES...
"...WE WERE EVENTUALLY ROUNDED UP AND PUT TO WORK TRYING TO TRACK OUR ANCESTORS."
AND?
WHAT DID YOU FIND?

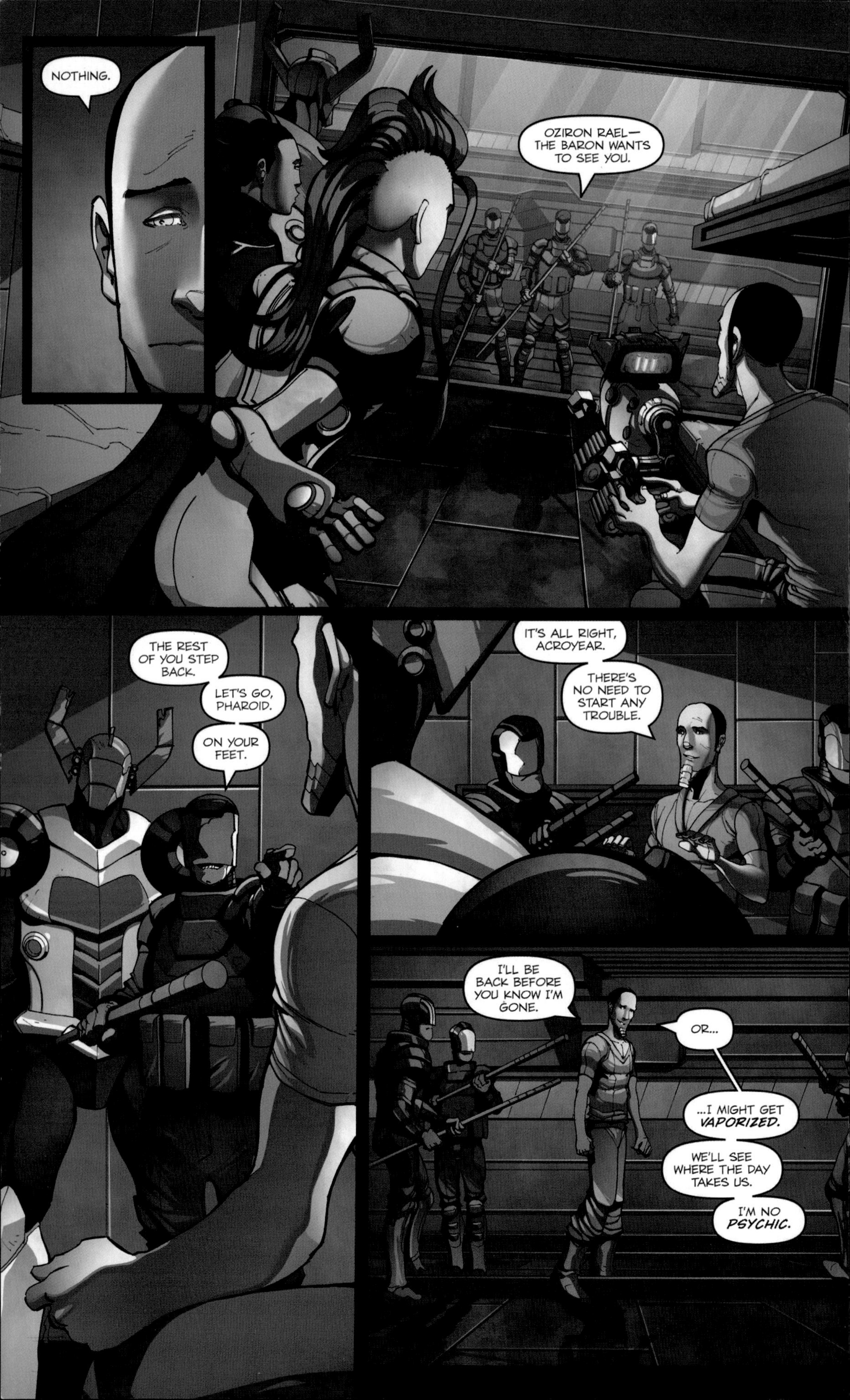
NOTHING.
OZIRON RAEL— THE BARON WANTS TO SEE YOU.
THE REST OF YOU STEP BACK.
LET'S GO, PHAROID.
ON YOUR FEET.
IT'S ALL RIGHT, ACROYEAR.
THERE'S NO NEED TO START ANY TROUBLE.
I'LL BE BACK BEFORE YOU KNOW I'M GONE.
OR...
...I MIGHT GET *VAPORIZED.*
WE'LL SEE WHERE THE DAY TAKES US.
I'M NO *PSYCHIC.*

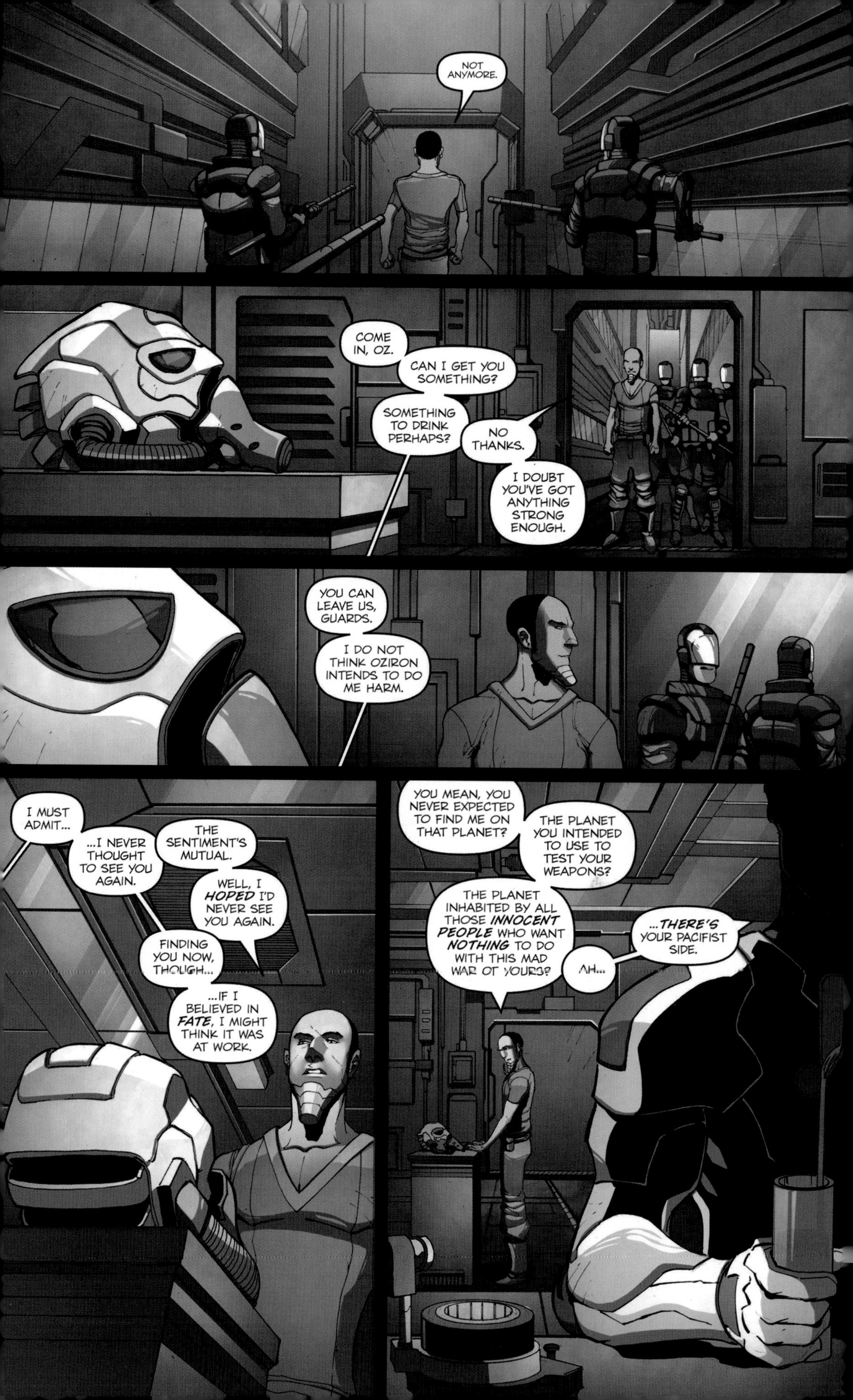

NOT ANYMORE.
COME IN, OZ.
CAN I GET YOU SOMETHING?
SOMETHING TO DRINK PERHAPS?
NO THANKS.
I DOUBT YOU'VE GOT ANYTHING STRONG ENOUGH.
YOU CAN LEAVE US, GUARDS.
I DO NOT THINK OZIRON INTENDS TO DO ME HARM.
I MUST ADMIT...
...I NEVER THOUGHT TO SEE YOU AGAIN.
THE SENTIMENT'S MUTUAL.
WELL, I *HOPED* I'D NEVER SEE YOU AGAIN.
FINDING YOU NOW, THOUGH...
...IF I BELIEVED IN *FATE*, I MIGHT THINK IT WAS AT WORK.
YOU MEAN, YOU NEVER EXPECTED TO FIND ME ON THAT PLANET?
THE PLANET YOU INTENDED TO USE TO TEST YOUR WEAPONS?
THE PLANET INHABITED BY ALL THOSE *INNOCENT PEOPLE* WHO WANT *NOTHING* TO DO WITH THIS MAD WAR OF YOURS?
AH...
...*THERE'S* YOUR PACIFIST SIDE.

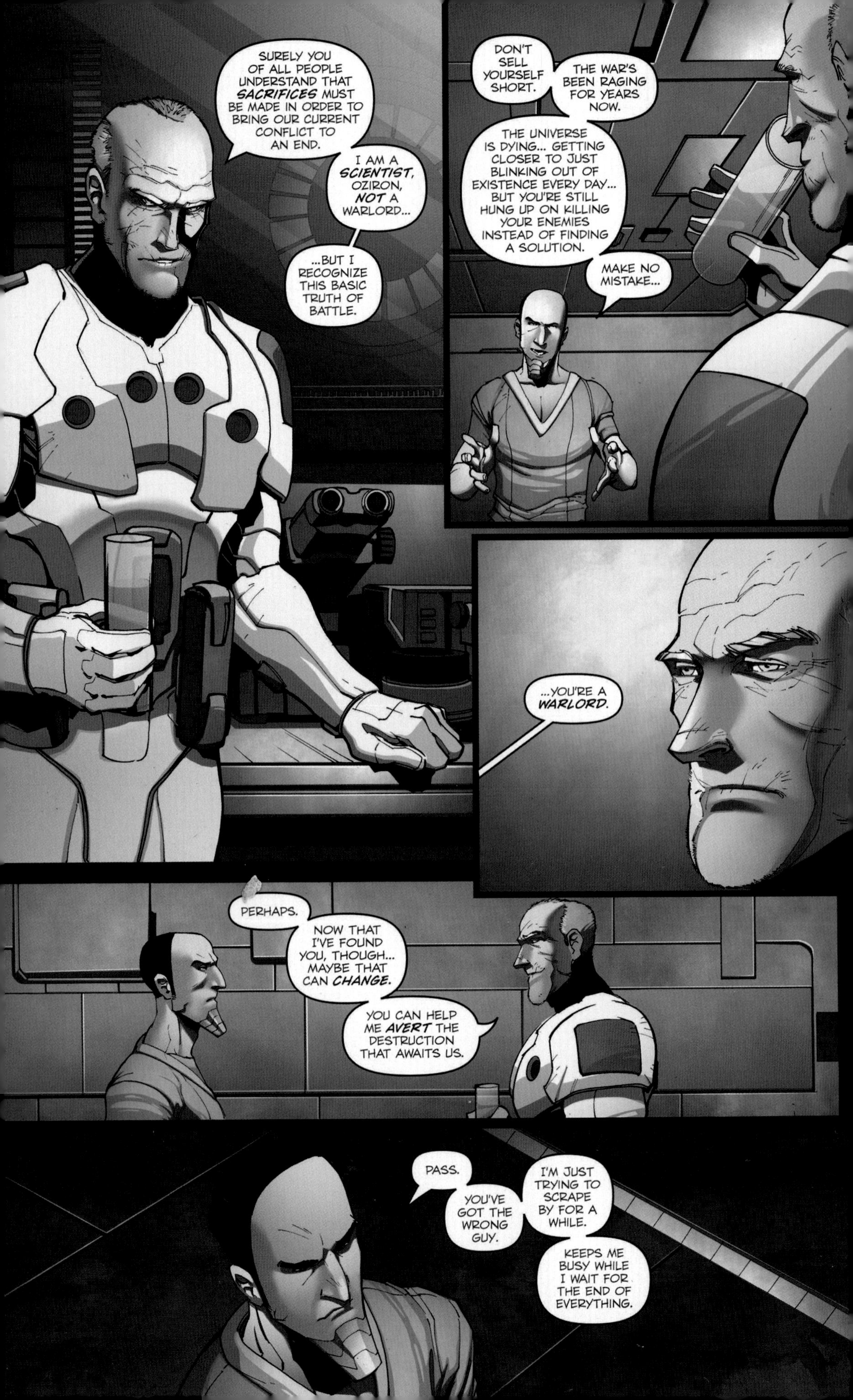
SURELY YOU OF ALL PEOPLE UNDERSTAND THAT SACRIFICES MUST BE MADE IN ORDER TO BRING OUR CURRENT CONFLICT TO AN END.
I AM A SCIENTIST, OZIRON, NOT A WARLORD...
...BUT I RECOGNIZE THIS BASIC TRUTH OF BATTLE.
DON'T SELL YOURSELF SHORT.
THE WAR'S BEEN RAGING FOR YEARS NOW.
THE UNIVERSE IS DYING... GETTING CLOSER TO JUST BLINKING OUT OF EXISTENCE EVERY DAY... BUT YOU'RE STILL HUNG UP ON KILLING YOUR ENEMIES INSTEAD OF FINDING A SOLUTION.
MAKE NO MISTAKE...
...YOU'RE A WARLORD.
PERHAPS.
NOW THAT I'VE FOUND YOU, THOUGH... MAYBE THAT CAN CHANGE.
YOU CAN HELP ME AVERT THE DESTRUCTION THAT AWAITS US.
PASS.
YOU'VE GOT THE WRONG GUY.
I'M JUST TRYING TO SCRAPE BY FOR A WHILE.
KEEPS ME BUSY WHILE I WAIT FOR THE END OF EVERYTHING.

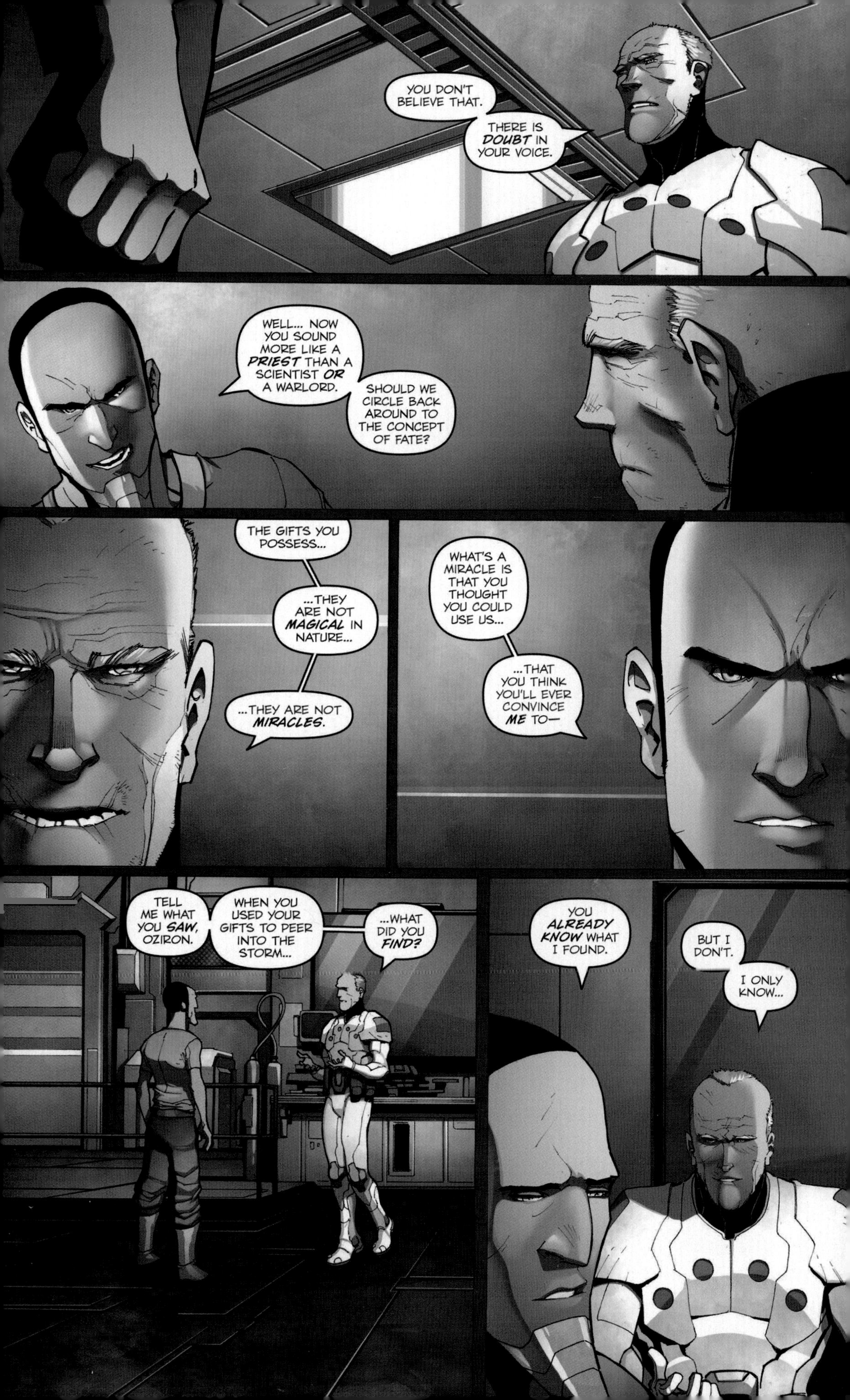
YOU DON'T BELIEVE THAT.
THERE IS DOUBT IN YOUR VOICE.
WELL... NOW YOU SOUND MORE LIKE A PRIEST THAN A SCIENTIST OR A WARLORD.
SHOULD WE CIRCLE BACK AROUND TO THE CONCEPT OF FATE?
THE GIFTS YOU POSSESS...
...THEY ARE NOT MAGICAL IN NATURE...
...THEY ARE NOT MIRACLES.
WHAT'S A MIRACLE IS THAT YOU THOUGHT YOU COULD USE US...
...THAT YOU THINK YOU'LL EVER CONVINCE ME TO—
TELL ME WHAT YOU SAW, OZIRON.
WHEN YOU USED YOUR GIFTS TO PEER INTO THE STORM...
...WHAT DID YOU FIND?
YOU ALREADY KNOW WHAT I FOUND.
BUT I DON'T.
I ONLY KNOW...

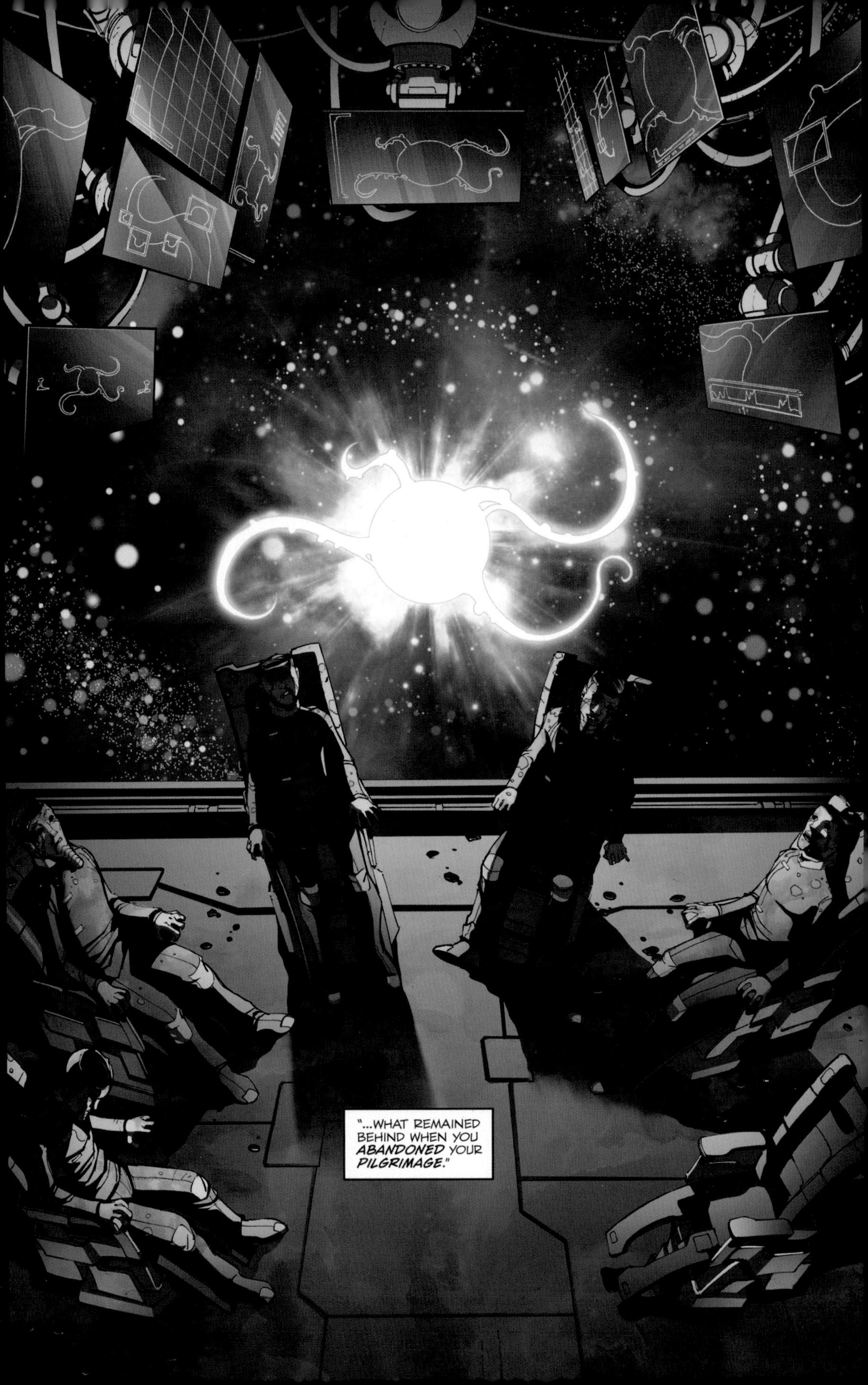
"...WHAT REMAINED BEHIND WHEN YOU *ABANDONED* YOUR *PILGRIMAGE*."

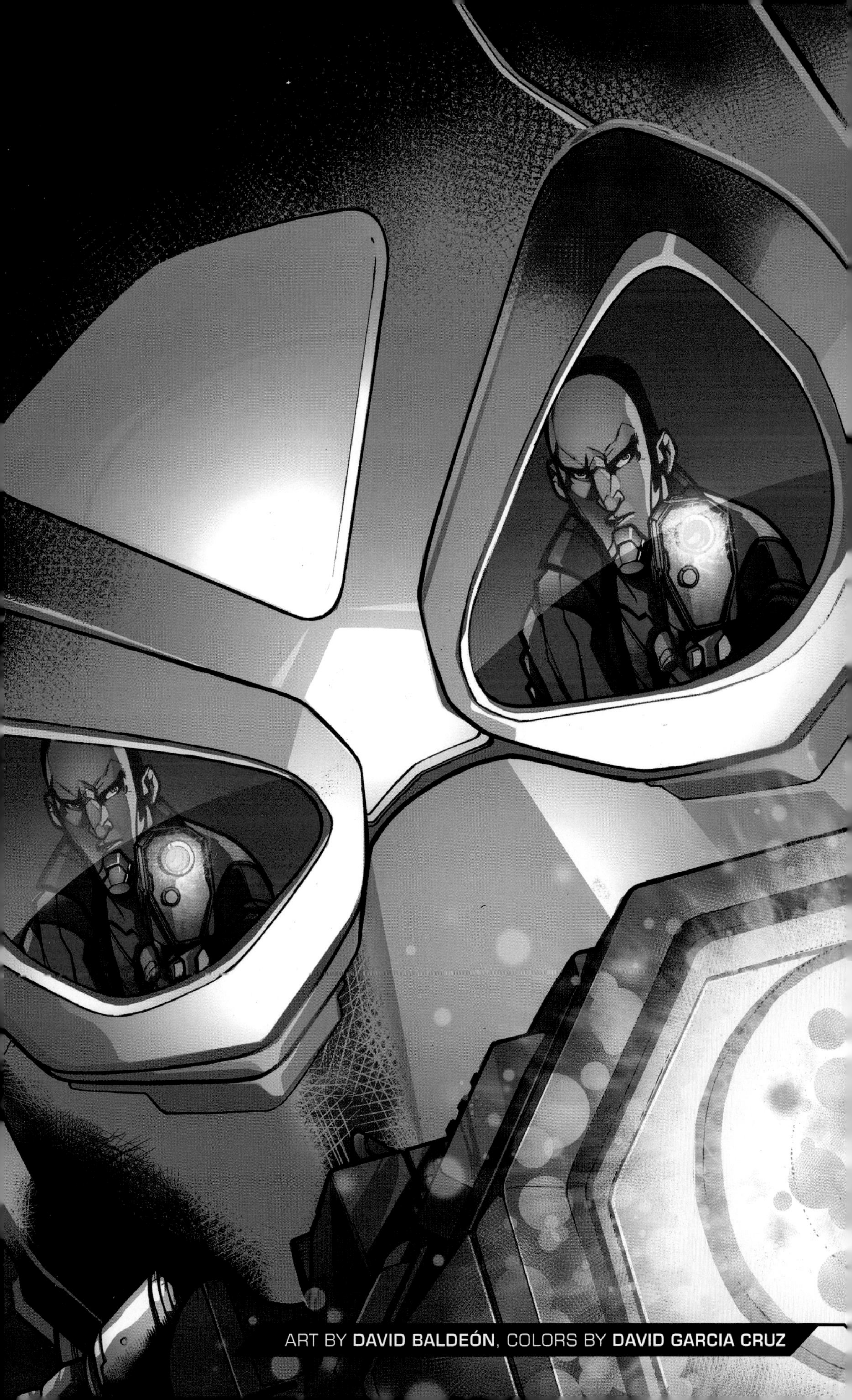

ART BY **DAVID BALDEÓN**, COLORS BY **DAVID GARCIA CRUZ**

04

ART BY J.H. WILLIAMS III

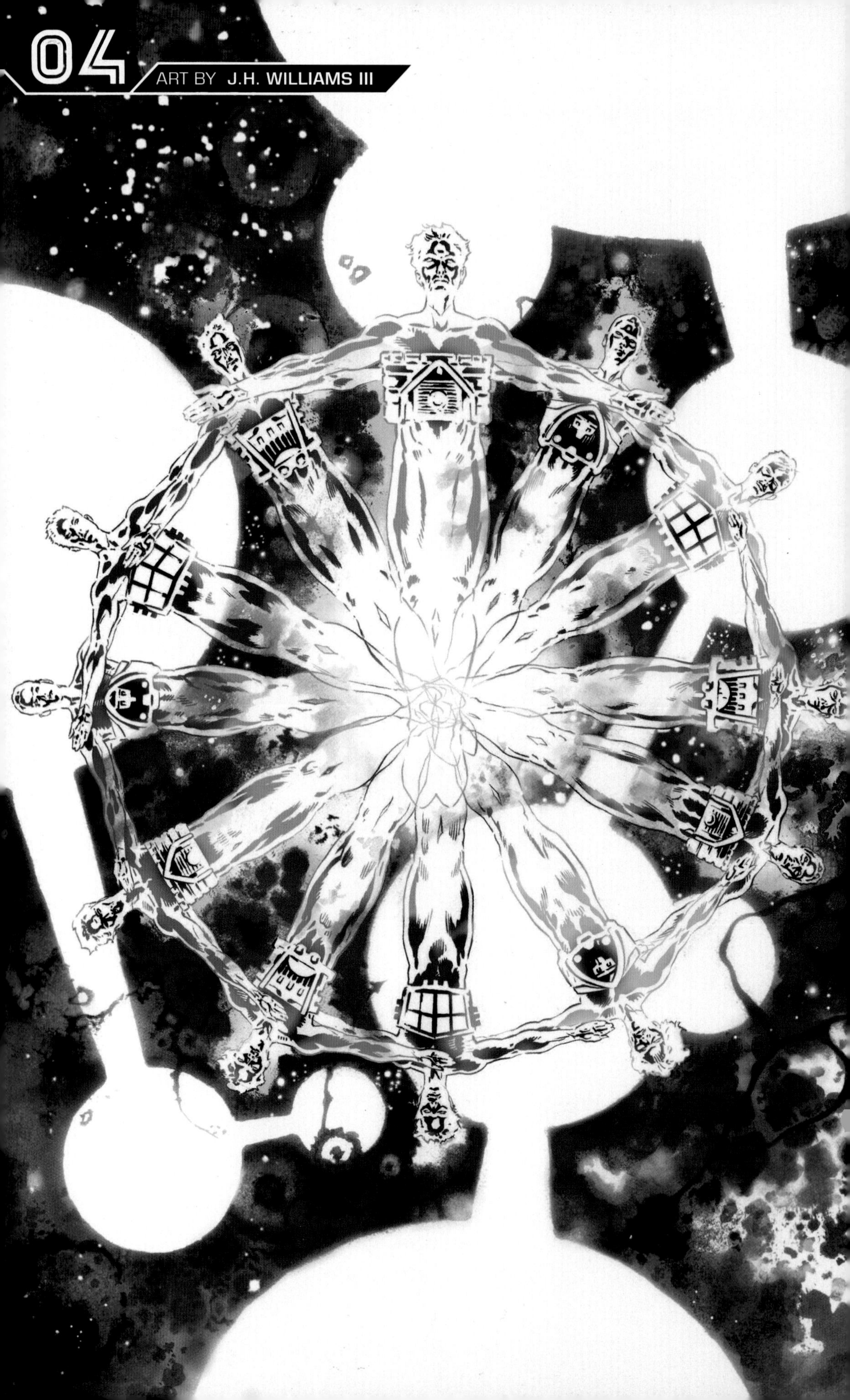

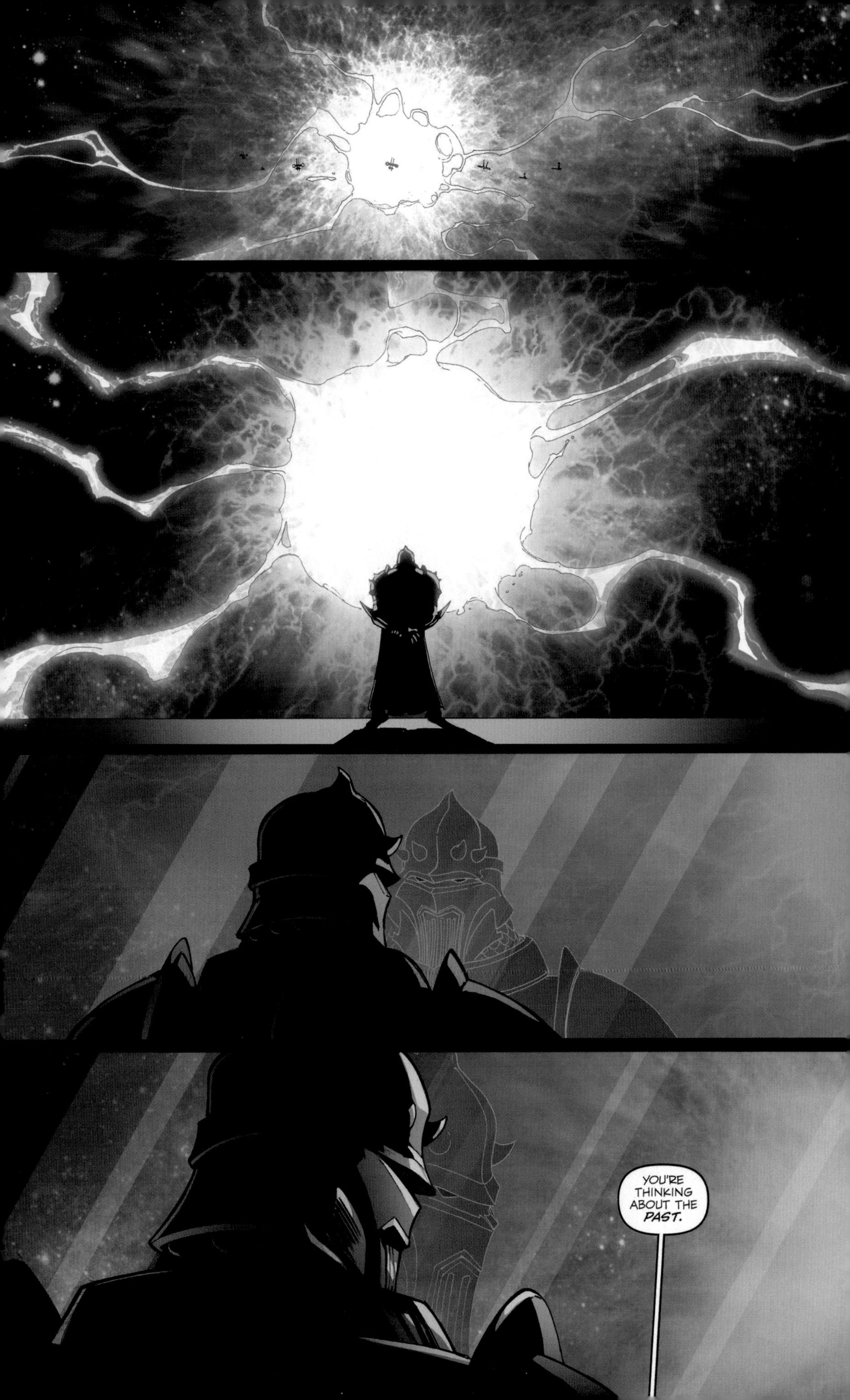
YOU'RE THINKING ABOUT THE PAST.

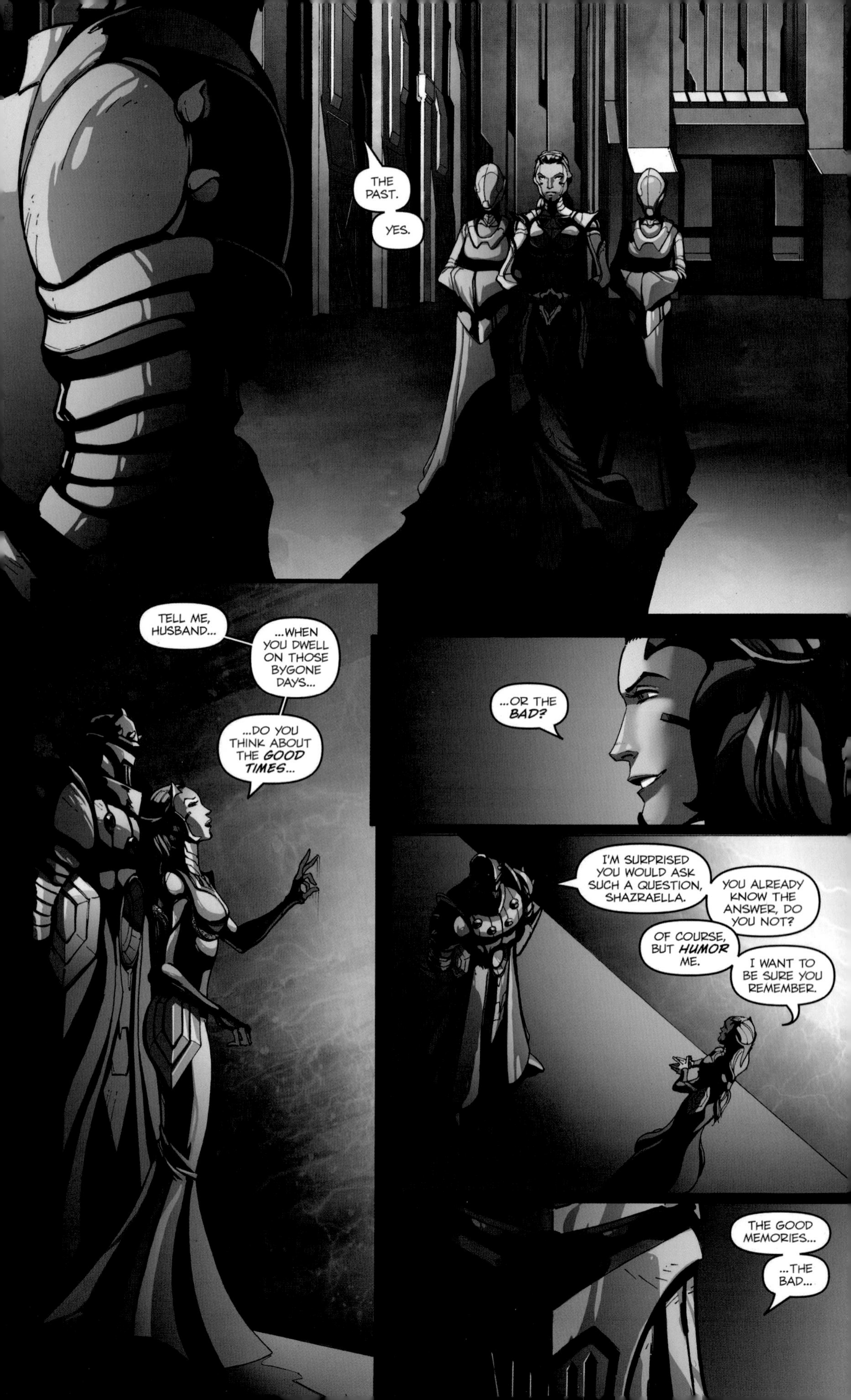
THE PAST.
YES.
TELL ME, HUSBAND...
...WHEN YOU DWELL ON THOSE BYGONE DAYS...
...DO YOU THINK ABOUT THE *GOOD TIMES*...
...OR THE *BAD?*
I'M SURPRISED YOU WOULD ASK SUCH A QUESTION, SHAZRAELLA.
YOU ALREADY KNOW THE ANSWER, DO YOU NOT?
OF COURSE, BUT *HUMOR* ME.
I WANT TO BE SURE YOU REMEMBER.
THE GOOD MEMORIES...
...THE BAD...

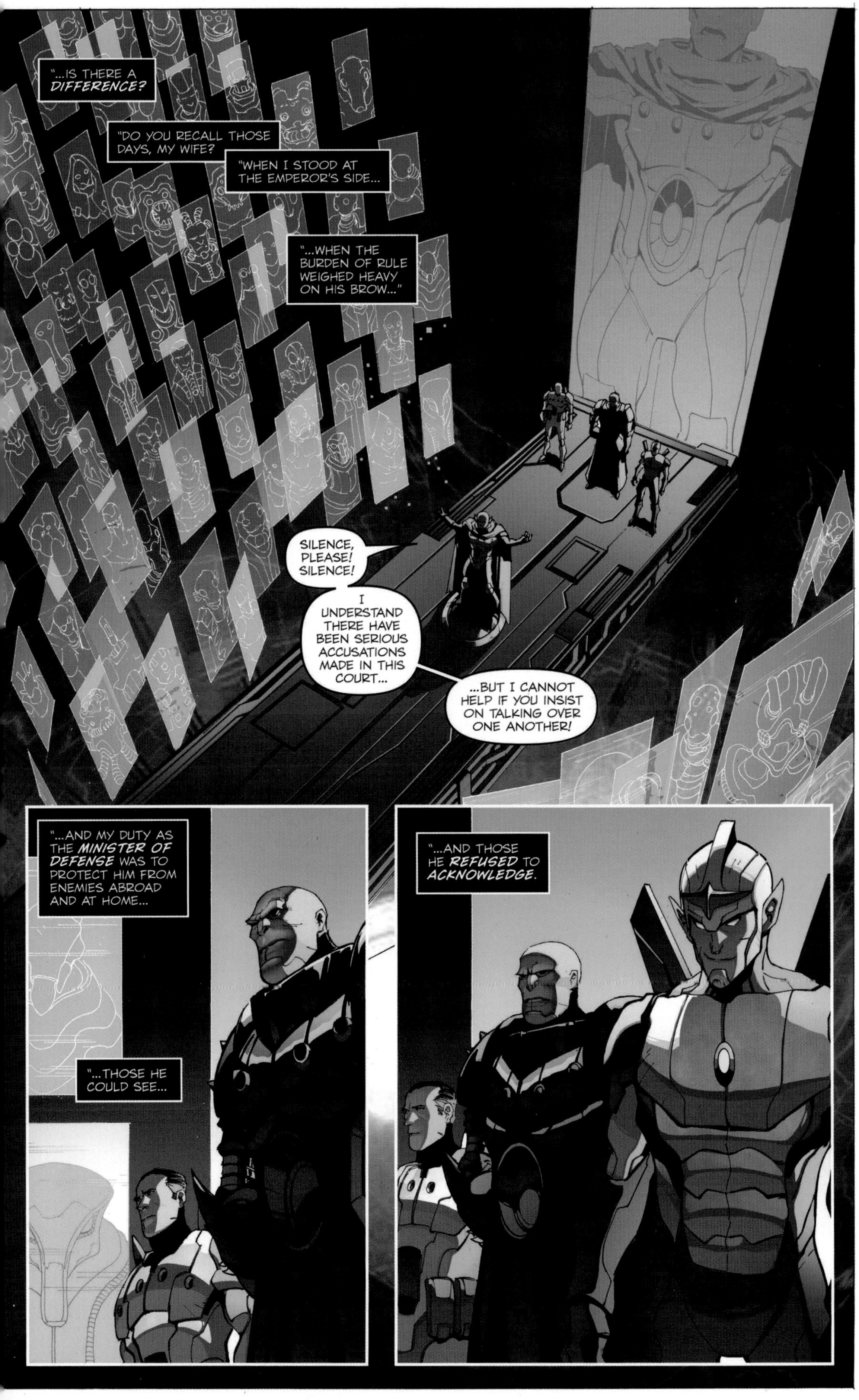
"...IS THERE A DIFFERENCE?
"DO YOU RECALL THOSE DAYS, MY WIFE?
"WHEN I STOOD AT THE EMPEROR'S SIDE...
"...WHEN THE BURDEN OF RULE WEIGHED HEAVY ON HIS BROW..."
SILENCE, PLEASE! SILENCE!
I UNDERSTAND THERE HAVE BEEN SERIOUS ACCUSATIONS MADE IN THIS COURT...
...BUT I CANNOT HELP IF YOU INSIST ON TALKING OVER ONE ANOTHER!
"...AND MY DUTY AS THE MINISTER OF DEFENSE WAS TO PROTECT HIM FROM ENEMIES ABROAD AND AT HOME...
"...THOSE HE COULD SEE...
"...AND THOSE HE REFUSED TO ACKNOWLEDGE.

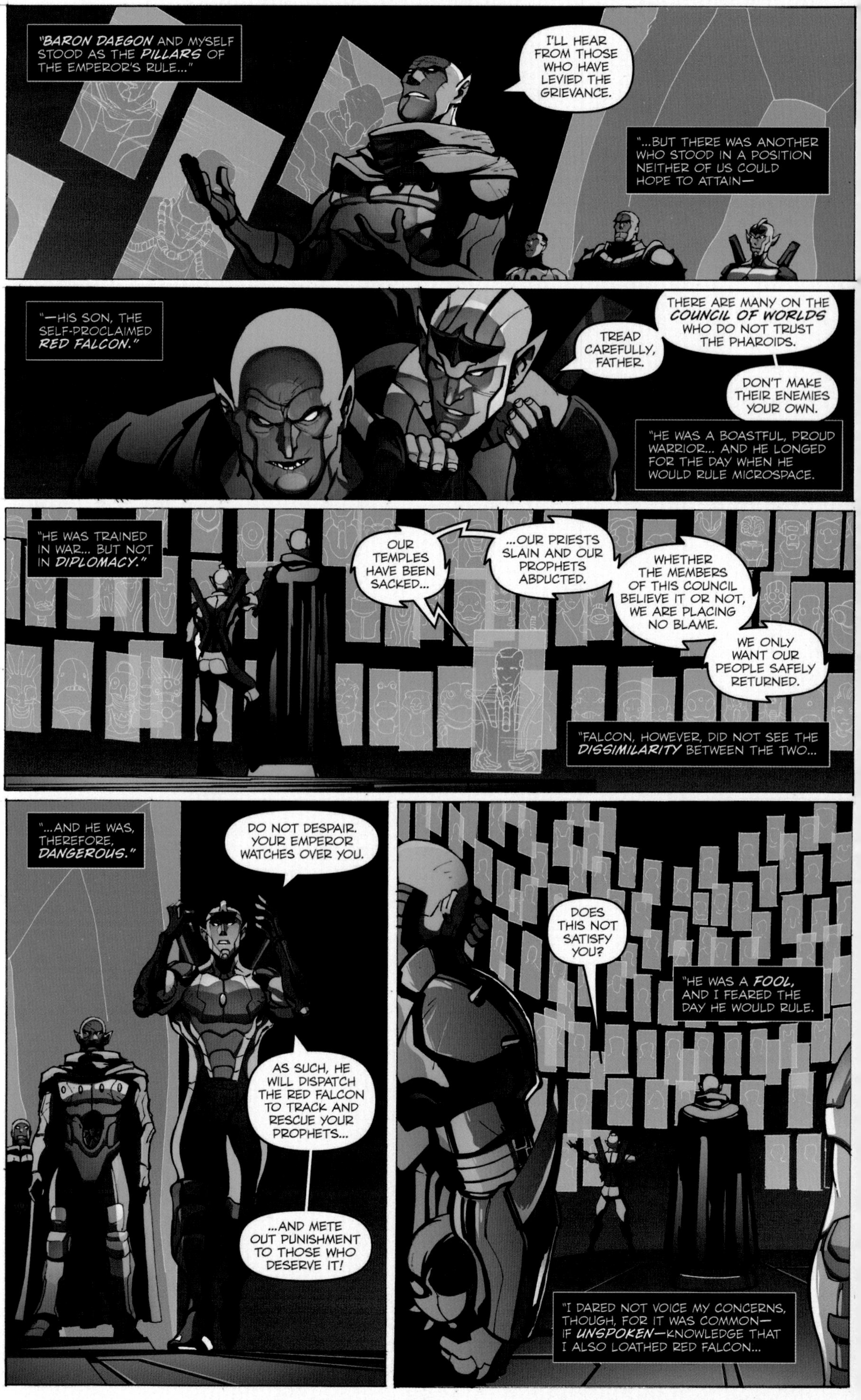
"BARON DAEGON AND MYSELF STOOD AS THE PILLARS OF THE EMPEROR'S RULE..."
I'LL HEAR FROM THOSE WHO HAVE LEVIED THE GRIEVANCE.
"...BUT THERE WAS ANOTHER WHO STOOD IN A POSITION NEITHER OF US COULD HOPE TO ATTAIN—
"—HIS SON, THE SELF-PROCLAIMED RED FALCON."
TREAD CAREFULLY, FATHER.
THERE ARE MANY ON THE COUNCIL OF WORLDS WHO DO NOT TRUST THE PHAROIDS.
DON'T MAKE THEIR ENEMIES YOUR OWN.
"HE WAS A BOASTFUL, PROUD WARRIOR... AND HE LONGED FOR THE DAY WHEN HE WOULD RULE MICROSPACE.
"HE WAS TRAINED IN WAR... BUT NOT IN DIPLOMACY."
OUR TEMPLES HAVE BEEN SACKED...
...OUR PRIESTS SLAIN AND OUR PROPHETS ABDUCTED.
WHETHER THE MEMBERS OF THIS COUNCIL BELIEVE IT OR NOT, WE ARE PLACING NO BLAME.
WE ONLY WANT OUR PEOPLE SAFELY RETURNED.
"FALCON, HOWEVER, DID NOT SEE THE DISSIMILARITY BETWEEN THE TWO...
"...AND HE WAS, THEREFORE, DANGEROUS."
DO NOT DESPAIR. YOUR EMPEROR WATCHES OVER YOU.
AS SUCH, HE WILL DISPATCH THE RED FALCON TO TRACK AND RESCUE YOUR PROPHETS...
...AND METE OUT PUNISHMENT TO THOSE WHO DESERVE IT!
DOES THIS NOT SATISFY YOU?
"HE WAS A FOOL, AND I FEARED THE DAY HE WOULD RULE.
"I DARED NOT VOICE MY CONCERNS, THOUGH, FOR IT WAS COMMON—IF UNSPOKEN—KNOWLEDGE THAT I ALSO LOATHED RED FALCON...

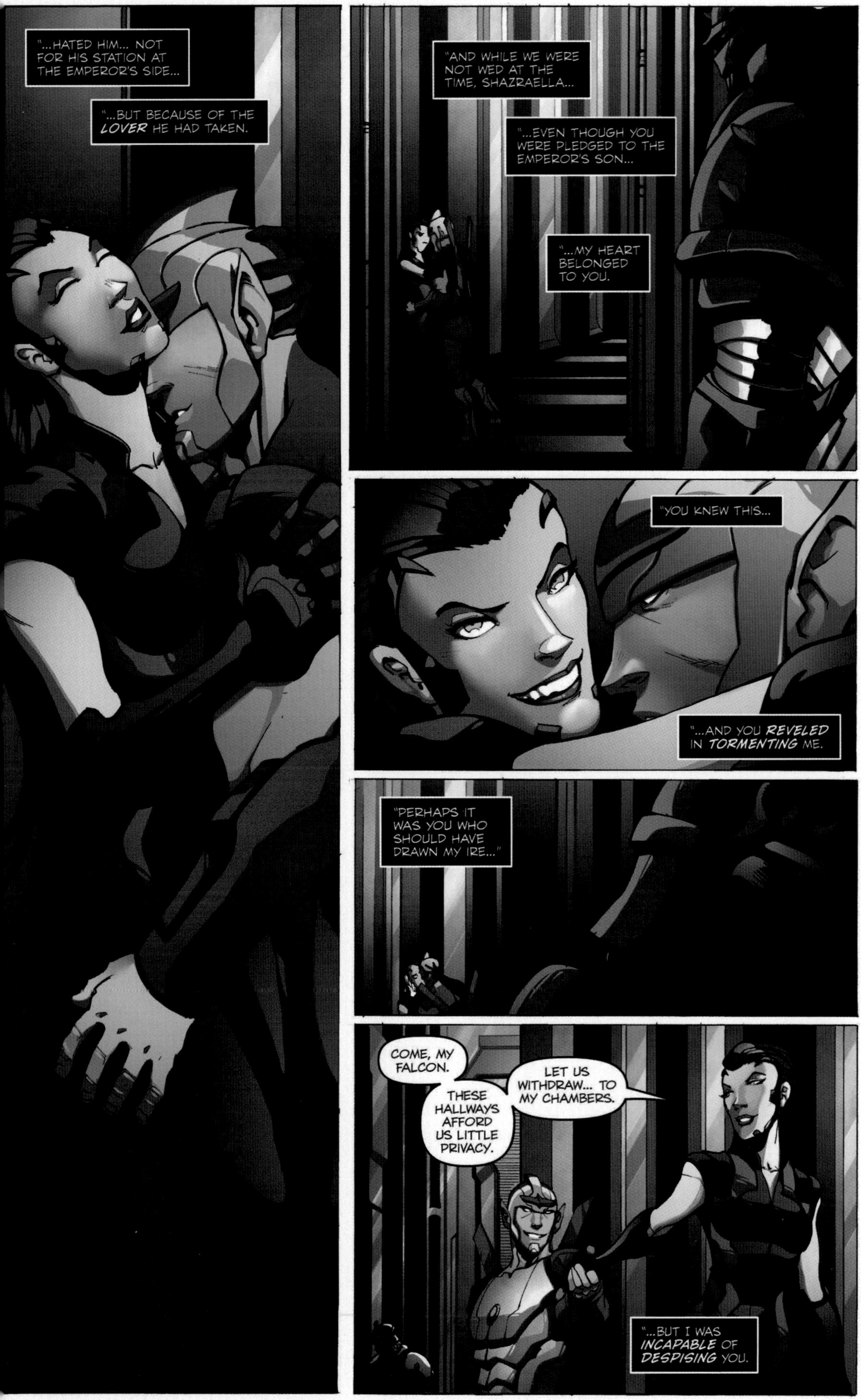
"...HATED HIM... NOT FOR HIS STATION AT THE EMPEROR'S SIDE...
"...BUT BECAUSE OF THE LOVER HE HAD TAKEN.
"AND WHILE WE WERE NOT WED AT THE TIME, SHAZRAELLA...
"...EVEN THOUGH YOU WERE PLEDGED TO THE EMPEROR'S SON...
"...MY HEART BELONGED TO YOU.
"YOU KNEW THIS...
"...AND YOU REVELED IN TORMENTING ME.
"PERHAPS IT WAS YOU WHO SHOULD HAVE DRAWN MY IRE..."
COME, MY FALCON.
THESE HALLWAYS AFFORD US LITTLE PRIVACY.
LET US WITHDRAW... TO MY CHAMBERS.
"...BUT I WAS INCAPABLE OF DESPISING YOU.

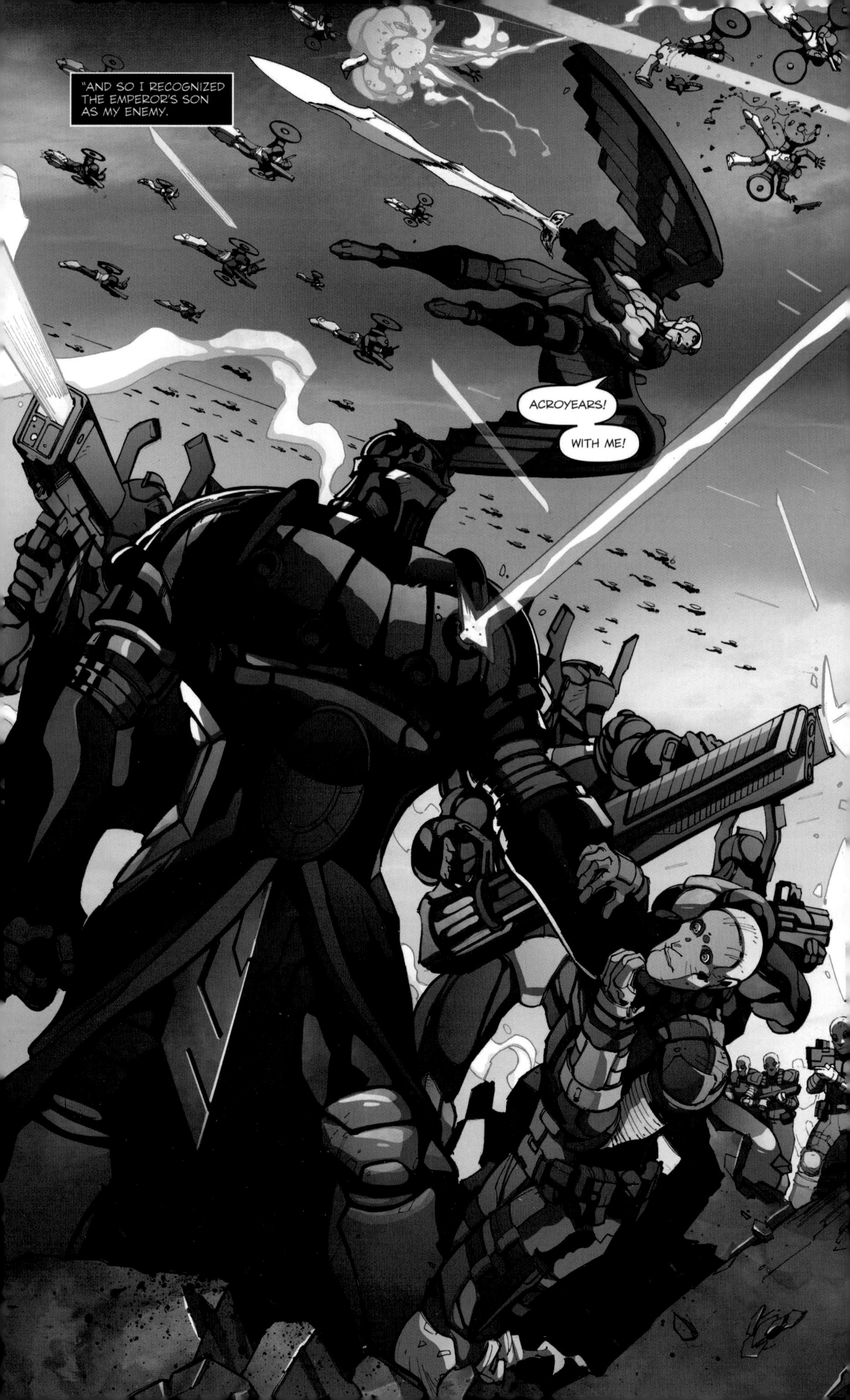
"AND SO I RECOGNIZED THE EMPEROR'S SON AS MY ENEMY.
ACROYEARS!
WITH ME!

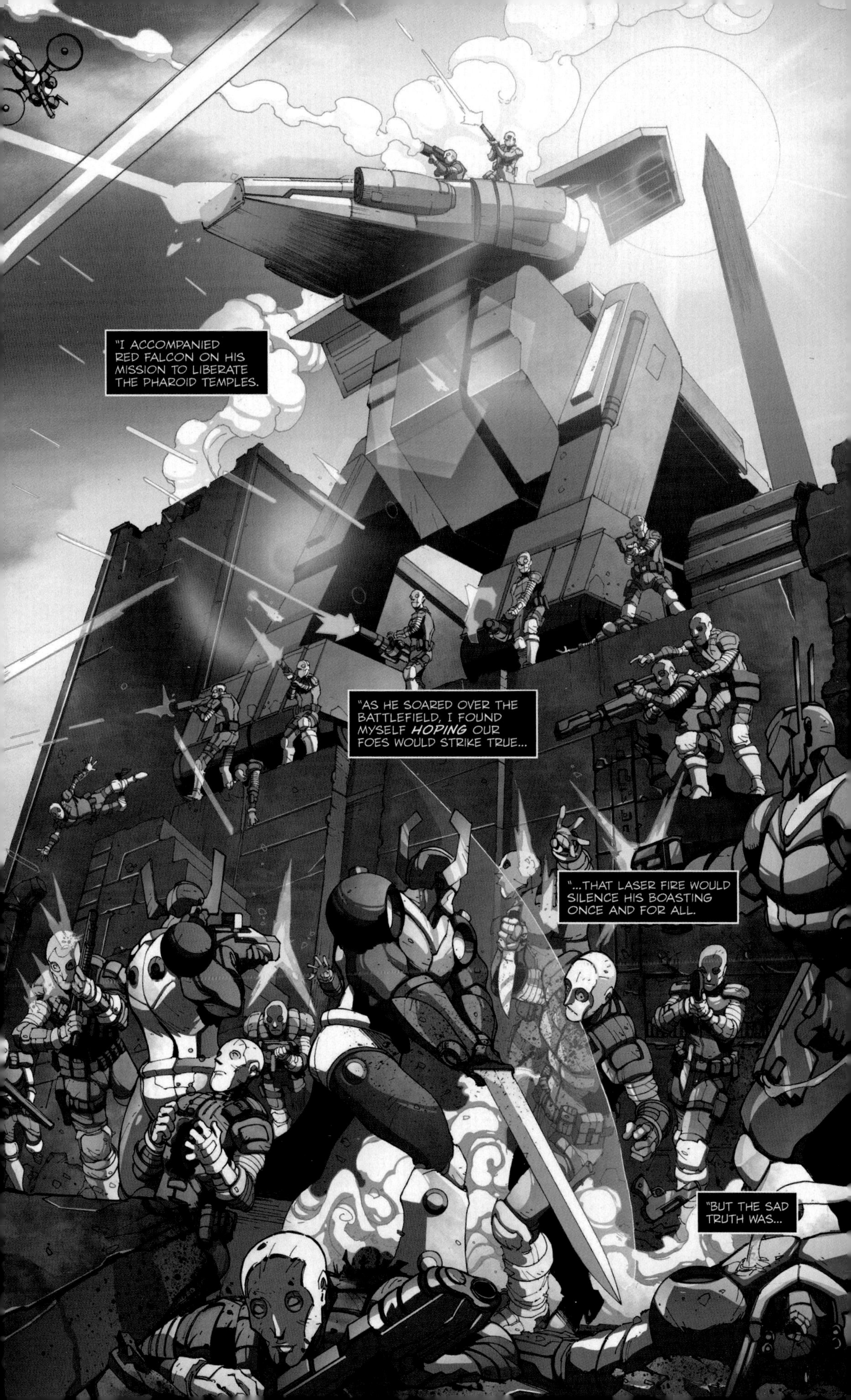
"I ACCOMPANIED RED FALCON ON HIS MISSION TO LIBERATE THE PHAROID TEMPLES.
"AS HE SOARED OVER THE BATTLEFIELD, I FOUND MYSELF *HOPING* OUR FOES WOULD STRIKE TRUE...
"...THAT LASER FIRE WOULD SILENCE HIS BOASTING ONCE AND FOR ALL.
"BUT THE SAD TRUTH WAS...

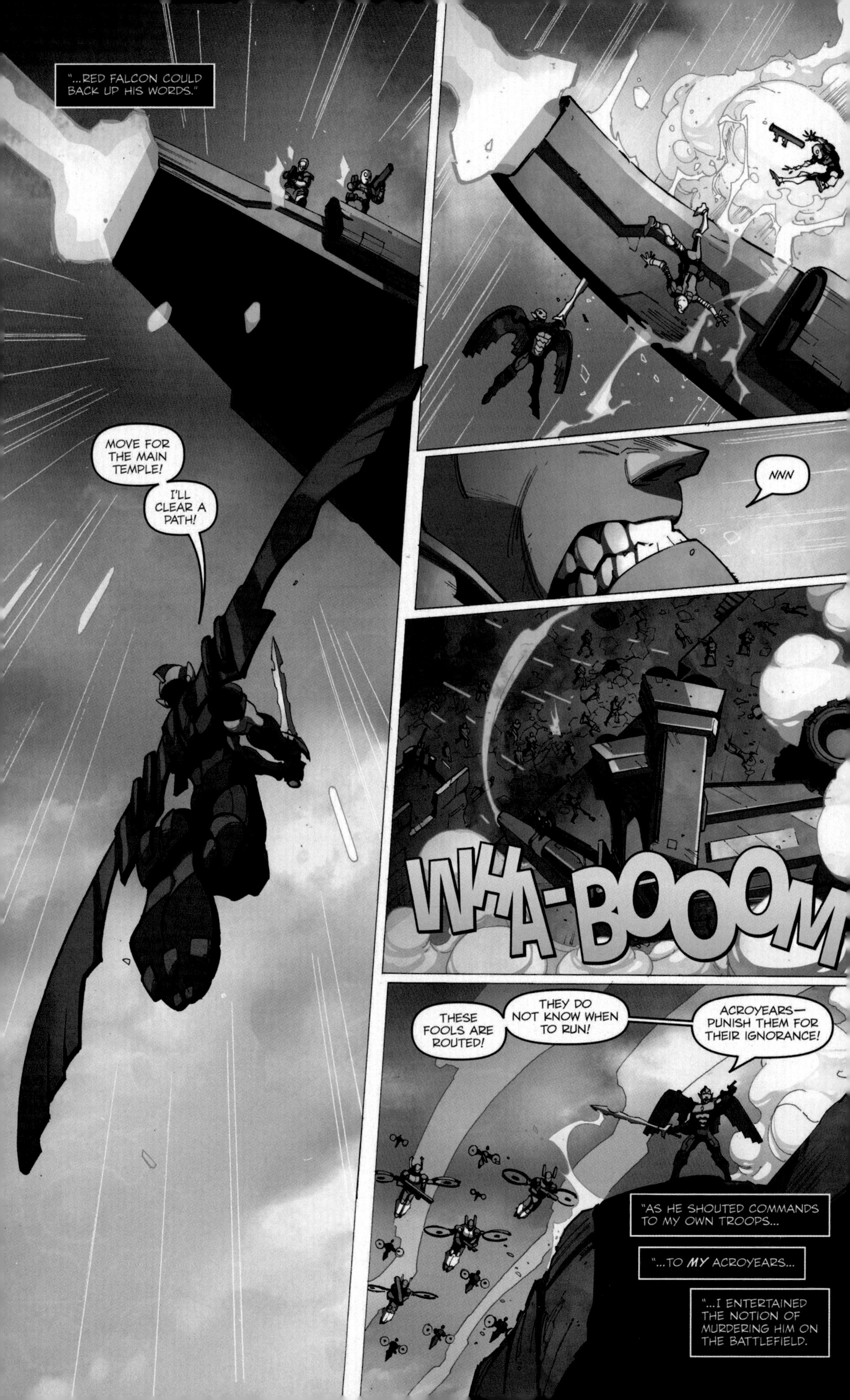
"...RED FALCON COULD BACK UP HIS WORDS."
MOVE FOR THE MAIN TEMPLE!
I'LL CLEAR A PATH!
NNN
WHA-BOOOM
THESE FOOLS ARE ROUTED!
THEY DO NOT KNOW WHEN TO RUN!
ACROYEARS— PUNISH THEM FOR THEIR IGNORANCE!
"AS HE SHOUTED COMMANDS TO MY OWN TROOPS...
"...TO *MY* ACROYEARS...
"...I ENTERTAINED THE NOTION OF MURDERING HIM ON THE BATTLEFIELD.

"IF OUR ADVERSARIES COULD NOT BYPASS HIS BLADE OR PIERCE HIS ARMOR...

"...PERHAPS I COULD.

"I WAS NOT PROUD OF MY TRAITOROUS THOUGHTS.

"I WAS EVEN LESS PROUD OF THE *FEAR* AND *DOUBT* THAT STAYED MY HAND."

P-PLEASE...

...PLEASE, LISTEN...

Y-YOU HAVE TO UNDERSTAND...

...THEY'RE NOT SAFE...

...IF YOU ONLY KNEW WHAT THEY WILL BECOME...

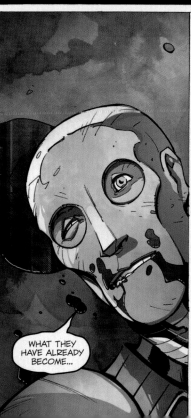

WHAT THEY HAVE ALREADY BECOME...

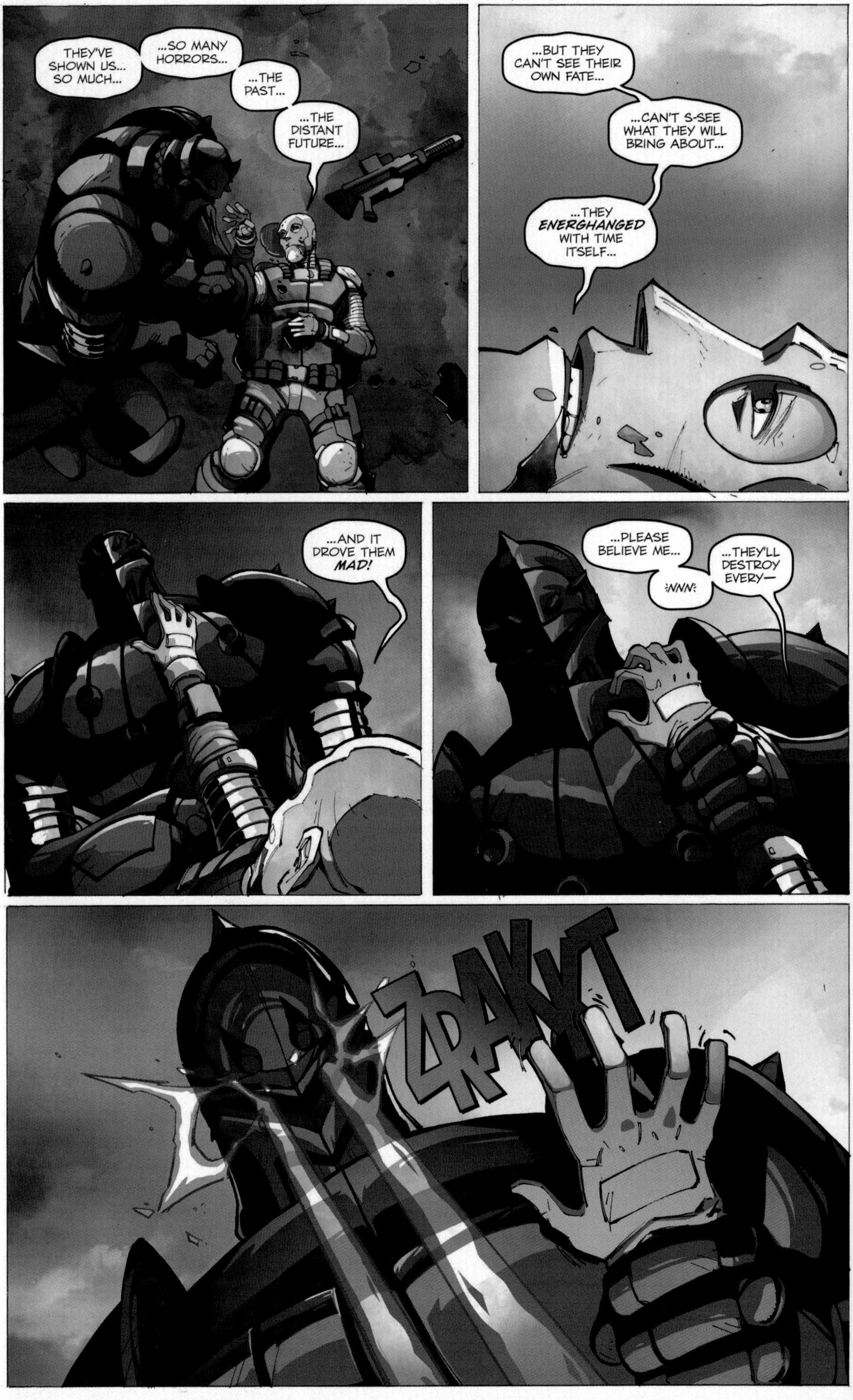
THEY'VE SHOWN US... SO MUCH...
...SO MANY HORRORS...
...THE PAST...
...THE DISTANT FUTURE...
...BUT THEY CAN'T SEE THEIR OWN FATE...
...CAN'T S-SEE WHAT THEY WILL BRING ABOUT...
...THEY ENERGHANGED WITH TIME ITSELF...
...AND IT DROVE THEM MAD!
...PLEASE BELIEVE ME...
NNN
...THEY'LL DESTROY EVERY—
ZRAKT

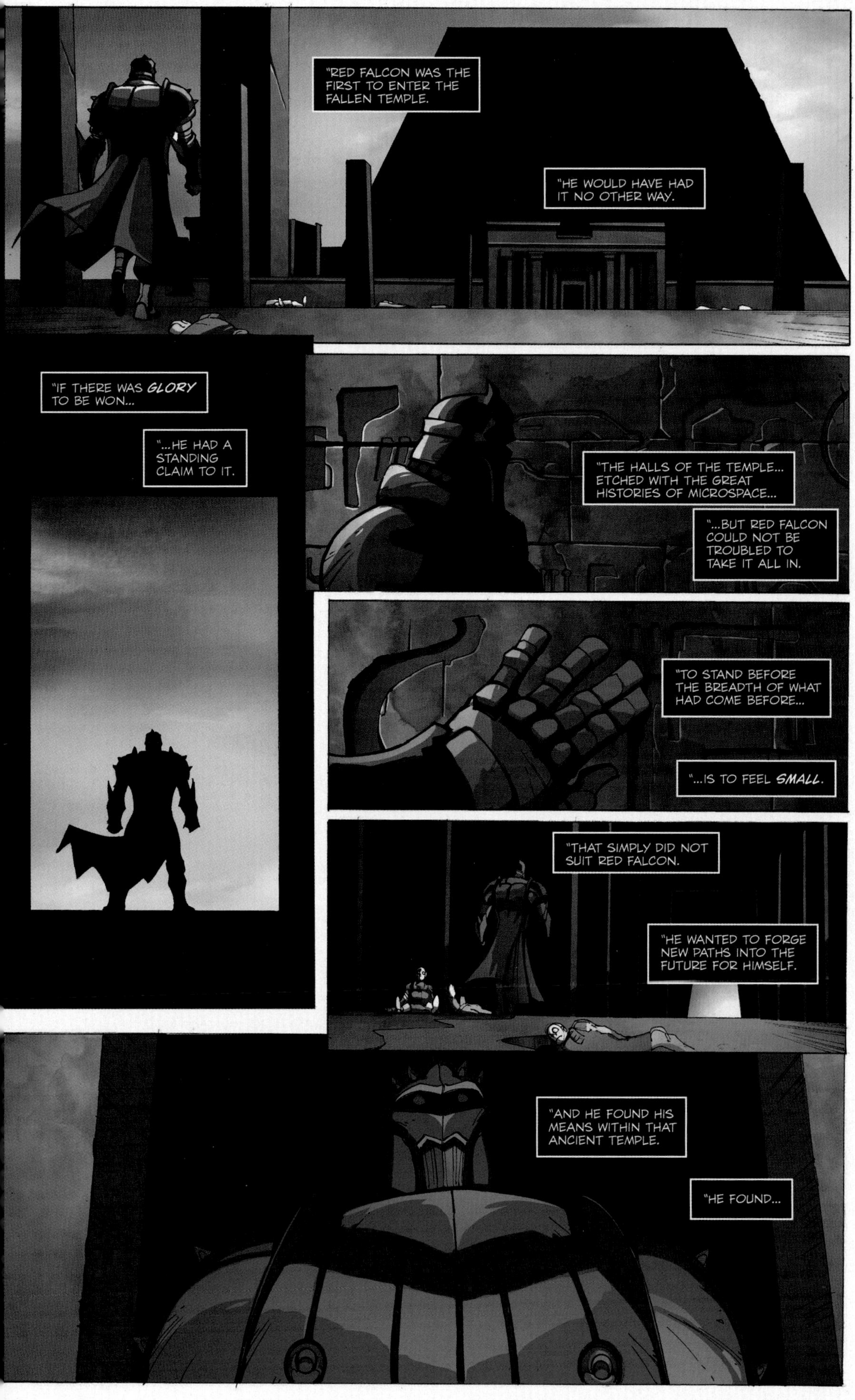
"RED FALCON WAS THE FIRST TO ENTER THE FALLEN TEMPLE.
"HE WOULD HAVE HAD IT NO OTHER WAY.
"IF THERE WAS GLORY TO BE WON...
"...HE HAD A STANDING CLAIM TO IT.
"THE HALLS OF THE TEMPLE... ETCHED WITH THE GREAT HISTORIES OF MICROSPACE...
"...BUT RED FALCON COULD NOT BE TROUBLED TO TAKE IT ALL IN.
"TO STAND BEFORE THE BREADTH OF WHAT HAD COME BEFORE...
"...IS TO FEEL SMALL.
"THAT SIMPLY DID NOT SUIT RED FALCON.
"HE WANTED TO FORGE NEW PATHS INTO THE FUTURE FOR HIMSELF.
"AND HE FOUND HIS MEANS WITHIN THAT ANCIENT TEMPLE.
"HE FOUND...

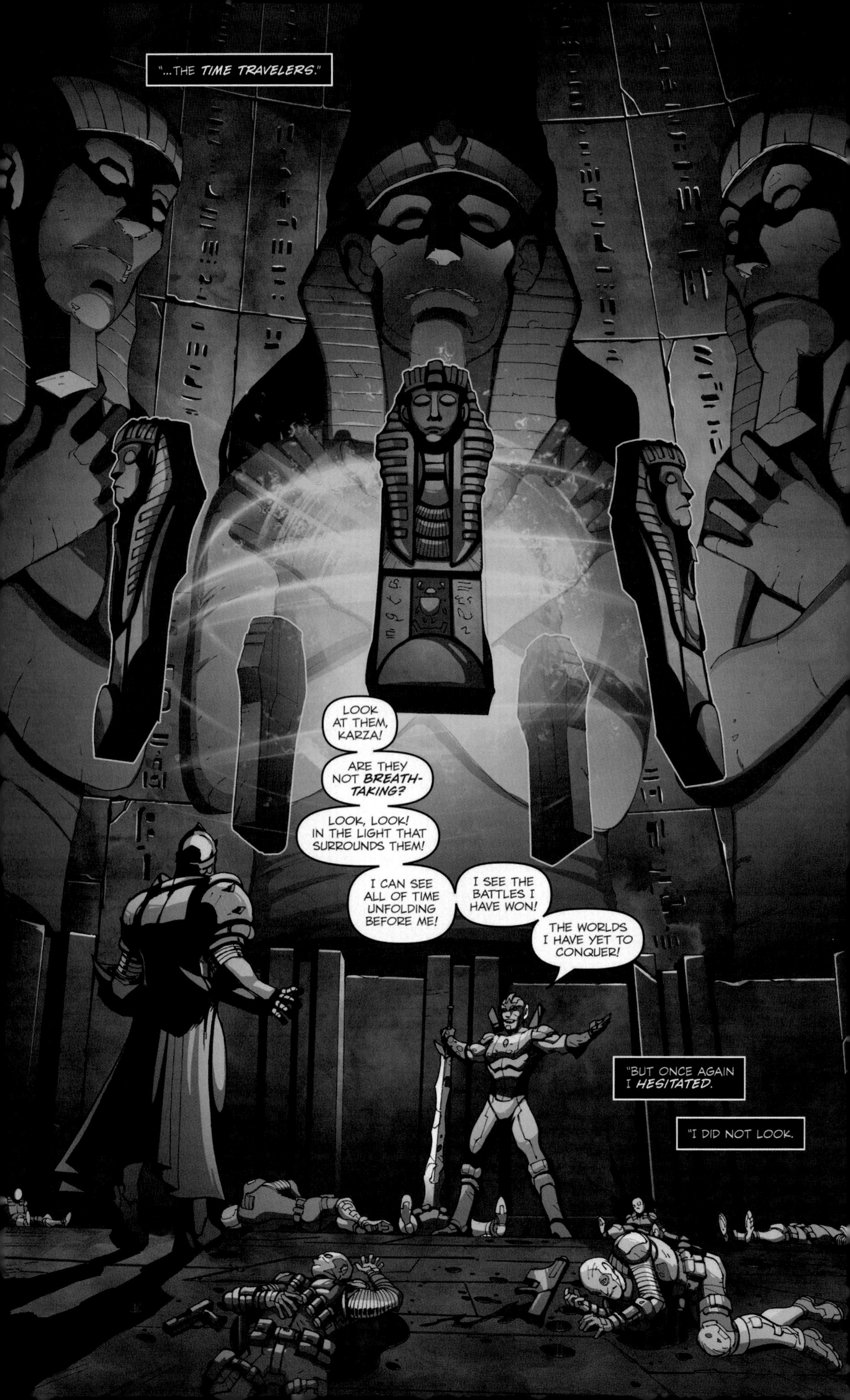
"...THE TIME TRAVELERS."
LOOK AT THEM, KARZA!
ARE THEY NOT BREATH-TAKING?
LOOK, LOOK! IN THE LIGHT THAT SURROUNDS THEM!
I CAN SEE ALL OF TIME UNFOLDING BEFORE ME!
I SEE THE BATTLES I HAVE WON!
THE WORLDS I HAVE YET TO CONQUER!
"BUT ONCE AGAIN I HESITATED.
"I DID NOT LOOK.

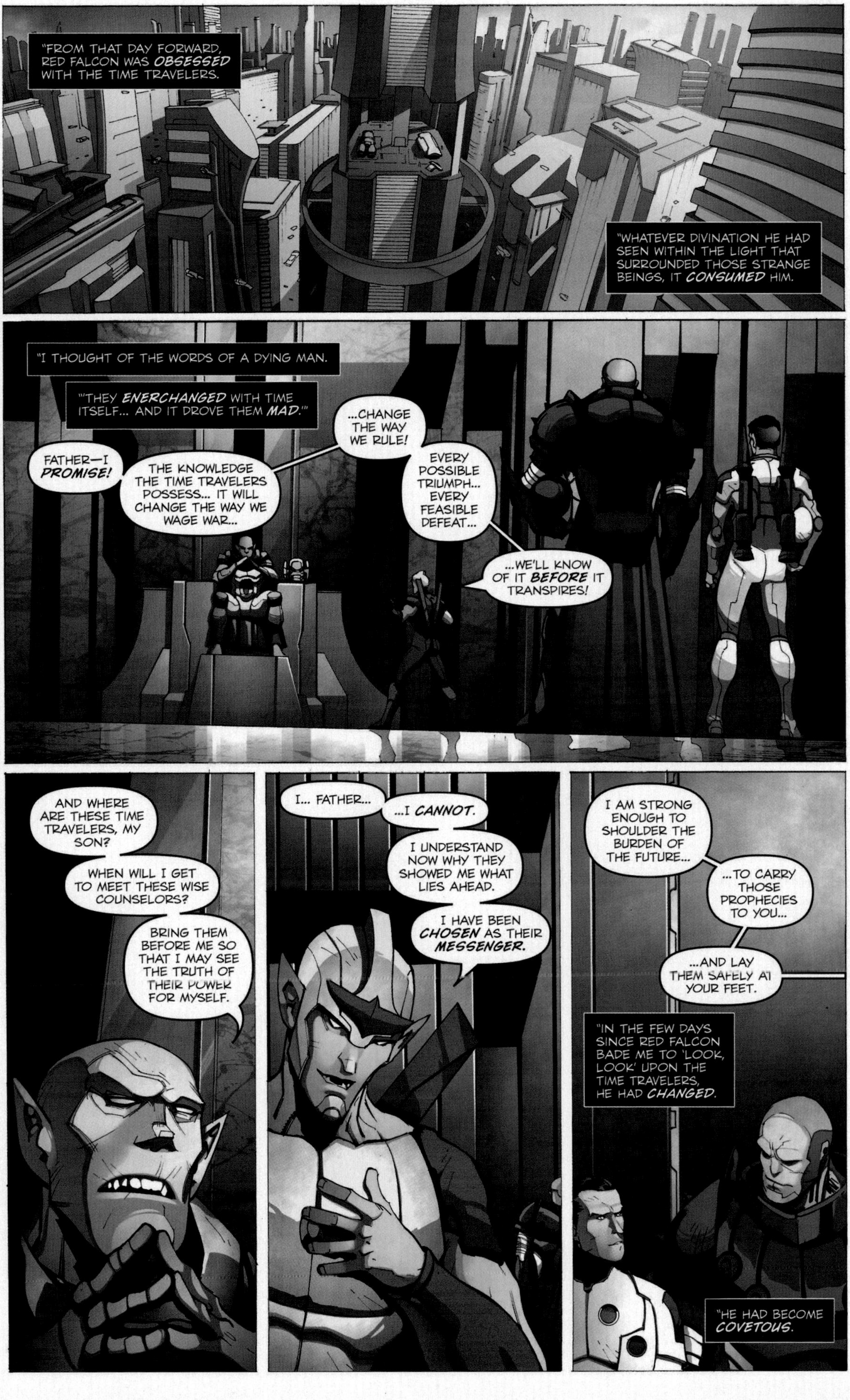
"FROM THAT DAY FORWARD, RED FALCON WAS OBSESSED WITH THE TIME TRAVELERS.
"WHATEVER DIVINATION HE HAD SEEN WITHIN THE LIGHT THAT SURROUNDED THOSE STRANGE BEINGS, IT CONSUMED HIM.
"I THOUGHT OF THE WORDS OF A DYING MAN.
"'THEY ENERCHANGED WITH TIME ITSELF... AND IT DROVE THEM MAD.'"
FATHER—I PROMISE!
THE KNOWLEDGE THE TIME TRAVELERS POSSESS... IT WILL CHANGE THE WAY WE WAGE WAR...
...CHANGE THE WAY WE RULE!
EVERY POSSIBLE TRIUMPH... EVERY FEASIBLE DEFEAT...
...WE'LL KNOW OF IT BEFORE IT TRANSPIRES!
AND WHERE ARE THESE TIME TRAVELERS, MY SON?
WHEN WILL I GET TO MEET THESE WISE COUNSELORS?
BRING THEM BEFORE ME SO THAT I MAY SEE THE TRUTH OF THEIR POWER FOR MYSELF.
I... FATHER...
...I CANNOT.
I UNDERSTAND NOW WHY THEY SHOWED ME WHAT LIES AHEAD.
I HAVE BEEN CHOSEN AS THEIR MESSENGER.
I AM STRONG ENOUGH TO SHOULDER THE BURDEN OF THE FUTURE...
...TO CARRY THOSE PROPHECIES TO YOU...
...AND LAY THEM SAFELY AT YOUR FEET.
"IN THE FEW DAYS SINCE RED FALCON BADE ME TO 'LOOK, LOOK' UPON THE TIME TRAVELERS, HE HAD CHANGED.
"HE HAD BECOME COVETOUS.

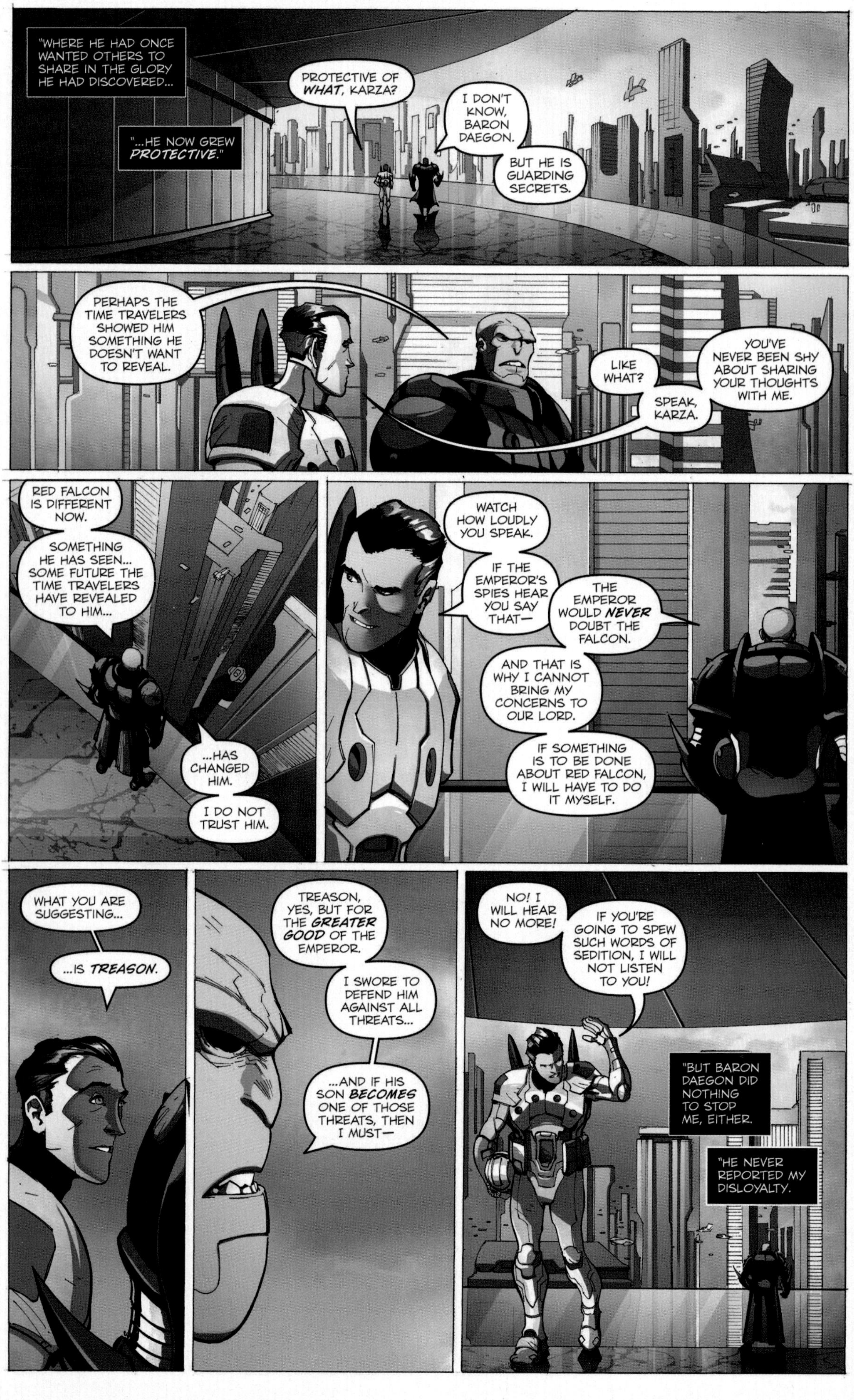
"WHERE HE HAD ONCE WANTED OTHERS TO SHARE IN THE GLORY HE HAD DISCOVERED...
"...HE NOW GREW *PROTECTIVE*."
PROTECTIVE OF *WHAT*, KARZA?
I DON'T KNOW, BARON DAEGON.
BUT HE IS GUARDING SECRETS.
PERHAPS THE TIME TRAVELERS SHOWED HIM SOMETHING HE DOESN'T WANT TO REVEAL.
LIKE WHAT?
SPEAK, KARZA.
YOU'VE NEVER BEEN SHY ABOUT SHARING YOUR THOUGHTS WITH ME.
RED FALCON IS DIFFERENT NOW.
SOMETHING HE HAS SEEN... SOME FUTURE THE TIME TRAVELERS HAVE REVEALED TO HIM...
...HAS CHANGED HIM.
I DO NOT TRUST HIM.
WATCH HOW LOUDLY YOU SPEAK.
IF THE EMPEROR'S SPIES HEAR YOU SAY THAT—
THE EMPEROR WOULD ***NEVER*** DOUBT THE FALCON.
AND THAT IS WHY I CANNOT BRING MY CONCERNS TO OUR LORD.
IF SOMETHING IS TO BE DONE ABOUT RED FALCON, I WILL HAVE TO DO IT MYSELF.
WHAT YOU ARE SUGGESTING...
...IS ***TREASON***.
TREASON, YES, BUT FOR THE ***GREATER GOOD*** OF THE EMPEROR.
I SWORE TO DEFEND HIM AGAINST ALL THREATS...
...AND IF HIS SON ***BECOMES*** ONE OF THOSE THREATS, THEN I MUST—
NO! I WILL HEAR NO MORE!
IF YOU'RE GOING TO SPEW SUCH WORDS OF SEDITION, I WILL NOT LISTEN TO YOU!
"BUT BARON DAEGON DID NOTHING TO STOP ME, EITHER.
"HE NEVER REPORTED MY DISLOYALTY.

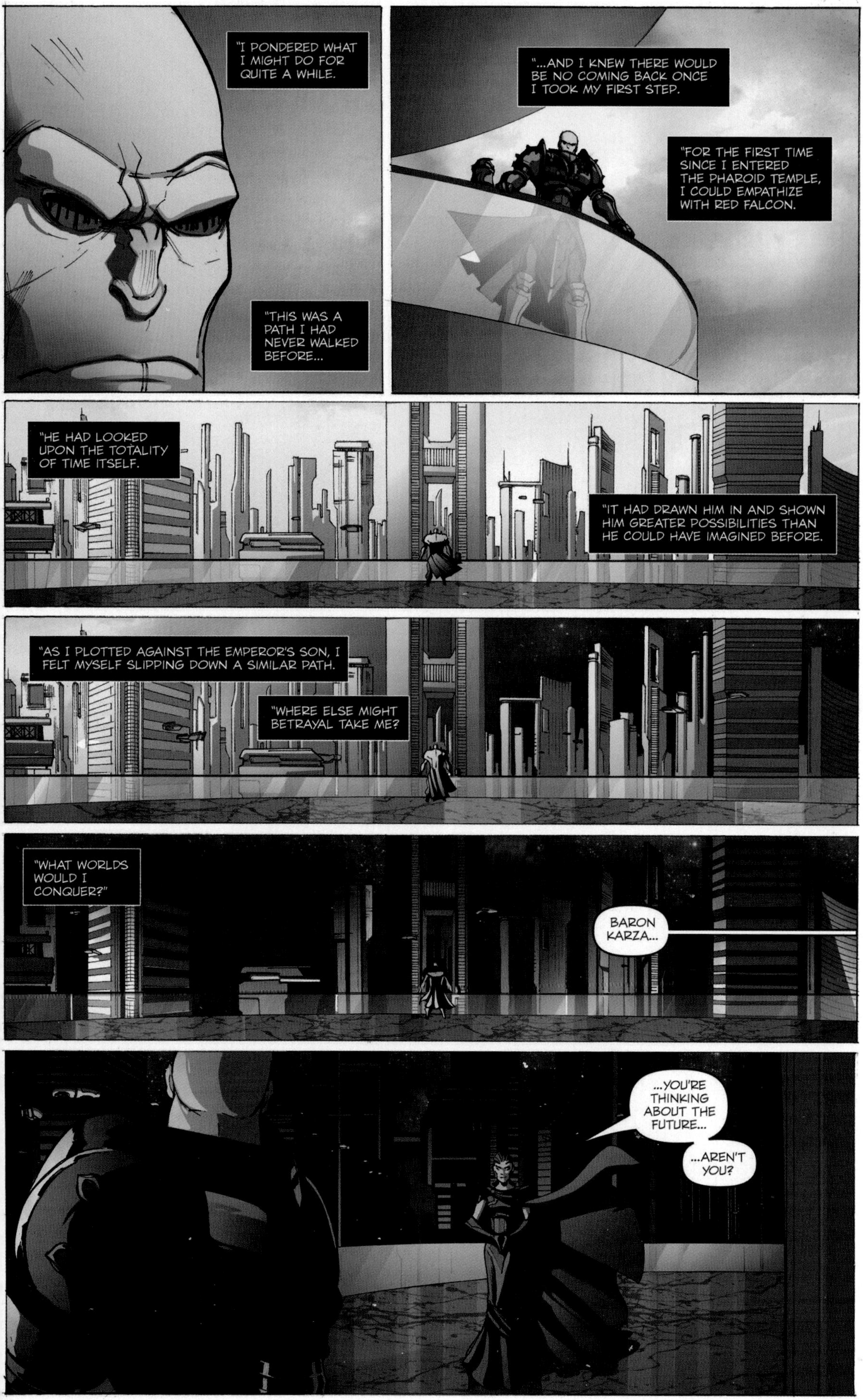
"I PONDERED WHAT I MIGHT DO FOR QUITE A WHILE.
"THIS WAS A PATH I HAD NEVER WALKED BEFORE...
"...AND I KNEW THERE WOULD BE NO COMING BACK ONCE I TOOK MY FIRST STEP.
"FOR THE FIRST TIME SINCE I ENTERED THE PHAROID TEMPLE, I COULD EMPATHIZE WITH RED FALCON.
"HE HAD LOOKED UPON THE TOTALITY OF TIME ITSELF.
"IT HAD DRAWN HIM IN AND SHOWN HIM GREATER POSSIBILITIES THAN HE COULD HAVE IMAGINED BEFORE.
"AS I PLOTTED AGAINST THE EMPEROR'S SON, I FELT MYSELF SLIPPING DOWN A SIMILAR PATH.
"WHERE ELSE MIGHT BETRAYAL TAKE ME?
"WHAT WORLDS WOULD I CONQUER?"
BARON KARZA...
...YOU'RE THINKING ABOUT THE FUTURE...
...AREN'T YOU?

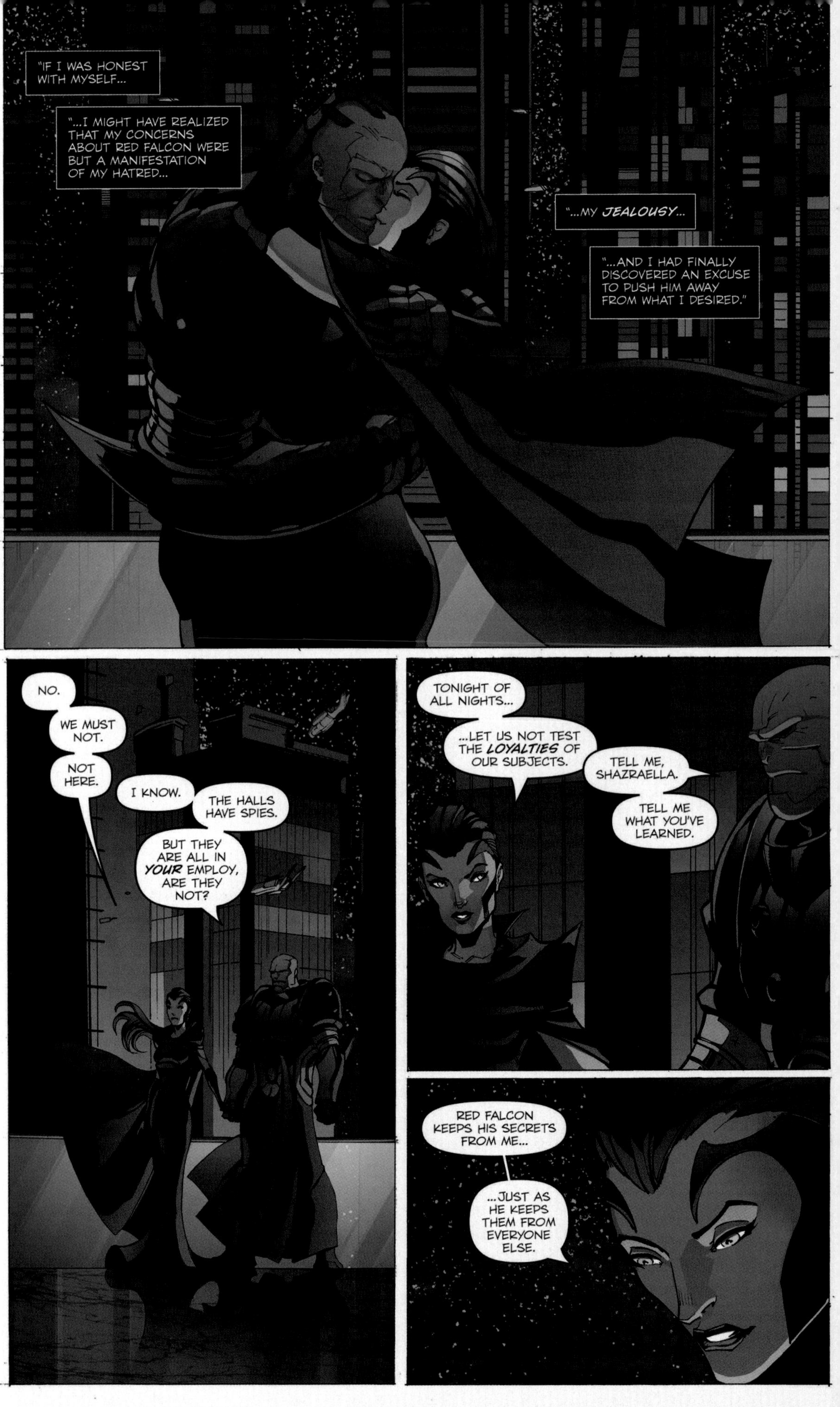
"IF I WAS HONEST WITH MYSELF...
"...I MIGHT HAVE REALIZED THAT MY CONCERNS ABOUT RED FALCON WERE BUT A MANIFESTATION OF MY HATRED...
"...MY *JEALOUSY*...
"...AND I HAD FINALLY DISCOVERED AN EXCUSE TO PUSH HIM AWAY FROM WHAT I DESIRED."
NO.
WE MUST NOT.
NOT HERE.
I KNOW.
THE HALLS HAVE SPIES.
BUT THEY ARE ALL IN *YOUR* EMPLOY, ARE THEY NOT?
TONIGHT OF ALL NIGHTS...
...LET US NOT TEST THE *LOYALTIES* OF OUR SUBJECTS.
TELL ME, SHAZRAELLA.
TELL ME WHAT YOU'VE LEARNED.
RED FALCON KEEPS HIS SECRETS FROM ME...
...JUST AS HE KEEPS THEM FROM EVERYONE ELSE.

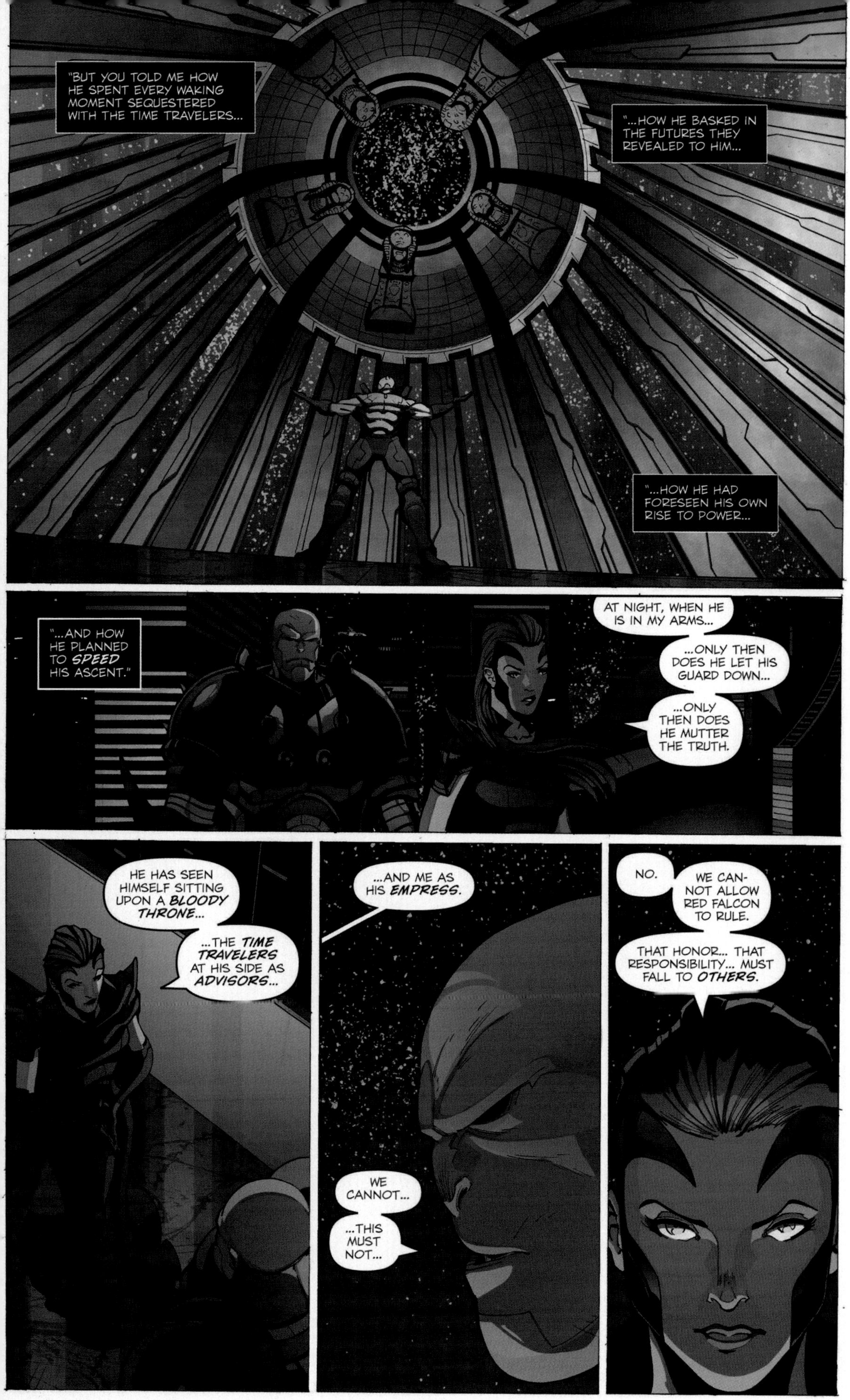
"BUT YOU TOLD ME HOW HE SPENT EVERY WAKING MOMENT SEQUESTERED WITH THE TIME TRAVELERS...
"...HOW HE BASKED IN THE FUTURES THEY REVEALED TO HIM...
"...HOW HE HAD FORESEEN HIS OWN RISE TO POWER...
"...AND HOW HE PLANNED TO SPEED HIS ASCENT."
AT NIGHT, WHEN HE IS IN MY ARMS...
...ONLY THEN DOES HE LET HIS GUARD DOWN...
...ONLY THEN DOES HE MUTTER THE TRUTH.
HE HAS SEEN HIMSELF SITTING UPON A BLOODY THRONE...
...THE TIME TRAVELERS AT HIS SIDE AS ADVISORS...
...AND ME AS HIS EMPRESS.
WE CANNOT...
...THIS MUST NOT...
NO.
WE CAN-NOT ALLOW RED FALCON TO RULE.
THAT HONOR... THAT RESPONSIBILITY... MUST FALL TO OTHERS.

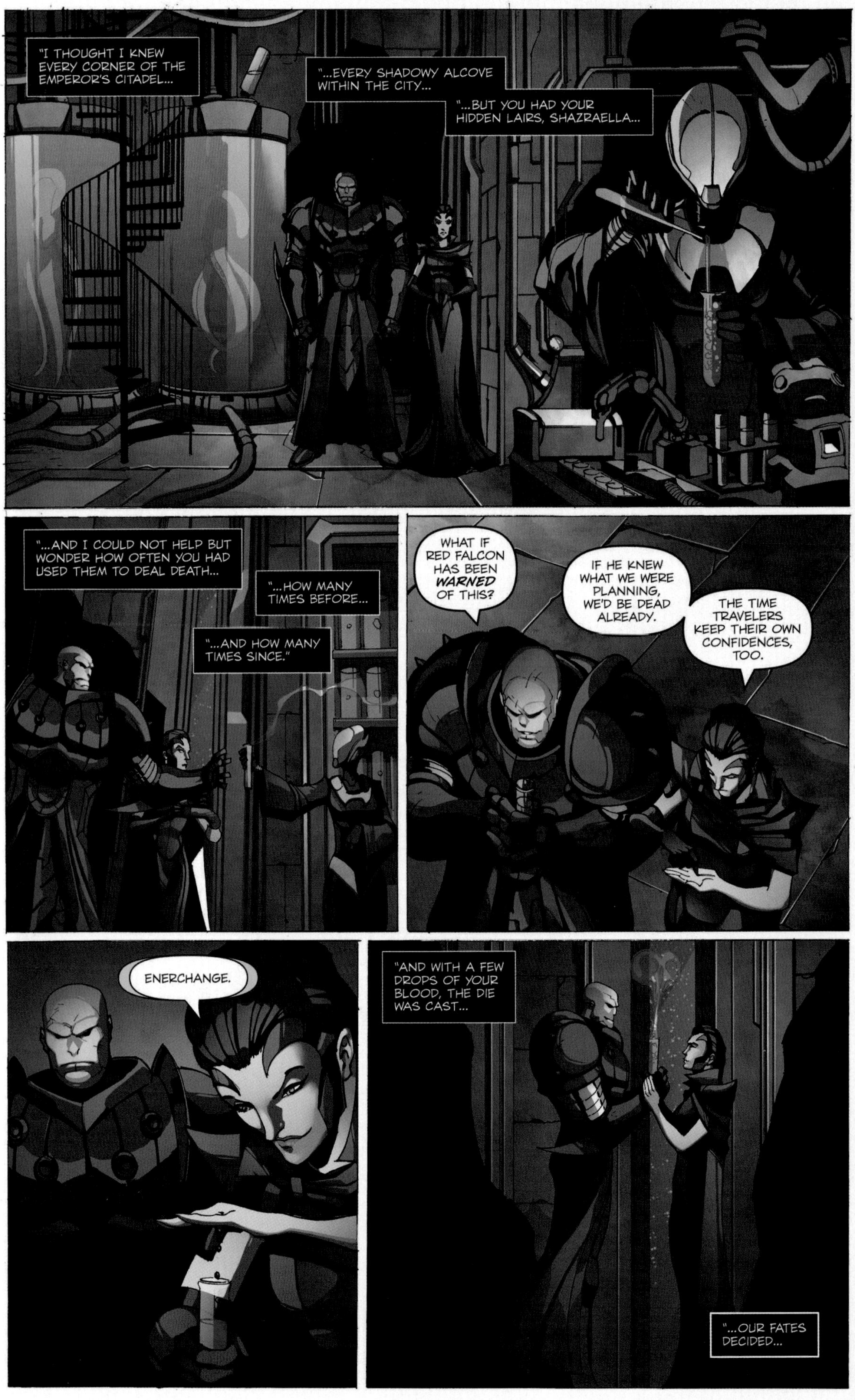
"I THOUGHT I KNEW EVERY CORNER OF THE EMPEROR'S CITADEL...
"...EVERY SHADOWY ALCOVE WITHIN THE CITY...
"...BUT YOU HAD YOUR HIDDEN LAIRS, SHAZRAELLA...
"...AND I COULD NOT HELP BUT WONDER HOW OFTEN YOU HAD USED THEM TO DEAL DEATH...
"...HOW MANY TIMES BEFORE...
"...AND HOW MANY TIMES SINCE."
WHAT IF RED FALCON HAS BEEN *WARNED* OF THIS?
IF HE KNEW WHAT WE WERE PLANNING, WE'D BE DEAD ALREADY.
THE TIME TRAVELERS KEEP THEIR OWN CONFIDENCES, TOO.
ENERCHANGE.
"AND WITH A FEW DROPS OF YOUR BLOOD, THE DIE WAS CAST...
"...OUR FATES DECIDED...

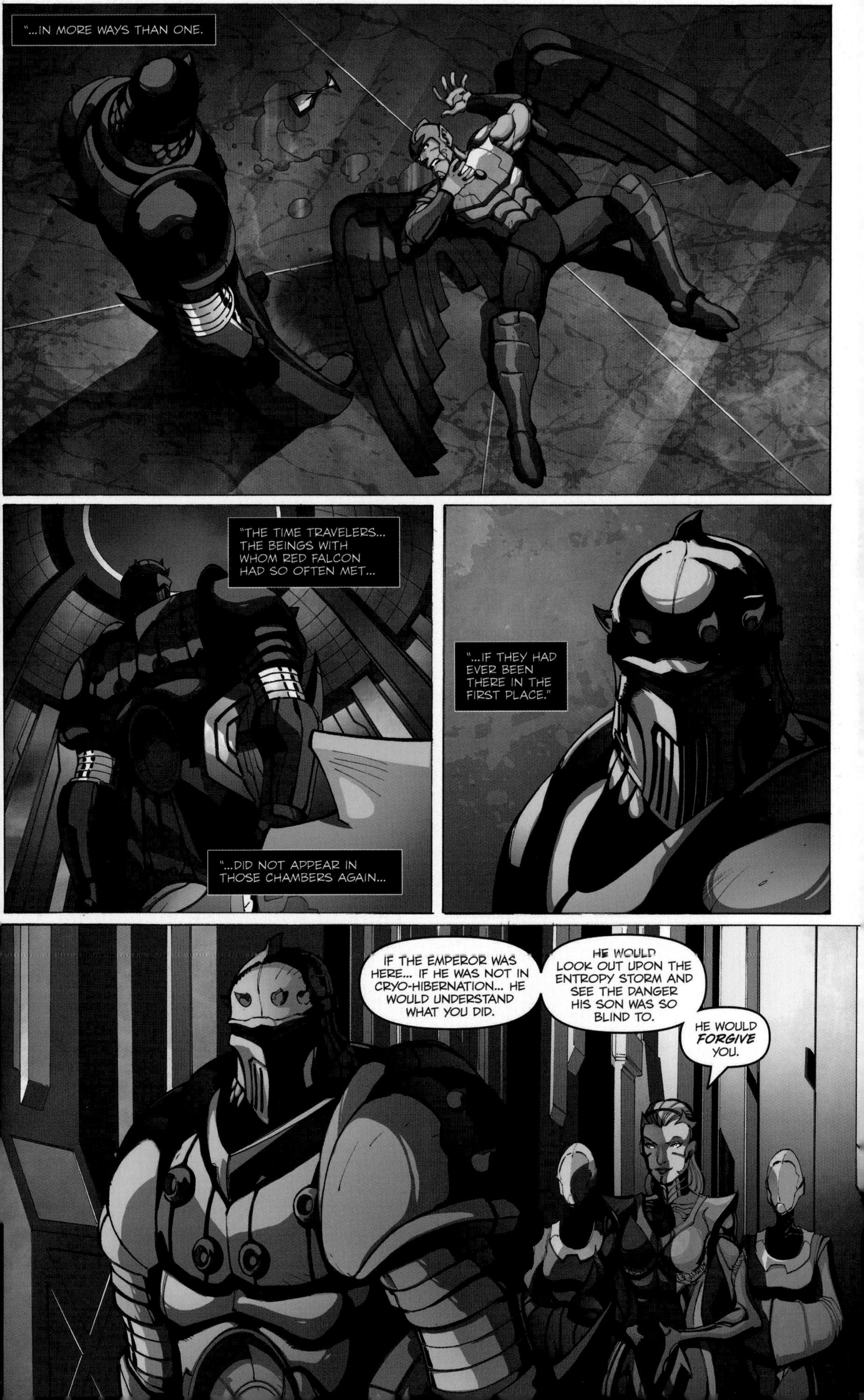
"...IN MORE WAYS THAN ONE.
"THE TIME TRAVELERS... THE BEINGS WITH WHOM RED FALCON HAD SO OFTEN MET...
"...DID NOT APPEAR IN THOSE CHAMBERS AGAIN...
"...IF THEY HAD EVER BEEN THERE IN THE FIRST PLACE."
IF THE EMPEROR WAS HERE... IF HE WAS NOT IN CRYO-HIBERNATION... HE WOULD UNDERSTAND WHAT YOU DID.
HE WOULD LOOK OUT UPON THE ENTROPY STORM AND SEE THE DANGER HIS SON WAS SO BLIND TO.
HE WOULD *FORGIVE* YOU.

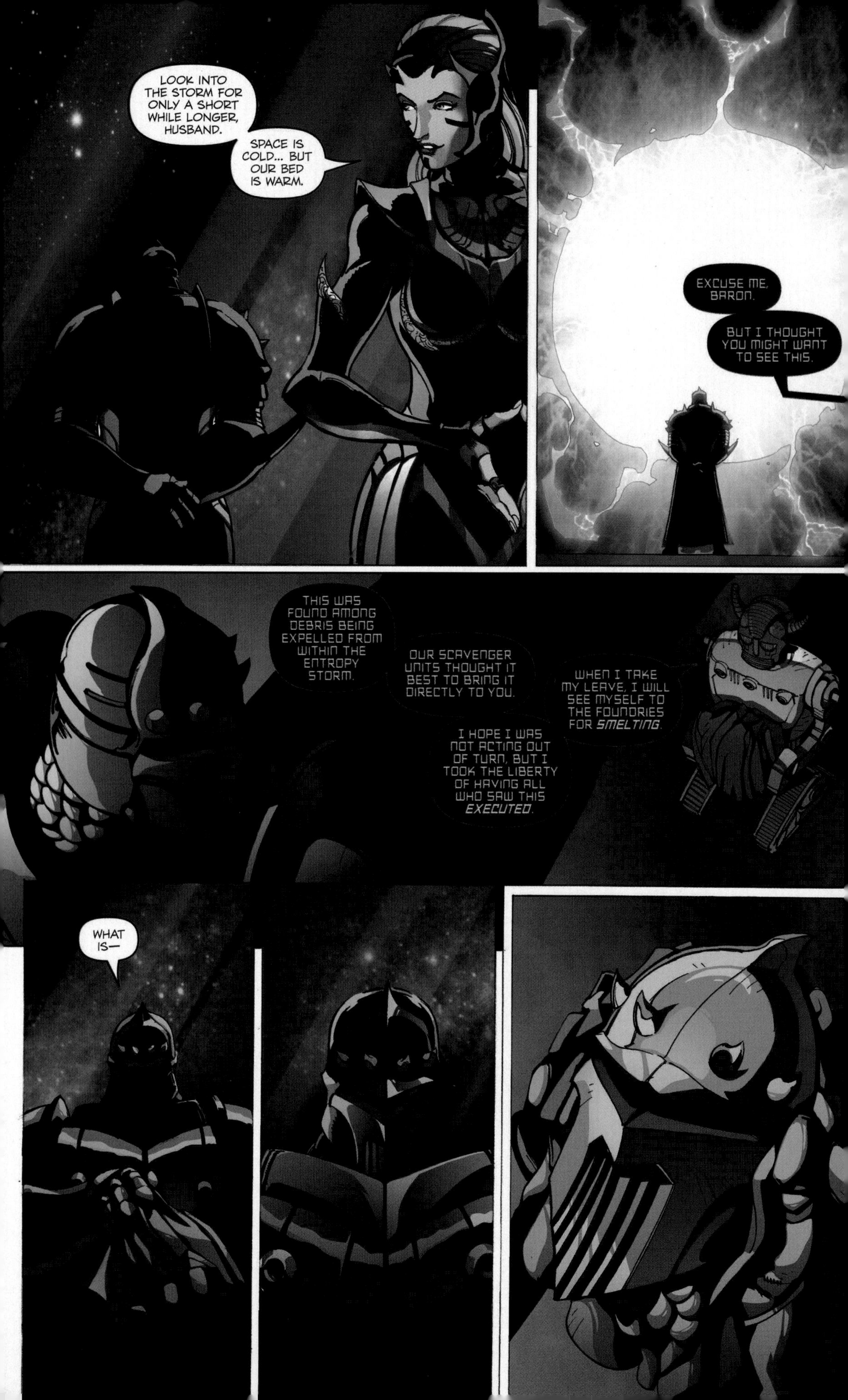
LOOK INTO THE STORM FOR ONLY A SHORT WHILE LONGER, HUSBAND.
SPACE IS COLD... BUT OUR BED IS WARM.
EXCUSE ME, BARON.
BUT I THOUGHT YOU MIGHT WANT TO SEE THIS.
THIS WAS FOUND AMONG DEBRIS BEING EXPELLED FROM WITHIN THE ENTROPY STORM.
OUR SCAVENGER UNITS THOUGHT IT BEST TO BRING IT DIRECTLY TO YOU.
I HOPE I WAS NOT ACTING OUT OF TURN, BUT I TOOK THE LIBERTY OF HAVING ALL WHO SAW THIS *EXECUTED*.
WHEN I TAKE MY LEAVE, I WILL SEE MYSELF TO THE FOUNDRIES FOR *SMELTING*.
WHAT IS—

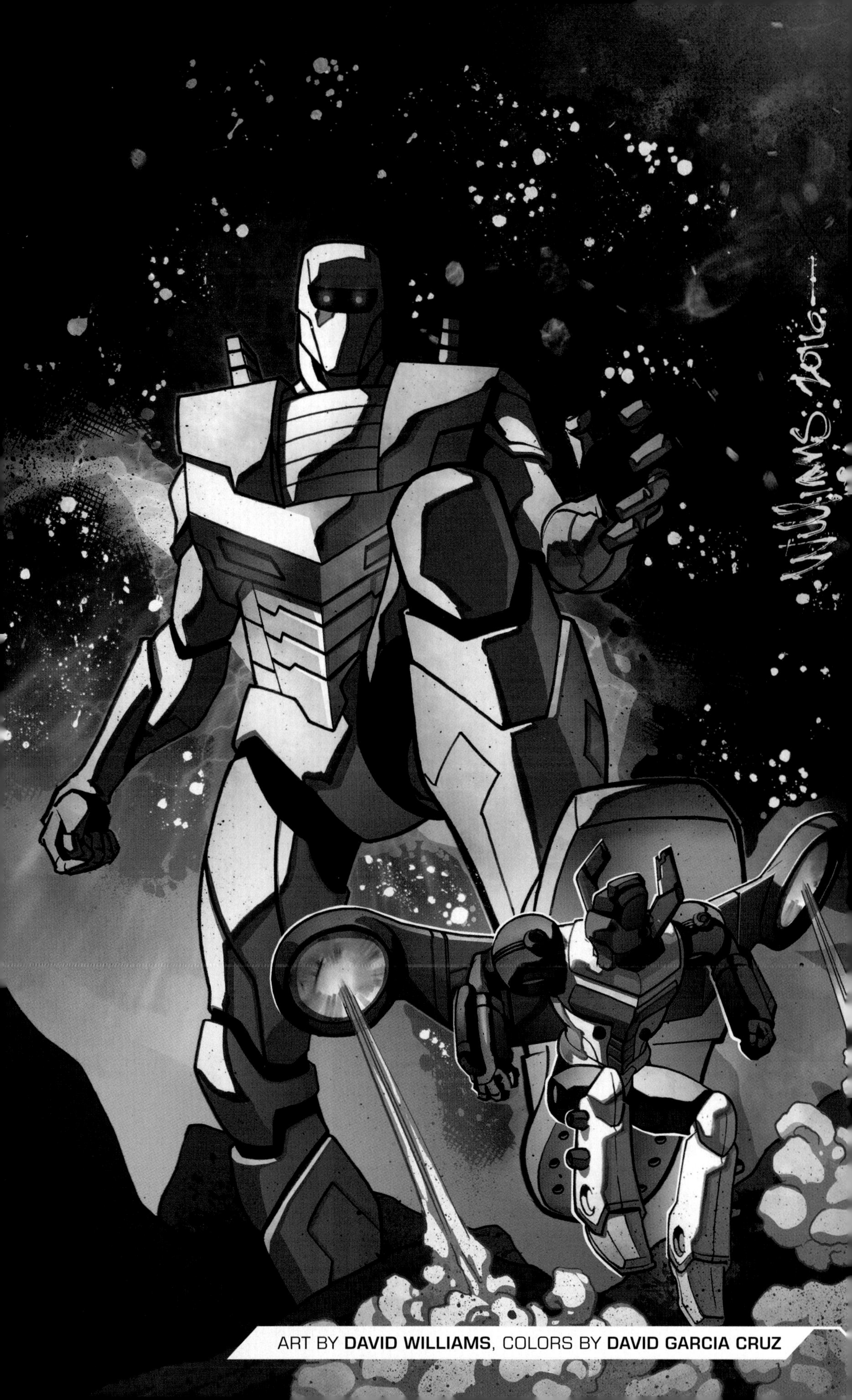

ART BY **DAVID WILLIAMS**, COLORS BY **DAVID GARCIA CRUZ**

05

ART BY **MAX DUNBAR**, COLORS BY **THOMAS DEER**

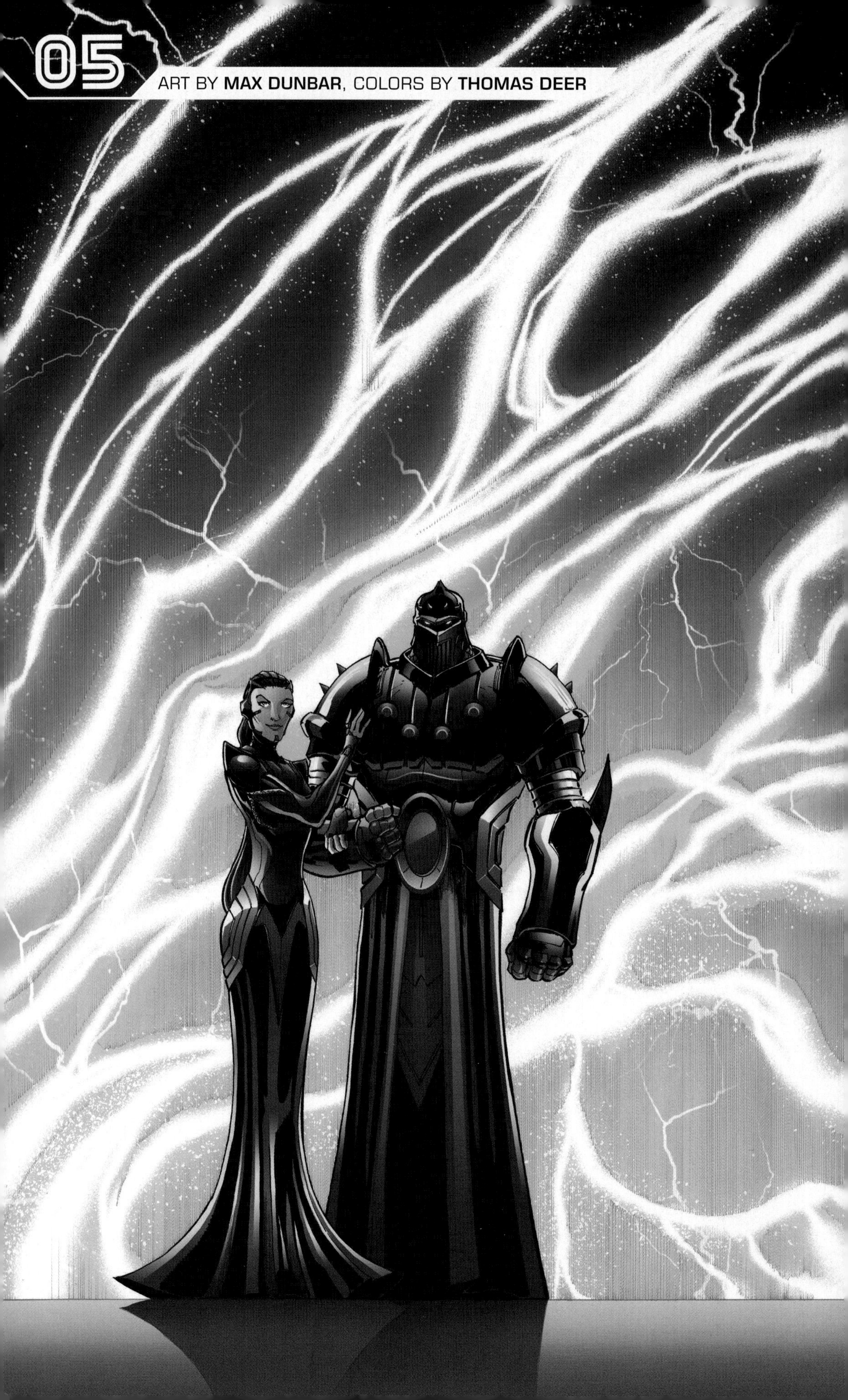

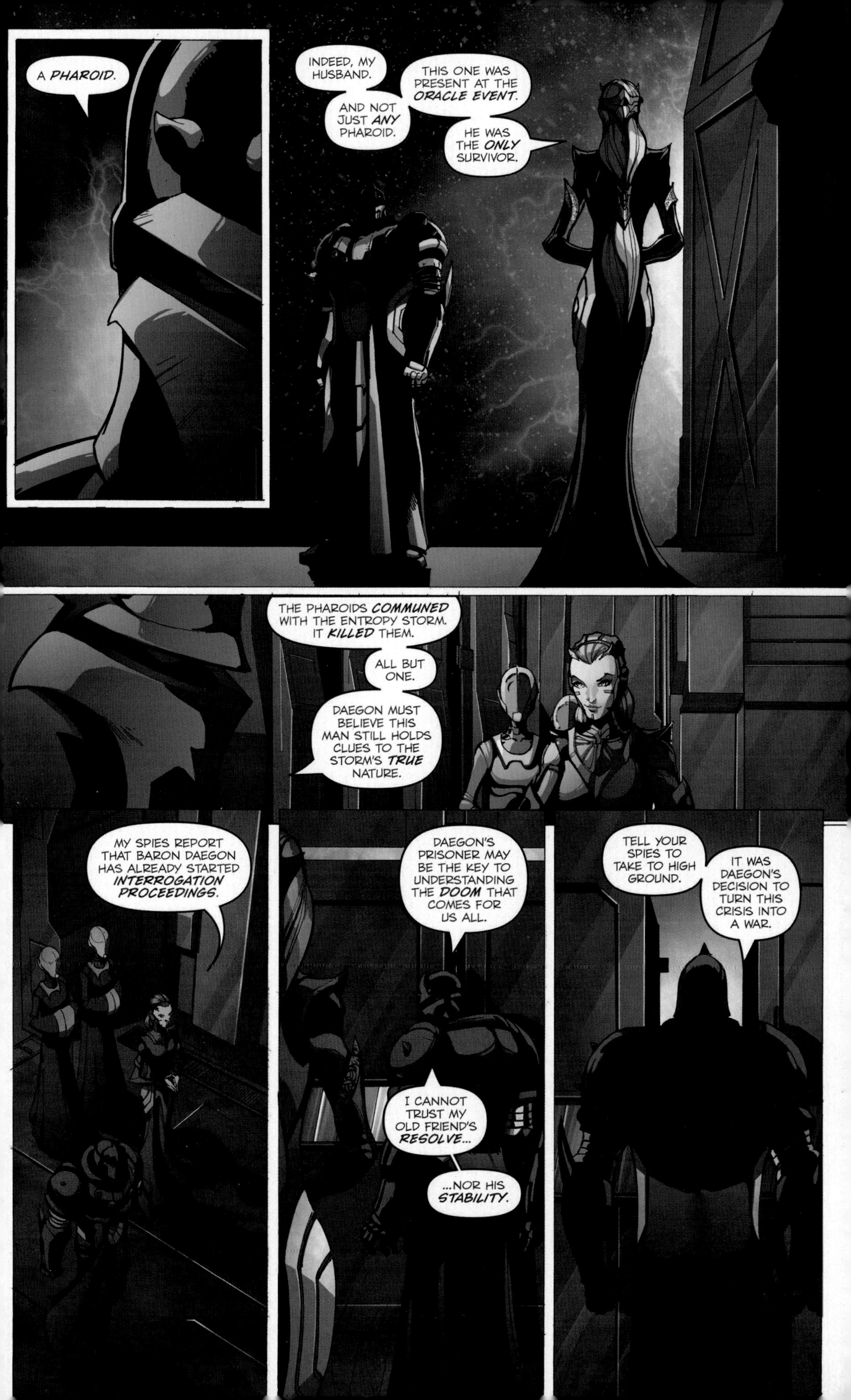
A PHAROID.
INDEED, MY HUSBAND.
AND NOT JUST ANY PHAROID.
THIS ONE WAS PRESENT AT THE ORACLE EVENT.
HE WAS THE ONLY SURVIVOR.
THE PHAROIDS COMMUNED WITH THE ENTROPY STORM. IT KILLED THEM.
ALL BUT ONE.
DAEGON MUST BELIEVE THIS MAN STILL HOLDS CLUES TO THE STORM'S TRUE NATURE.
MY SPIES REPORT THAT BARON DAEGON HAS ALREADY STARTED INTERROGATION PROCEEDINGS.
DAEGON'S PRISONER MAY BE THE KEY TO UNDERSTANDING THE DOOM THAT COMES FOR US ALL.
I CANNOT TRUST MY OLD FRIEND'S RESOLVE...
...NOR HIS STABILITY.
TELL YOUR SPIES TO TAKE TO HIGH GROUND.
IT WAS DAEGON'S DECISION TO TURN THIS CRISIS INTO A WAR.

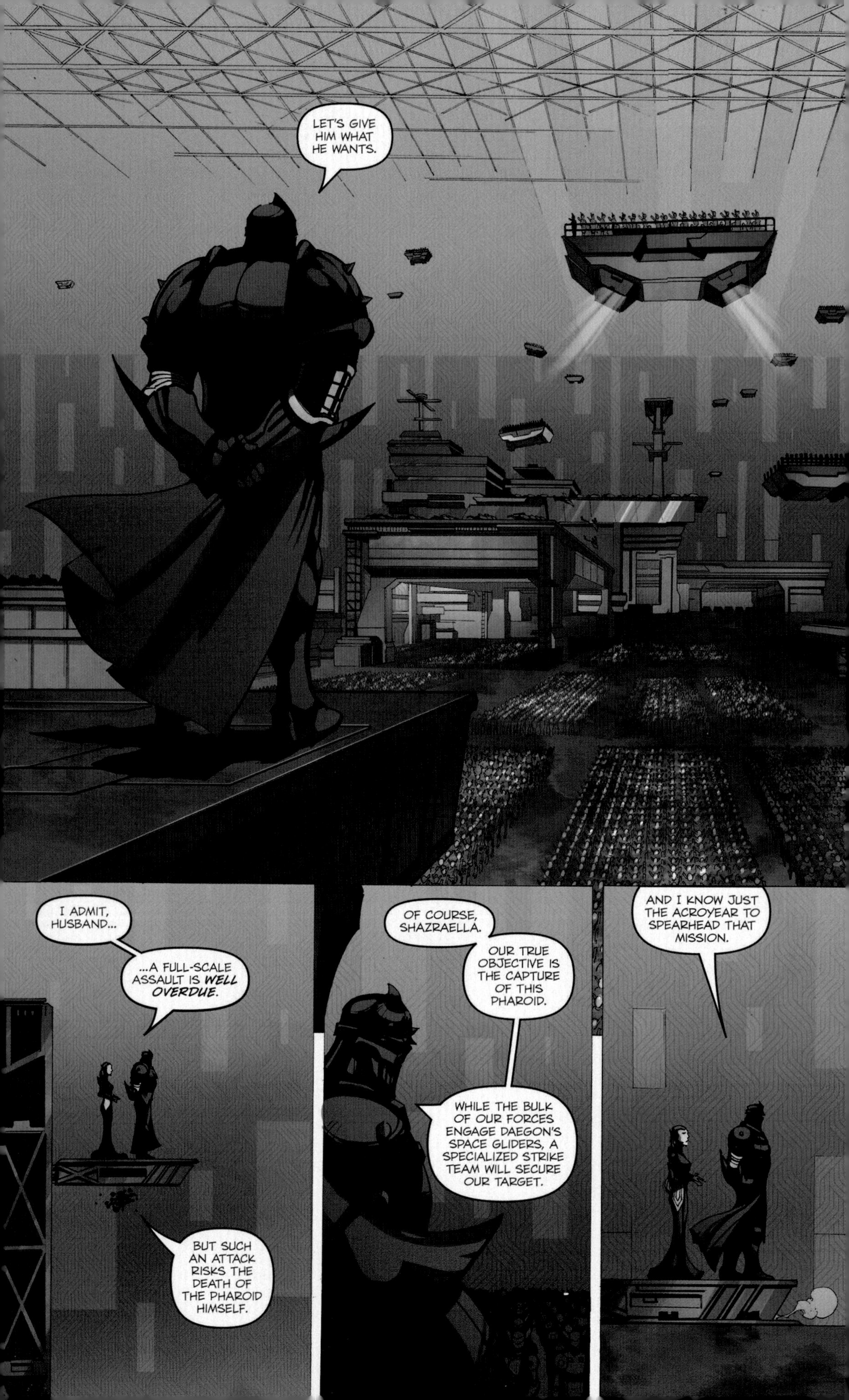
LET'S GIVE HIM WHAT HE WANTS.
I ADMIT, HUSBAND...
...A FULL-SCALE ASSAULT IS **WELL OVERDUE**.
BUT SUCH AN ATTACK RISKS THE DEATH OF THE PHAROID HIMSELF.
OF COURSE, SHAZRAELLA.
OUR TRUE OBJECTIVE IS THE CAPTURE OF THIS PHAROID.
WHILE THE BULK OF OUR FORCES ENGAGE DAEGON'S SPACE GLIDERS, A SPECIALIZED STRIKE TEAM WILL SECURE OUR TARGET.
AND I KNOW JUST THE ACROYEAR TO SPEARHEAD THAT MISSION.

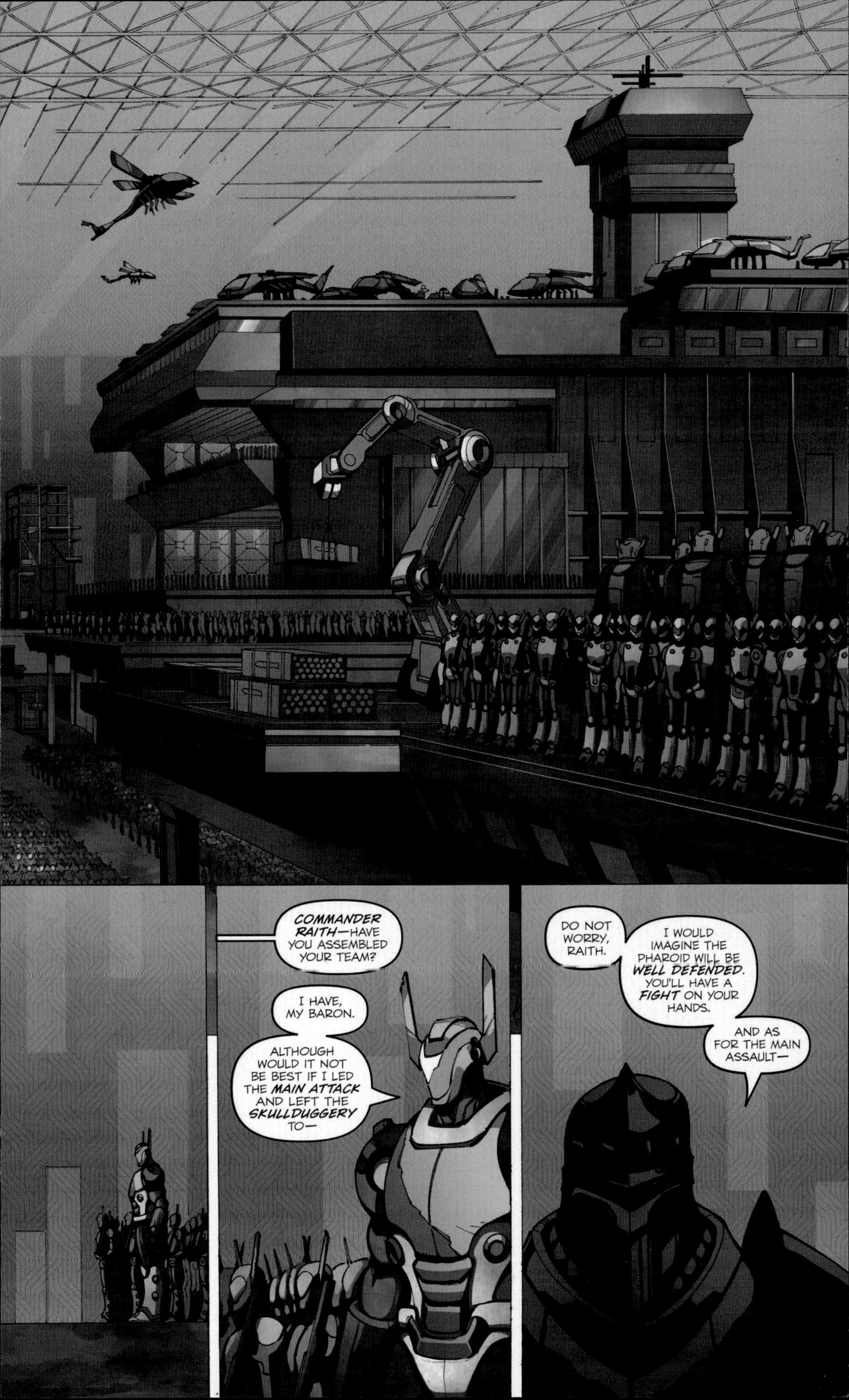
COMMANDER RAITH—HAVE YOU ASSEMBLED YOUR TEAM?
I HAVE, MY BARON.
ALTHOUGH WOULD IT NOT BE BEST IF I LED THE MAIN ATTACK AND LEFT THE SKULLDUGGERY TO—
DO NOT WORRY, RAITH.
I WOULD IMAGINE THE PHAROID WILL BE WELL DEFENDED. YOU'LL HAVE A FIGHT ON YOUR HANDS.
AND AS FOR THE MAIN ASSAULT—

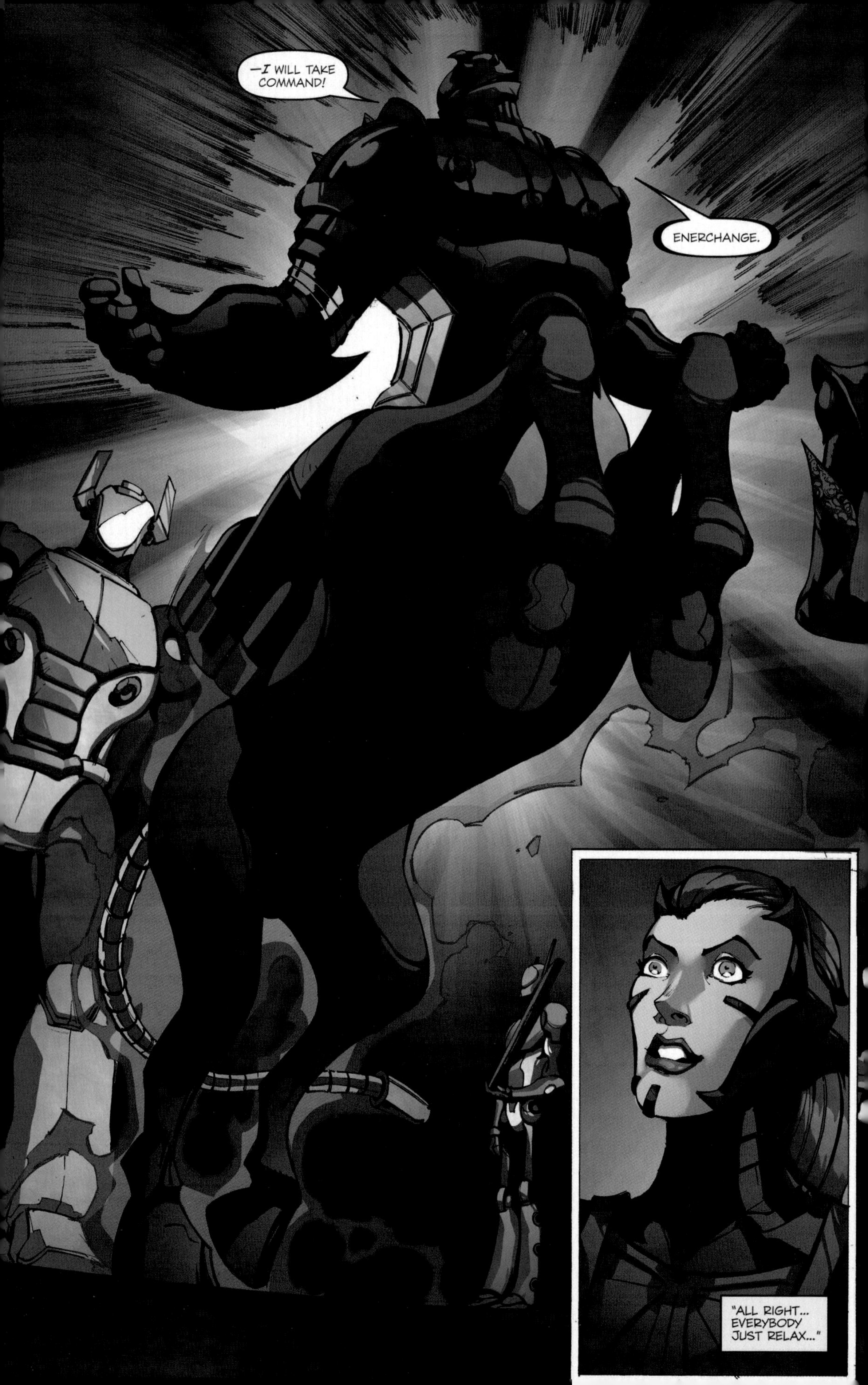
—I WILL TAKE COMMAND!
ENERCHANGE.
"ALL RIGHT... EVERYBODY JUST RELAX..."

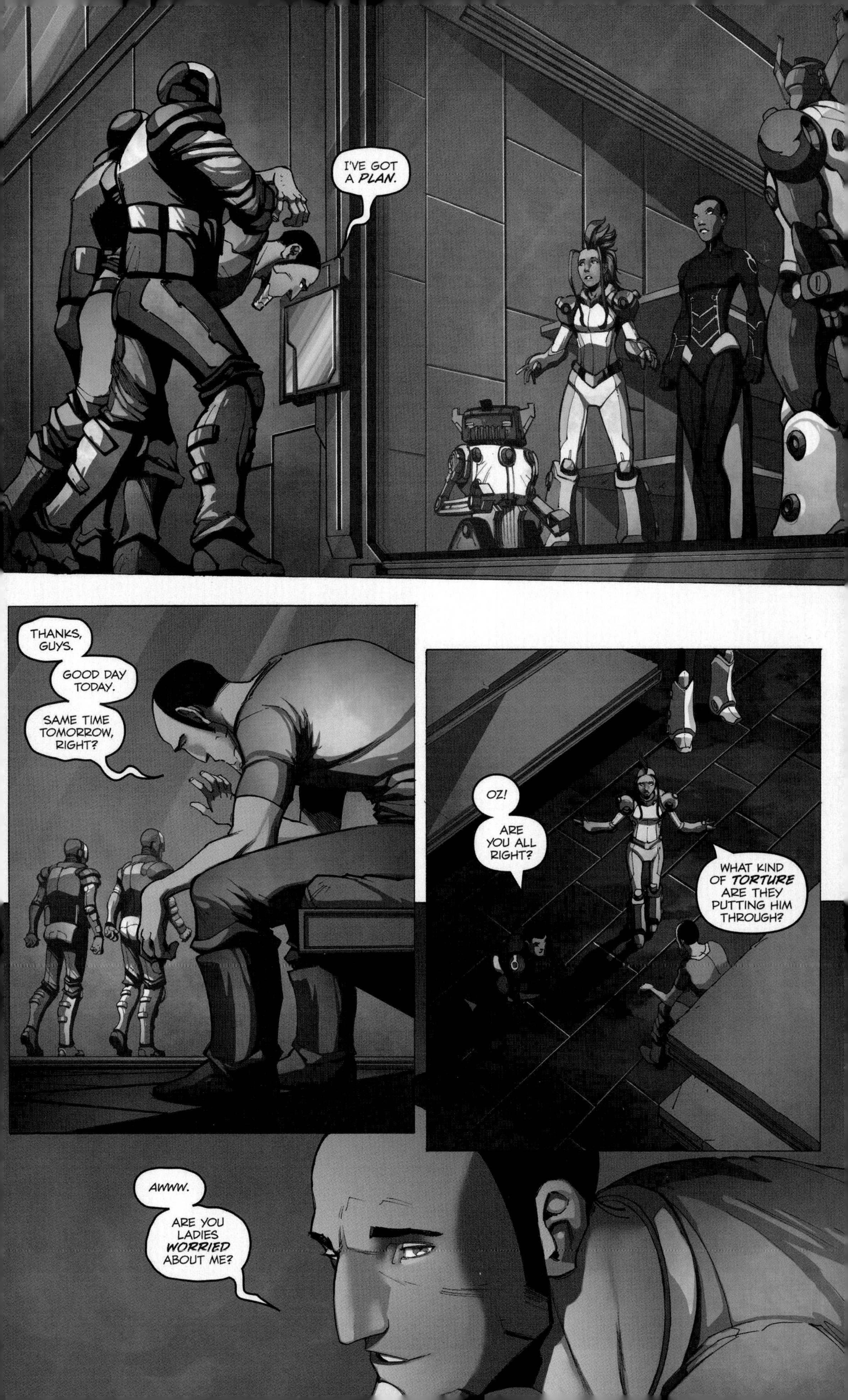
I'VE GOT A *PLAN*.
THANKS, GUYS.
GOOD DAY TODAY.
SAME TIME TOMORROW, RIGHT?
OZ!
ARE YOU ALL RIGHT?
WHAT KIND OF *TORTURE* ARE THEY PUTTING HIM THROUGH?
AWWW.
ARE YOU LADIES *WORRIED* ABOUT ME?

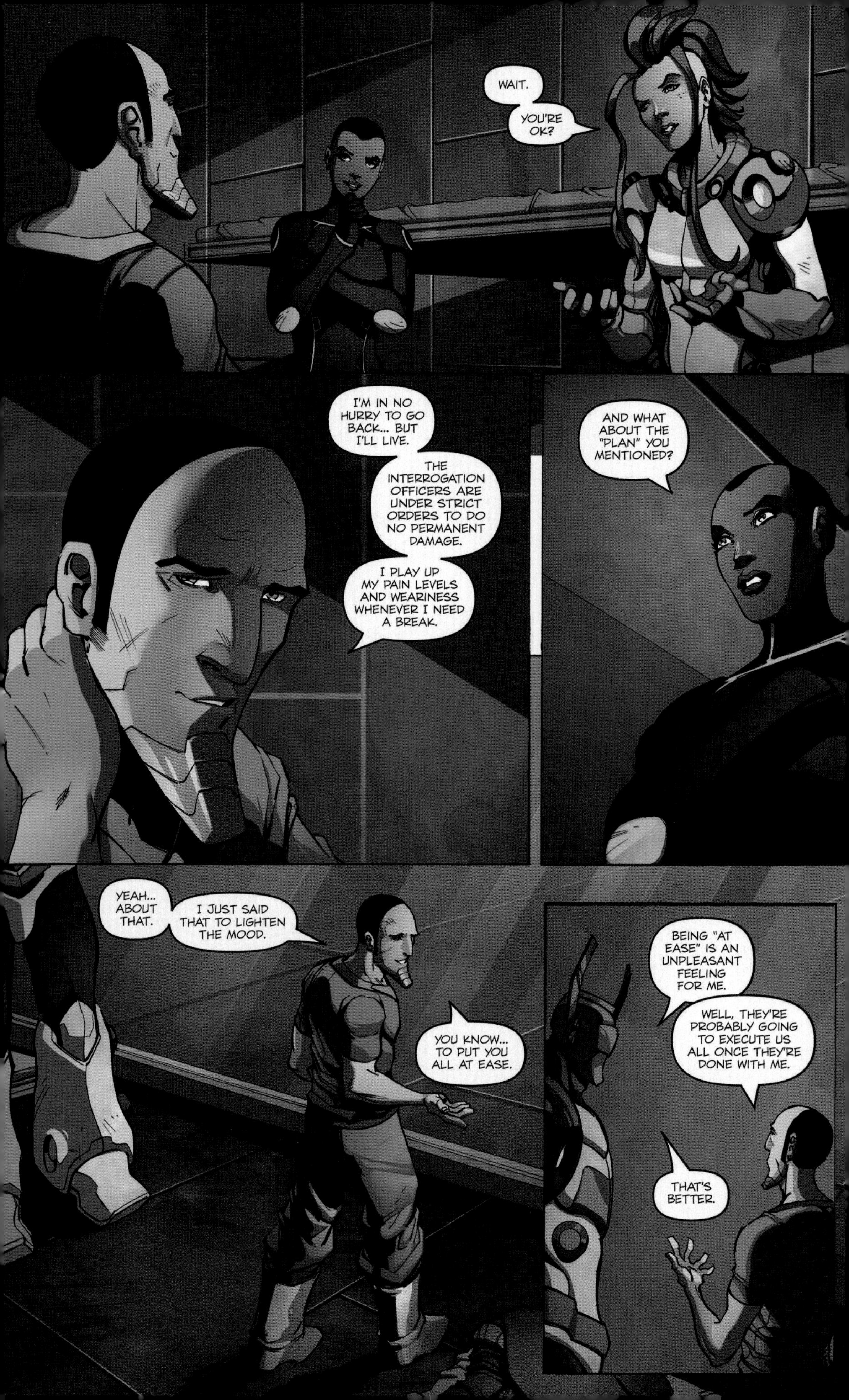
WAIT.
YOU'RE OK?
I'M IN NO HURRY TO GO BACK... BUT I'LL LIVE.
THE INTERROGATION OFFICERS ARE UNDER STRICT ORDERS TO DO NO PERMANENT DAMAGE.
I PLAY UP MY PAIN LEVELS AND WEARINESS WHENEVER I NEED A BREAK.
AND WHAT ABOUT THE "PLAN" YOU MENTIONED?
YEAH... ABOUT THAT.
I JUST SAID THAT TO LIGHTEN THE MOOD.
YOU KNOW... TO PUT YOU ALL AT EASE.
BEING "AT EASE" IS AN UNPLEASANT FEELING FOR ME.
WELL, THEY'RE PROBABLY GOING TO EXECUTE US ALL ONCE THEY'RE DONE WITH ME.
THAT'S BETTER.

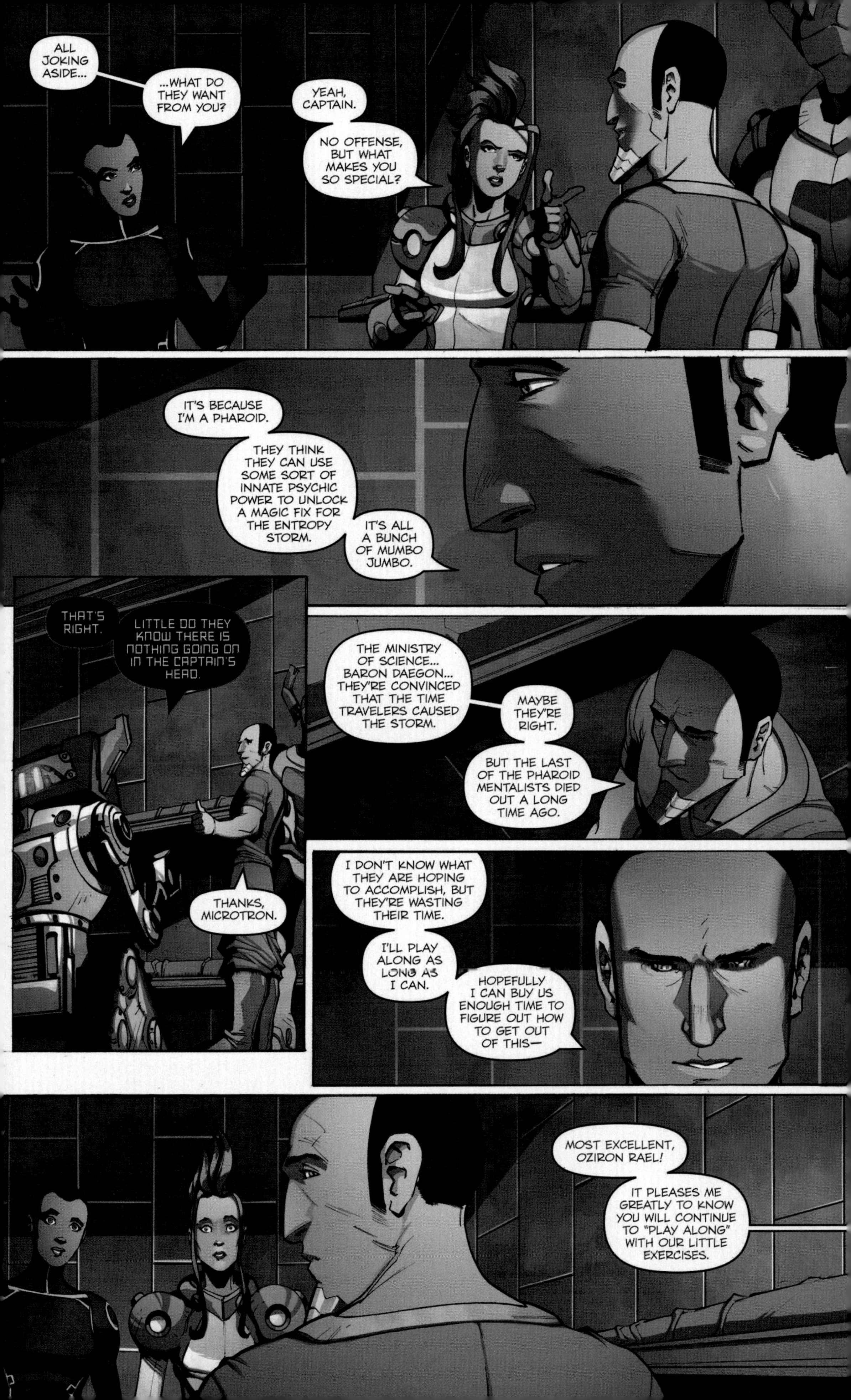
ALL JOKING ASIDE...
...WHAT DO THEY WANT FROM YOU?
YEAH, CAPTAIN.
NO OFFENSE, BUT WHAT MAKES YOU SO SPECIAL?
IT'S BECAUSE I'M A PHAROID.
THEY THINK THEY CAN USE SOME SORT OF INNATE PSYCHIC POWER TO UNLOCK A MAGIC FIX FOR THE ENTROPY STORM.
IT'S ALL A BUNCH OF MUMBO JUMBO.
THAT'S RIGHT.
LITTLE DO THEY KNOW THERE IS NOTHING GOING ON IN THE CAPTAIN'S HEAD.
THANKS, MICROTRON.
THE MINISTRY OF SCIENCE... BARON DAEGON... THEY'RE CONVINCED THAT THE TIME TRAVELERS CAUSED THE STORM.
MAYBE THEY'RE RIGHT.
BUT THE LAST OF THE PHAROID MENTALISTS DIED OUT A LONG TIME AGO.
I DON'T KNOW WHAT THEY ARE HOPING TO ACCOMPLISH, BUT THEY'RE WASTING THEIR TIME.
I'LL PLAY ALONG AS LONG AS I CAN.
HOPEFULLY I CAN BUY US ENOUGH TIME TO FIGURE OUT HOW TO GET OUT OF THIS—
MOST EXCELLENT, OZIRON RAEL!
IT PLEASES ME GREATLY TO KNOW YOU WILL CONTINUE TO "PLAY ALONG" WITH OUR LITTLE EXERCISES.

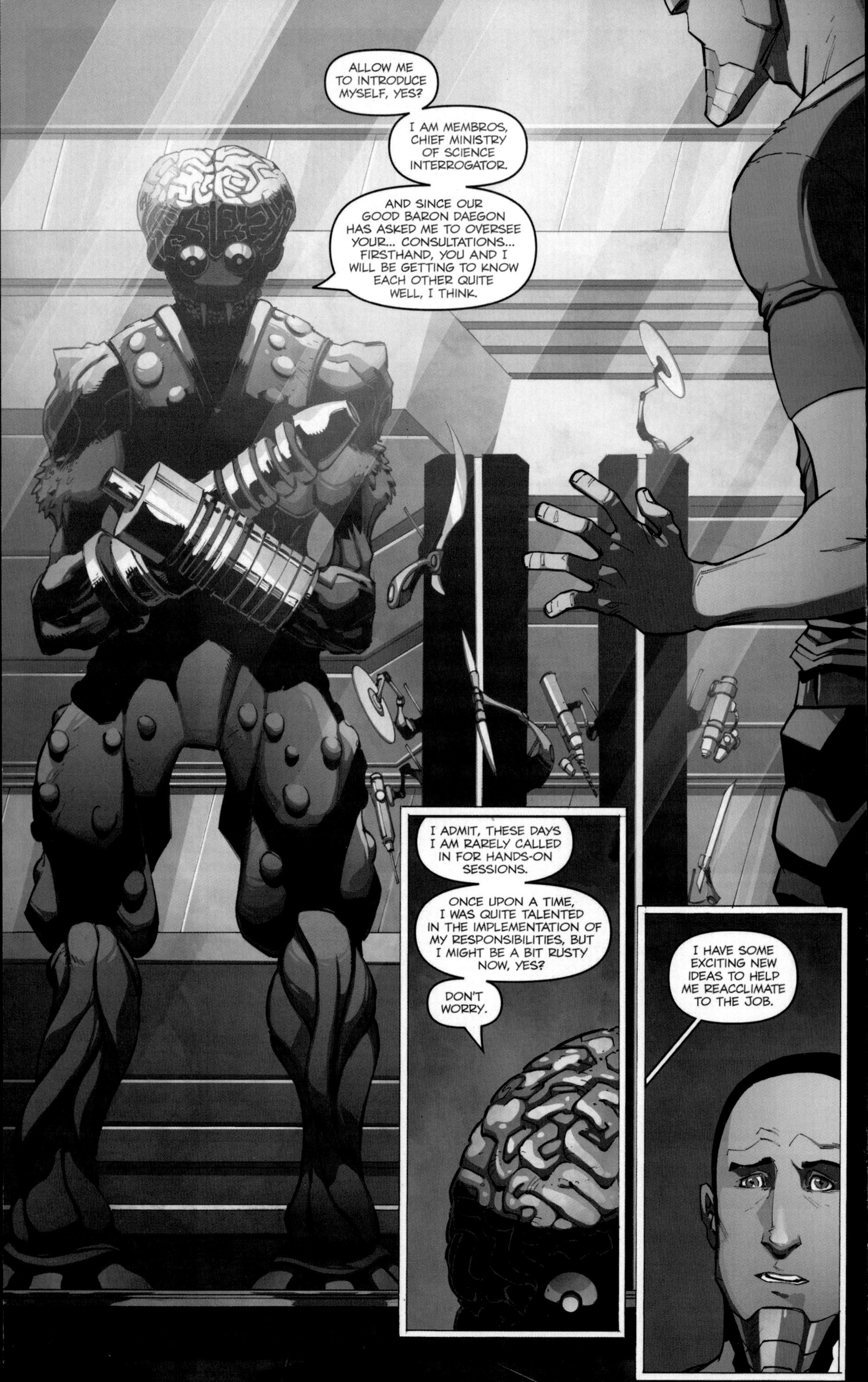
ALLOW ME TO INTRODUCE MYSELF, YES?
I AM MEMBROS, CHIEF MINISTRY OF SCIENCE INTERROGATOR.
AND SINCE OUR GOOD BARON DAEGON HAS ASKED ME TO OVERSEE YOUR... CONSULTATIONS... FIRSTHAND, YOU AND I WILL BE GETTING TO KNOW EACH OTHER QUITE WELL, I THINK.
I ADMIT, THESE DAYS I AM RARELY CALLED IN FOR HANDS-ON SESSIONS.
ONCE UPON A TIME, I WAS QUITE TALENTED IN THE IMPLEMENTATION OF MY RESPONSIBILITIES, BUT I MIGHT BE A BIT RUSTY NOW, YES?
DON'T WORRY.
I HAVE SOME EXCITING NEW IDEAS TO HELP ME REACCLIMATE TO THE JOB.

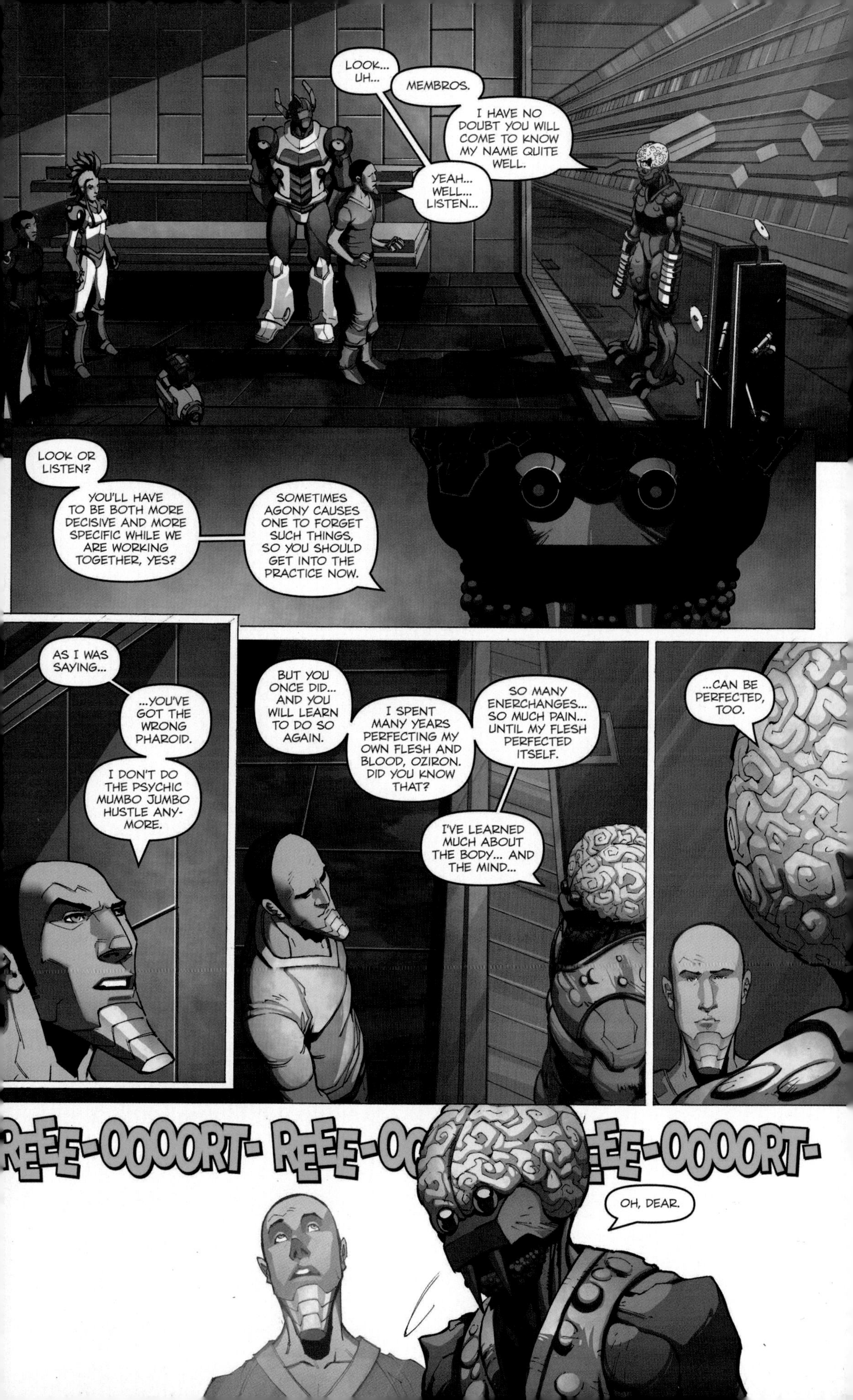
LOOK... UH...
MEMBROS.
I HAVE NO DOUBT YOU WILL COME TO KNOW MY NAME QUITE WELL.
YEAH... WELL... LISTEN...
LOOK OR LISTEN?
YOU'LL HAVE TO BE BOTH MORE DECISIVE AND MORE SPECIFIC WHILE WE ARE WORKING TOGETHER, YES?
SOMETIMES AGONY CAUSES ONE TO FORGET SUCH THINGS, SO YOU SHOULD GET INTO THE PRACTICE NOW.
AS I WAS SAYING...
...YOU'VE GOT THE WRONG PHAROID.
I DON'T DO THE PSYCHIC MUMBO JUMBO HUSTLE ANY-MORE.
BUT YOU ONCE DID... AND YOU WILL LEARN TO DO SO AGAIN.
I SPENT MANY YEARS PERFECTING MY OWN FLESH AND BLOOD, OZIRON. DID YOU KNOW THAT?
SO MANY ENERCHANGES... SO MUCH PAIN... UNTIL MY FLESH PERFECTED ITSELF.
I'VE LEARNED MUCH ABOUT THE BODY... AND THE MIND...
...CAN BE PERFECTED, TOO.
REEE-OOOORT- REEE-OO EEE-OOOORT-
OH, DEAR.

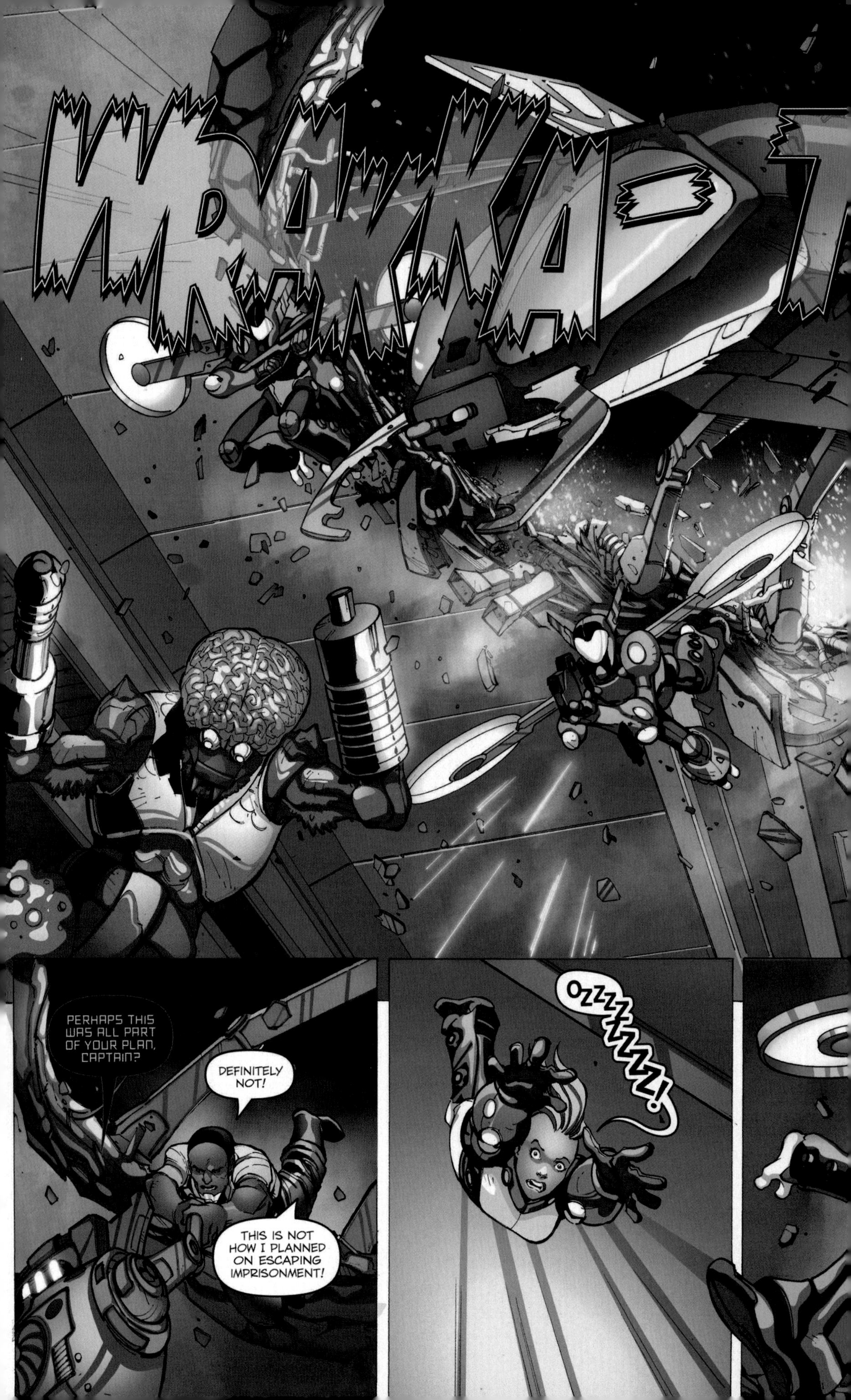
PERHAPS THIS WAS ALL PART OF YOUR PLAN, CAPTAIN?
DEFINITELY NOT!
THIS IS NOT HOW I PLANNED ON ESCAPING IMPRISONMENT!
OZZZZZZZZ!

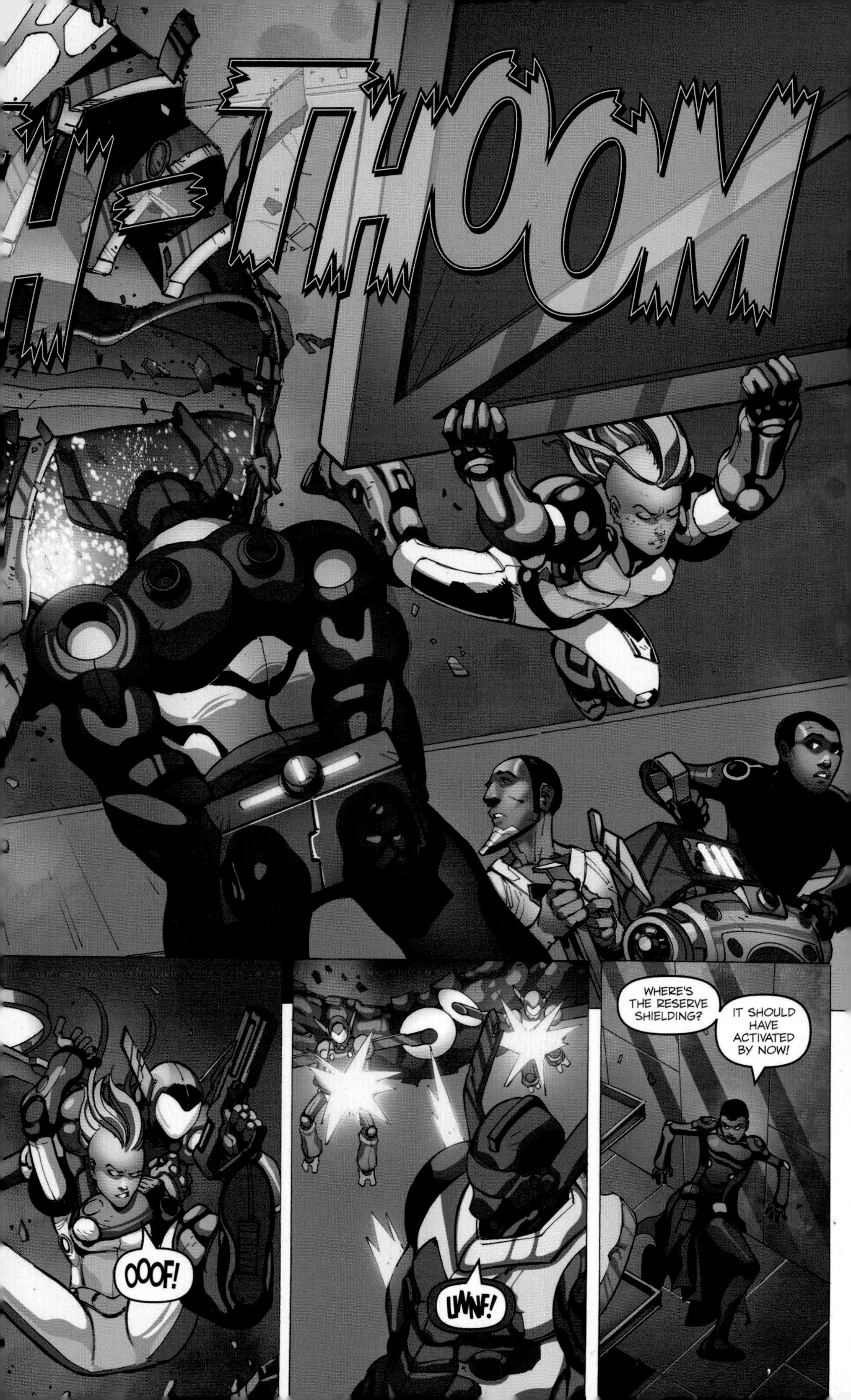
THOOM
OOOF!
UWNF!
WHERE'S THE RESERVE SHIELDING?
IT SHOULD HAVE ACTIVATED BY NOW!

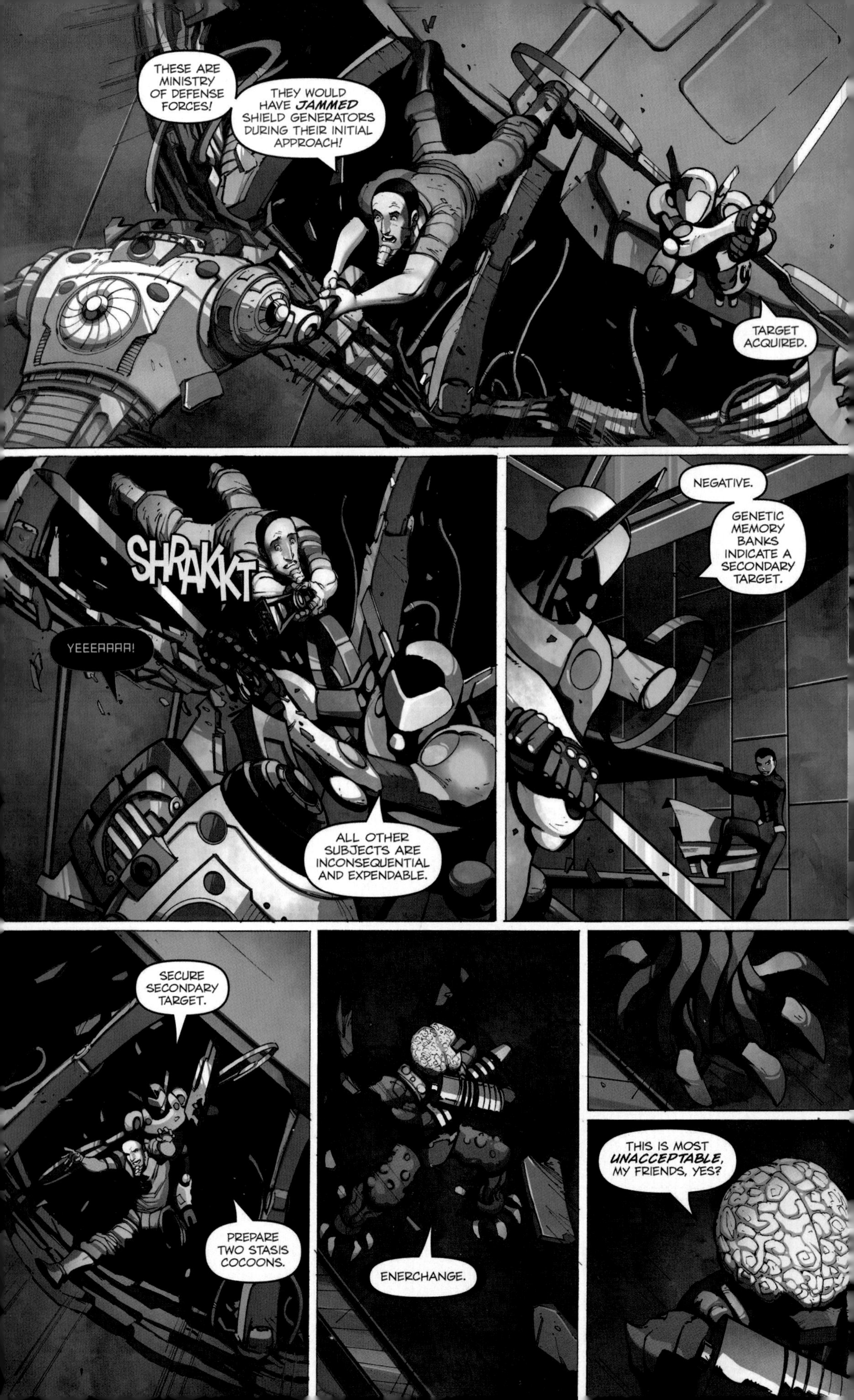
THESE ARE MINISTRY OF DEFENSE FORCES!
THEY WOULD HAVE JAMMED SHIELD GENERATORS DURING THEIR INITIAL APPROACH!
TARGET ACQUIRED.
SHRAKKT
YEEEAAAA!
ALL OTHER SUBJECTS ARE INCONSEQUENTIAL AND EXPENDABLE.
NEGATIVE.
GENETIC MEMORY BANKS INDICATE A SECONDARY TARGET.
SECURE SECONDARY TARGET.
PREPARE TWO STASIS COCOONS.
ENERCHANGE.
THIS IS MOST UNACCEPTABLE, MY FRIENDS, YES?

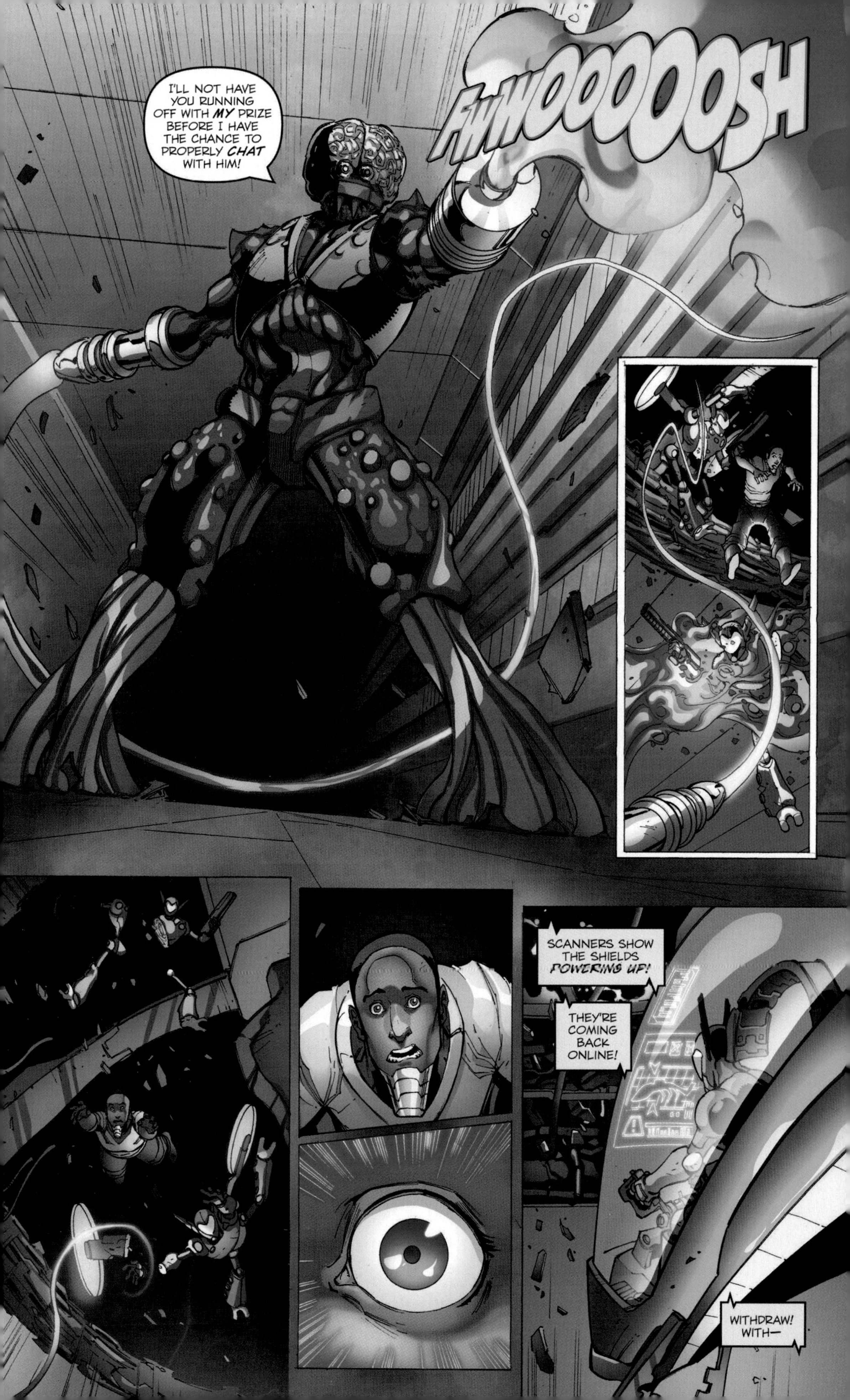
I'LL NOT HAVE YOU RUNNING OFF WITH MY PRIZE BEFORE I HAVE THE CHANCE TO PROPERLY CHAT WITH HIM!
FWWOOOOOOSH
SCANNERS SHOW THE SHIELDS POWERING UP!
THEY'RE COMING BACK ONLINE!
WITHDRAW! WITH—

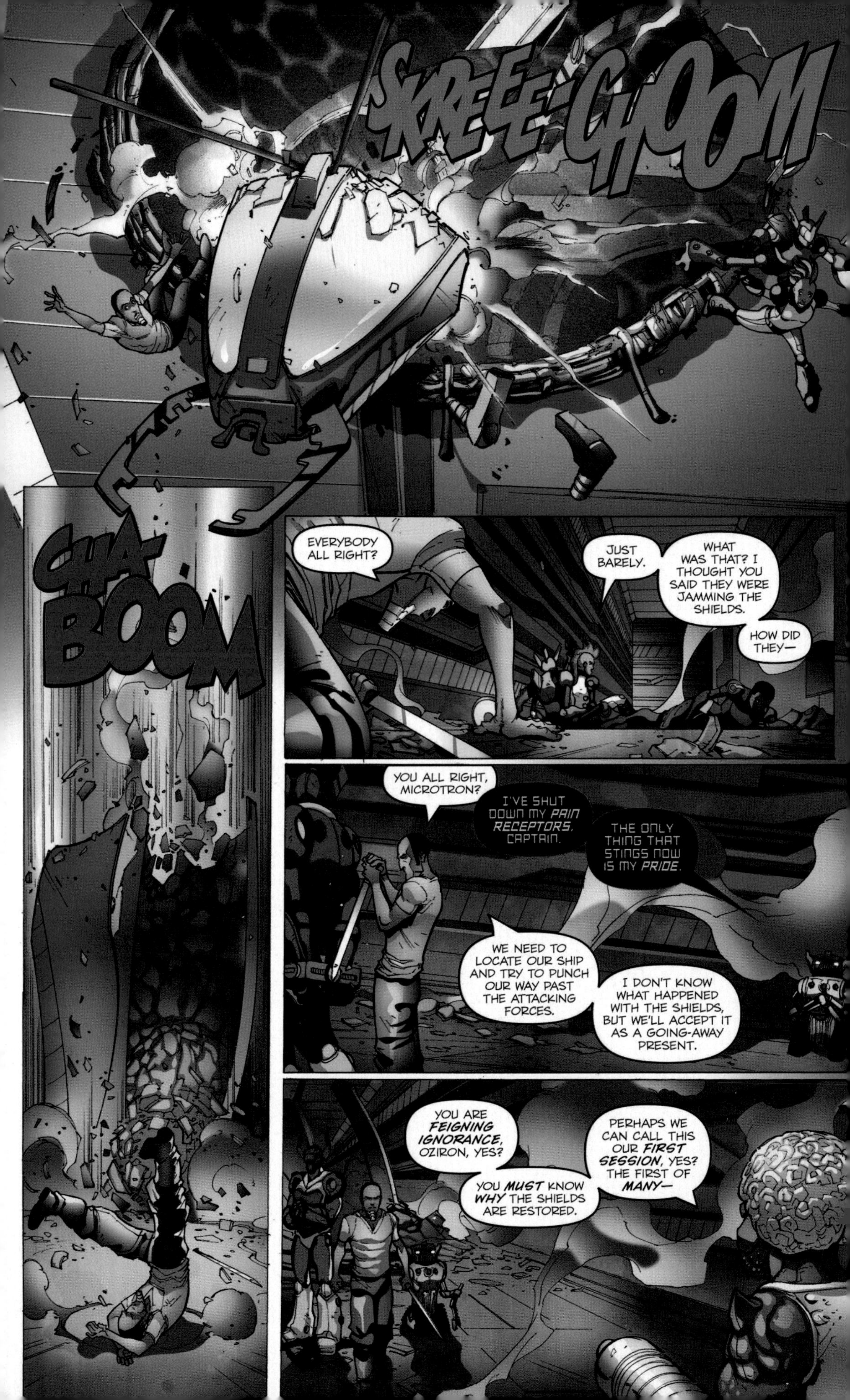
SKREEE-CHOOM
CHA-BOOM
EVERYBODY ALL RIGHT?
JUST BARELY.
WHAT WAS THAT? I THOUGHT YOU SAID THEY WERE JAMMING THE SHIELDS.
HOW DID THEY—
YOU ALL RIGHT, MICROTRON?
I'VE SHUT DOWN MY PAIN RECEPTORS, CAPTAIN.
THE ONLY THING THAT STINGS NOW IS MY PRIDE.
WE NEED TO LOCATE OUR SHIP AND TRY TO PUNCH OUR WAY PAST THE ATTACKING FORCES.
I DON'T KNOW WHAT HAPPENED WITH THE SHIELDS, BUT WE'LL ACCEPT IT AS A GOING-AWAY PRESENT.
YOU ARE FEIGNING IGNORANCE, OZIRON, YES?
YOU MUST KNOW WHY THE SHIELDS ARE RESTORED.
PERHAPS WE CAN CALL THIS OUR FIRST SESSION, YES? THE FIRST OF MANY—

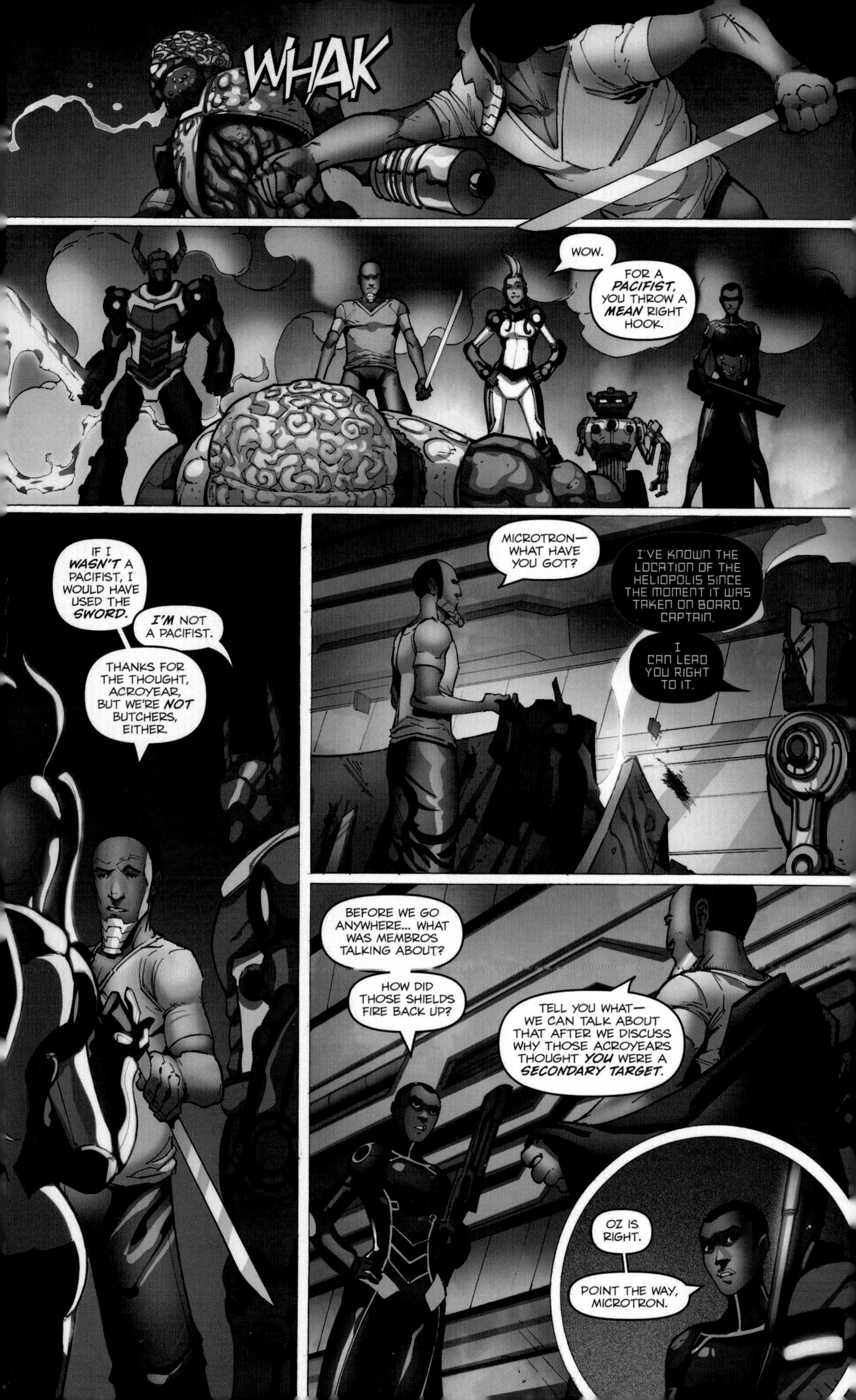
WHAK
WOW.
FOR A PACIFIST, YOU THROW A MEAN RIGHT HOOK.
IF I WASN'T A PACIFIST, I WOULD HAVE USED THE SWORD.
I'M NOT A PACIFIST.
THANKS FOR THE THOUGHT, ACROYEAR, BUT WE'RE NOT BUTCHERS, EITHER.
MICROTRON— WHAT HAVE YOU GOT?
I'VE KNOWN THE LOCATION OF THE HELIOPOLIS SINCE THE MOMENT IT WAS TAKEN ON BOARD, CAPTAIN.
I CAN LEAD YOU RIGHT TO IT.
BEFORE WE GO ANYWHERE... WHAT WAS MEMBROS TALKING ABOUT?
HOW DID THOSE SHIELDS FIRE BACK UP?
TELL YOU WHAT— WE CAN TALK ABOUT THAT AFTER WE DISCUSS WHY THOSE ACROYEARS THOUGHT YOU WERE A SECONDARY TARGET.
OZ IS RIGHT.
POINT THE WAY, MICROTRON.

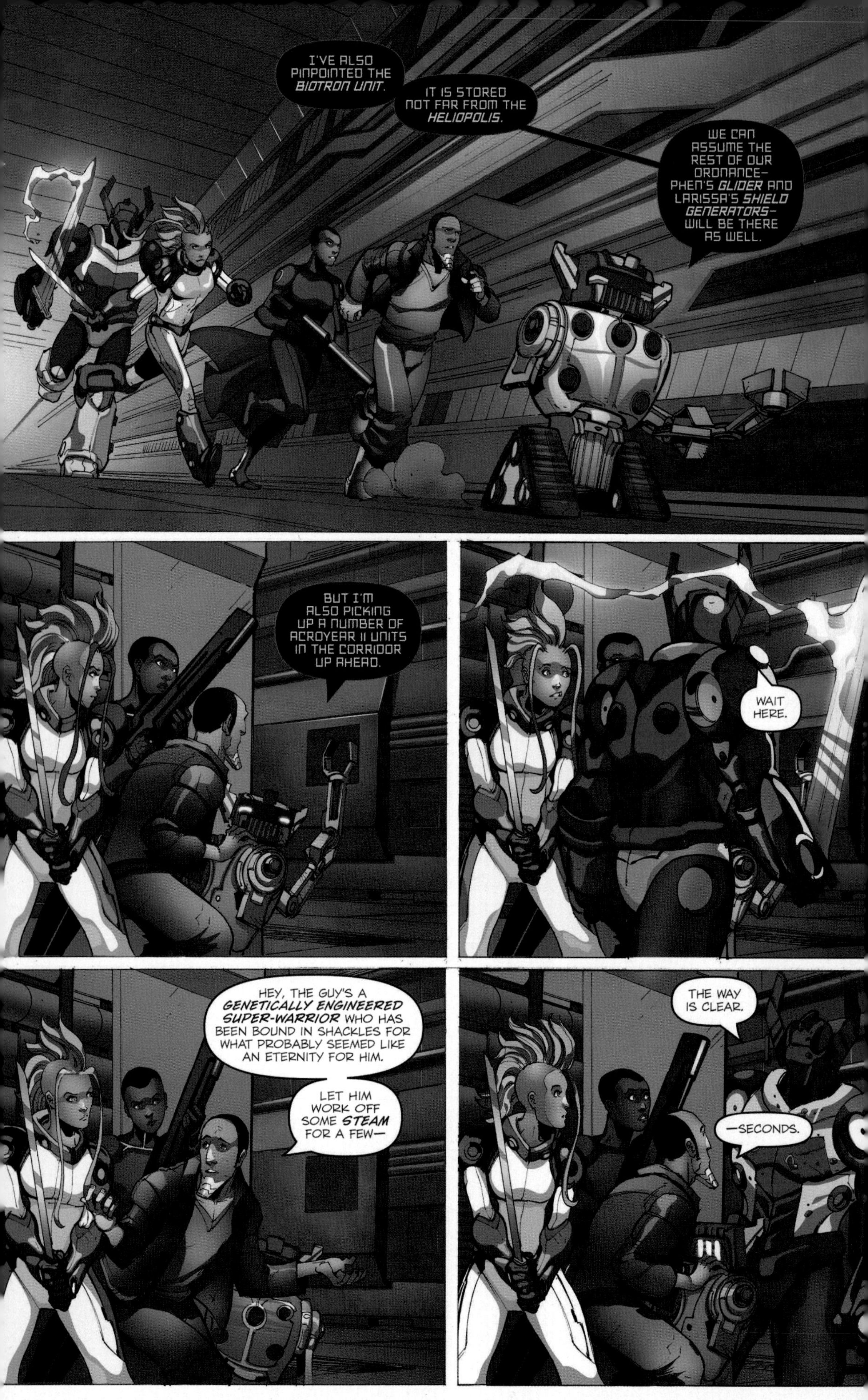
I'VE ALSO PINPOINTED THE BIOTRON UNIT.
IT IS STORED NOT FAR FROM THE HELIOPOLIS.
WE CAN ASSUME THE REST OF OUR ORDNANCE– PHEN'S GLIDER AND LARISSA'S SHIELD GENERATORS– WILL BE THERE AS WELL.
BUT I'M ALSO PICKING UP A NUMBER OF ACROYEAR II UNITS IN THE CORRIDOR UP AHEAD.
WAIT HERE.
HEY, THE GUY'S A GENETICALLY ENGINEERED SUPER-WARRIOR WHO HAS BEEN BOUND IN SHACKLES FOR WHAT PROBABLY SEEMED LIKE AN ETERNITY FOR HIM.
LET HIM WORK OFF SOME STEAM FOR A FEW—
THE WAY IS CLEAR.
—SECONDS.

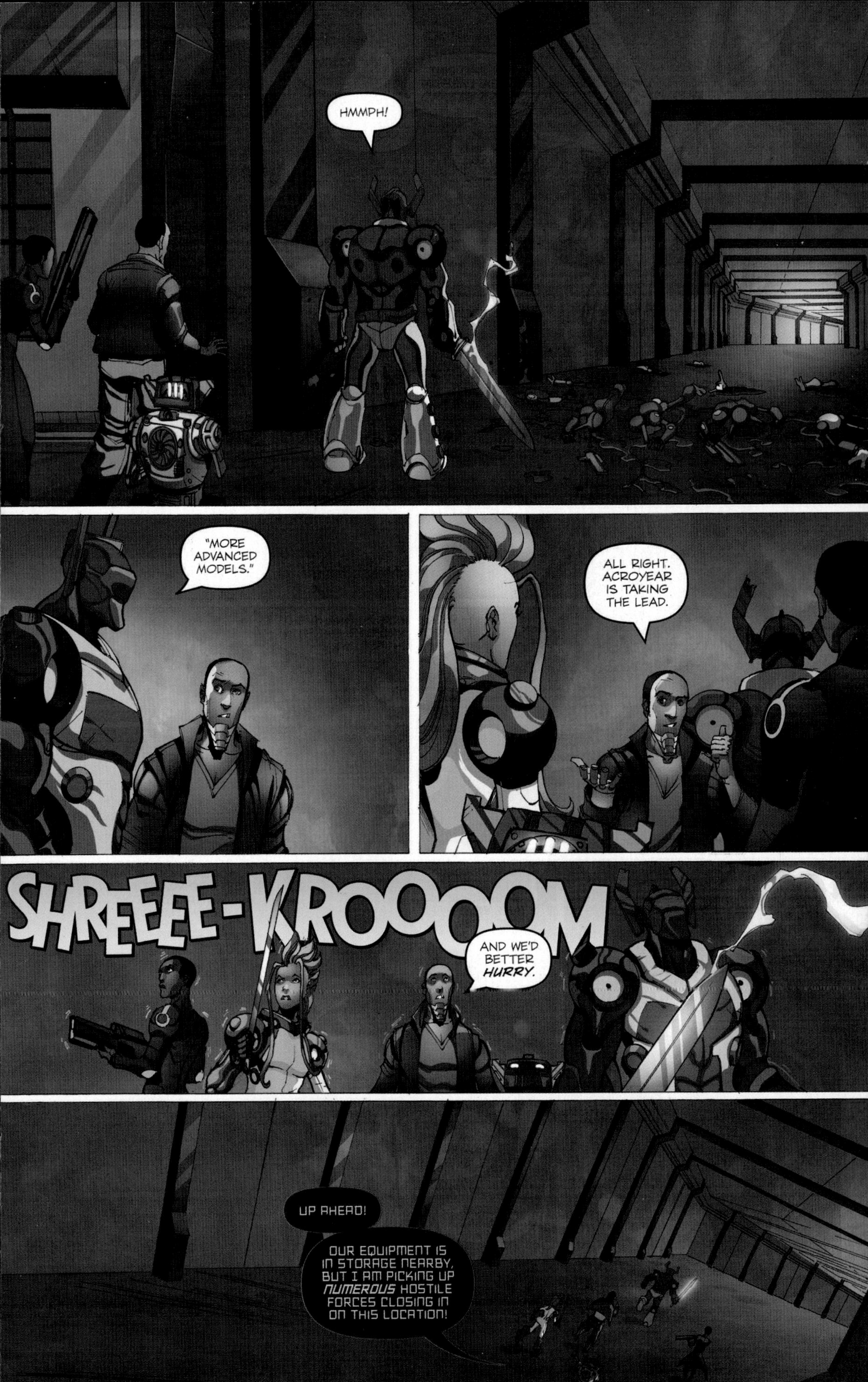
HMMPH!
"MORE ADVANCED MODELS."
ALL RIGHT. ACROYEAR IS TAKING THE LEAD.
SHREEEE-KROOOOOM
AND WE'D BETTER *HURRY*.
UP AHEAD!
OUR EQUIPMENT IS IN STORAGE NEARBY, BUT I AM PICKING UP *NUMEROUS* HOSTILE FORCES CLOSING IN ON THIS LOCATION!

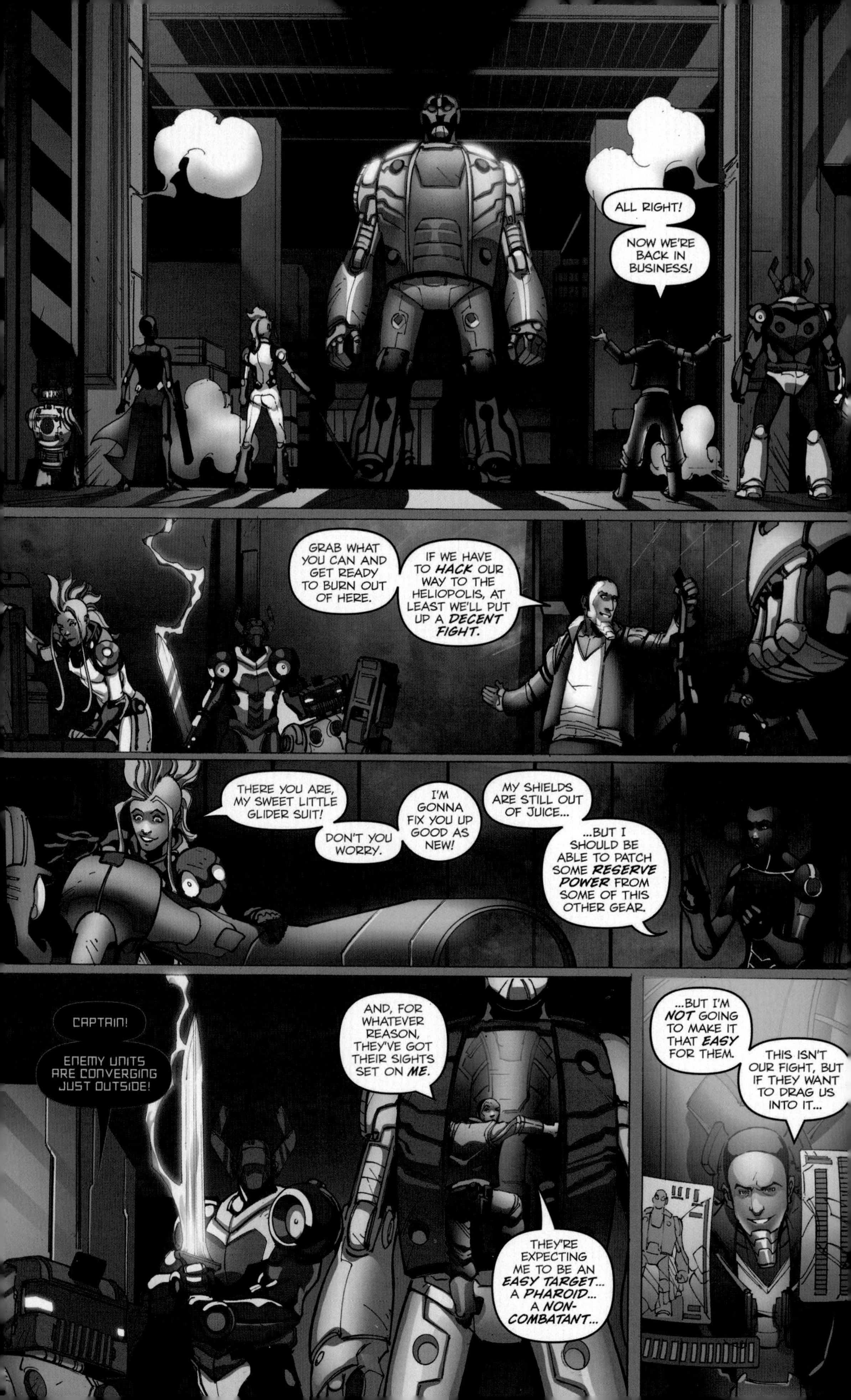
ALL RIGHT!
NOW WE'RE BACK IN BUSINESS!
GRAB WHAT YOU CAN AND GET READY TO BURN OUT OF HERE.
IF WE HAVE TO HACK OUR WAY TO THE HELIOPOLIS, AT LEAST WE'LL PUT UP A DECENT FIGHT.
THERE YOU ARE, MY SWEET LITTLE GLIDER SUIT!
DON'T YOU WORRY.
I'M GONNA FIX YOU UP GOOD AS NEW!
MY SHIELDS ARE STILL OUT OF JUICE...
...BUT I SHOULD BE ABLE TO PATCH SOME RESERVE POWER FROM SOME OF THIS OTHER GEAR.
CAPTAIN!
ENEMY UNITS ARE CONVERGING JUST OUTSIDE!
AND, FOR WHATEVER REASON, THEY'VE GOT THEIR SIGHTS SET ON ME.
THEY'RE EXPECTING ME TO BE AN EASY TARGET... A PHAROID... A NON-COMBATANT...
...BUT I'M NOT GOING TO MAKE IT THAT EASY FOR THEM.
THIS ISN'T OUR FIGHT, BUT IF THEY WANT TO DRAG US INTO IT...

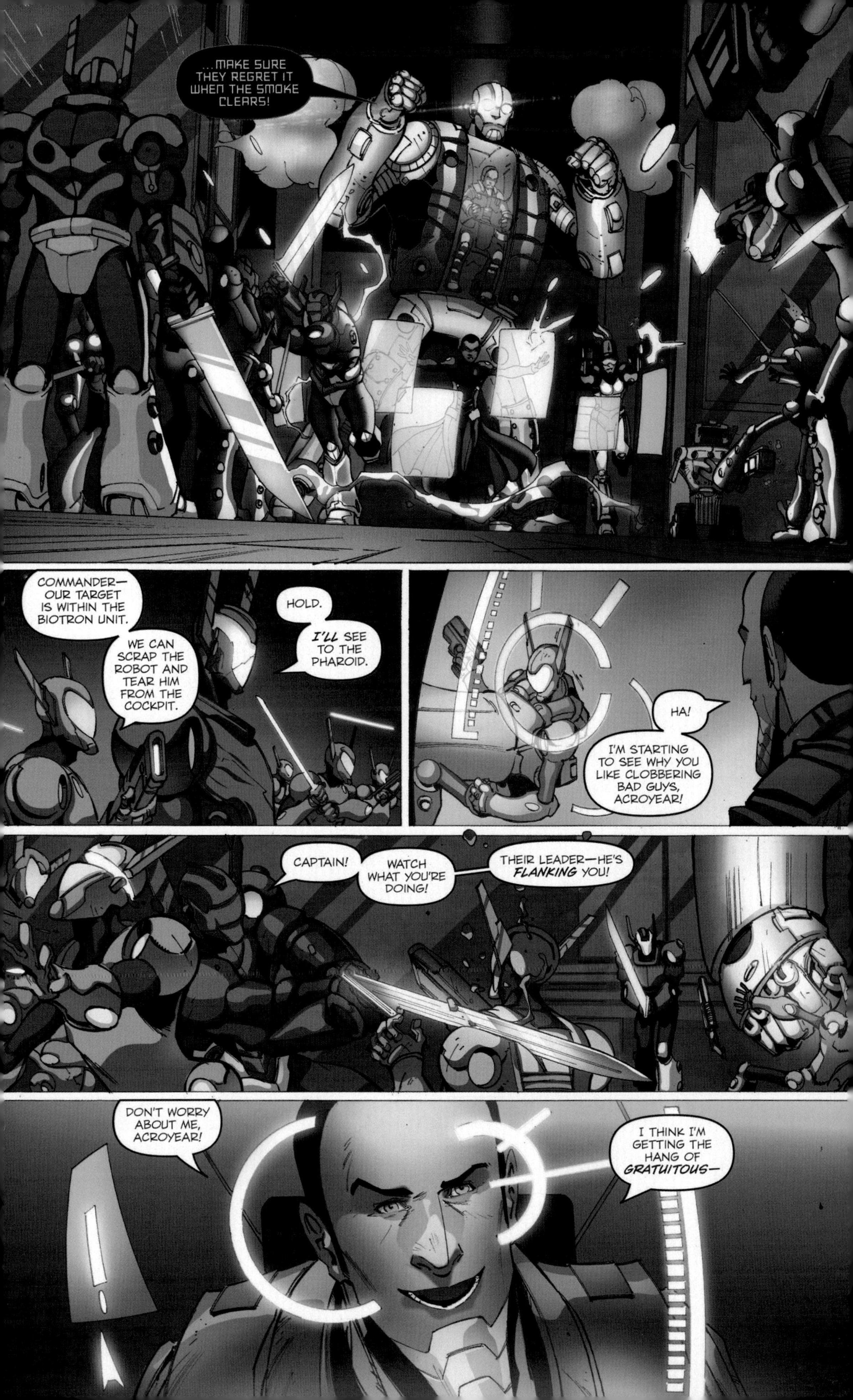
...MAKE SURE THEY REGRET IT WHEN THE SMOKE CLEARS!
COMMANDER— OUR TARGET IS WITHIN THE BIOTRON UNIT.
WE CAN SCRAP THE ROBOT AND TEAR HIM FROM THE COCKPIT.
HOLD.
I'LL SEE TO THE PHAROID.
HA!
I'M STARTING TO SEE WHY YOU LIKE CLOBBERING BAD GUYS, ACROYEAR!
CAPTAIN!
WATCH WHAT YOU'RE DOING!
THEIR LEADER—HE'S FLANKING YOU!
DON'T WORRY ABOUT ME, ACROYEAR!
I THINK I'M GETTING THE HANG OF GRATUITOUS—

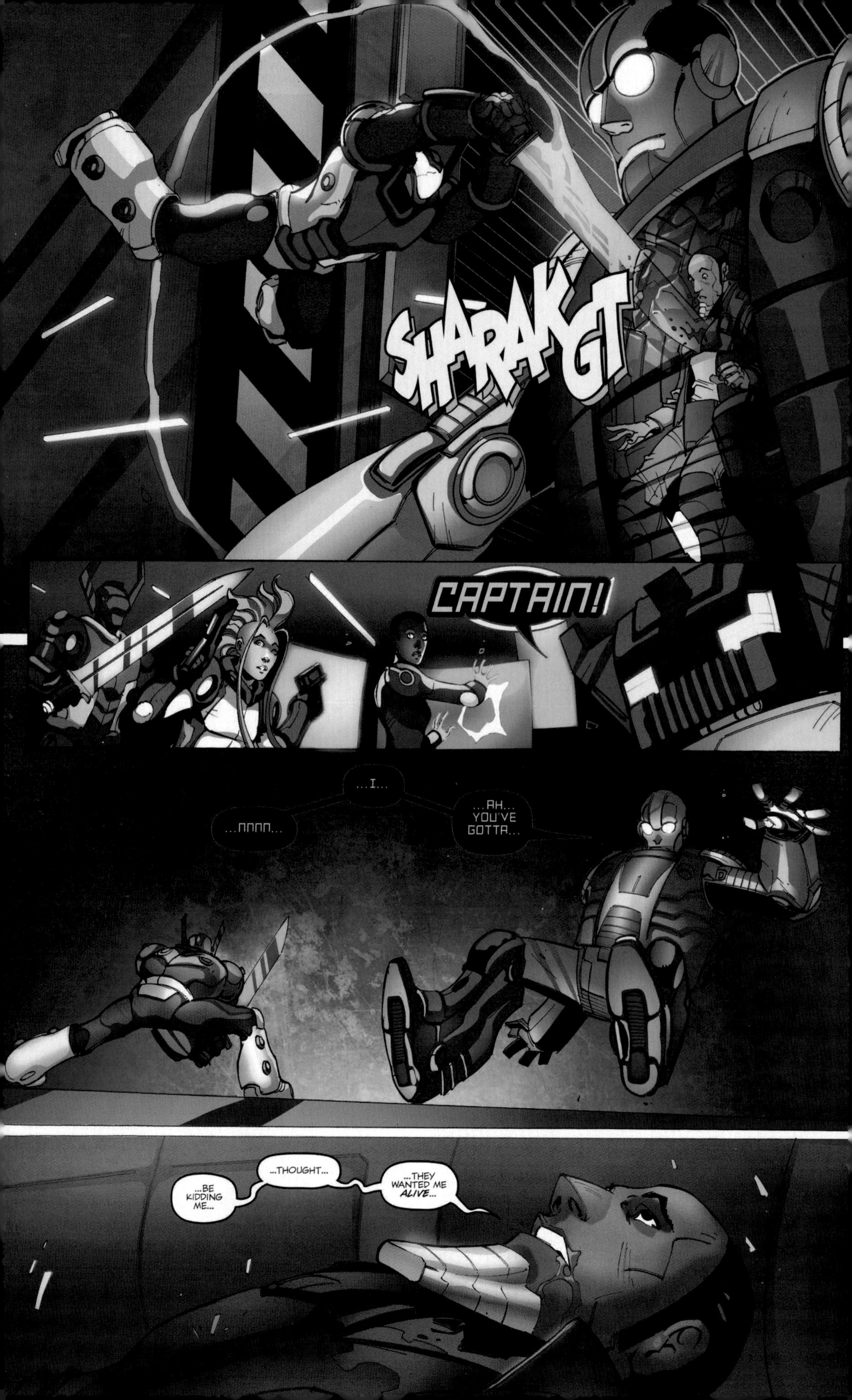
SHARAKGT
CAPTAIN!
...NNNN...
...I...
...AH... YOU'VE GOTTA...
...BE KIDDING ME...
...THOUGHT...
...THEY WANTED ME ALIVE...

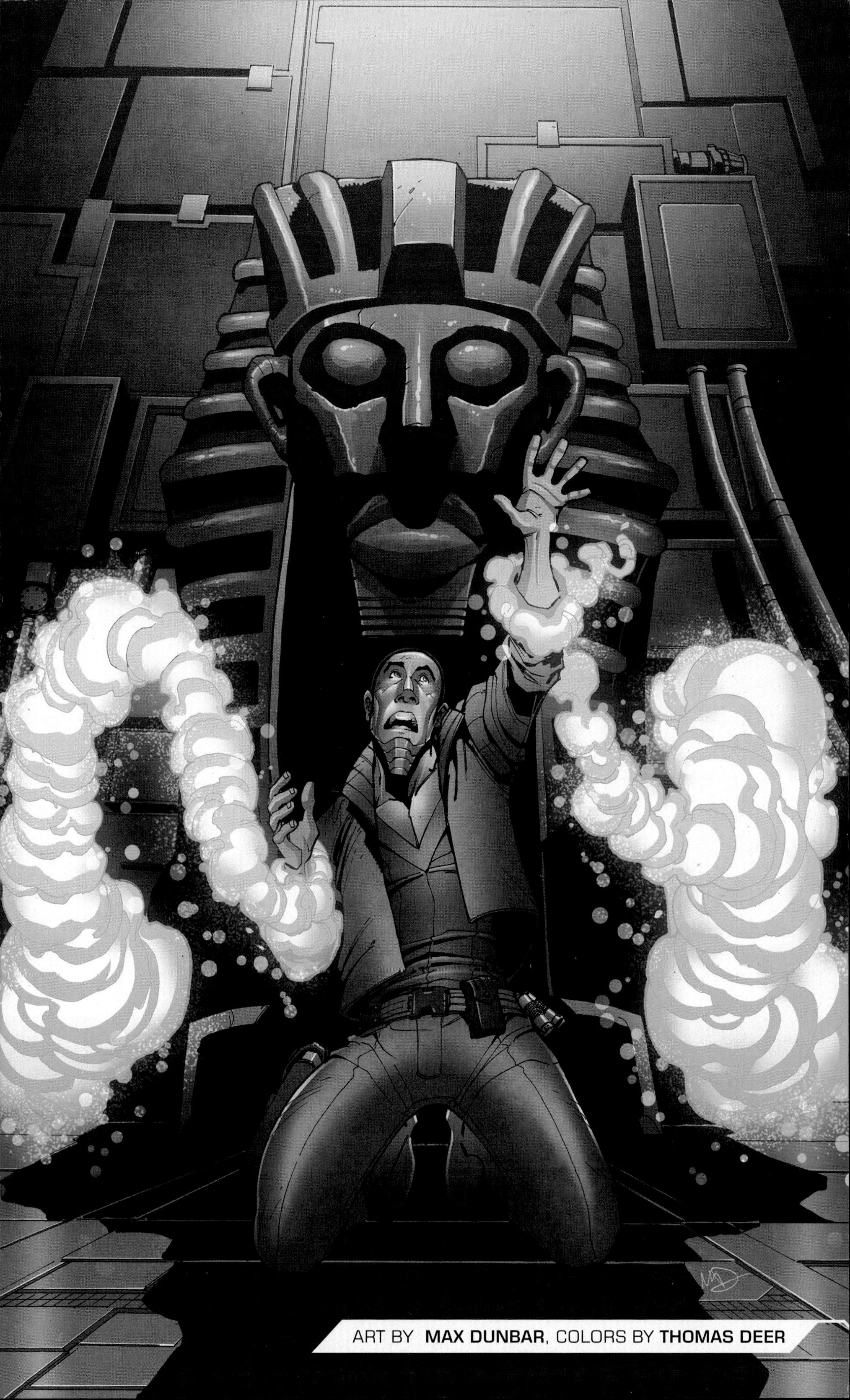

ART BY **MAX DUNBAR**, COLORS BY **THOMAS DEER**

06

ART BY **MAX DUNBAR**, COLORS BY **THOMAS DEER**

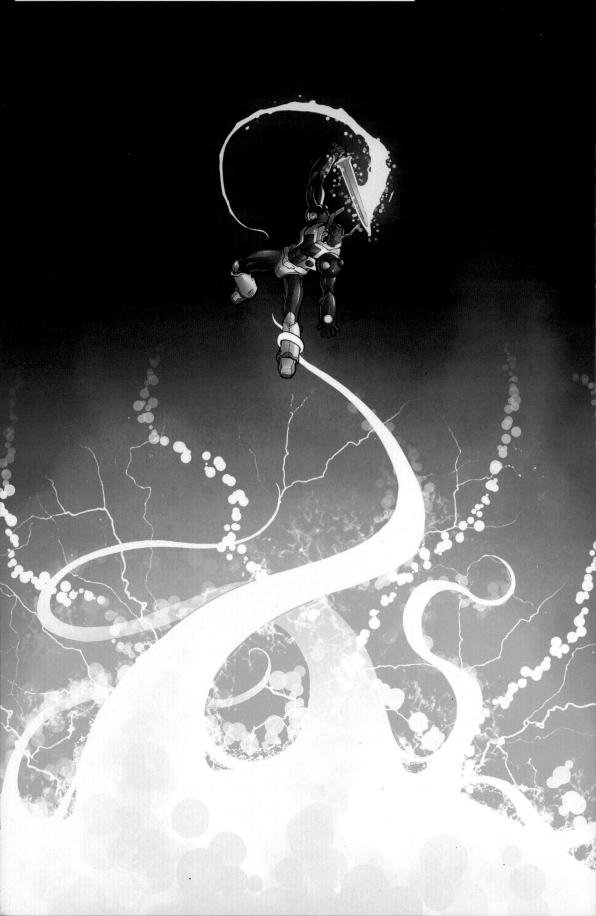

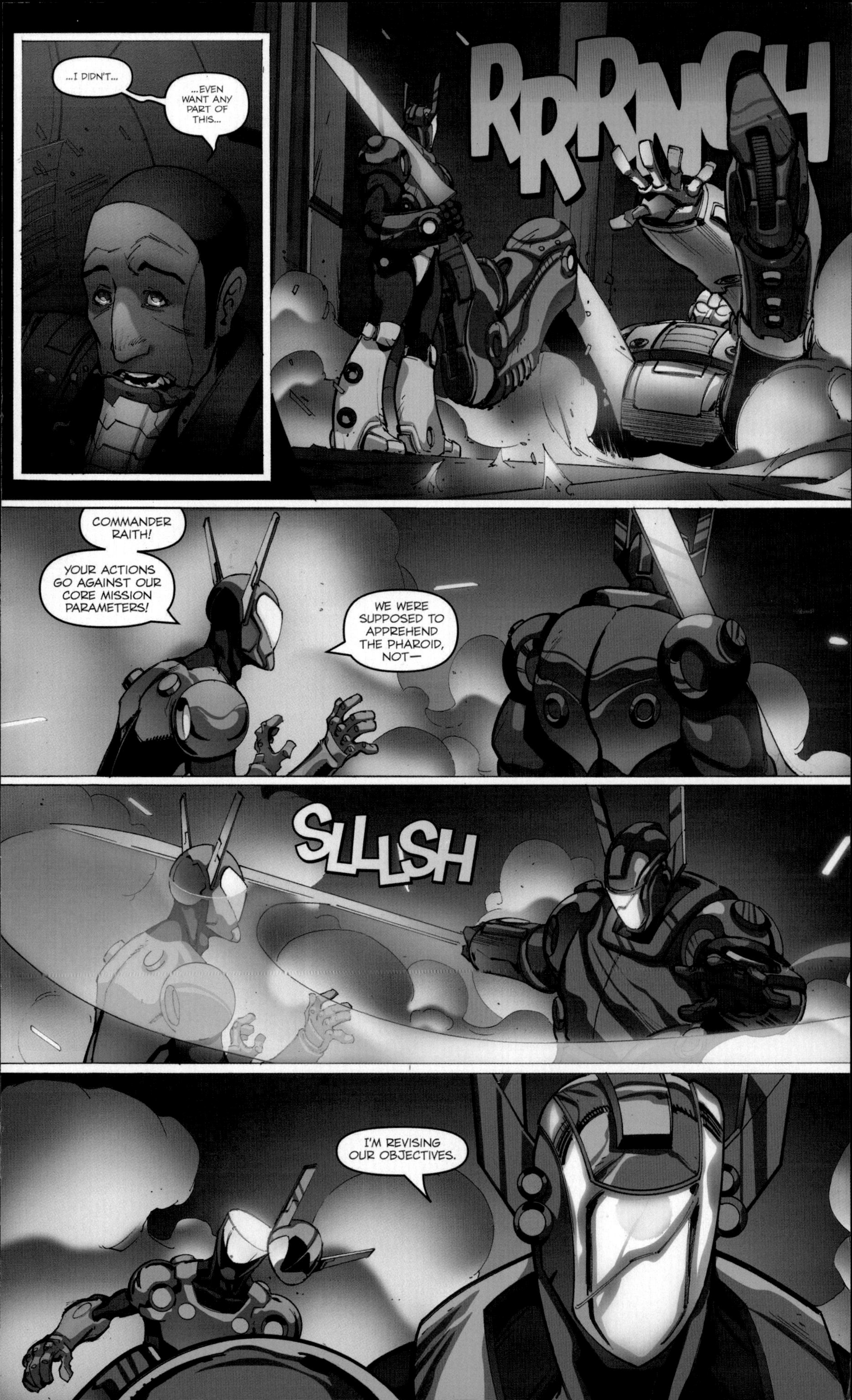
...I DIDN'T...
...EVEN WANT ANY PART OF THIS...
RRRNCH
COMMANDER RAITH!
YOUR ACTIONS GO AGAINST OUR CORE MISSION PARAMETERS!
WE WERE SUPPOSED TO APPREHEND THE PHAROID, NOT—
SLLLSH
I'M REVISING OUR OBJECTIVES.

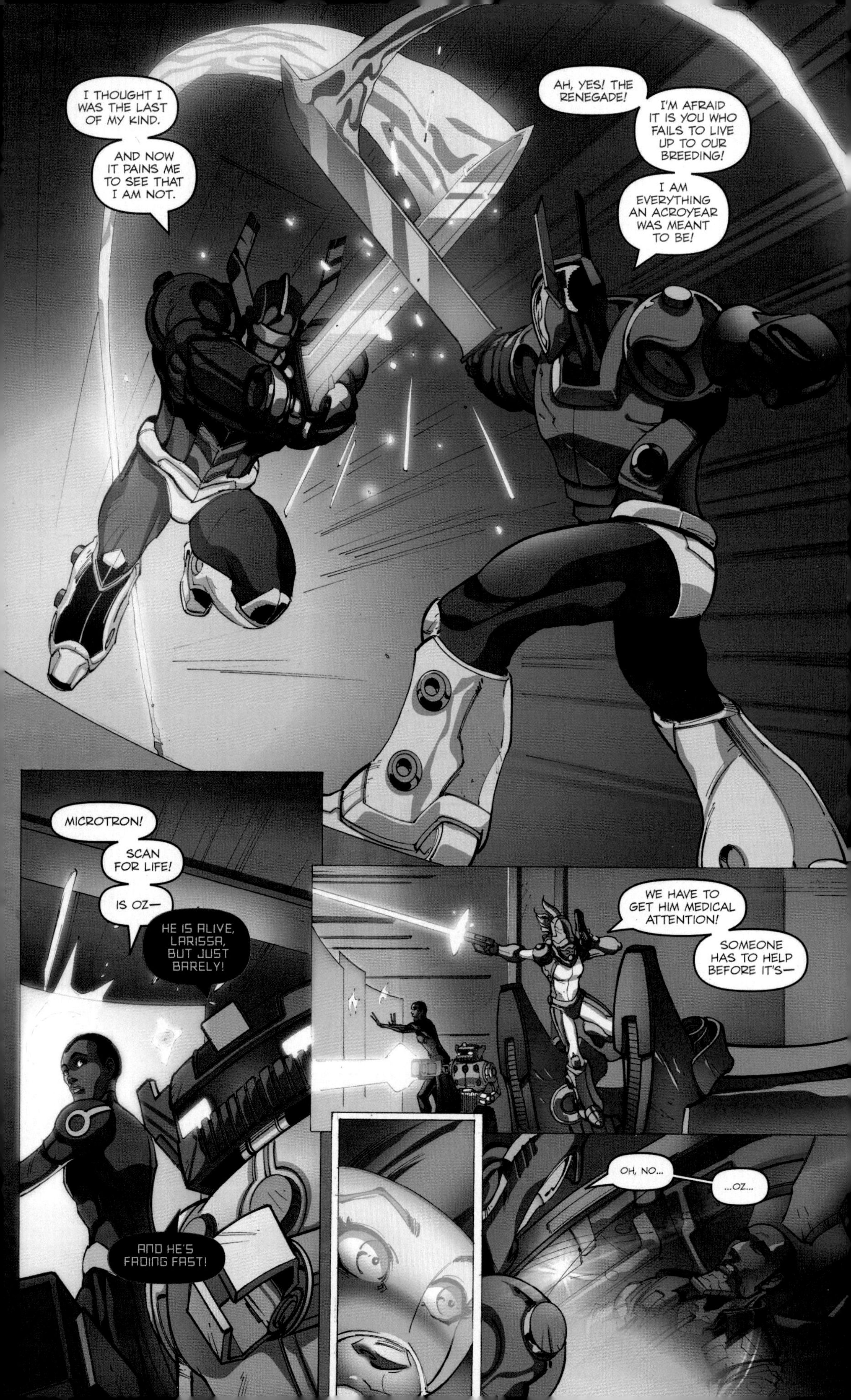
I THOUGHT I WAS THE LAST OF MY KIND.
AND NOW IT PAINS ME TO SEE THAT I AM NOT.
AH, YES! THE RENEGADE!
I'M AFRAID IT IS YOU WHO FAILS TO LIVE UP TO OUR BREEDING!
I AM EVERYTHING AN ACROYEAR WAS MEANT TO BE!
MICROTRON!
SCAN FOR LIFE!
IS OZ—
HE IS ALIVE, LARISSA, BUT JUST BARELY!
AND HE'S FADING FAST!
WE HAVE TO GET HIM MEDICAL ATTENTION!
SOMEONE HAS TO HELP BEFORE IT'S—
OH, NO...
...OZ...

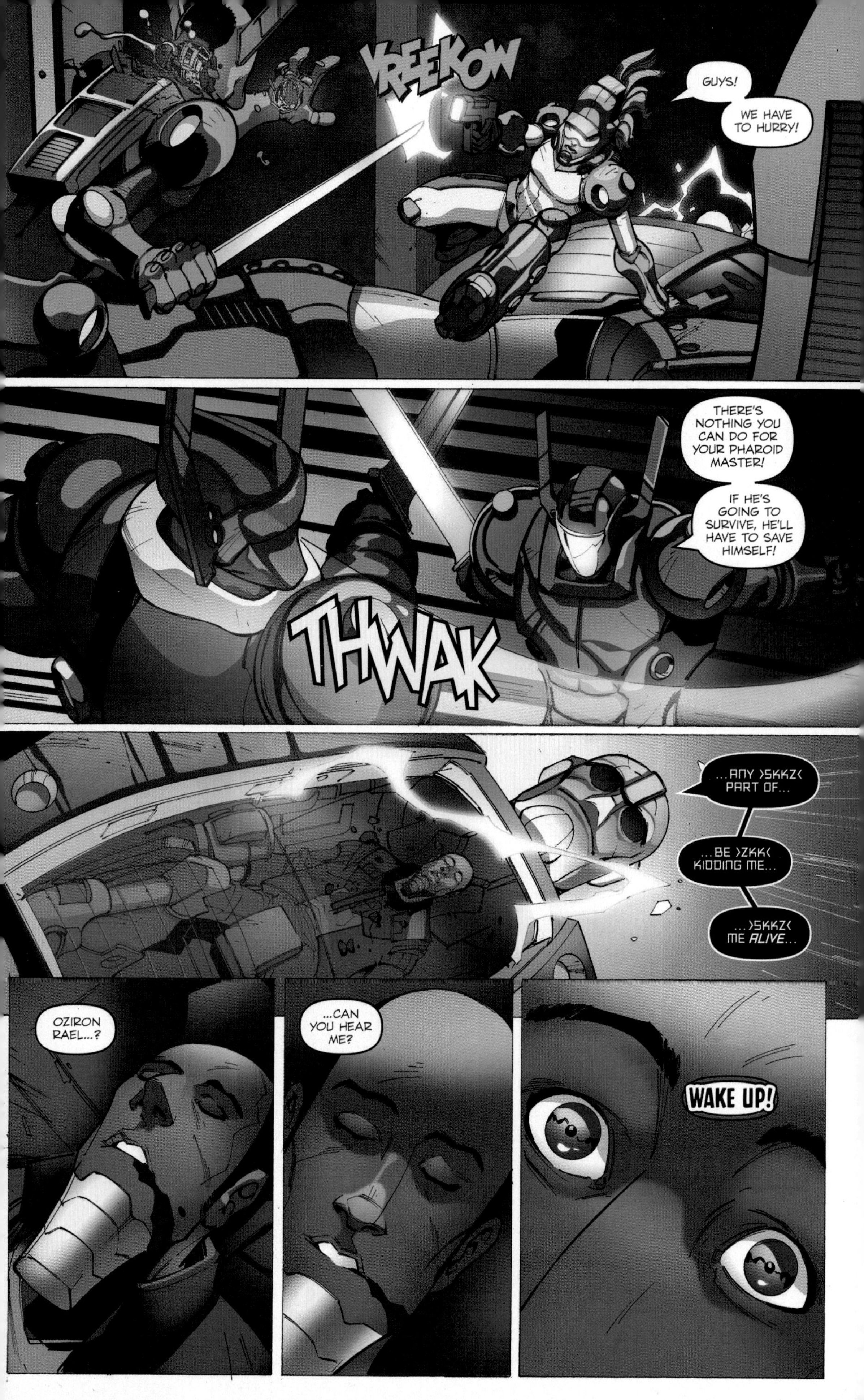
VREEKOW
GUYS!
WE HAVE TO HURRY!
THERE'S NOTHING YOU CAN DO FOR YOUR PHAROID MASTER!
IF HE'S GOING TO SURVIVE, HE'LL HAVE TO SAVE HIMSELF!
THWAK
...ANY >SKKZ< PART OF...
...BE >ZKK< KIDDING ME...
...>SKKZ< ME *ALIVE*...
OZIRON RAEL...?
...CAN YOU HEAR ME?
WAKE UP!

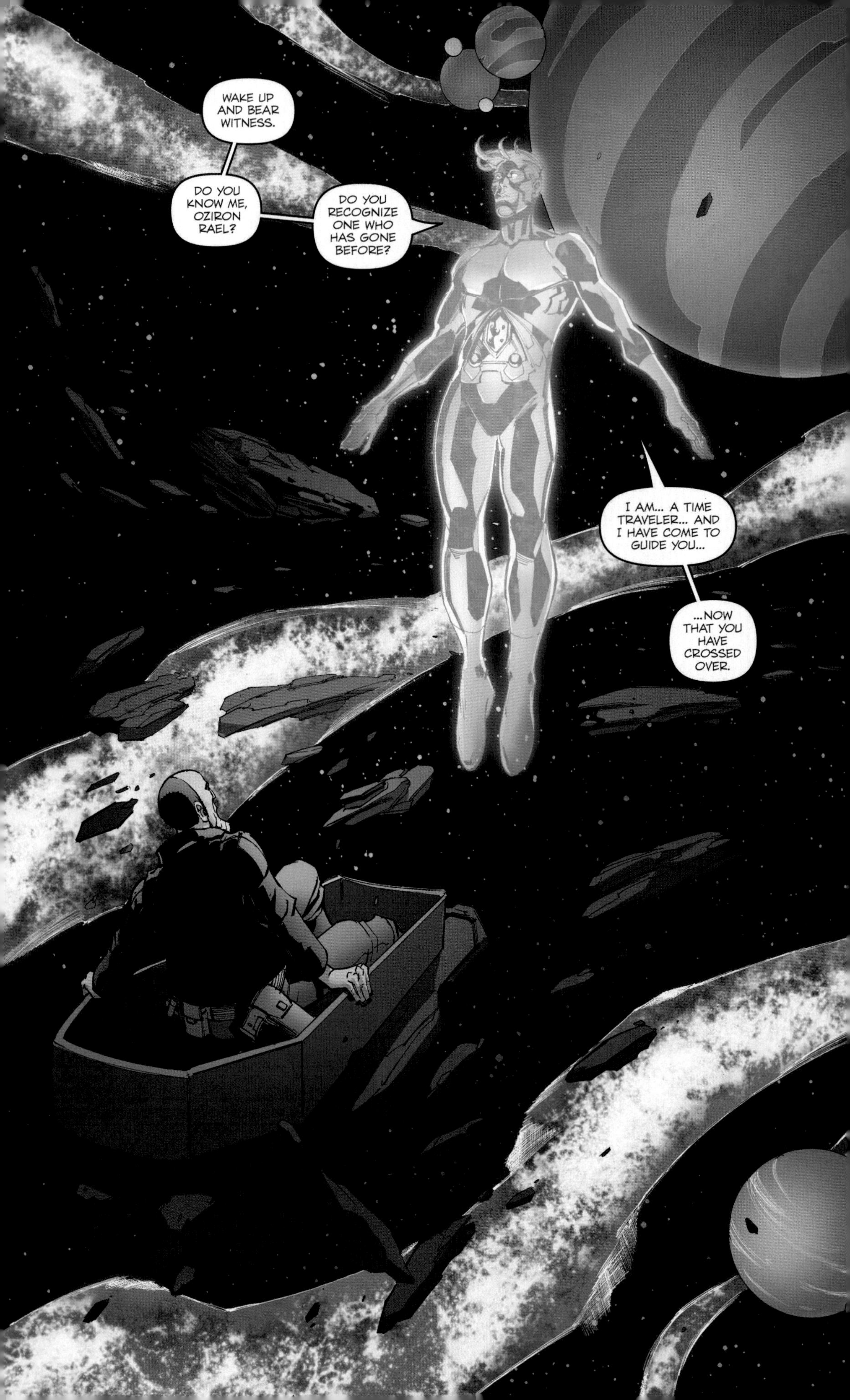
WAKE UP AND BEAR WITNESS.
DO YOU KNOW ME, OZIRON RAEL?
DO YOU RECOGNIZE ONE WHO HAS GONE BEFORE?
I AM... A TIME TRAVELER... AND I HAVE COME TO GUIDE YOU...
...NOW THAT YOU HAVE CROSSED OVER.

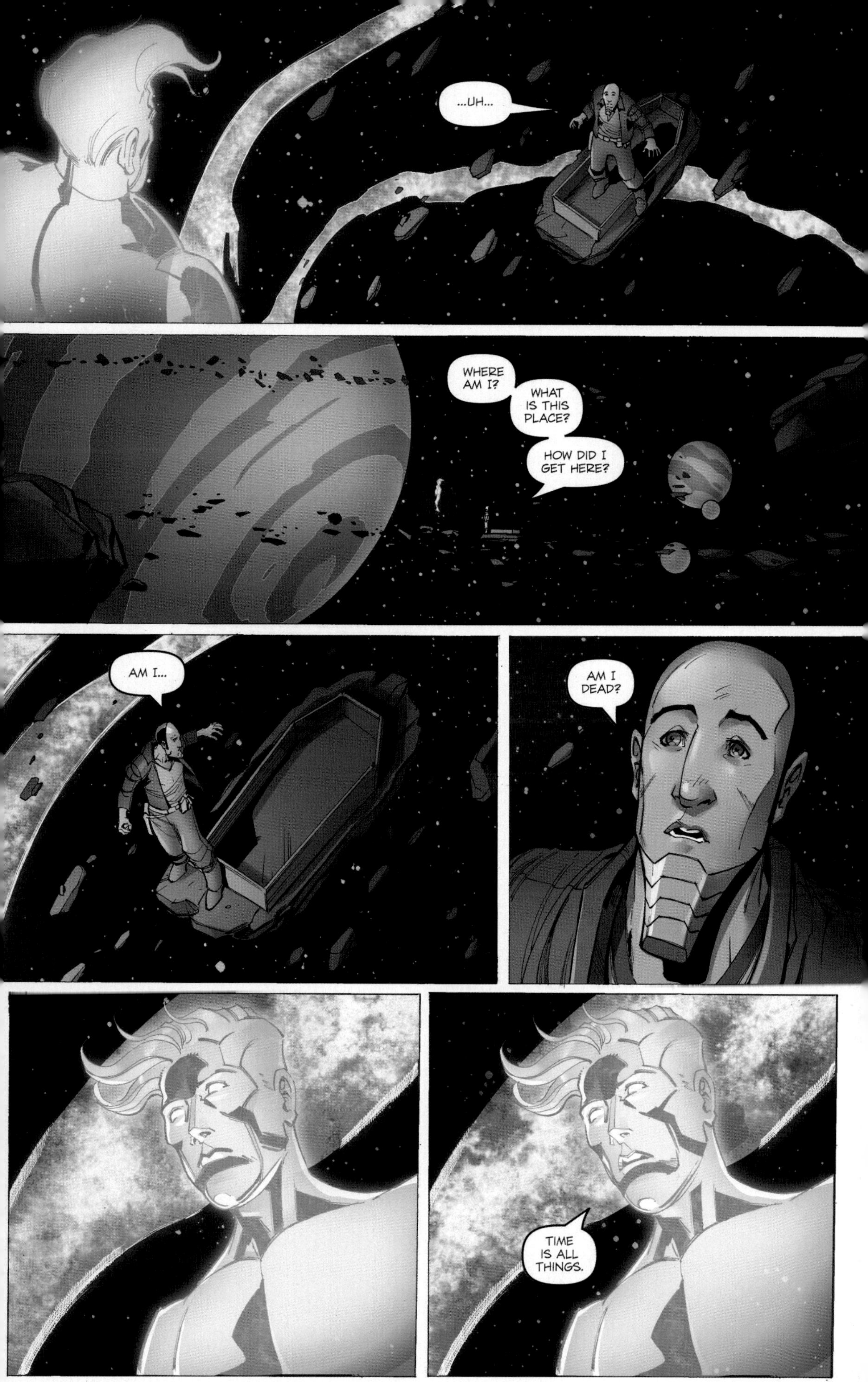
...UH...
WHERE AM I?
WHAT IS THIS PLACE?
HOW DID I GET HERE?
AM I...
AM I DEAD?
TIME IS ALL THINGS.

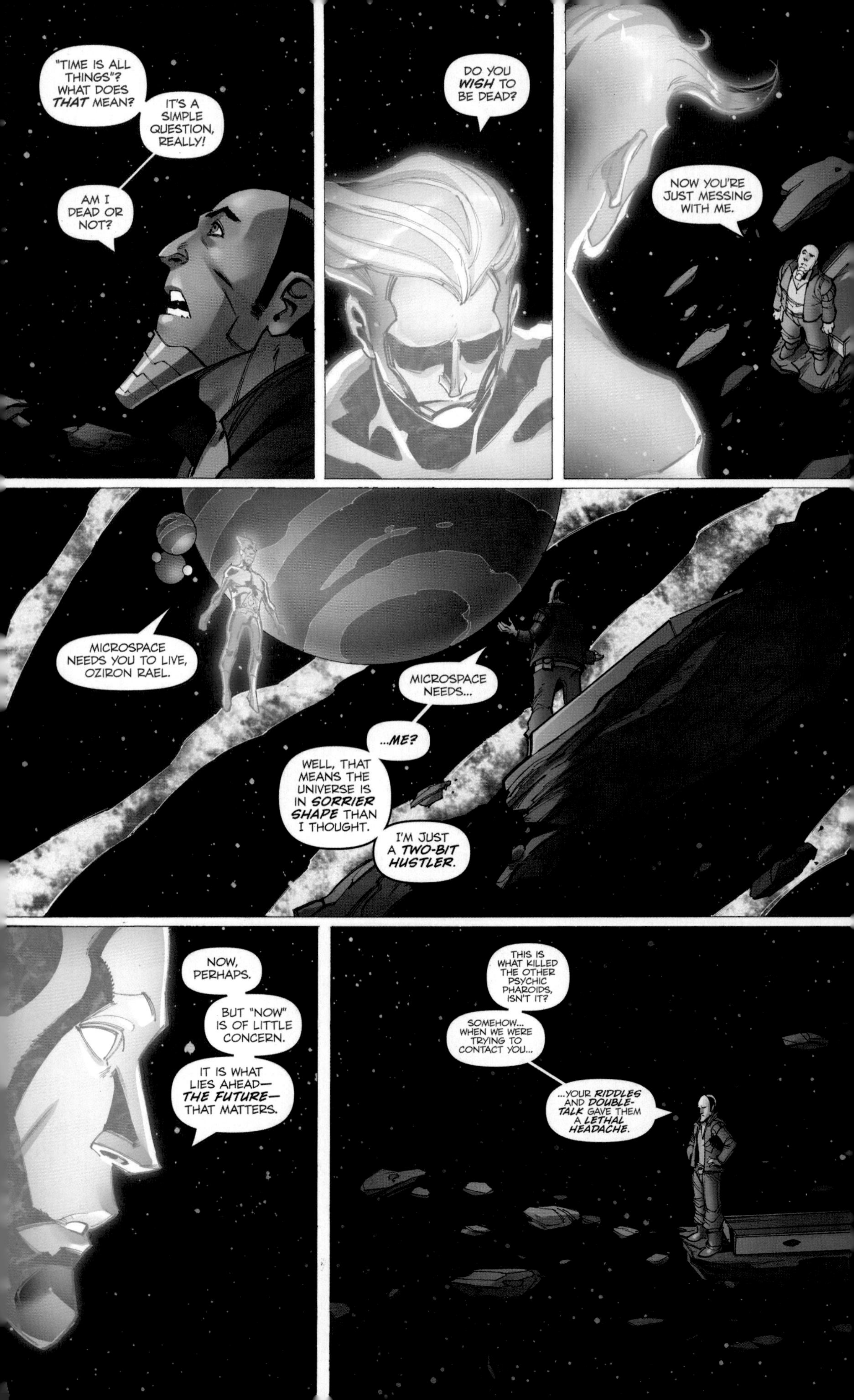
"TIME IS ALL THINGS"? WHAT DOES THAT MEAN?
IT'S A SIMPLE QUESTION, REALLY!
AM I DEAD OR NOT?
DO YOU WISH TO BE DEAD?
NOW YOU'RE JUST MESSING WITH ME.
MICROSPACE NEEDS YOU TO LIVE, OZIRON RAEL.
MICROSPACE NEEDS...
...ME?
WELL, THAT MEANS THE UNIVERSE IS IN SORRIER SHAPE THAN I THOUGHT.
I'M JUST A TWO-BIT HUSTLER.
NOW, PERHAPS.
BUT "NOW" IS OF LITTLE CONCERN.
IT IS WHAT LIES AHEAD— THE FUTURE— THAT MATTERS.
THIS IS WHAT KILLED THE OTHER PSYCHIC PHAROIDS, ISN'T IT?
SOMEHOW... WHEN WE WERE TRYING TO CONTACT YOU...
...YOUR RIDDLES AND DOUBLE-TALK GAVE THEM A LETHAL HEADACHE.

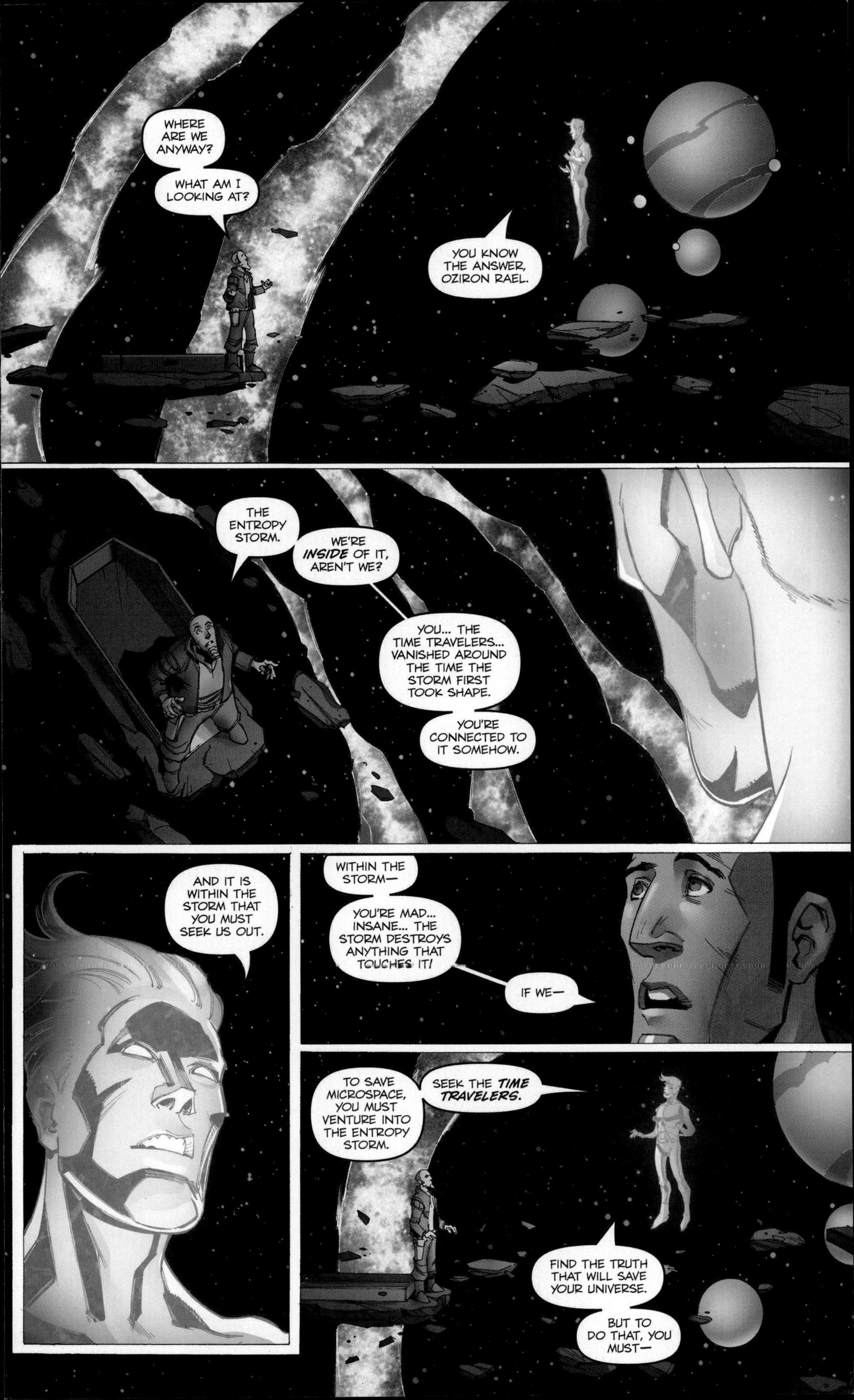
WHERE ARE WE ANYWAY?
WHAT AM I LOOKING AT?
YOU KNOW THE ANSWER, OZIRON RAEL.
THE ENTROPY STORM.
WE'RE *INSIDE* OF IT, AREN'T WE?
YOU... THE TIME TRAVELERS... VANISHED AROUND THE TIME THE STORM FIRST TOOK SHAPE.
YOU'RE CONNECTED TO IT SOMEHOW.
AND IT IS WITHIN THE STORM THAT YOU MUST SEEK US OUT.
WITHIN THE STORM—
YOU'RE MAD... INSANE... THE STORM DESTROYS ANYTHING THAT TOUCHES IT!
IF WE—
TO SAVE MICROSPACE, YOU MUST VENTURE INTO THE ENTROPY STORM.
SEEK THE *TIME TRAVELERS.*
FIND THE TRUTH THAT WILL SAVE YOUR UNIVERSE.
BUT TO DO THAT, YOU MUST—

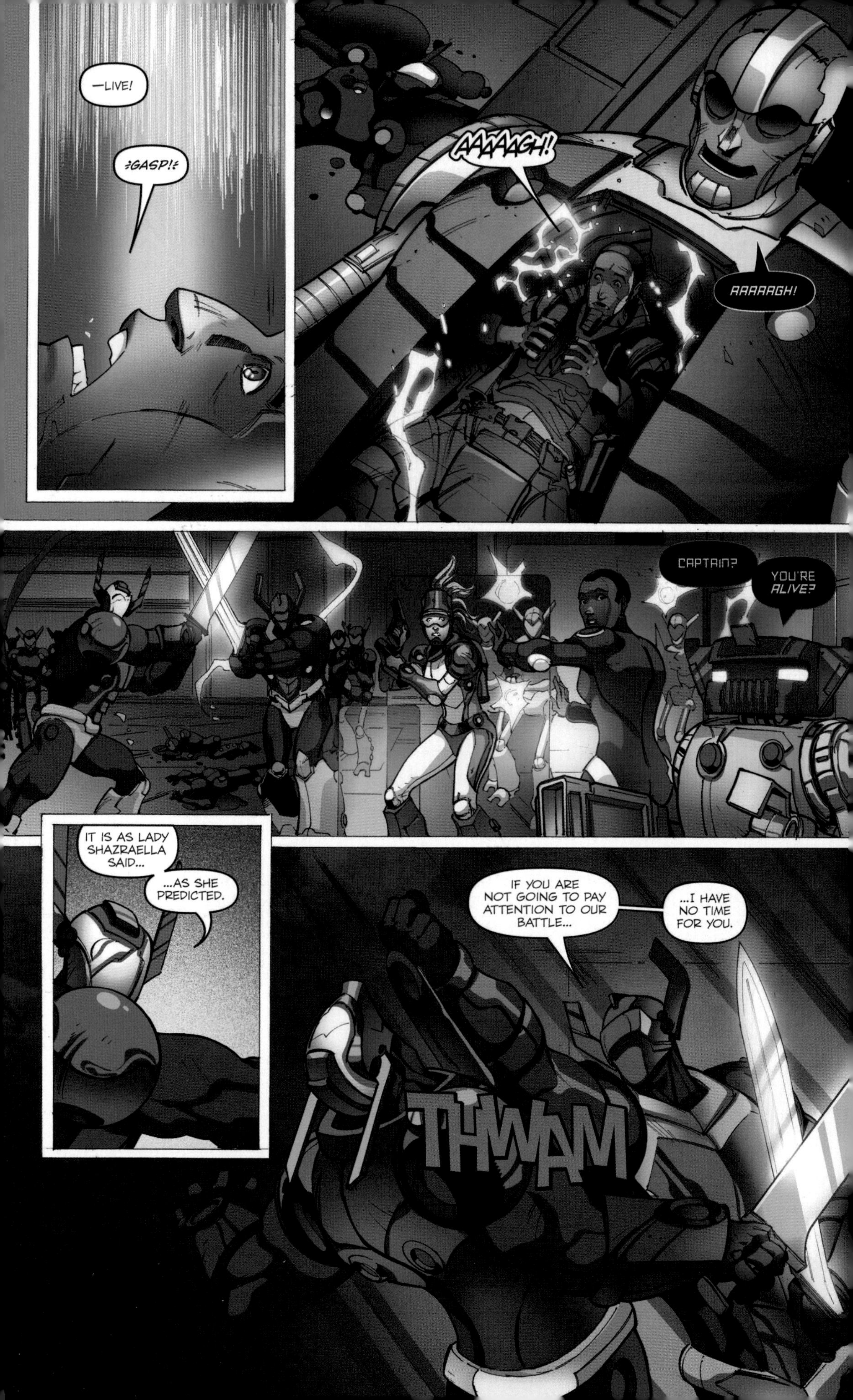
—LIVE!
GASP!
AAAAAGH!
AAAAAGH!
CAPTAIN?
YOU'RE ALIVE?
IT IS AS LADY SHAZRAELLA SAID...
...AS SHE PREDICTED.
IF YOU ARE NOT GOING TO PAY ATTENTION TO OUR BATTLE...
...I HAVE NO TIME FOR YOU.
THWAM

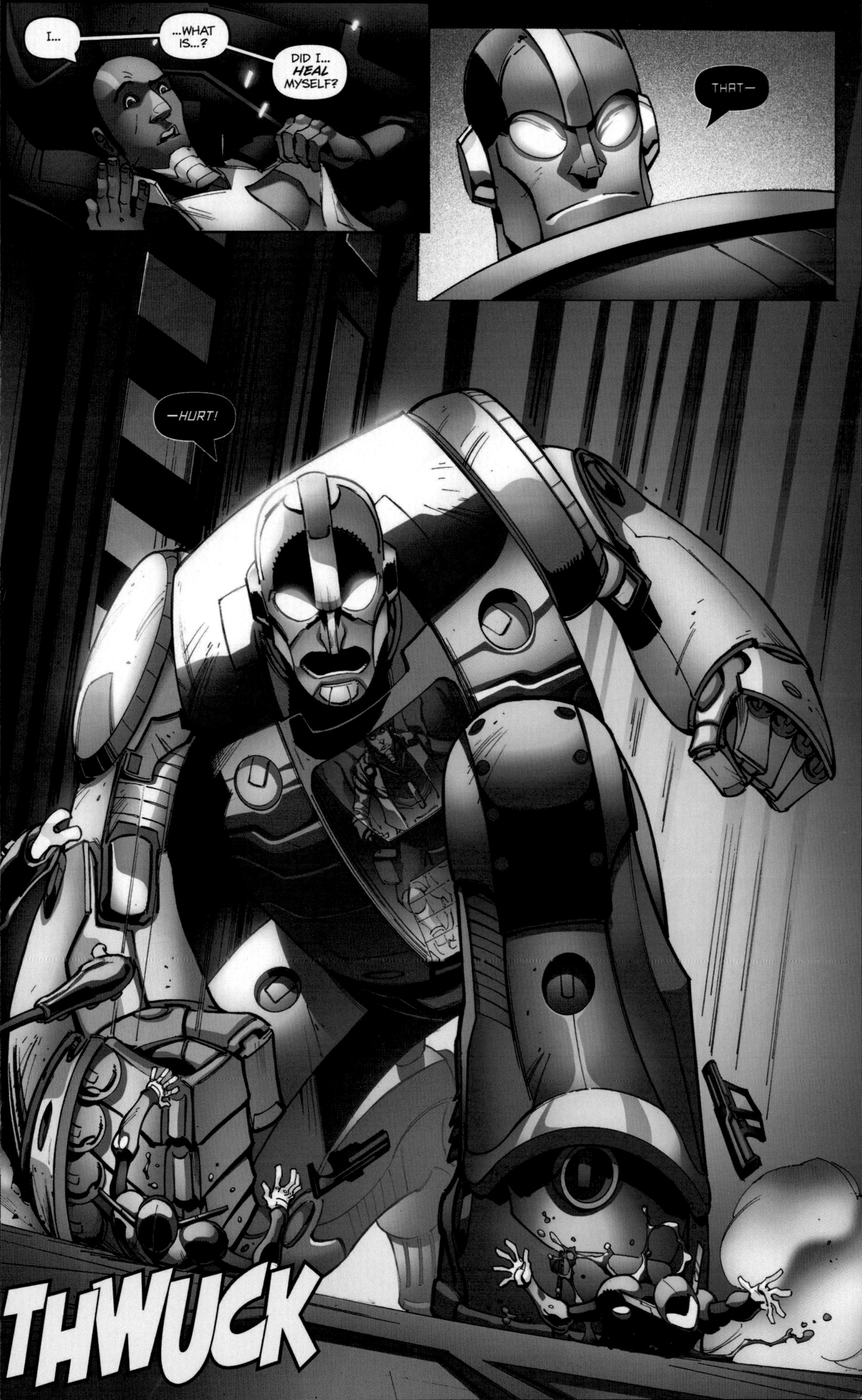
I...
...WHAT IS...?
DID I... HEAL MYSELF?
THAT—
—HURT!
THWUCK

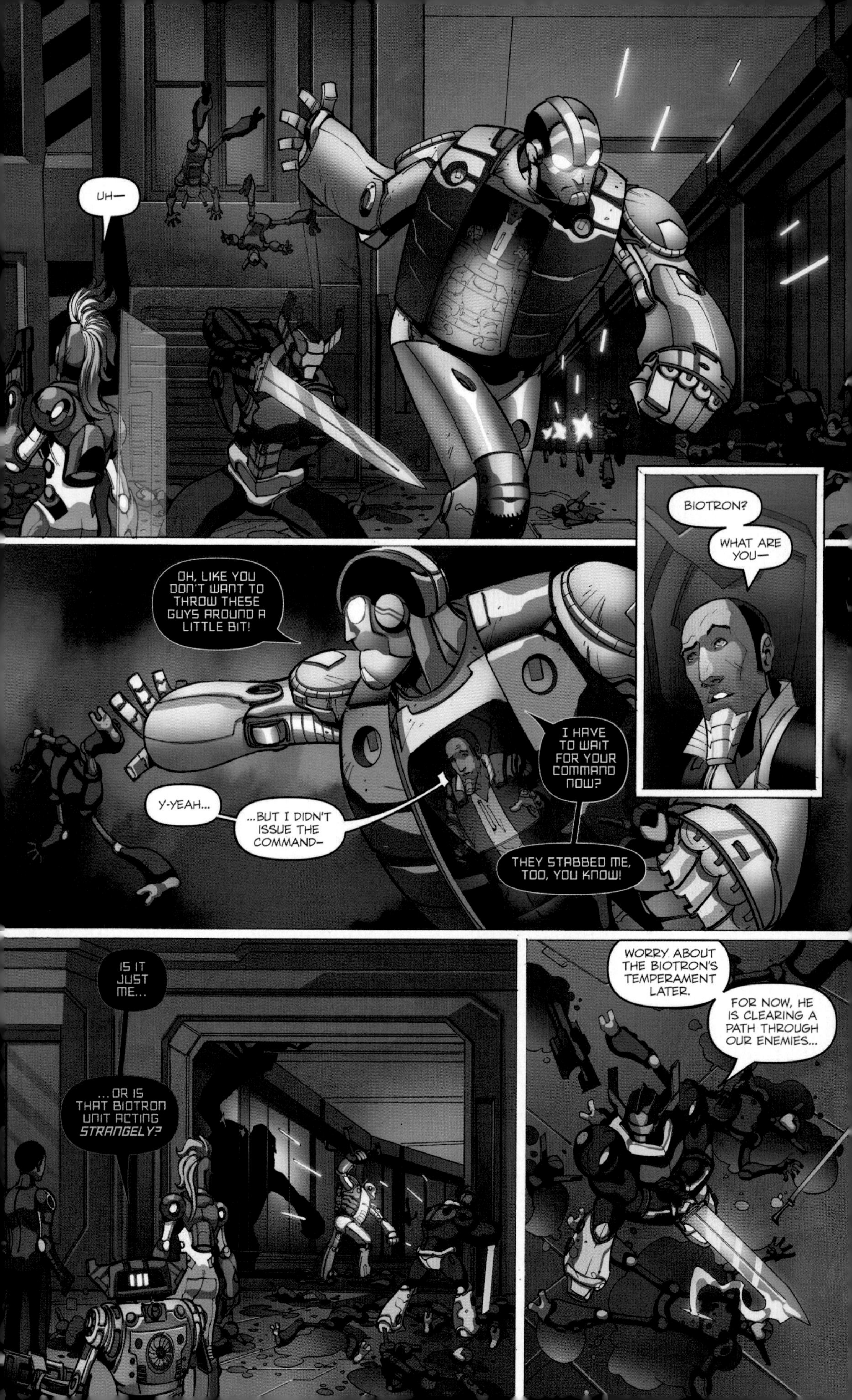
UH—
BIOTRON?
WHAT ARE YOU—
OH, LIKE YOU DON'T WANT TO THROW THESE GUYS AROUND A LITTLE BIT!
Y-YEAH...
...BUT I DIDN'T ISSUE THE COMMAND—
I HAVE TO WAIT FOR YOUR COMMAND NOW?
THEY STABBED ME, TOO, YOU KNOW!
IS IT JUST ME...
...OR IS THAT BIOTRON UNIT ACTING *STRANGELY?*
WORRY ABOUT THE BIOTRON'S TEMPERAMENT LATER.
FOR NOW, HE IS CLEARING A PATH THROUGH OUR ENEMIES...

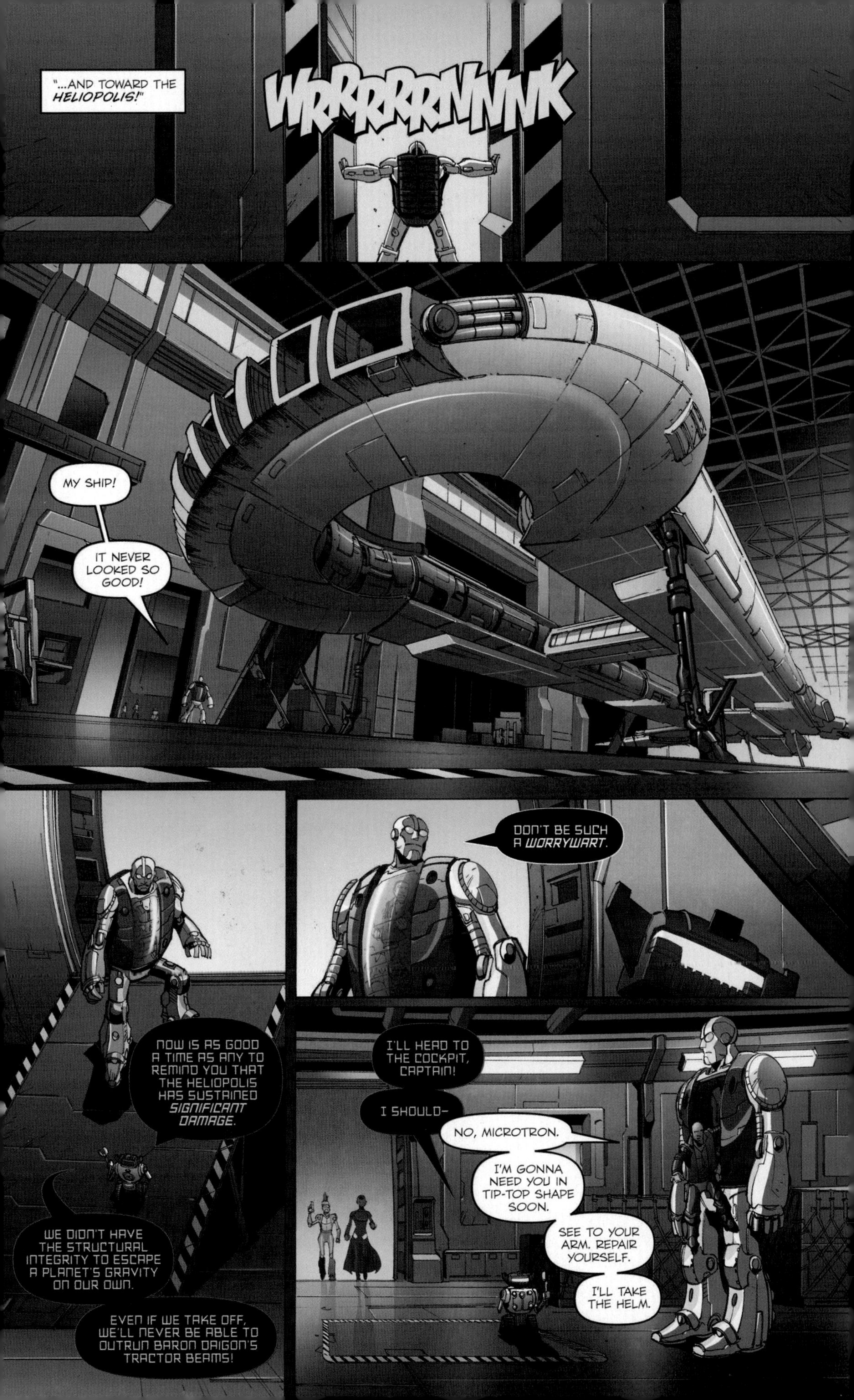

"...AND TOWARD THE *HELIOPOLIS!*"
WRRRRRNNNK
MY SHIP!
IT NEVER LOOKED SO GOOD!
NOW IS AS GOOD A TIME AS ANY TO REMIND YOU THAT THE HELIOPOLIS HAS SUSTAINED *SIGNIFICANT DAMAGE.*
WE DIDN'T HAVE THE STRUCTURAL INTEGRITY TO ESCAPE A PLANET'S GRAVITY ON OUR OWN.
EVEN IF WE TAKE OFF, WE'LL NEVER BE ABLE TO OUTRUN BARON DAIGON'S TRACTOR BEAMS!
DON'T BE SUCH A *WORRYWART.*
I'LL HEAD TO THE COCKPIT, CAPTAIN!
I SHOULD–
NO, MICROTRON.
I'M GONNA NEED YOU IN TIP-TOP SHAPE SOON.
SEE TO YOUR ARM. REPAIR YOURSELF.
I'LL TAKE THE HELM.

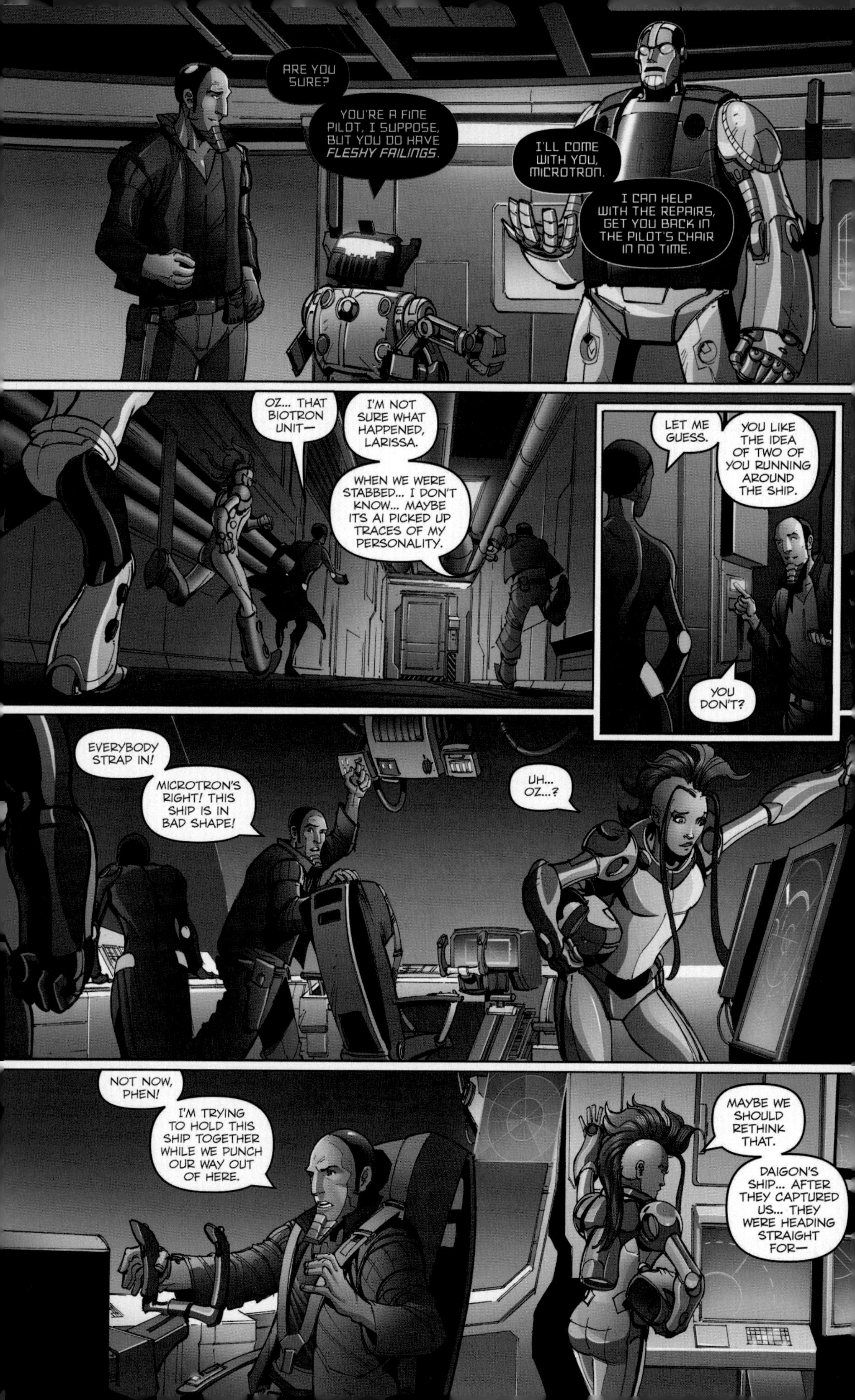
ARE YOU SURE?
YOU'RE A FINE PILOT, I SUPPOSE, BUT YOU DO HAVE FLESHY FAILINGS.
I'LL COME WITH YOU, MICROTRON.
I CAN HELP WITH THE REPAIRS, GET YOU BACK IN THE PILOT'S CHAIR IN NO TIME.
OZ... THAT BIOTRON UNIT—
I'M NOT SURE WHAT HAPPENED, LARISSA.
WHEN WE WERE STABBED... I DON'T KNOW... MAYBE ITS AI PICKED UP TRACES OF MY PERSONALITY.
LET ME GUESS.
YOU LIKE THE IDEA OF TWO OF YOU RUNNING AROUND THE SHIP.
YOU DON'T?
EVERYBODY STRAP IN!
MICROTRON'S RIGHT! THIS SHIP IS IN BAD SHAPE!
UH... OZ...?
NOT NOW, PHEN!
I'M TRYING TO HOLD THIS SHIP TOGETHER WHILE WE PUNCH OUR WAY OUT OF HERE.
MAYBE WE SHOULD RETHINK THAT.
DAIGON'S SHIP... AFTER THEY CAPTURED US... THEY WERE HEADING STRAIGHT FOR—

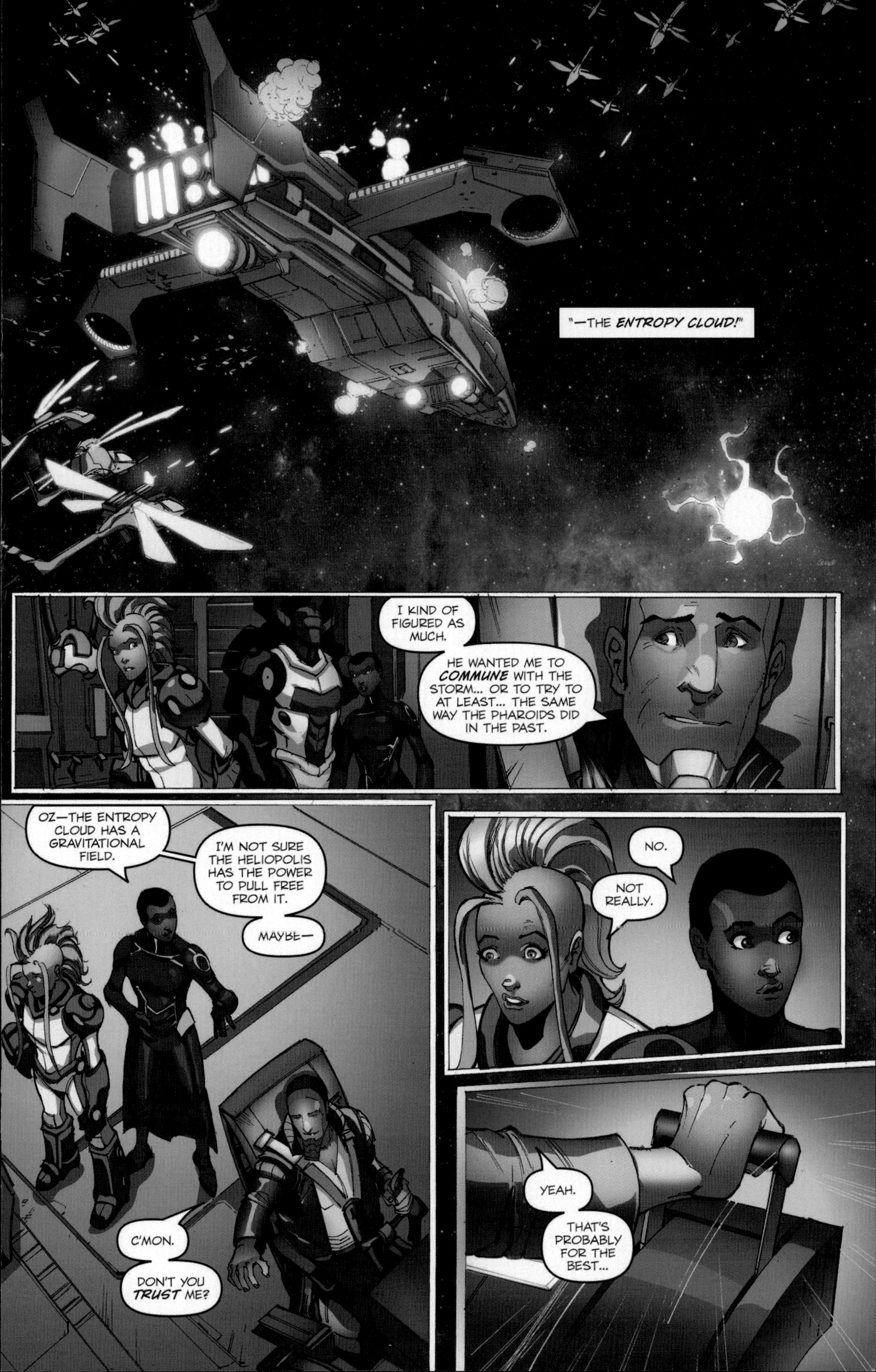
"—THE ENTROPY CLOUD!"
I KIND OF FIGURED AS MUCH.
HE WANTED ME TO COMMUNE WITH THE STORM... OR TO TRY TO AT LEAST... THE SAME WAY THE PHAROIDS DID IN THE PAST.
OZ—THE ENTROPY CLOUD HAS A GRAVITATIONAL FIELD.
I'M NOT SURE THE HELIOPOLIS HAS THE POWER TO PULL FREE FROM IT.
MAYBE—
C'MON.
DON'T YOU TRUST ME?
NO.
NOT REALLY.
YEAH.
THAT'S PROBABLY FOR THE BEST...

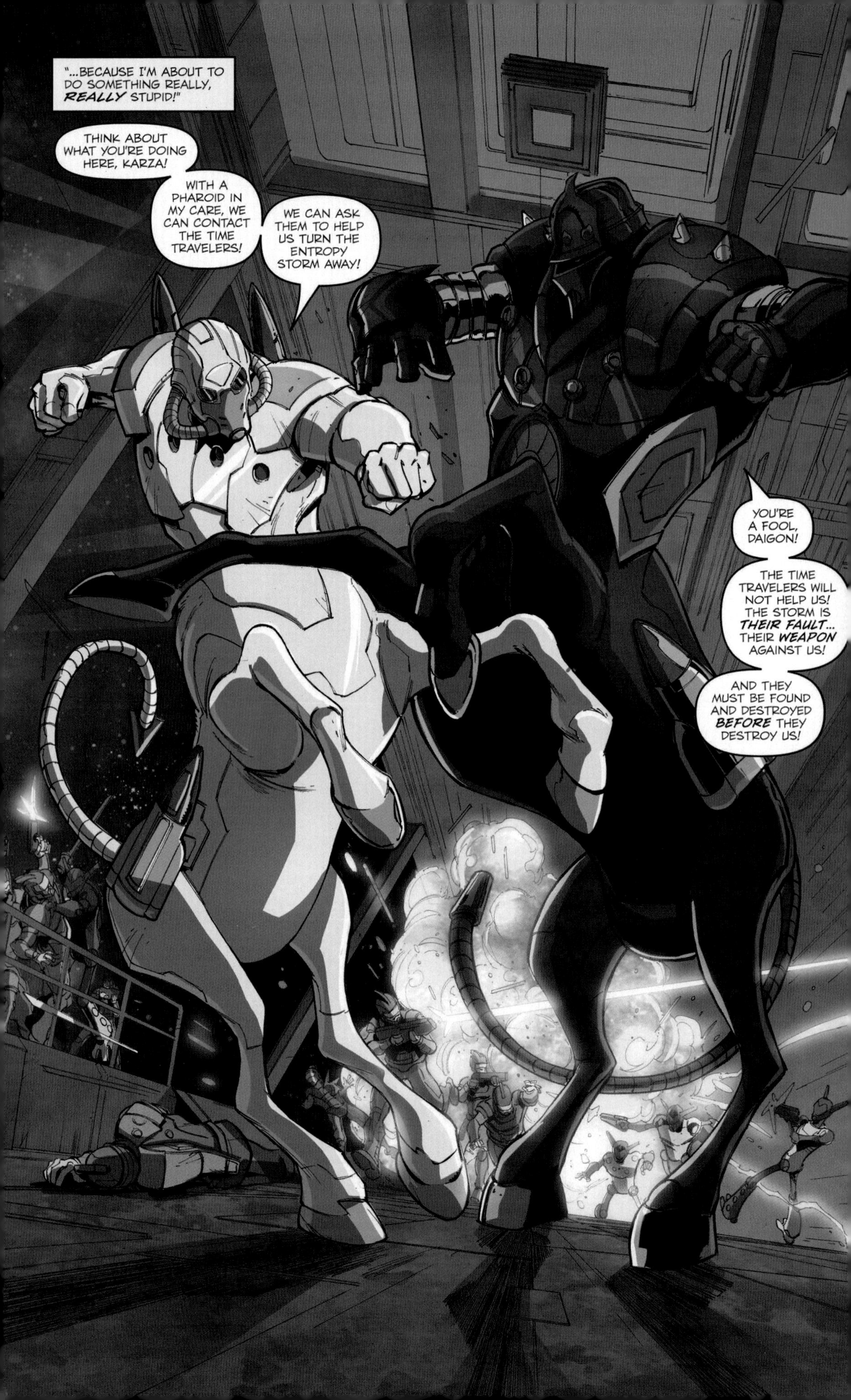
"...BECAUSE I'M ABOUT TO DO SOMETHING REALLY, ***REALLY*** STUPID!"
THINK ABOUT WHAT YOU'RE DOING HERE, KARZA!
WITH A PHAROID IN MY CARE, WE CAN CONTACT THE TIME TRAVELERS!
WE CAN ASK THEM TO HELP US TURN THE ENTROPY STORM AWAY!
YOU'RE A FOOL, DAIGON!
THE TIME TRAVELERS WILL NOT HELP US! THE STORM IS ***THEIR FAULT***... THEIR ***WEAPON*** AGAINST US!
AND THEY MUST BE FOUND AND DESTROYED ***BEFORE*** THEY DESTROY US!

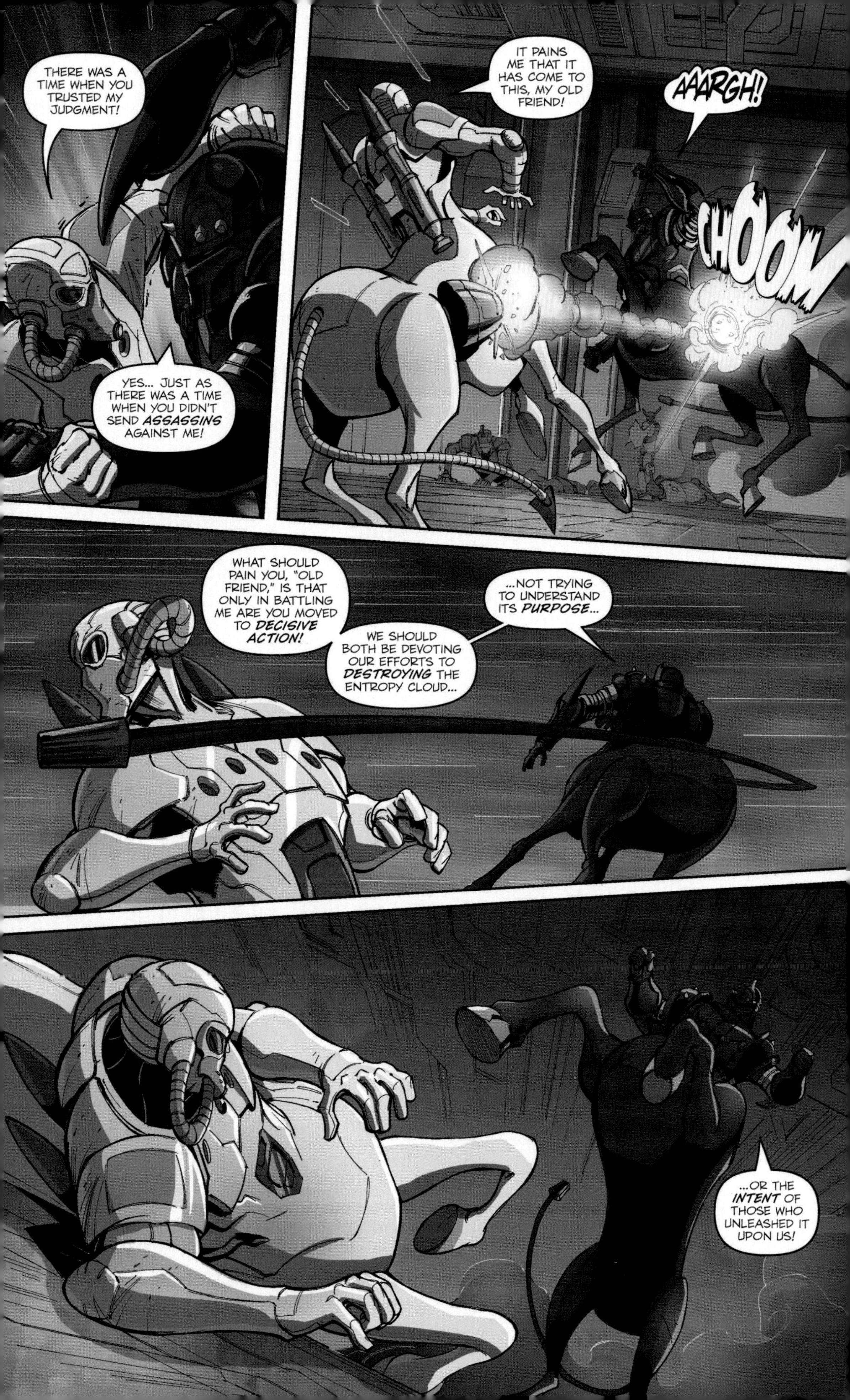
THERE WAS A TIME WHEN YOU TRUSTED MY JUDGMENT!
YES... JUST AS THERE WAS A TIME WHEN YOU DIDN'T SEND ASSASSINS AGAINST ME!
IT PAINS ME THAT IT HAS COME TO THIS, MY OLD FRIEND!
AAARGH!
CHOOOM
WHAT SHOULD PAIN YOU, "OLD FRIEND," IS THAT ONLY IN BATTLING ME ARE YOU MOVED TO DECISIVE ACTION!
WE SHOULD BOTH BE DEVOTING OUR EFFORTS TO DESTROYING THE ENTROPY CLOUD...
...NOT TRYING TO UNDERSTAND ITS PURPOSE...
...OR THE INTENT OF THOSE WHO UNLEASHED IT UPON US!

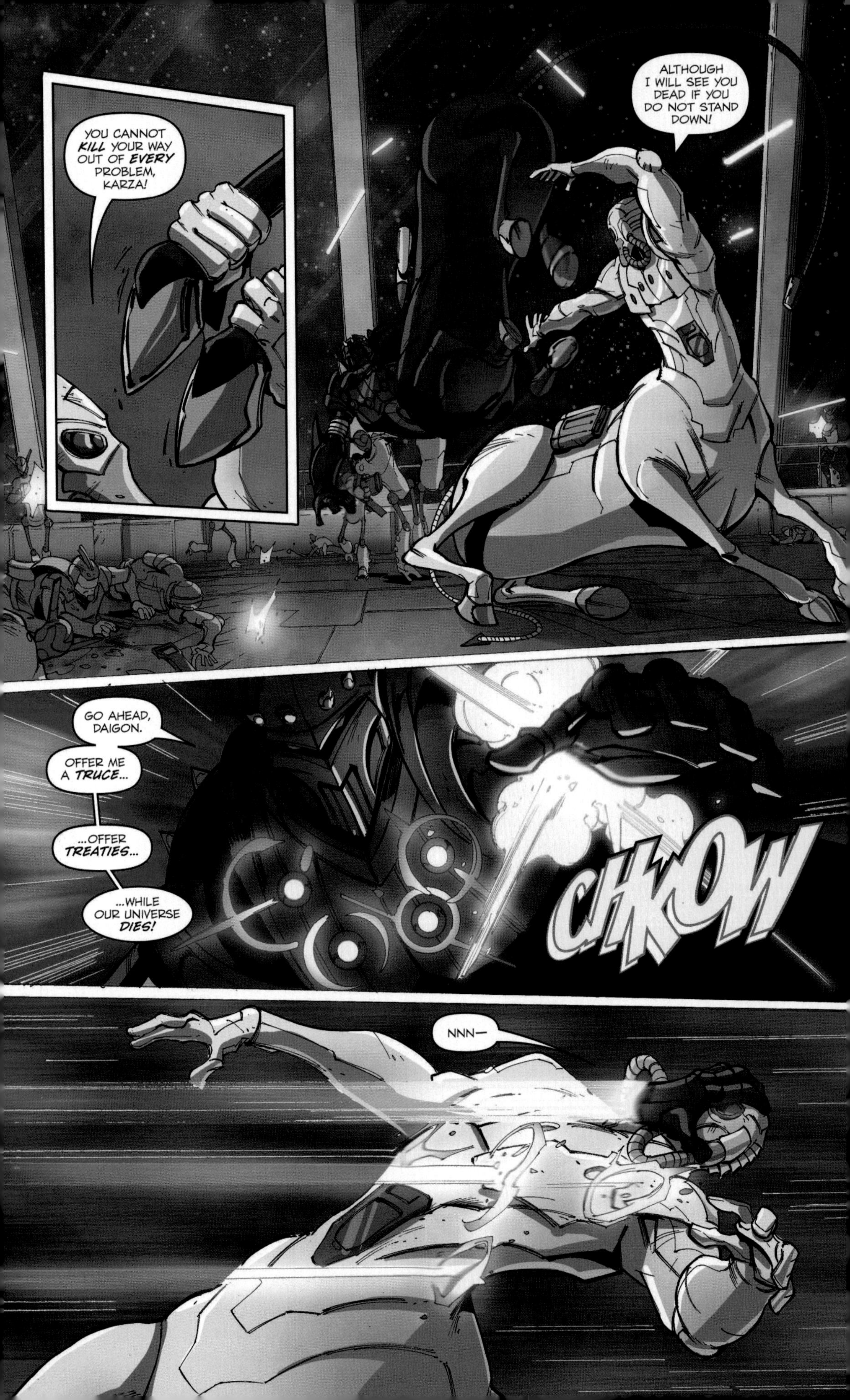
YOU CANNOT KILL YOUR WAY OUT OF EVERY PROBLEM, KARZA!
ALTHOUGH I WILL SEE YOU DEAD IF YOU DO NOT STAND DOWN!
GO AHEAD, DAIGON.
OFFER ME A TRUCE...
...OFFER TREATIES...
...WHILE OUR UNIVERSE DIES!
CHOW
NNN—

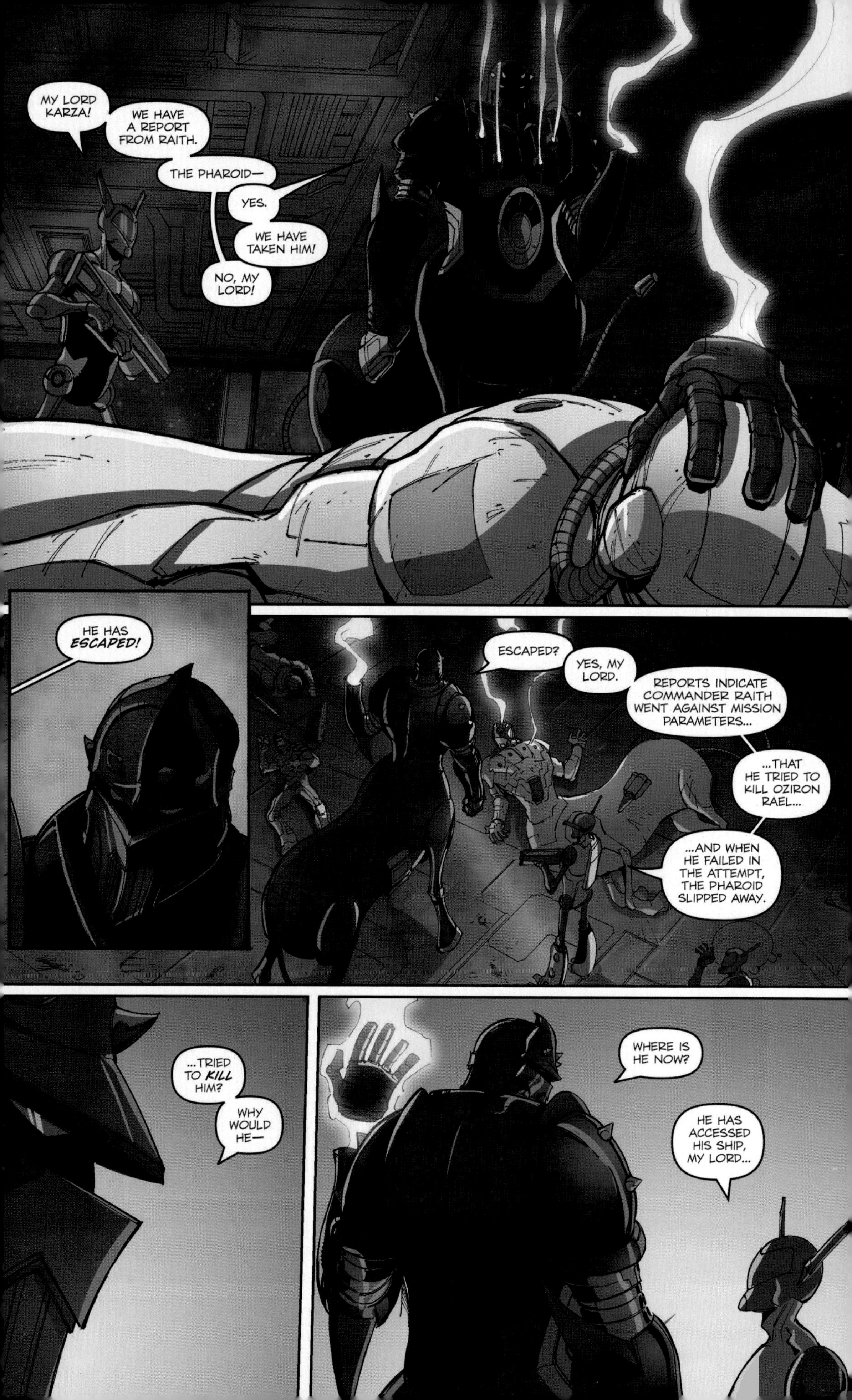
MY LORD KARZA!
WE HAVE A REPORT FROM RAITH.
THE PHAROID—
YES.
WE HAVE TAKEN HIM!
NO, MY LORD!
HE HAS ESCAPED!
ESCAPED?
YES, MY LORD.
REPORTS INDICATE COMMANDER RAITH WENT AGAINST MISSION PARAMETERS...
...THAT HE TRIED TO KILL OZIRON RAEL...
...AND WHEN HE FAILED IN THE ATTEMPT, THE PHAROID SLIPPED AWAY.
...TRIED TO KILL HIM?
WHY WOULD HE—
WHERE IS HE NOW?
HE HAS ACCESSED HIS SHIP, MY LORD...

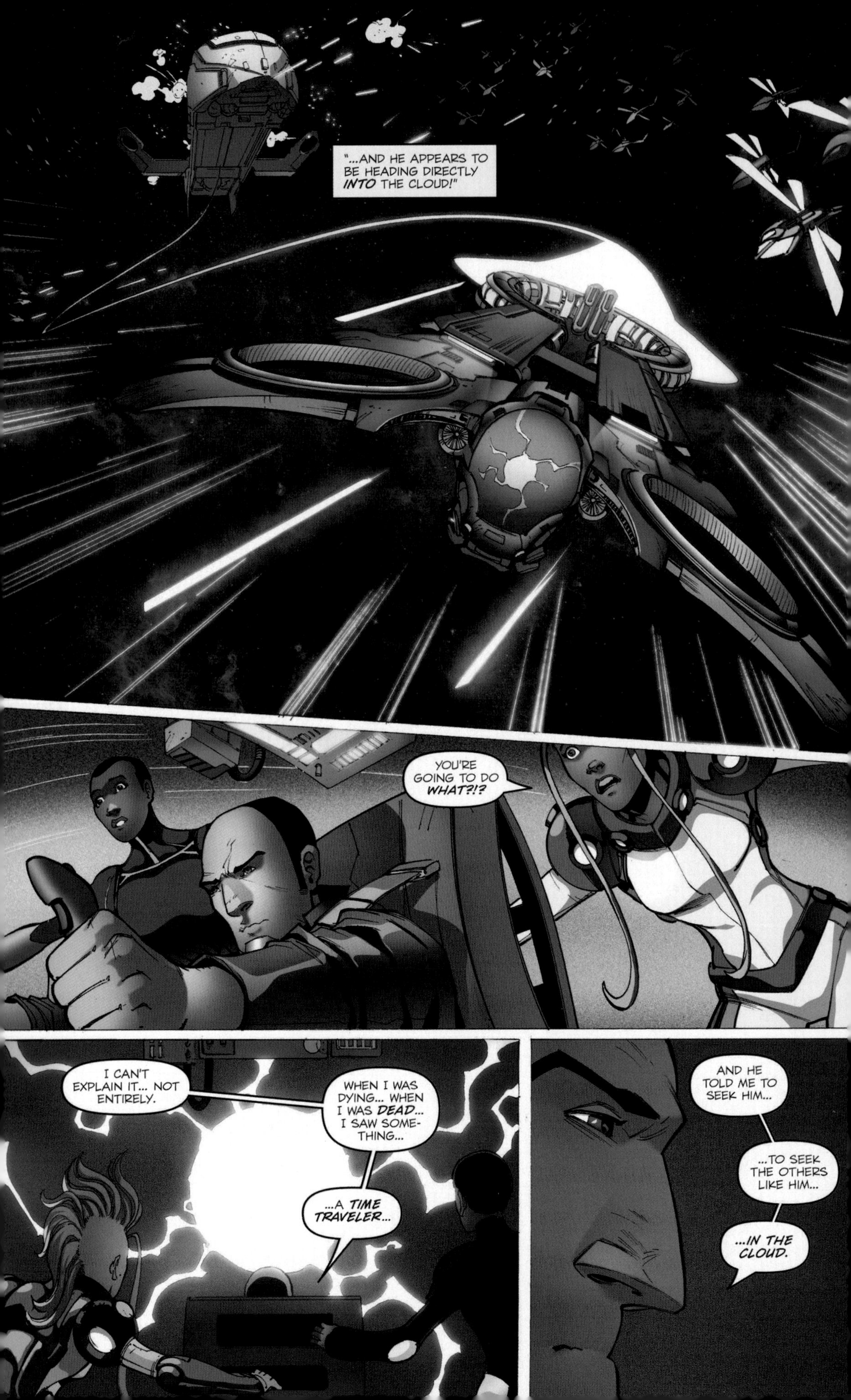
"...AND HE APPEARS TO BE HEADING DIRECTLY INTO THE CLOUD!"
YOU'RE GOING TO DO WHAT?!?
I CAN'T EXPLAIN IT... NOT ENTIRELY.
WHEN I WAS DYING... WHEN I WAS DEAD... I SAW SOME-THING...
...A TIME TRAVELER...
AND HE TOLD ME TO SEEK HIM...
...TO SEEK THE OTHERS LIKE HIM...
...IN THE CLOUD.

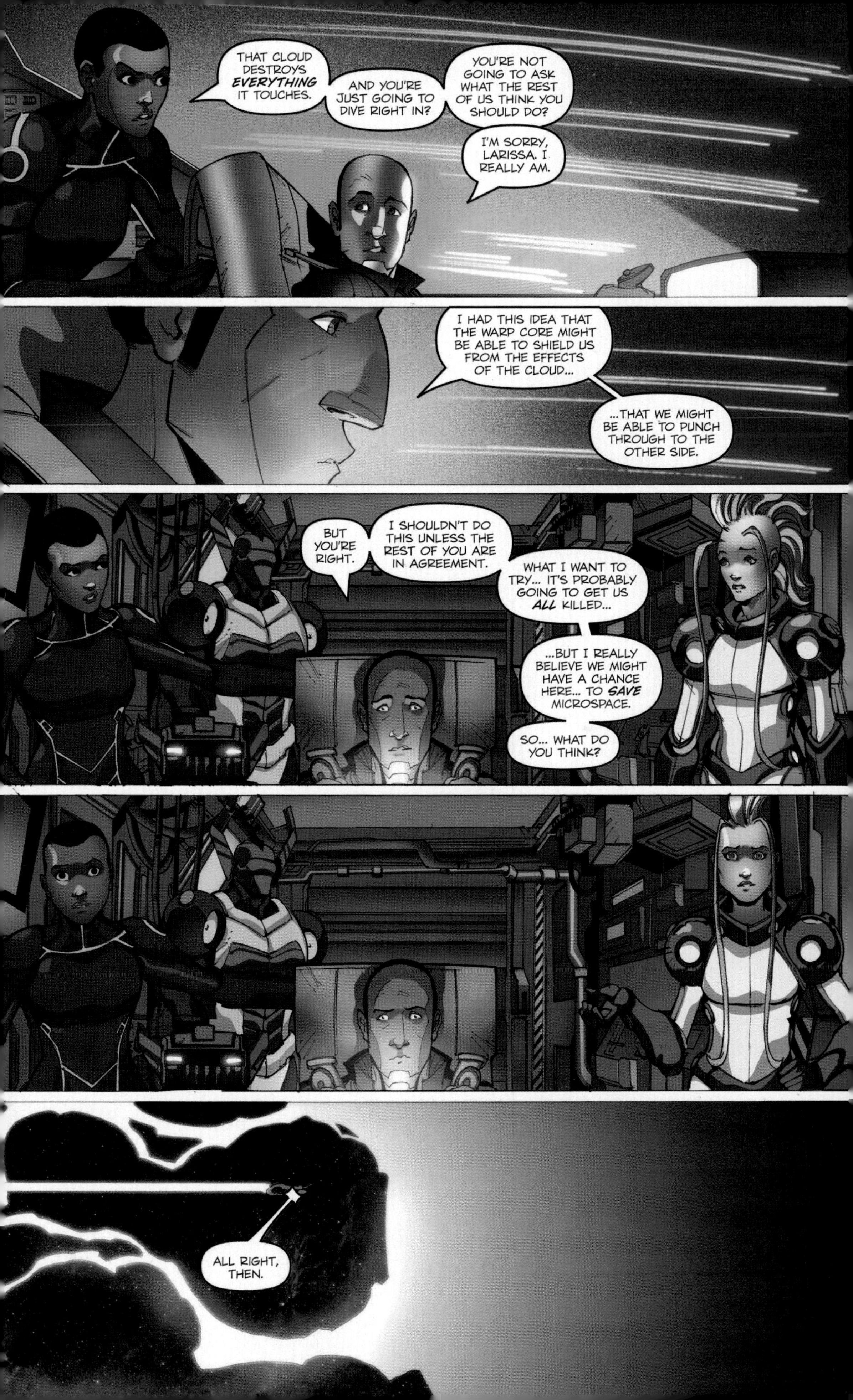
THAT CLOUD DESTROYS EVERYTHING IT TOUCHES.
AND YOU'RE JUST GOING TO DIVE RIGHT IN?
YOU'RE NOT GOING TO ASK WHAT THE REST OF US THINK YOU SHOULD DO?
I'M SORRY, LARISSA. I REALLY AM.
I HAD THIS IDEA THAT THE WARP CORE MIGHT BE ABLE TO SHIELD US FROM THE EFFECTS OF THE CLOUD...
...THAT WE MIGHT BE ABLE TO PUNCH THROUGH TO THE OTHER SIDE.
BUT YOU'RE RIGHT.
I SHOULDN'T DO THIS UNLESS THE REST OF YOU ARE IN AGREEMENT.
WHAT I WANT TO TRY... IT'S PROBABLY GOING TO GET US ALL KILLED...
...BUT I REALLY BELIEVE WE MIGHT HAVE A CHANCE HERE... TO SAVE MICROSPACE.
SO... WHAT DO YOU THINK?
ALL RIGHT, THEN.

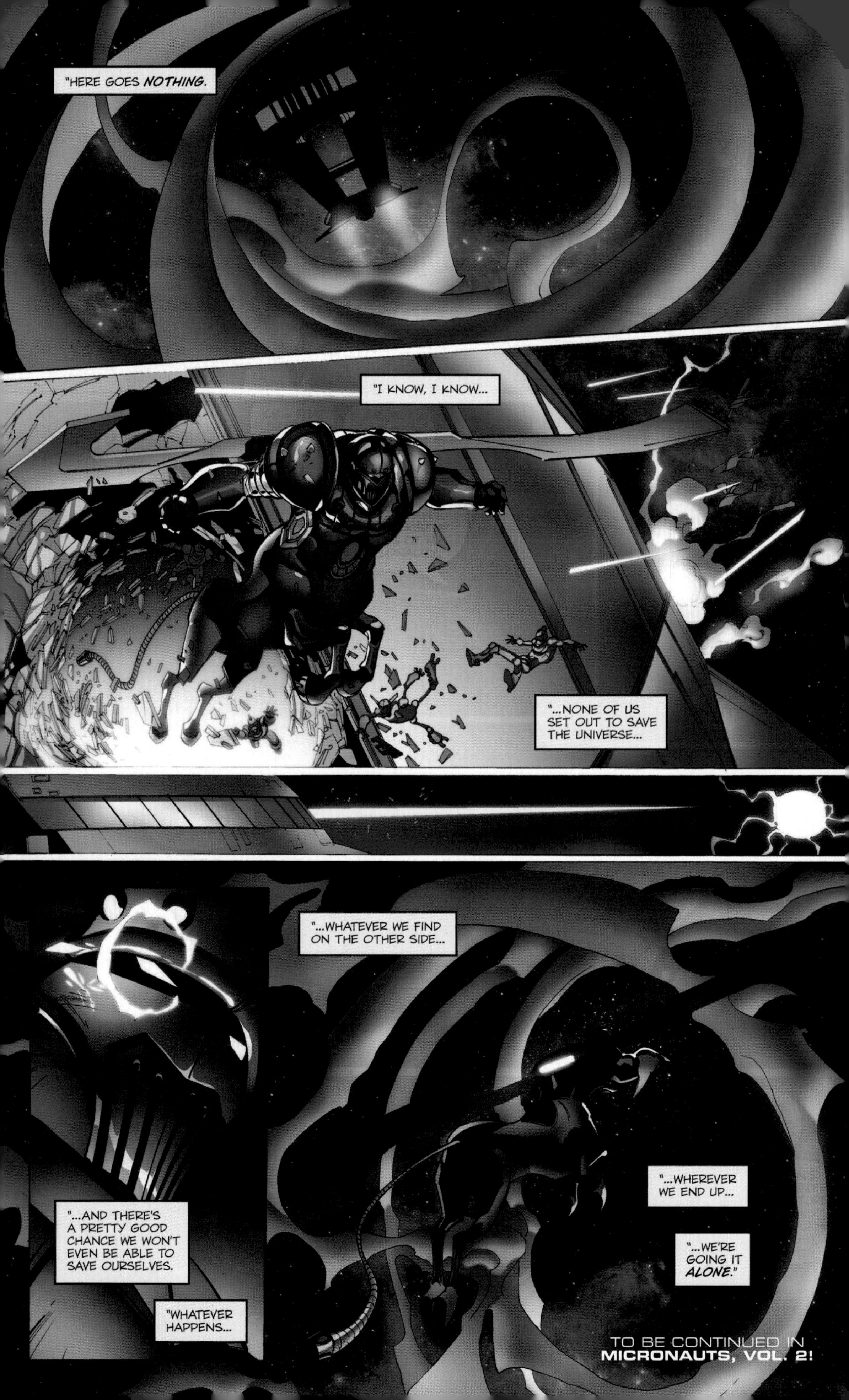

"HERE GOES NOTHING.
"I KNOW, I KNOW...
"...NONE OF US SET OUT TO SAVE THE UNIVERSE...
"...WHATEVER WE FIND ON THE OTHER SIDE...
"...AND THERE'S A PRETTY GOOD CHANCE WE WON'T EVEN BE ABLE TO SAVE OURSELVES.
"WHATEVER HAPPENS...
"...WHEREVER WE END UP...
"...WE'RE GOING IT ALONE."
TO BE CONTINUED IN MICRONAUTS, VOL. 2!

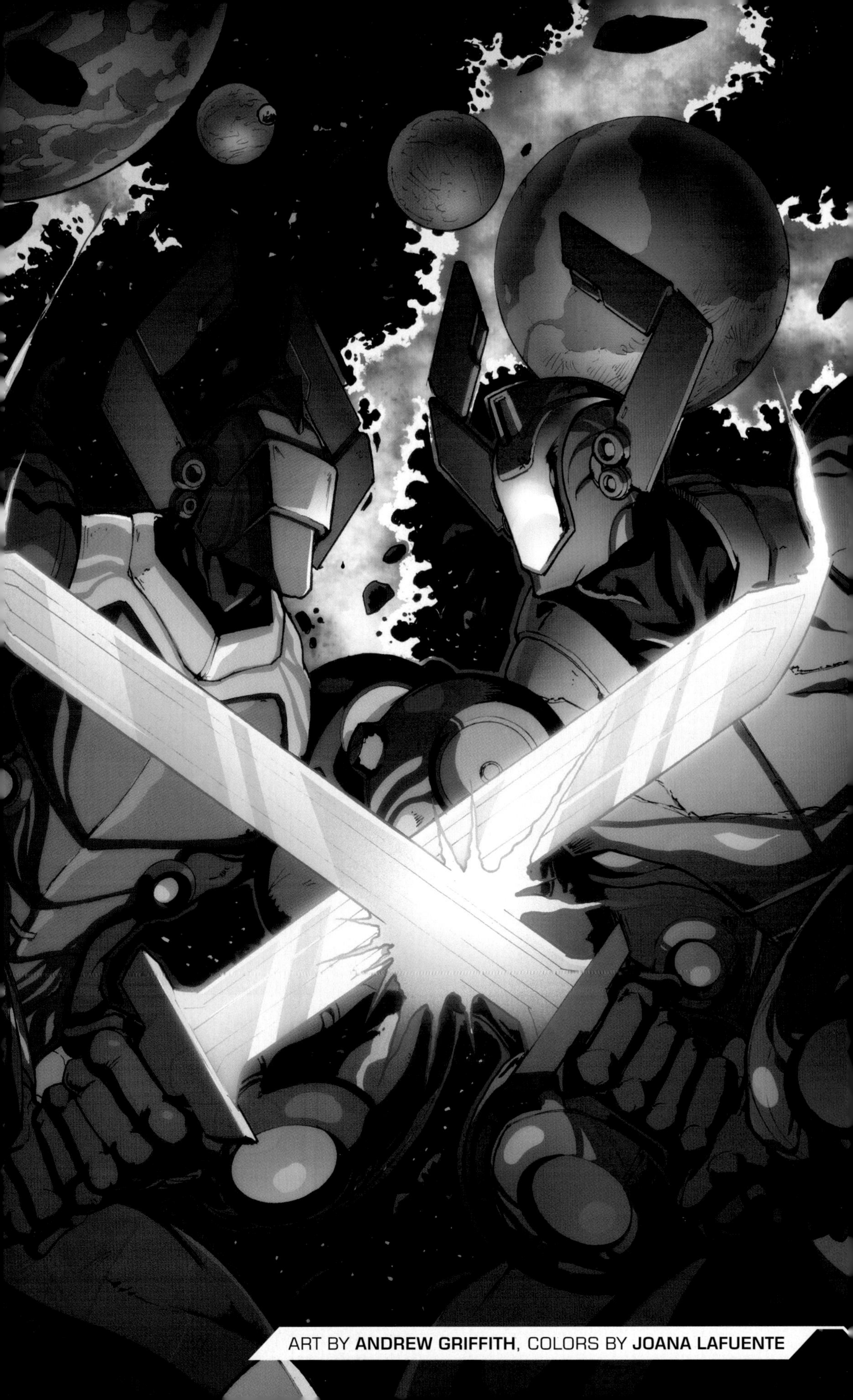

ART BY **ANDREW GRIFFITH**, COLORS BY **JOANA LAFUENTE**

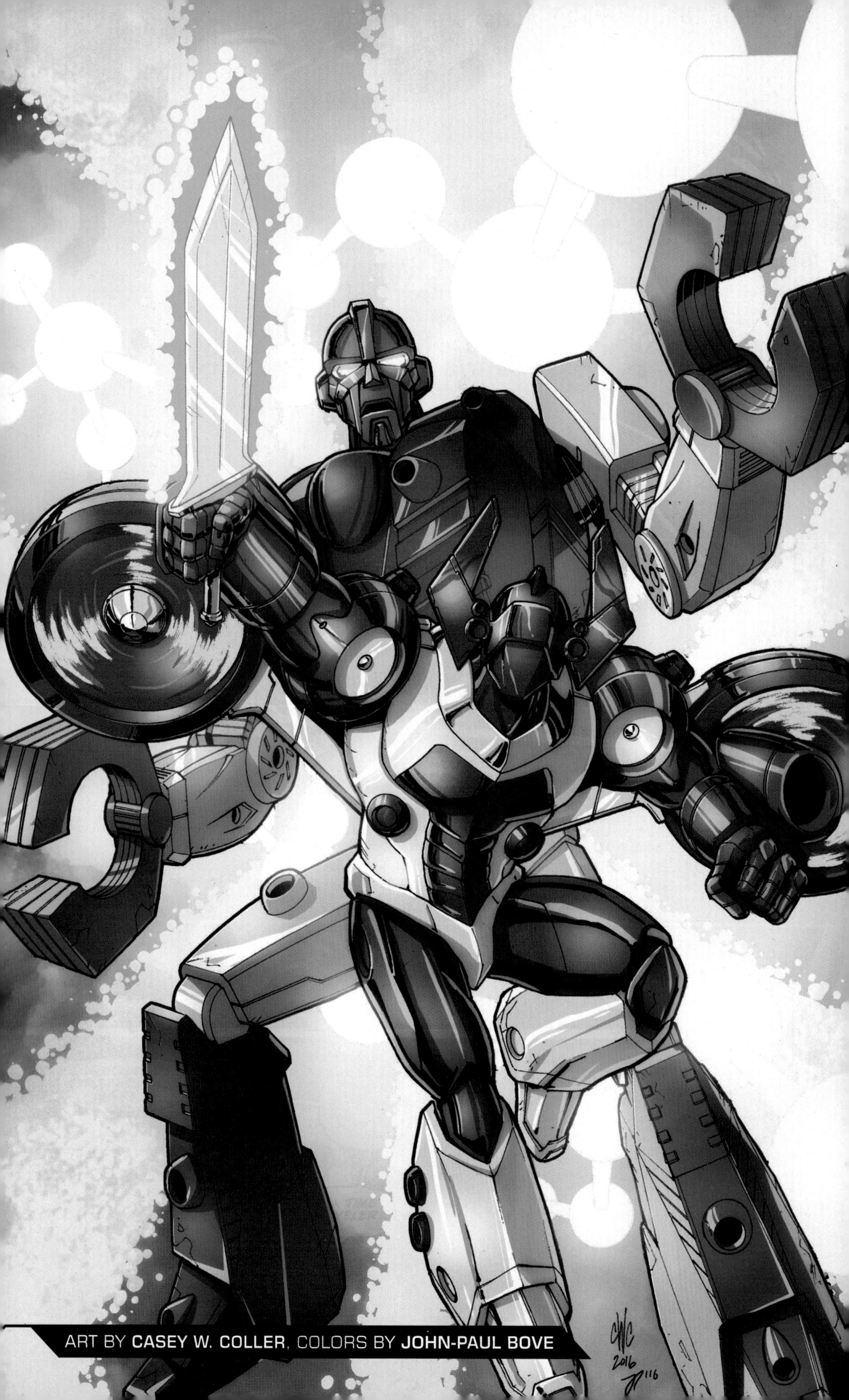

ART BY **CASEY W. COLLER**, COLORS BY **JOHN-PAUL BOVE**

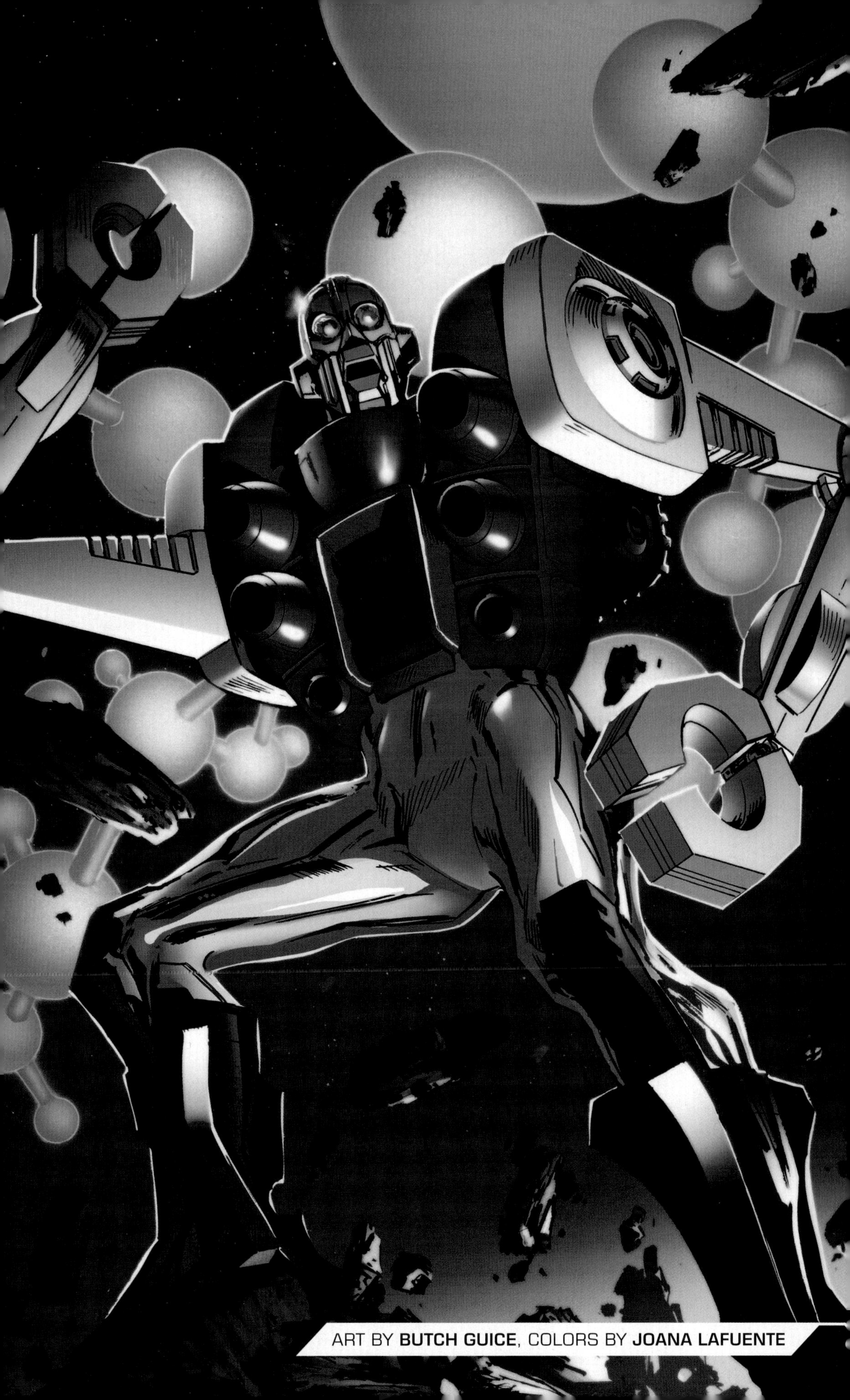

ART BY **BUTCH GUICE**, COLORS BY **JOANA LAFUENTE**

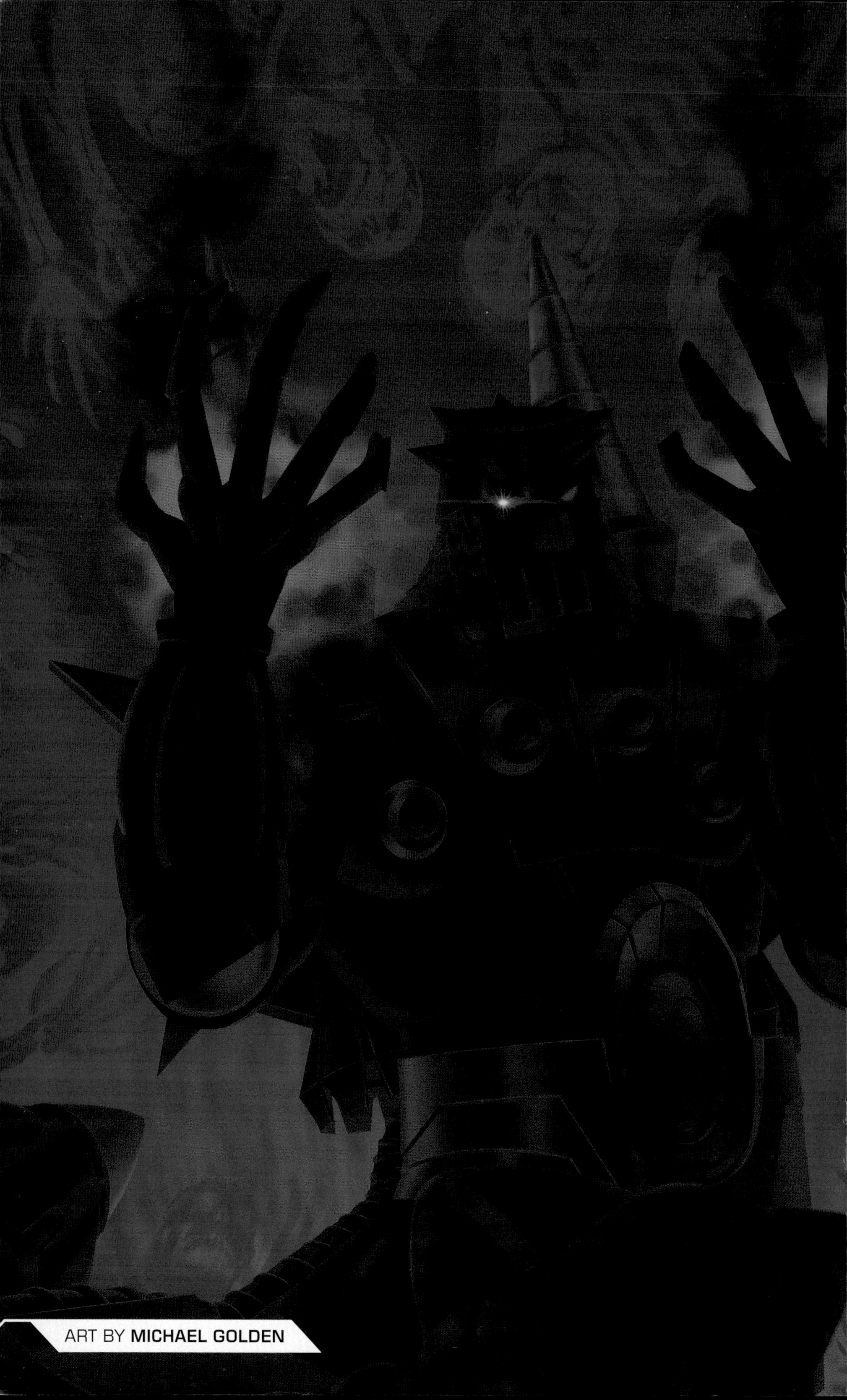

ART BY **MICHAEL GOLDEN**

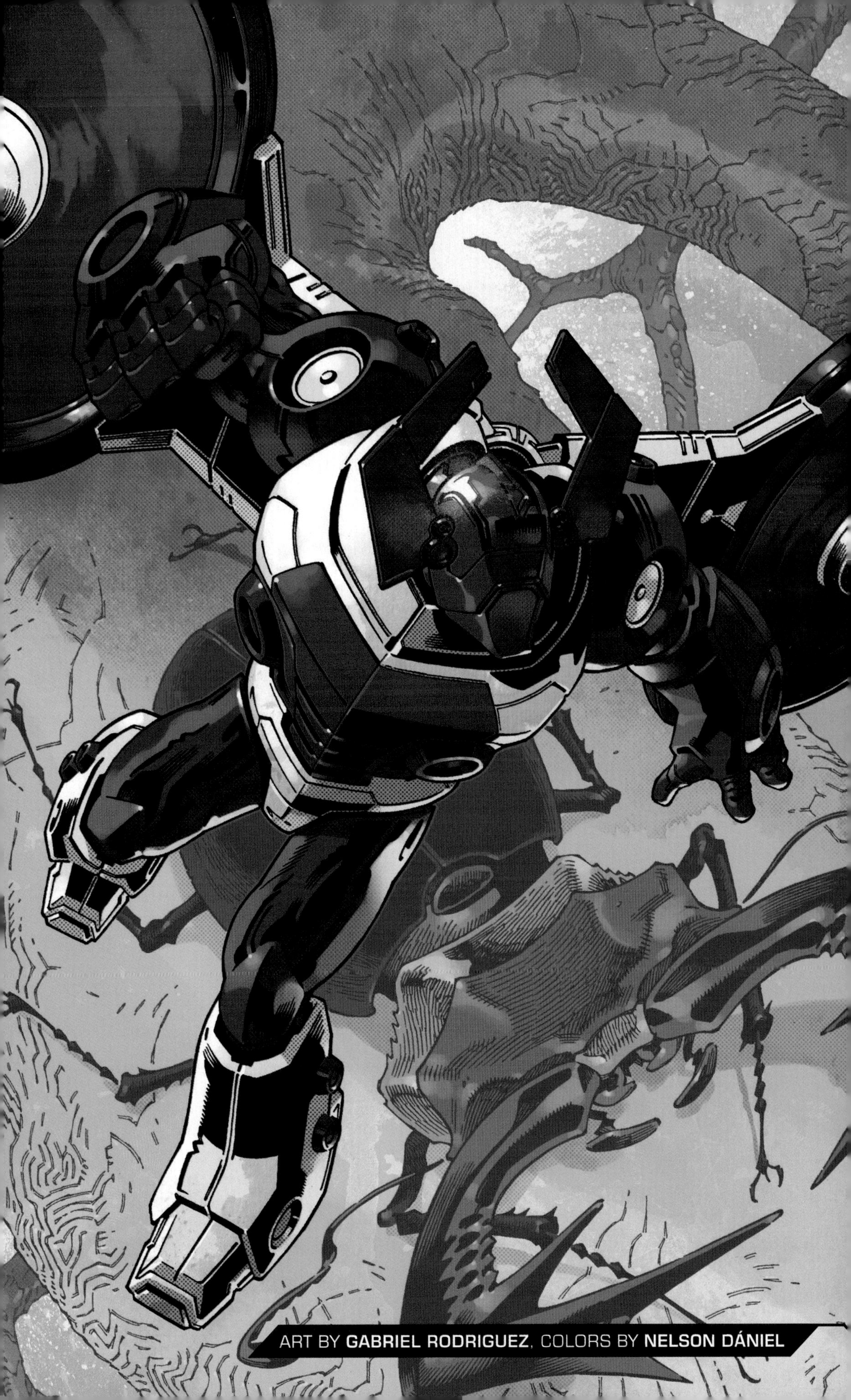

ART BY **GABRIEL RODRIGUEZ**, COLORS BY **NELSON DÁNIEL**

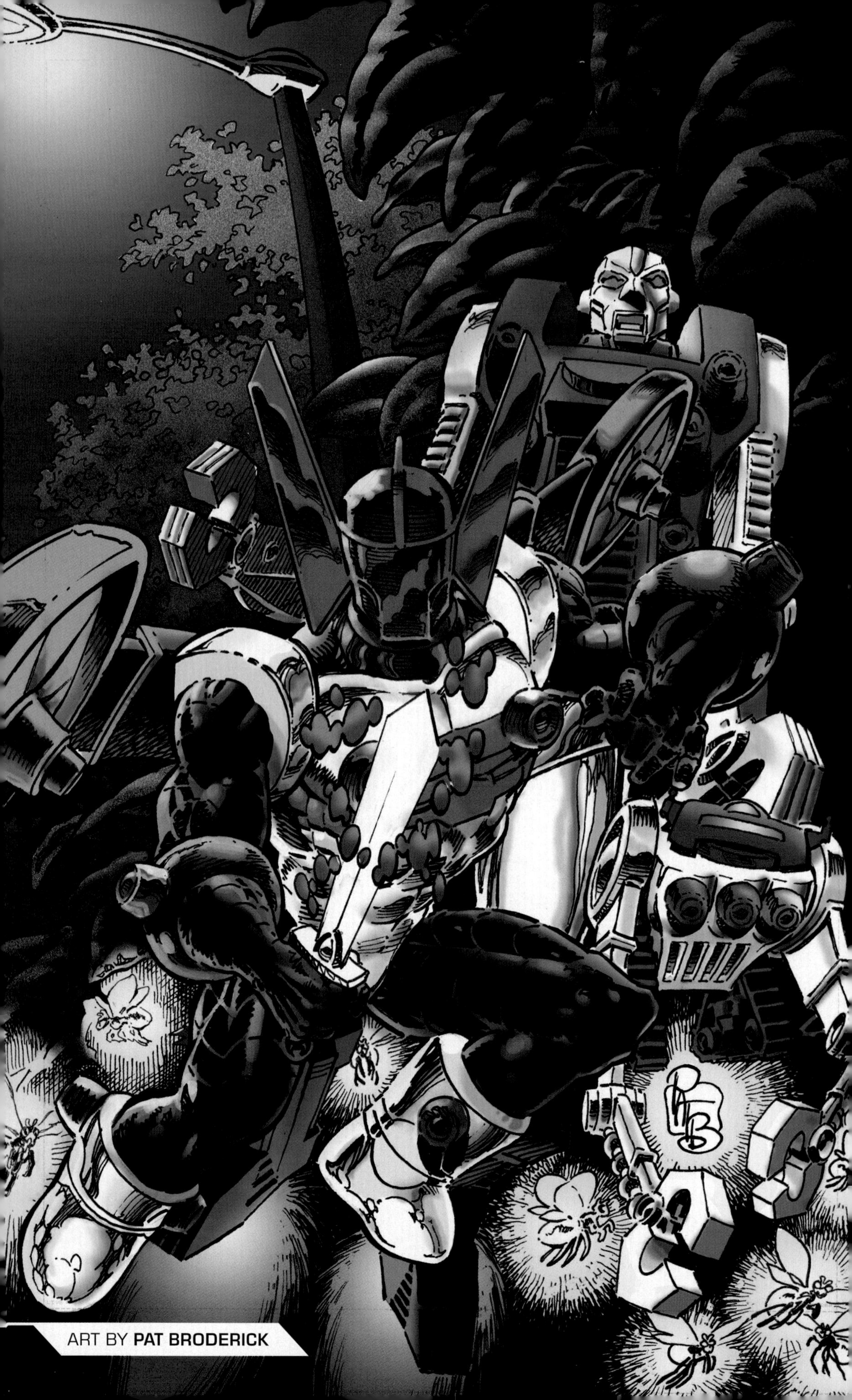

ART BY **PAT BRODERICK**

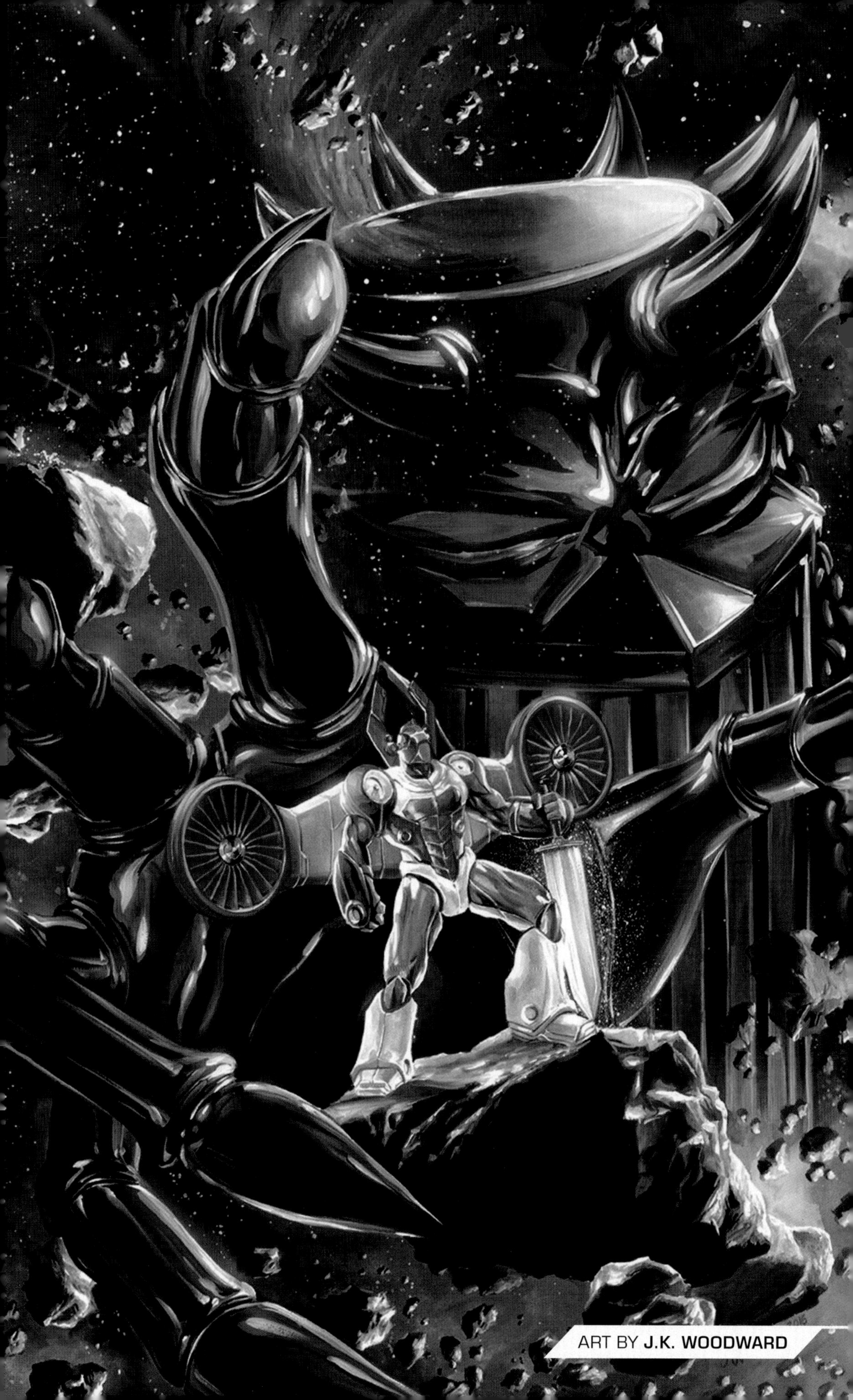

ART BY **J.K. WOODWARD**

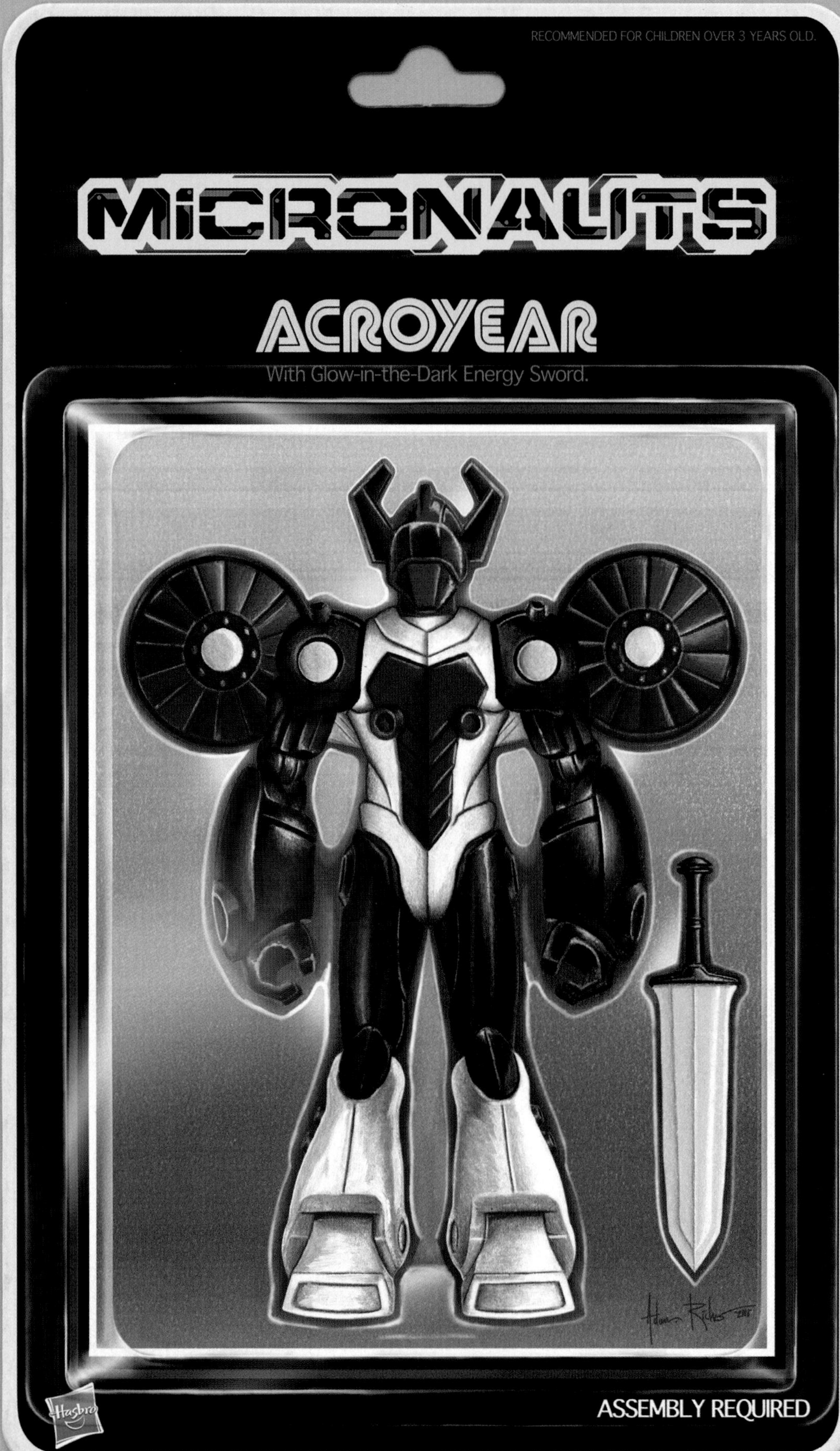
RECOMMENDED FOR CHILDREN OVER 3 YEARS OLD.
MICRONAUTS
ACROYEAR
With Glow-in-the-Dark Energy Sword.
Hasbro
ASSEMBLY REQUIRED

ART BY **ADAM RICHES**

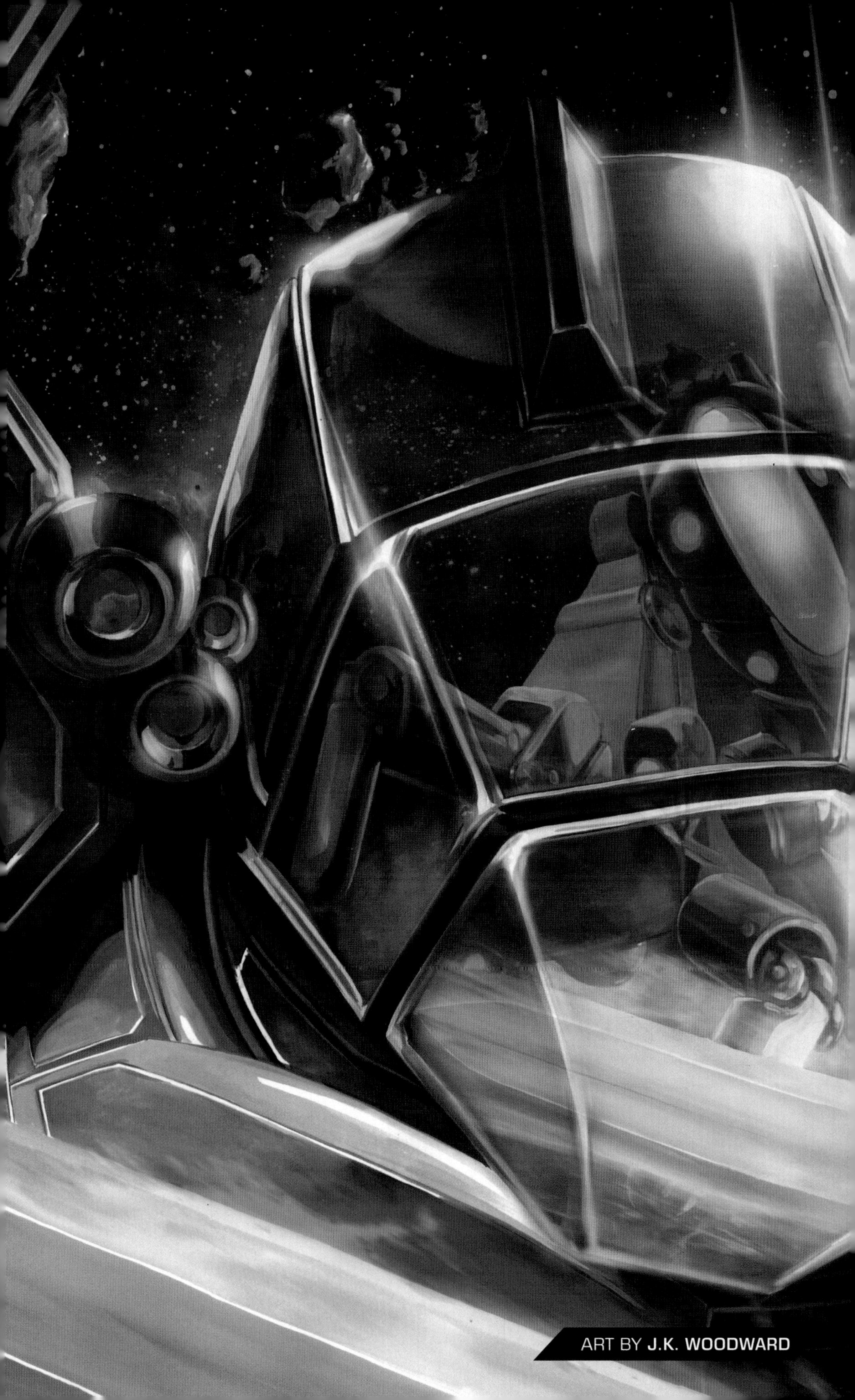
ART BY J.K. WOODWARD

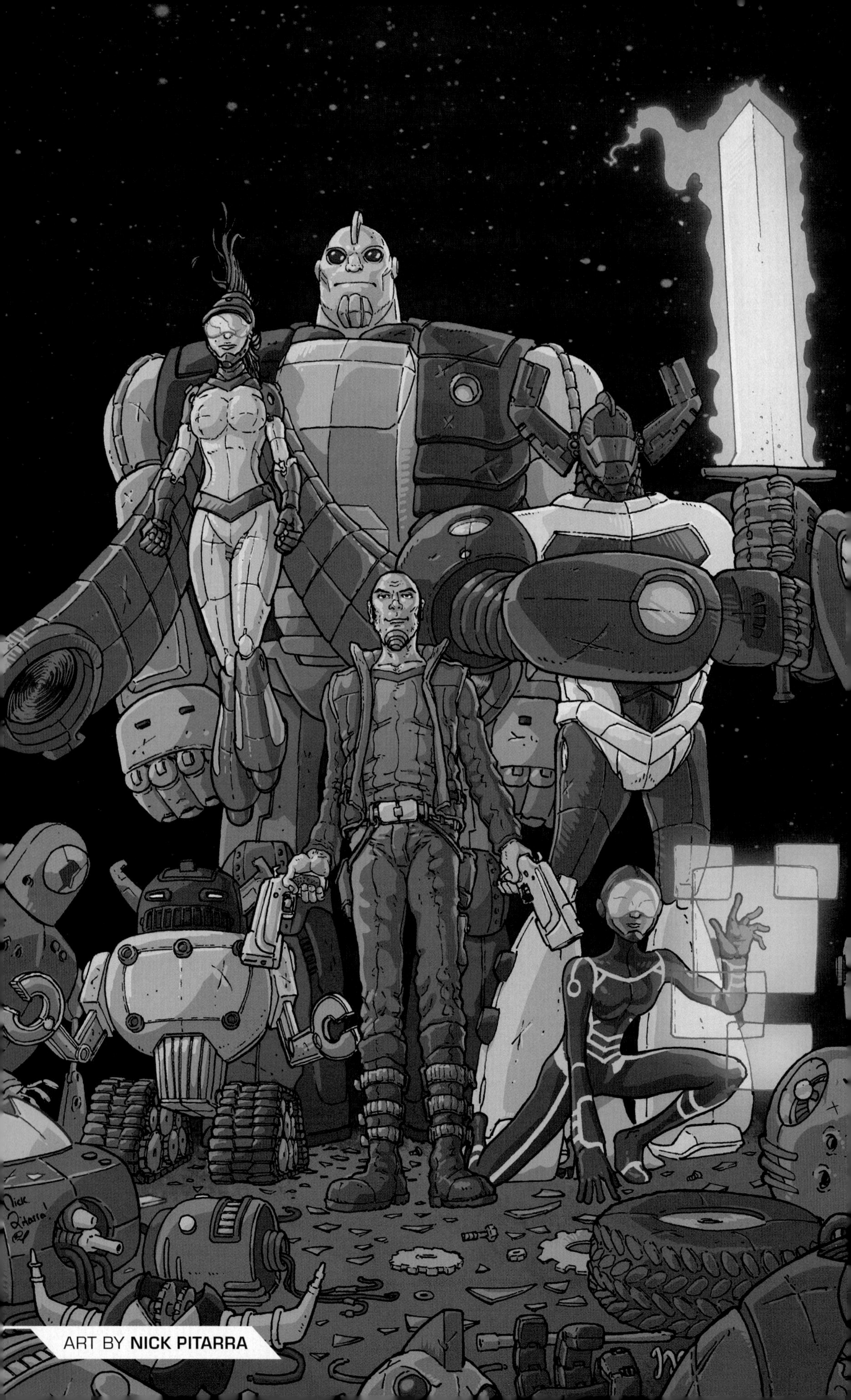

ART BY **NICK PITARRA**

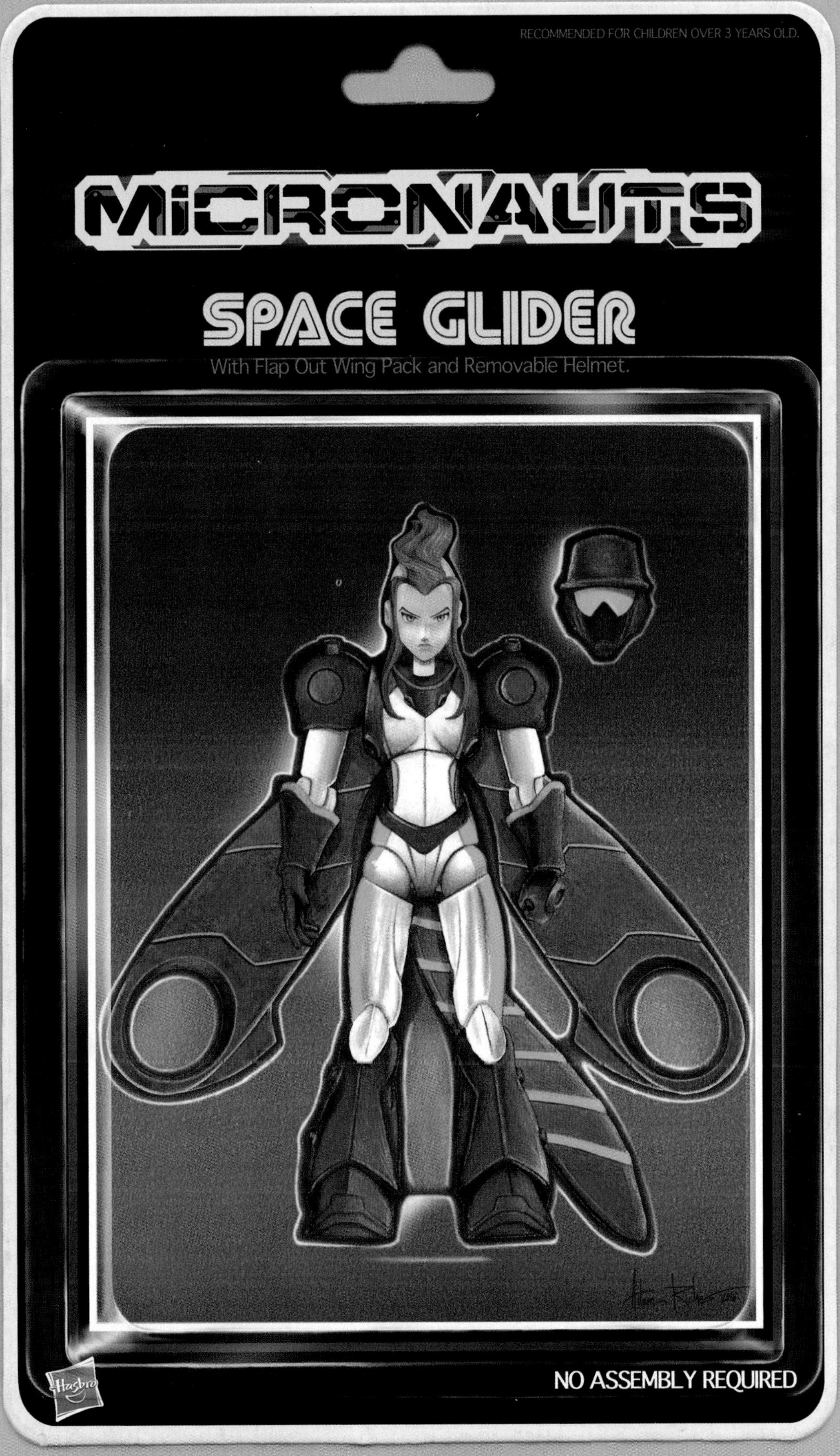
RECOMMENDED FOR CHILDREN OVER 3 YEARS OLD.
MICRONAUTS
SPACE GLIDER
With Flap Out Wing Pack and Removable Helmet.
Hasbro
NO ASSEMBLY REQUIRED

ART BY **ADAM RICHES**

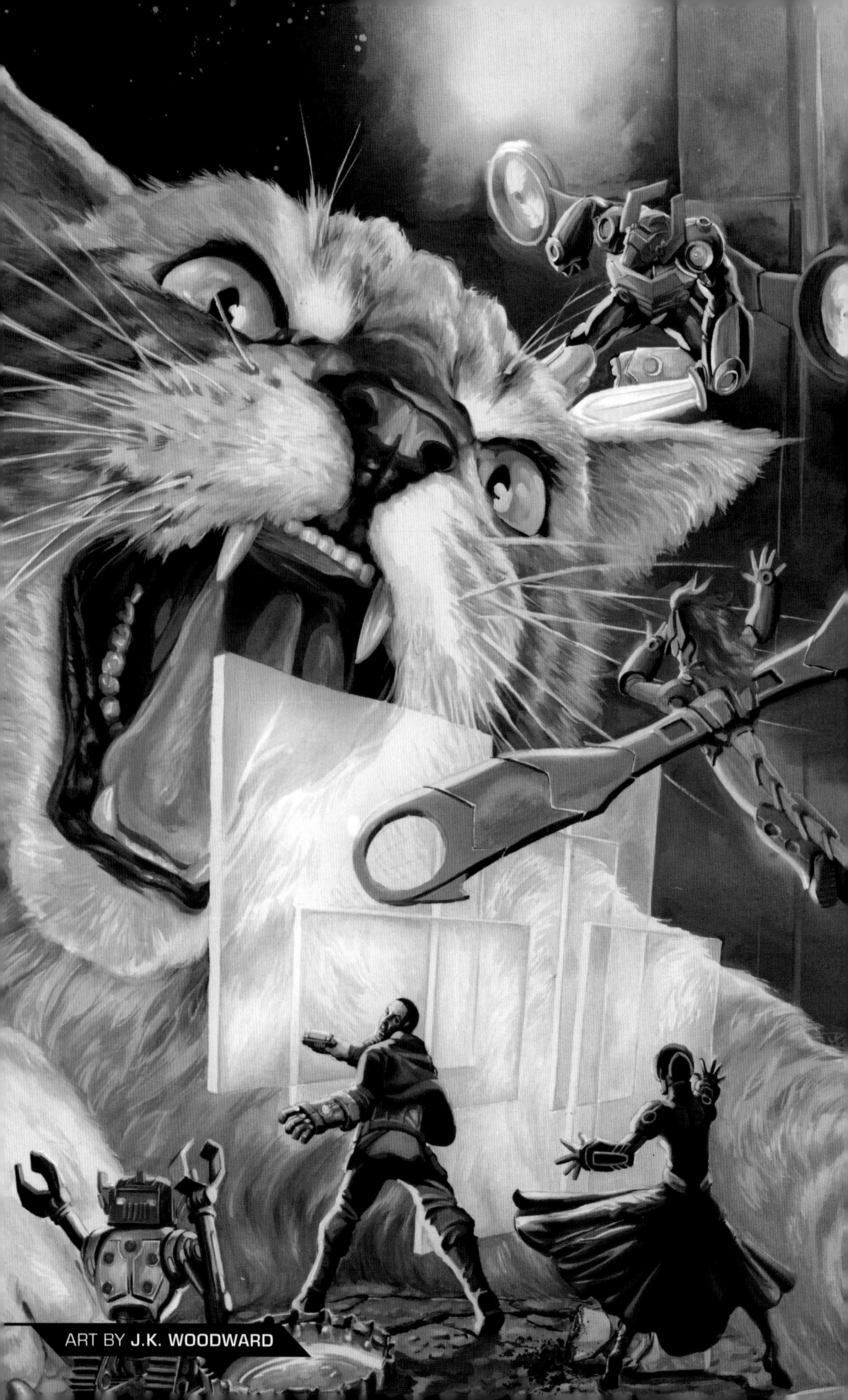

ART BY **J.K. WOODWARD**

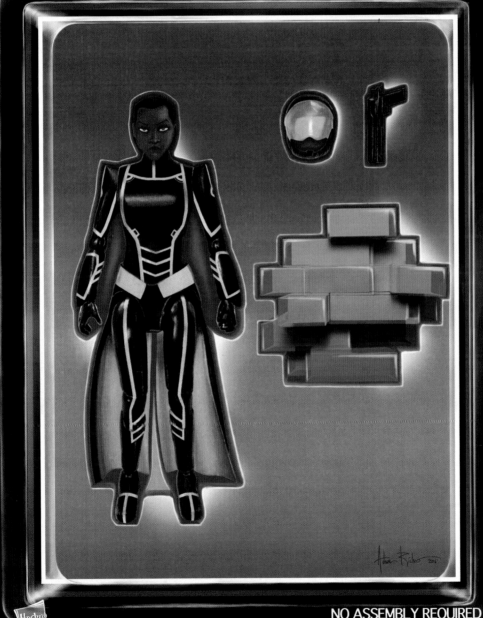

MICRONAUTS

ORBITAL DEFENDER
With Helmet, Blaster, and Force Fields.

RECOMMENDED FOR CHILDREN OVER 3 YEARS OLD.

NO ASSEMBLY REQUIRED

Hasbro

ART BY **ADAM RICHES**

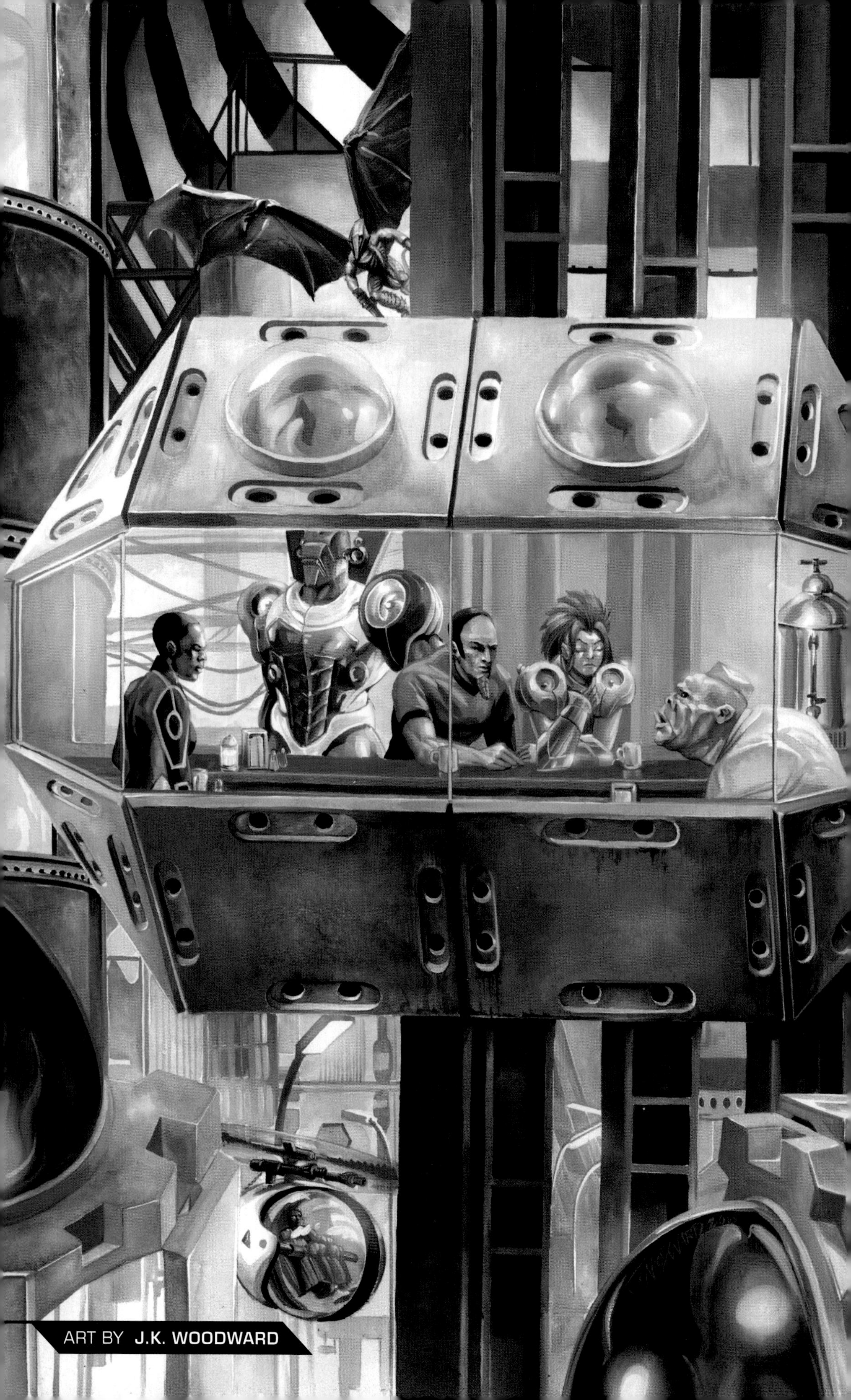

ART BY J.K. WOODWARD

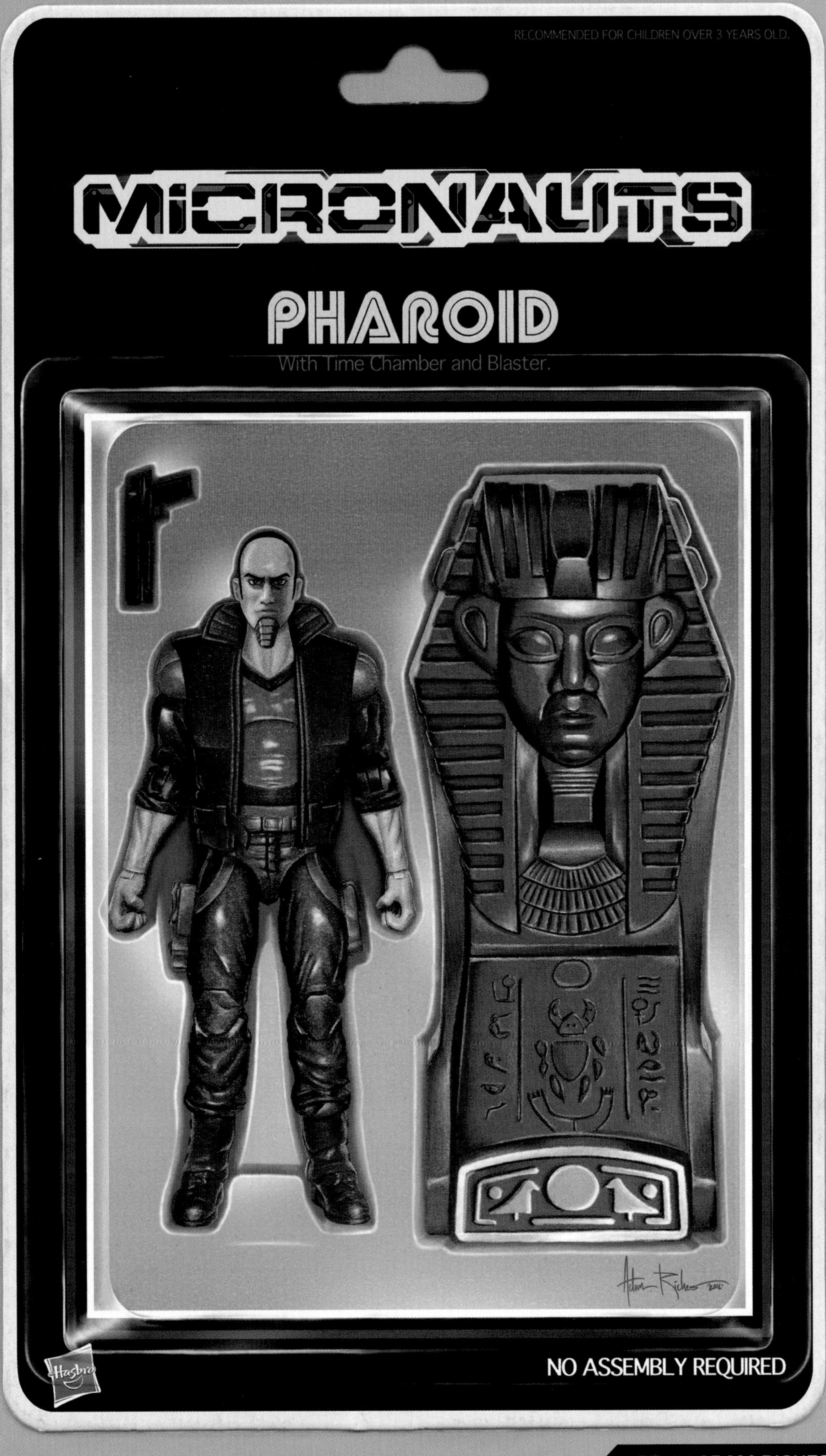

RECOMMENDED FOR CHILDREN OVER 3 YEARS OLD.
MICRONAUTS
PHAROID
With Time Chamber and Blaster.
Hasbro
NO ASSEMBLY REQUIRED

ART BY **ADAM RICHES**

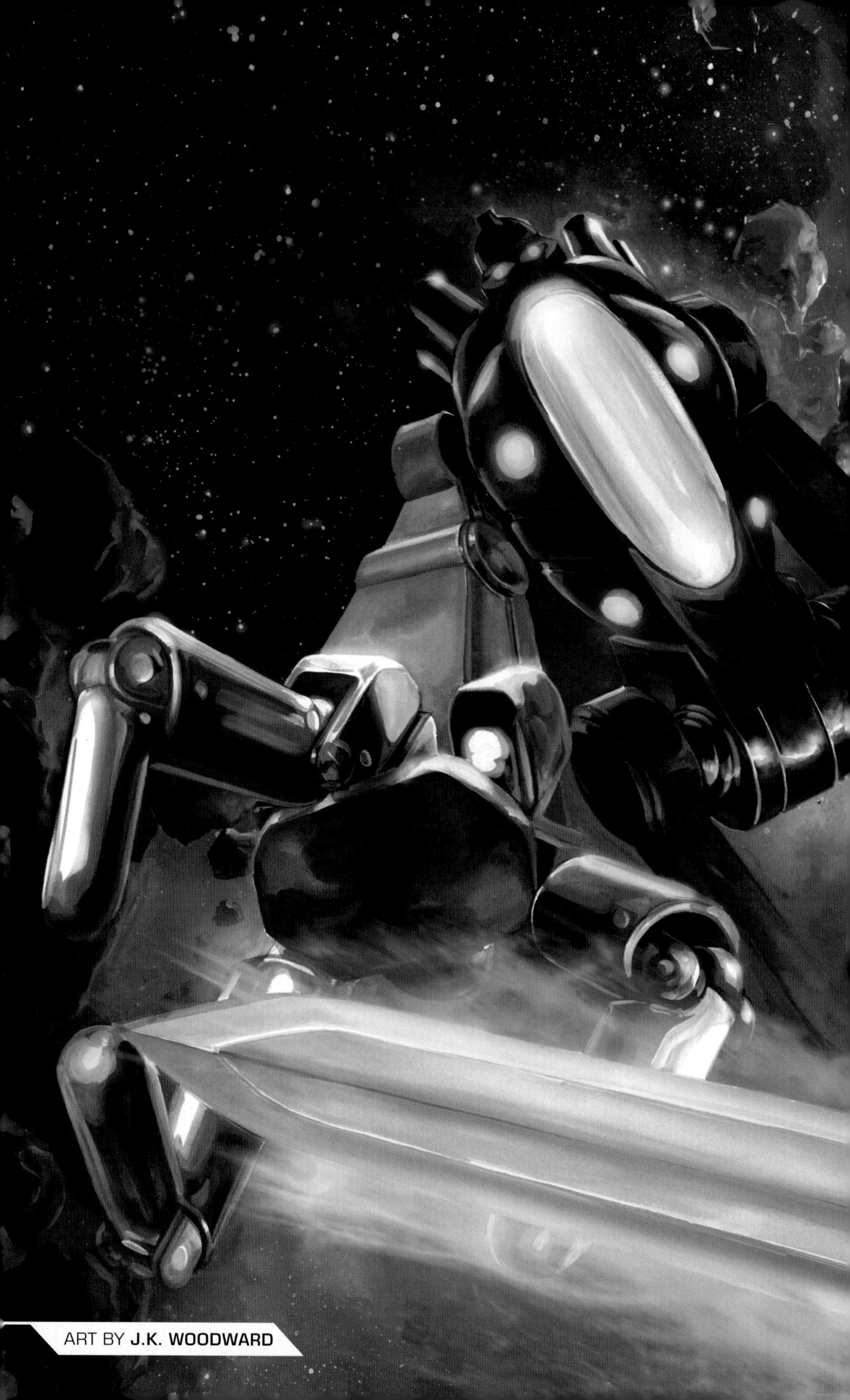

ART BY **J.K. WOODWARD**

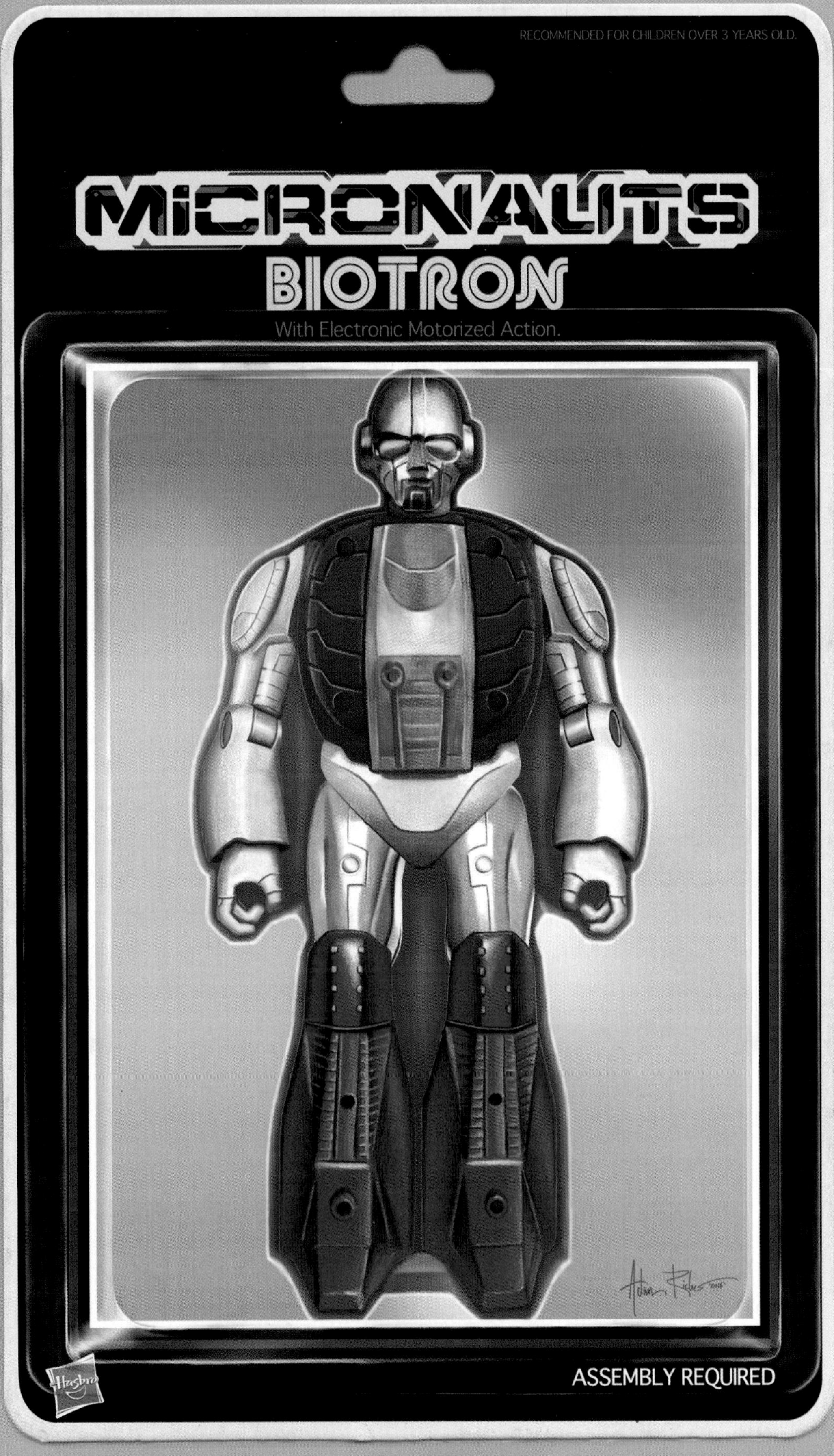
RECOMMENDED FOR CHILDREN OVER 3 YEARS OLD.
MICRONAUTS
BIOTRON
With Electronic Motorized Action.
Hasbro
ASSEMBLY REQUIRED

ART BY **ADAM RICHES**

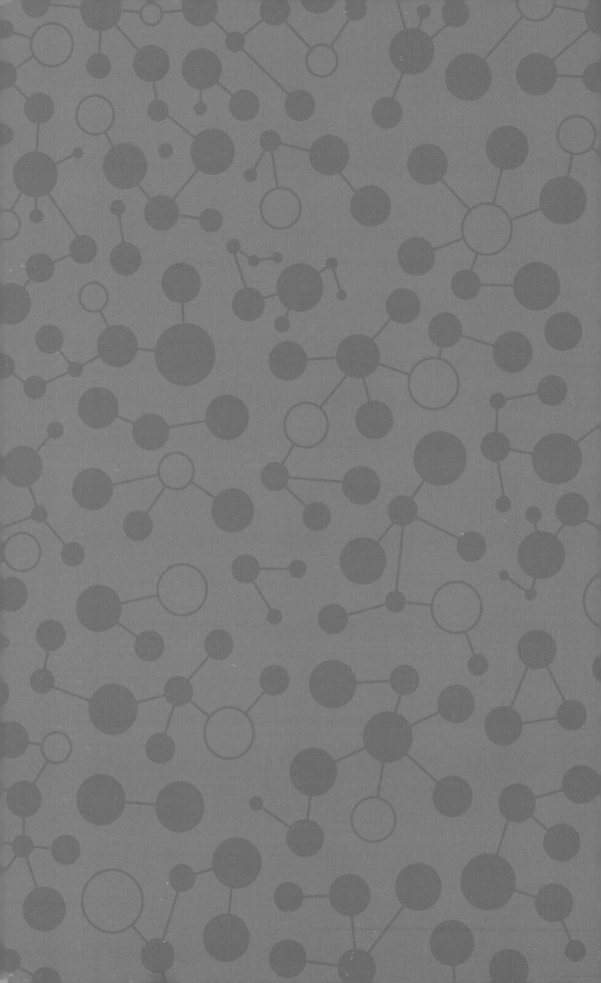